Last Among Equals is the first detailed account of Hawaii's quest for statehood. It is a story of struggle and accommodation, of how Hawaii was gradually absorbed into the political, economic, and ideological structures of American life. It also recounts the complex process that came into play when the states of the Union were confronted with the difficulty of granting admission to a non-contiguous territory with an overwhelmingly non-Caucasian population. More than any previous study of modern Hawaii, this book explains why Hawaii's legitimate claims to equality and autonomy as a state were frustrated for more than half a century.

Beginning with the efforts of Hawaii's small white elite to overthrow its Polynesian rulers and shelter under the protection of Washington, Roger Bell traces the changing patterns of support for and opposition to statehood. He examines these patterns as they developed within the context of both island and national American politics.

Hawaii itself was divided by conflicting interests, ethnic and economic as well as political. Americans of Asian descent in particular viewed statehood as the only means by which they could shed their second-class status and gain political and social equality. When demands for civil rights by non-Caucasians on the mainland generated a domestic crisis after World War II, statehood for Hawaii was drawn inevitably into that bitter controversy. What Bell makes clear, however, is that the long frustration of Hawaii's political aspirations was rarely a matter of simple racism. Indeed, the question of Hawaiian statehood appeared constantly against the backdrop of some of the most emotional and divisive issues of the time: civil rights, states' rights, communist subversion, and, not least, contests of party strength in Congress.

Last Among Equals is sure to remain a standard reference for modern Hawaiian and American political historians. As important, it will require a re-evaluation of two commonly held myths: that of racial harmony in Hawaii and that of automatic equality under the Constitution of the United States.

Roger Bell, who has a Ph.D. from the University of Sydney, teaches U.S. history and comparative history of multicultural society at the University of New South Wales in Sydney, Australia. He is the author of *Unequal Allies: Australian-American Relations and the Pacific War*. In 1983 he received the Louis Knott Koontz Award from the West Coast Branch of the American Historical Association for his article titled "Testing the Open Door Thesis in Australia, 1941–1945."

LAST AMONG EQUALS

Last Among Equals

HAWAIIAN STATEHOOD
AND AMERICAN POLITICS

Roger Bell

University of Hawaii Press • Honolulu

Library of Congress Cataloging in Publication Data

Bell, Roger J. (Roger John), 1947–
 Last among equals.

 Bibliography: p.
 Includes index.
 1. Hawaii—Politics and government—1900–1959.
 2. United States—Politics and government—1901–1953.
 3. United States—Politics and government—1953–1961.
 4. Statehood (American politics)   I. Title.
 DU627.5.B44   1984   996.9'03   83–24330
 ISBN 0–8248–0847–9

For **Jan**

Contents

Acknowledgments

Over the years spent researching this book I have enjoyed the support and assistance of many people in Hawaii, mainland United States, and Australia. I am particularly indebted to the following people for granting me lengthy interviews: Hiram Fong, William Quinn, C. Nils Tavares, the late John Reinecke, and the late governor John A. Burns. Patience McDowell of Harvard University has recently completed a series of interviews on statehood, and I am grateful to her for permission to use her interviews with William Quinn, Elizabeth Farrington, Daniel Inouye, and Samuel P. King. I am also deeply indebted to Stuart Gerry Brown, Daniel Boylan, and Paul Hooper for undertaking the John A. Burns Oral History Project. This important and exhaustive series of interviews with people prominent in island politics represents oral history at its very best. In the years to come other researchers who use these interviews will doubtless share my gratitude. All those interviewed as part of this project have now given researchers unrestricted access to the transcripts of their interviews. Apart from the various interviews with John Burns, those most helpful to my research were conducted with Elizabeth Farrington, Daniel Aoki, Chuck Mau, Sakae Takahashi, Mitsuyuki Kido, Robert Oshiro, George Chaplin, Seichi Hirai, Ernest Murai, and William Richardson.

I am also extremely grateful to the staff of the Hawaiian and Pacific Collection, Sinclair Library, University of Hawaii, particularly Michaelyn Chou, David Kittelson, and Ashby Fristoe, for help in locating sources. The staff of the Hawaiian Archives, especially Mrs. Dabagh and Ms. Conrad, also gave friendly assistance in identifying and using manuscript sources during the early phases of my research. John E. Wickman of the Eisenhower Library, Philip D. Lagerquist of the Truman Library, and Claudia Anderson of the Johnson Library have each given generous help. For financial support, and an enlightened attitude toward sabbatical leave, I am indebted to the University of New South Wales, Sydney, Australia. My thanks also go to Maureen Kelleher and Faye Sutherland for tireless assistance with research and typing, and to Daniel Boylan, Philip Bell, Neville Meaney, Hilary Golder, and Lucy Taksa for their most helpful comments on the manuscript. Finally, I wish to express my deep appreciation to Iris Wiley, executive editor of the University of Hawaii Press, for constant encouragement and guidance.

Despite this indebtedness, responsibility for any errors of fact, or peculiarities of interpretation, rests solely with me.

Introduction

The power to create States belongs to the people
who inhabit them; the power to admit them into
the Union belongs to Congress.
Senator Lewis Cass, speaking on the admission
of California, 1850.

It is said they [the Hawaiian Islands] will come
in as a State some time. But they will not come in
as a State unless they are fit to be a State. . . .
We never have been in a hurry about this thing.
Senator George Frisbie Hoar, speaking on annexation of Hawaii, 1898.

In the century after Captain James Cook's fatal landing at Kealakekua
Bay, Hawaii's political sovereignty and traditional social fabric were
eroded by white penetration which its native peoples were unable to
resist. The islands were drawn inexorably toward the United States.
Planters, missionaries, and traders carried to the distant islands the
political and ideological imperatives of "manifest destiny." As early as
the 1840s the Monroe Doctrine was, in effect, extended to Hawaii, and
some European diplomats anticipated that it would soon be annexed to
the United States. In the following decades officials in Washington were
adamant that the independent kingdom must not be "cut adrift" from
the "American system" by the exploits of any ambitious European or
Asian state.[1] At the close of the nineteenth century, as the United States
won its new empire in the Pacific, Far East, and Caribbean, Hawaii's
independence formally ended. Its monarchy was overthrown in 1893 by
a tiny but powerful minority of whites. Five years later, against a background of war with Spain and unprecedented enthusiasm for expansion, the United States annexed the islands. Until 1959, when it was
belatedly accepted as a state, Hawaii remained a semi-colonial appendage of the United States. It was incorporated as a territory in 1900, and
governed under terms derived largely from the Northwest Ordinance of
1787 which had previously been reserved for America's continental possessions. By acquiring an overseas empire at the turn of the century the
United States irreversibly broke the constraints implicit in the Monroe
Doctrine, and conveniently submerged its traditional disdain for the
corrupt practices of old-world imperialism. Westward expansion and
settlements were projected forcefully beyond continental limits.

These events have been discussed by many historians. Annexation of Hawaii was a pivotal episode in America's thrust for empire and a symbol of its determination to join the European imperialist powers on the world stage. This book does not aim to duplicate the literature on this intensively studied initial phase of American expansion abroad.[2] Nor is it intended as a general history of the islands since annexation, although it necessarily covers a variety of developments, both local and national, since the 1890s. Any analysis of Hawaii during this period must be informed by the rich historical and sociological literature of authors such as Ralph S. Kuykendall, Romanzo Adams, Andrew Lind, Lawrence Fuchs, and Gavan Daws. But previous studies of modern Hawaii have devoted little attention to the statehood issue.[3] Certainly they have not treated the issue thoroughly, nor considered it within the wider framework of American politics.

Hawaii's annexation, Americanization, and eventual statehood are relatively recent fragments of a much broader theme embracing white settlement and transformation of the New World. In this context the traditional island community can be seen as the object of American penetration and settlement. It was gradually absorbed into the political and ideological spheres of that major power. In contrast to the colonial possessions of the various European nations, Hawaii after annexation was never anxious to win political sovereignty as an independent nation. Nor did Washington ever encourage such an aspiration, or contemplate granting independence to the islands. As an incorporated territory Hawaii enjoyed greater autonomy than most colonies under the control of European powers. Rather than sever its political associations with the metropolitan power and seek independence, Hawaii chose to win unqualified political equality within the American body politic. It thus followed a path unusual among colonial possessions—a path leading to equality with the existing American states, not sovereign independence on the world stage.

The explanation for this development lies partly in the particular nature of Hawaii's annexation and incorporation as an American territory at the turn of the century. But any analysis of Hawaii's political evolution and statehood must also take account of its gradual Americanization—a process begun early in the nineteenth century. Thus, in tracing the formal and informal integration of Hawaii into the United States, my study has been obliged to cast its net very wide. While the forces which transformed the island community are central to my book, developments within the nation-at-large must also be explored. Links between the two areas multiplied throughout the nineteenth century. Whalers, missionaries, planters, and entrepreneurs brought new ideas, practices, and institutions from the United States. These provided the foundations for annexation and eventual statehood. The political, cultural, social, and economic systems of traditional Hawaii were eroded, eclipsed, and ultimately replaced. A Polynesian kingdom became an American territory and, in turn, an American state.

The poet John Masefield observed that "States are not made, nor patched; they grow."[4] In part this book is a history of Hawaii's growth —a study of its development, modernization, and gradual adaptation to America's political norms and values. Yet in the final analysis, states of the Union are "made," as admission depends on legislative action by Congress. A territory has only the right to petition for statehood; the authority to accept or reject such initiatives rests with Congress. This study, then, is a detailed history of the way in which Hawaii was brought under the American flag, first as a territory and later, after a long and difficult struggle, as a state. It seeks to explain Washington's ambivalence to Hawaii's claims for statehood during more than half a century. Beginning with the overthrow of the Hawaiian monarchy, it traces the changing patterns of support for, and resistance to, statehood within the island community. Gradually, a traditional Pacific island community became part of America's political system, cultural norms, and economic arrangements. Statehood was a belated, formal manifestation of this larger, almost imperceptible trend. It both symbolized and made irreversible the Americanization of the island community.

The question of statehood for Hawaii was not simply about home rule. It was also about who should rule at home.[5] It centered on demands for sovereign equality as a state within the Union, but it also involved attempts to establish full-fledged democracy within the island community itself. Those who resisted statehood locally were generally hostile to any substantial change in the political, social, or economic status quo which they had long controlled to their own advantage. In addition, some native Hawaiians clung desperately to territorial government, believing that it might at least delay the final victory of foreign influences, both Asian and Caucasian, which their ancestors had vainly attempted to resist in the late nineteenth century. On the other hand, support for statehood was increasingly synonymous with enthusiasm for truly representative government which would reflect both the islands' unique ethnic patterns and the more liberal political aspirations of its recently Americanized people. It was not until after the war against Japan, however, that the entrenched authority of the old white elite was seriously challenged by an assertive, confident, and essentially nonwhite majority. In large part these new forces, which ultimately achieved statehood, were identified with the burgeoning Democratic party. Supported largely by the descendents of Asian immigrants, who had long been denied equality in island life, the Democrats fervently believed that equality as a state in the Union would pave the way for genuine democracy and equality of opportunity at home. For many of

Hawaii's nonwhite peoples, especially those of Japanese descent who had borne the brunt of hostility and suspicion, statehood was much more than a guarantee of unqualified political rights: by the 1940s it had become an emotive symbol of genuine acceptance into the wider American society.

Thirty-seven areas were accepted as states after confederation. But of these, the noncontiguous, multiracial territory of Hawaii was the most thoroughly studied, the most exhaustively investigated, and the most frequently rejected by Congress. The islands were subject to territorial rule for longer than all but one incorporated area, New Mexico. A mountain of testimony and information was collected through more than thirty congressional hearings and reports. Beginning shortly after annexation, Hawaii ritualistically, but with little initial enthusiasm, petitioned Congress for admission. After 1919 statehood bills were frequently introduced into Congress by the territory's nonvoting delegate. In 1935 economic difficulties confronting "King Sugar" prompted Hawaii to begin an organized, forceful, and expensive campaign for political equality with the existing states. Five years later, against a background of war in Europe and mounting tensions in the Pacific, a plebiscite indicated that more than two-thirds of Hawaii's electorate favored statehood. All Gallup polls conducted in the United States after 1945 also revealed that a substantial majority consistently favored immediate admission. Before the outbreak of World War II, a congressional committee had concluded that Hawaii was entitled to statehood because it fulfilled the traditional requirements for entry. After the war statehood was supported by both major national political parties, recommended by Truman and Eisenhower, and endorsed by an overwhelming majority of national editorial opinions. In addition, as Donald Dedmon concluded, those on the side of statehood always presented the stronger case in the exhaustive debates on the issue.[6] Yet Congress continued to deny Hawaii equality within the Union. Hawaii's statehood hopes were constantly dashed on the rocks of national politics in Washington.

An understanding of Hawaii's long-frustrated bid for statehood demands an appreciation of the ways in which it impinged on wider national controversies. These disputes determined its fate in Congress, especially during the war against Japan, the cold war, and the drive for desegregation and civil rights during the 1940s and 1950s. Consequently, the interplay of local and national developments provides the organizing structure of this book. Locally the struggle over statehood ranged those who viewed it as a legitimate and urgent democratic aspiration against those determined to stifle disruptive change. Nationally it sharpened conflict over such fundamental questions as minority rights in wartime, states' rights, internal subversion, appropriate patterns of

Americanization, racial equality, and relative party strengths in Congress. Statehood was withheld until it was finally extricated from these deep national conflicts.

Hawaii was always much more than an irritating political thorn in the side of the American body politic. Once annexed and incorporated as a territory, Hawaii presented Congress with an unprecedented dilemma: it raised unavoidably the question of equality under the nation's Constitution for a noncontiguous area with an essentially nonwhite population. The issue remained embarrassingly unresolved for sixty years. Hawaii's status within the Union, as well as its unique racial composition and ambiguous Americanization, provoked deep controversy, even hostility, in Washington. In particular, its diverse ethnic composition and tolerant social practices challenged the patterns of race relations imposed in many mainland states, notably those still segregated. On the other hand, the islands' dependent and restricted political status contradicted popular American notions of anti-colonialism, not to mention basic tenets of the Constitution and Bill of Rights. Appeals for statehood invariably highlighted these glaring contradictions. But in Washington the merits of Hawaii's case were much less persuasive than were the self-interested influences of certain geographic sections and party factions.

America's most prolonged and violent domestic crisis, the conflict between the North and the South which resulted in the bloody civil war of 1861–1865, was in part a result of political and racial tensions deriving from the issue of statehood for its territories. Moreover, contests over constitutional principles, moral and racial assumptions, expansion of the Union, and the balance of political or sectional forces within Congress were frequently translated into congressional debate on the nature and number of potential new states. Territories and their statehood aspirations were burning political questions in antebellum America. "Indeed," William R. Brock concluded recently, "the problem of governing distant territories was at the heart of much controversy during the period" leading up to the war.[7] The question of slavery versus freedom for such territories was obviously the most divisive dispute. But concern over this issue stemmed from mounting tension over the very nature of American federalism, involving the sovereignty of states within the Union as well as the racial complexion and social practices appropriate for new states. The elevation of territories to statehood had direct implications for this contest between the industrial North and the rural South, as new states might disrupt the delicate congressional balance which existed after the Missouri Compromise.

The considerations which confused and fuelled the controversy over continental expansion and states' rights were not buried with the North's hard-won victory over the South. They resurfaced, although usually in muted and rhetorical forms, whenever Congress contemplated giving an existing territory statehood. In the case of Hawaii, these considerations were more explicit and divisive than for any territory admitted after the Civil War. Yet even before the war, compromises between the sections and political parties sometimes brought territories into the Union fairly quickly. As Louisiana and Texas demonstrated, statehood was conferred rapidly when powerful factions could exploit the opportunity to boost their voting strength in Congress. By contrast, Hawaii was repeatedly denied admission so that the sectional and political status quo on Capitol Hill would not be disrupted. The racial and political complexion of Hawaii's voters, and the anticipated impact they would have on the fortunes of the conservative and racially sensitive factions of Congress, were the central reasons why it was for so long denied equality as a state. Cynical political partisanship, combined with Southern hostility to civil rights for nonwhite Americans, induced Congress to withhold statehood from Hawaii's heterogenous people until 1959.

Under the Constitution and the Northwest Ordinance, Congress has the power to admit new states and to "dispose of and make all needful Rules and Regulations respecting the Territory or other Property belonging to the United States." While America's expansion remained continental, precedent and judicial opinion ensured that territoriality was an intermediate step to full and equal statehood. Even during the heated, widening conflict over the admissions of such territories as Missouri and Maine or Kansas and Nebraska this principle was generally accepted. Dispute centered on the economic, racial, and political preferences of such territories, rather than on the ultimate entitlement of the inhabitants of these areas to statehood under the Constitution. The entry of Vermont and Kentucky as a pair of states in 1791 suggested very early in the history of the new republic that practical politics would override constitutional principles in determining the fate of America's many territories. States like Indiana and Mississippi (1816–1817) or Illinois and Alabama (1818–1819) were also accepted in pairs in order to maintain the delicate political and sectional balance in Congress. Yet this difficult juggling act was ultimately unable to prevent a bloody war between the states—a conflict fuelled at every level by issues relating to expansion of the Union, statehood for territories, and states' rights.

Despite the tragic consequences of sectional rivalry over admission of new states, constitutional historians like John Mathews have argued that Congress displayed a surprising willingness to accept them.[8] Nationalist historians like Daniel Boorstin, ever anxious to stress the unifying experience of nineteenth-century American democracy, have asserted that the Northwest Ordinance reduced state making to straightforward, simply followed procedures. For Boorstin, and indeed most American historians, his country's rapid spread westward was not synonymous with imperialist or colonial expansion but with the growth of democracy. "Over a broad continent," he concluded, " 'self-government' was created in place after place with perfunctory simplicity."[9] In this view territorial rule was but a brief, welcome interlude on the way to equality under the uniquely flexible American political system. But as slavery and segregation, the Civil War, and the fate of North American Indians all demonstrated, any consensus over the entitlement of all citizens to equality was fragile indeed. Even after the Civil War, statehood for some Western territories was determined by what might be considered irrelevant partisan concerns. These included the relative strengths of various parties and regions in Congress, opposition to alleged Western radicalism, and the perceived threat to dominant religious and social customs posed by groups such as Utah's Mormons.

As America expanded beyond continental boundaries in the 1890s, its overt democratic principles were again sharply challenged by the administrative and political structures it imposed on its newly dependent peoples. Washington moved very slowly after 1898 to resolve this contradiction. America remained a colonial power for a shorter time than the major European states; but this was largely a result of its late entry into the race for overseas possessions. If limited representative government came quickly to some parts of America's new empire, responsible government or sovereign equality did not. Hawaii's people lived under the inequalities of territorial rule until long after World War II. By deferring statehood, Congress openly tolerated this situation. Ironically, America's self-conscious anti-colonialism was not translated into an early resolution of Hawaii's dependent status. Indeed statehood came to America's island possession only after much of Asia and Africa had won independence from their European overlords.

Chapter 1
Toward Annexation

Foreign Penetration and Settlement

During the nineteenth century Hawaii's isolated native peoples found that distance was not a barrier to foreign penetration and settlement. In the face of mounting European and American expansion into the Pacific the Hawaiian kingdom was gradually transformed, its sovereignty eroded, its culture and social fabric undermined. The future of the islands was shaped increasingly by forces and values foreign to the small Polynesian population of this remote archipelago. And, as the century wore on, the United States rather than Europe became the principal source of the powerful influences which cut across every facet of island life. Annexation, territorial government, and eventually statehood were the tangible symbols of this gradual absorption into an expanding America.

The influence and power of American settlers in Hawaii grew steadily throughout the nineteenth century. At the same time mainland interest in the islands intensified. Hawaii's survival as an independent monarchy was increasingly threatened by American settlers in the islands and expansionists on the mainland. Yet even before its monarchy was overthrown, Hawaii enjoyed, at most, a very tenuous independence. The principal forces undermining Hawaii's autonomy were associated with the development of a single crop, sugar. More than any other factor this crop transformed the islands. It brought radical changes to their demographic and social structures, and concentrated economic and political power in the hands of a few immigrant families.

As early as the 1840s American commercial influence surpassed that of any other nation. It was estimated, for example, that more than 80 percent of all ships entering island ports in this decade were American owned.[1] Missionaries, who arrived in substantial numbers after the first Congregationalists reached Oahu in 1820, were also overwhelmingly American. Traders and missionaries quickly transformed the economic and cultural base of the islands, competing unashamedly for the allegiances of the native population. Even so, as late as 1850 whites comprised less than 3 percent of the total population of about eighty thousand.[2] New settlers were quick to exploit their rich new environment. As the seemingly unlimited potential of sugar production was realized, landownership soon came to be concentrated in the hands of European and American settlers and their descendents, or haoles as they were locally known. Many of those who eagerly reaped this new harvest were missionaries or their descendents. Transporting the Protestant ethic to tropical conditions may have confused and demoralized the indigenous population, but it generated very tangible rewards for the carriers of Christianity. "They came to do good, and they did well," was a comment widely used in the islands; it captures well the feelings of many Hawaiians about the consequences of these missionary activities. By the 1880s second-generation missionary families like the Baldwins, Cookes, Alexanders, Rices, Wilcoxes, and Hancocks dominated the plantation economy and were diversifying into other business and trading activities.[3]

White penetration and settlement of the island kingdom brought rapid changes, and tragic consequences, for its native inhabitants. Disease and conquest reduced a Hawaiian population of perhaps 300,000* in the 1770s to less than 135,000 fifty years later, and to about 70,000 at the time of the first formal census in 1853. The old quasi-feudalistic social order was undermined by practices and assumptions imported by those who came to trade, plant, or to carry out missionary work in the islands. The role of the monarch and the influence of native Hawaiians were gradually eroded. Although it is not the aim of this study to discuss in detail the impact of white settlement on nineteenth-century Hawaiian society and culture, it nevertheless must be emphasized that the commercial and political triumph of Caucasian settlers over the natives, symbolized so unambiguously in the overthrow of the monarchy and annexation during the 1890s, was a fundamental result of the destruction and demoralization of the aboriginal populations of the islands during the preceding century. It was fortuitous indeed for the white settlers, haoles, who journeyed to Hawaii seeking land and wealth that foreign penetration reduced the numbers and cohesion of its native peoples. By the time of annexation, political control was indisputably in the hands of a small white, essentially American minority comprising only 5 percent of the total population; Christianity and capitalism dominated the cultural and economic fabrics of both Hawaiian and haole societies, and white men owned more than three-quarters of all land in the islands. Sixty years earlier David Malo, a Hawaiian scholar and nationalist, had commented prophetically: "The white man's ships have arrived with clever men from the big countries. They know our people are few in number and our country is small. They will devour us."[4]

Paradoxically, plantation agriculture—which demanded a plentiful, cheap, and controlled labor force—emerged at the time when Hawaii's native population was suffering a precipitous decline. Until the turn of the century when the native population, Hawaiians and part-Hawai-

*This figure is now widely disputed as being too high, perhaps by as much as 50,000 to 100,000.

ians, stabilized at about forty thousand, it declined annually by an estimated 2 percent. Even if the native population had not fallen so
sharply, it is unlikely that it would have provided an enthusiastic or adequate labor supply for the burgeoning plantations. Hawaiians and part-
Hawaiians were reluctant to sanction growing haole influence in government or the economy. Political cleavages in the late nineteenth
century, for example, were essentially along Hawaiian versus haole
lines, although both groups implicitly accepted that the political influence of Asians should be restricted. The native population also proudly
resisted subjugation as convenient labor under white control. Permanent work under a competitive economic system was alien to Hawaiian
traditions. "The whole idea of steady work for wages was so foreign to
their old culture that it had no value or appeal to them," Edwin Burrows has written. This reluctance to work as hired plantation laborers
also resulted from the fact that conditions on the plantation were usually harsh and exhausting, tolerated largely by those laborers tied to
contracts from which they could not escape.[5] But if the intractability of
Hawaiian workers was influenced by the nature of plantation work, it
also symbolized a broad hostility to the consequences of conquest and
dispossession during the nineteenth century.

Like their mainland counterparts before them, plantation owners
looked abroad for an appropriate labor force—one that was numerous,
inexpensive, and tractable. After the 1850s approximately four hundred
thousand workers and dependents, many of whom were bound by rigid
labor contracts, were recruited to work on Hawaii's plantations. In
1864 ad hoc private recruitments were replaced by an efficient system
of contract labor organized jointly by planters. In the following years
workers from East Asia arrived in large numbers. They became the
backbone of the islands' prosperous plantation economy, an economy
dominated by a wealthy group of plantation owners which historians
have appropriately labelled a "dynastic elite." The stability and profits
of this class were built on a labor force which it controlled by a combination of "perquisite paternalism" and, when necessary, outright
suppression of unrest and organized protest. Plantations operated as
essentially autonomous economic and social units, free from close government scrutiny—an ideal climate for enterprises which depended on
cheap, essentially unfree labor.[6]

Initially southern Chinese formed the nucleus of Hawaii's contract
labor force. Most arrived after the late 1870s. In 1882, when the U.S.
Congress passed its Chinese exclusion act, Chinese laborers comprised
about half of the total work force on Hawaii's plantations. However,
many returned home immediately upon expiration of their contracts.
Others disappointed their masters and at the first opportunity left the
plantation in search of more rewarding employment in Honolulu. Asian
immigration was indeed a thorny question. Many islanders were ambiv-

alent about it; they viewed it as both an economic necessity and a growing social threat. Haoles, Hawaiians, and part-Hawaiians generally
agreed that their community must not accept large numbers of laborers
from any one Asian nation. Even the mouthpiece of those who so fervently promoted contract labor, the *Planters' Monthly*, anticipated
problems. It was alarmed that uncontrolled Chinese immigration foreshadowed "an oversupply of this class." The journal argued that such an
influx could only be viewed as acceptable if the Chinese were tied to
contracts which compelled them to return eventually to their homeland. Despite efforts to find alternative workers, during the 1890s
about fifteen thousand more Chinese entered Hawaii, bringing the total
at the time of annexation to an estimated forty-six thousand.[7] Chinese
immigration ended abruptly with annexation as the islands were brought
under the authority of America's infamous Chinese exclusion act.

In the face of mounting opposition to the Chinese, planters looked
anxiously to other regions for labor. Initially they succeeded in recruit-
ing substantial numbers of Europeans (although, as Andrew Lind has
pointed out, these people were regarded and dealt with as a separate
racial group for as long as they stayed on the plantation). Portuguese
laborers were brought in from the Azores and Madeira Islands—twelve
thousand arrived in the decade after 1878; another six thousand in the
following twenty years. At the turn of the century other European or
part-European workers were imported, especially Spaniards (about
eight thousand) and Puerto Ricans (about six thousand).[8] In an age
accepting of social Darwinism and entrenched racism, Europeans were
reluctant to agree to labor contracts usually identified as appropriate
only for nonwhites, whether they were of Asian, African, or Pacific
island extraction. But if notions of white supremacy restricted the availability of cheap European labor, they also sustained and excused a rigid
system of contract labor for nonwhites.

In the absence of other adequate sources, Hawaii's planters continued
to look to Asia for laborers. With rural recession and starvation afflict-
ing many peasants in Honshu and Kyushu in the 1880s, owners induced
large numbers of Japanese to uproot themselves with the promise of
work and prosperity in Hawaii. From 1886, when the Meiji government
accepted new immigration levels, to 1924, when the Japanese exclusion
act was formally approved, about 180,000 Japanese arrived in Hawaii.
During these years also, about 8,000 Korean laborers were brought in.
Roughly half of the Japanese eventually returned to their homeland,
but the remainder and their descendents established permanent roots.
By 1900 they comprised the largest single ethnic component of Hawaii's
by then diverse population. Only slowly, however, did the Japanese
move from plantation to town or city, from the deprivations of contract
labor to the limited opportunities available to them in the wider community. Until they were supplanted by newer arrivals from the Philip-

pines, the Japanese remained the worst paid, least mobile, most separate and oppressed group in the islands.[9]

The history of Hawaii's annexation, and ultimate statehood, can only be understood against this background of racial and social change. The influx of plantation workers transformed the island community, giving it a unique ethnic mix and distinctive social patterns. These became central issues in every facet of the long struggle for statehood. By the 1890s, ethnic stratification and economic class systems were complicated and rigid. Solid class barriers separated a relatively small oligarchy of whites from much larger groups of nonwhite laborers. Pronounced divisions also cut across the laboring class, reflecting ethnic differences and the sequence of arrival of the various groups. Virtually no middle class existed, although some Chinese, poorer whites, and part-Hawaiians performed service and entrepreneurial functions usually associated with a middle class. Many Hawaiians and part-Hawaiians remained isolated geographically and socially, reluctant to work for white masters on plantations, ambivalent about the possible advantages of urban life or Western education and training, but resigned to the further erosion of their culture and traditions. "The social structure of Hawaii was a curious amalgam of a tropical European colony and a New England settlement," Fuchs has observed.

> In Hawaii, as in the European colonies, there was virtually no middle class. Oriental immigrants comprised almost 75 per cent of the population. There were many Chinese merchants and peddlers and a sprinkling of Japanese trade workers in town; but none of them could vote, few held land, and there was no social mixing with the upper-class haoles. . . . On top were the haoles, only slightly more than 5 per cent of the population, controlling politics, land, enterprise, and labor. . . . There was no middle class in the American sense of small independent landholders or small businessmen. Prestige, power and status were firmly in the possession of a small haole élite.[10]

Yet the authority of the haoles was somewhat tenuous. Certainly, many felt deeply insecure in the face of their physical isolation, ethnic separateness, and small numbers. These white settlers looked anxiously to Washington for assurances of support in the event of political or economic difficulties. In general, after the early 1870s Washington responded sympathetically to their appeals. Successive governments were anxious to secure a foothold in the islands and determined to exclude European countries or Japan from this vital Pacific outpost. The islands were a crucial link in America's strategic planning and commerce well before they were brought under its permanent control in 1898.

Hawaii and the Debate Over American Empire

During two distinct periods of expansion the United States developed into a large, powerful state with a substantial overseas empire.[11] The first phase of expansion was exclusively continental, linking the original Atlantic seaboard states with the western territories on the Pacific coast by the 1840s. The second, much briefer thrust at the turn of the century extended America's formal authority and informal influence across the vast waters of the Pacific and into the Caribbean. Each phase reflected a blend of economic, strategic, and jingoistic incentives. Although ultimately based on physical power, each stage was sanctioned and rationalized by notions of manifest destiny and a pervasive belief that it was the new nation's mission to assume moral leadership of a Western Hemisphere untainted by the Old World. All areas acquired during the first phase of expansion were quickly incorporated as territories and thereby constitutionally assured eventual statehood. Areas taken during America's outward thrust in the 1890s were governed very differently. Congress did not accept that these new possessions were necessarily entitled to eventual equality within the Union, or to sovereign independence as separate nations. The issues of political and civil rights for their inhabitants were not resolved in a uniform way. The Constitution and Bill of Rights no longer automatically followed the flag.[12] Government of America's new empire differed sharply from that exercised over contiguous areas previously incorporated as territories of the Union. Of these new possessions, only Hawaii was ever incorporated[13] or given statehood. Its unique fate was the result of particular pressures, both local and national in origin, which coalesced at the turn of the century.

Immigrants from the mainland had extended America's frontier to the Hawaiian islands by the 1840s, but European settlers and European powers also competed for influence and profits in the small kingdom. While Washington did not seek colonial authority over the islands, it was adamant that no other power be permitted to colonize them. Twenty years after the Monroe Doctrine attempted to exclude European imperialists from the Western Hemisphere, President John Tyler issued a similar warning to any nation which might covet the Hawaiian islands. A special relationship now existed between Hawaii and the United States, he implied in 1842, and his government would not tolerate any threat to Hawaii's independence. In the following year Secretary of State Daniel Webster affirmed that America's interest in Hawaii exceeded that of any nation. Shortly afterward President Millard Fillmore asserted that Hawaii "should not pass under the control of any other great maritime State, but should remain in an independent condition and so be accessible and useful to the commerce of all nations."[14] Against this background the French foreign minister predicted: "The Sandwich Islands seem inevitably destined to come under the direct influence if not a complete annexation on the part of the United States." In the same year, 1849, a New York newspaper, the *Northern Journal*, advocated statehood following immediate annexation of the islands by the United States. The Honolulu newspaper *Polynesia* was informed by its New York correspondent that a number of influential papers shared that sentiment.[15] Yet during the 1840s, despite unprecedented national fervor for expansion, Washington was content simply to apply the vague terms of the Monroe Doctrine in the hope of dissuading other nations from encroaching on the islands.

Such imprecise claims, however, did not appease the Americans who had settled in the islands. They attempted to secure either annexation by the United States or, failing this, a commercial monopoly for American settlers. Such proposals found growing sympathy on the mainland. Antebellum support for acquiring new territory in the Pacific developed against a background of direct naval, commercial, and missionary involvement in Asia. In 1853 Commodore Perry's gunboats opened Japan to Western penetration. Justifying this unprecedented action, Perry foreshadowed the extension of American power and territorial control beyond continental limits. "It is self-evident," he observed with rather curious logic, "that the course of coming events will ere long make it necessary for the United States to extend its jurisdiction beyond the limits of the Western continent."[16] For those who shared Perry's view, Hawaii was a unique stepping stone to Asia.

During the 1850s annexation, and even statehood, received serious consideration at the highest levels in Washington and Honolulu. In the following decades some native Hawaiians believed that annexation was synonymous with statehood. Few white settlers or American officials shared this view, but it did receive some encouragement from Washington. In 1852 the supporters of President Franklin Pierce celebrated his election with a toast to the islands, which included the wish: "May they soon be added to the galaxy of states." Following a petition from the ageing and insecure King Kauikeaouli (Kamehameha III), the Pierce administration drafted a treaty of annexation. But while the unsteady monarch and some of his white supporters were inclined to surrender Hawaii's sovereignty to the United States, many Hawaiians were not. To ensure that the kingdom's status did not change, and to overrule their king, the draft treaty finally negotiated by the Hawaiian officials in Washington anticipated not only annexation but immediate statehood as well. It stated, in part:

> [The] Hawaiian Islands shall be incorporated into the American Union as a State enjoying the same degree of sovereignty as other States, and admitted as such as soon as it can be done in consistency with the principles and requirements of the Federal Constitution, to all the rights, privileges and immunities of a State as aforesaid on a perfect equality with other States of the Union.[17]

The proposal to grant Hawaii equality was radical indeed: it would have given the largely non-Caucasian island peoples political equality with white mainland Americans. It must be remembered that Congress had not yet moved to abolish slavery; nor had Congress established real equality for some other minorities, notably native Americans. Clearly, the Hawaiian delegates recognized that while annexation might be approved, statehood would not. The statehood clause was inserted deliberately by the king's officials to jeopardize his rash initiative. Predictably, Congress refused to act. Kauikeaouli's death in December 1854 and his succession by the forceful pro-British Kamehameha IV abruptly ended these premature negotiations.[18]

In the following year, a reciprocal treaty abolishing duties on sugar imported from Hawaii also failed to gain approval by Congress. Fearing competition from such imports, sugar producers from the mainland South had lobbied heavily against the treaty. Again, in 1867, a reciprocal treaty was rejected. Protectionist sentiment in the plantation South again proved decisive, but other considerations were also significant. Despite Secretary of State William Seward's desire to annex the islands, expansionism did not yet command majority support in Congress or throughout the nation. In addition to commercial factors, racial considerations retarded efforts to forge closer permanent ties with Hawaii. Southern whites (and many Northerners also) remained convinced that all nonwhites, whether they be blacks or Asians, were inherently and irreversibly inferior to whites. Equally, they were adamant that racial difficulties and tensions had been compounded by emancipation and Reconstruction in the 1860s. These problems would be further aggravated, they argued, if additional non-Caucasians were incorporated into America's society. But racial questions cut across the early mainland debate on Hawaii's future in an ambivalent way. Some of the most liberal critics of the racial prejudices and stereotyping which afflicted Civil War America were also vigorously opposed to any expansion of their country's influence on the islands. Former abolitionist Charles Sumner, for example, opposed reciprocity for reasons which were very different from those advanced by most whites. He argued that closer economic or political ties would condemn Hawaii's nonwhite peoples to an inferior status in a new nation with an unfortunate record on racial issues, and deprive the islands and their inhabitants of eventual sovereign independence. Undoubtedly, many native Hawaiians shared Sumner's alarm. But as the nineteenth century drew to a close, such concerns had less and less impact on whites in either community.[19]

America's interest in the islands grew relentlessly throughout the nineteenth century. But other colonial powers also competed for Hawaii's resources. In 1843 a struggle between Britain and France resulted in a brief interlude of British colonial rule over the kingdom. Although British influence should not be overestimated, it did remain strong in the 1850s despite Washington's efforts to invoke the Monroe Doctrine against any European adventures in the islands. Kamehameha IV and Queen Emma were openly sympathetic to Britain, and ruled with the aid of numerous English advisers. As late as 1875 about one-third of Hawaii's sugar went to the British Empire. However, the European states and European settlers did not triumph. From the 1860s on Hawaii's economy and trade were dominated by American settlers and investors; and this group felt much less threatened by a residual European presence than by rising Japanese ambitions in the Pacific and by changes in the islands' racial mix. Numerical insecurity combined with a deep-seated belief in the inherent right of white men to rule over the uncivilized native races of such a tropical outpost led to growing demands that Hawaii be a de facto, if not an actual, protectorate of the United States. Fortunately for the white minority, such appeals were viewed with fresh sympathy in Washington after the Civil War. In 1868 President Andrew Johnson told Congress that the two Pacific countries should establish reciprocal free trade until Hawaii "shall . . . at no distant day, voluntarily apply for admission into the Union." President Grant went a step further and in 1871 asked Congress to consider annexation: "That such is to be the political destiny of this archipelago seems a foregone conclusion," he stated prophetically.[20] But Congress was not yet convinced of the logic of such pronouncements.

Perry's belief that America would win overseas possessions was not quickly realized. Although it purchased Alaska in 1867, America's actual military power and foreign adventures were still very limited.[21] Believing itself immune to the conflicts of the Old World and protected from foreign entanglements by the Monroe Doctrine, the United States remained essentially isolationist after the Civil War. Understandably, it was preoccupied with healing the wounds of its own recently ended internal conflict. Some prominent figures argued for Pacific colonies and an isthmian canal to boost access to East Asia. Nevertheless, Henry Cabot Lodge was scarcely exaggerating when he complained as late as 1889: "Our relations with foreign nations fill but a slight place in American politics, and excite generally only a languid interest."[22] Events in the 1890s quickly made this claim obsolete, as the United States hurriedly joined the major European states and Japan as a colonial and expansionist power.

After a century of conquest, purchase, and settlement, the thirteen original Eastern seaboard states had grown into a republic of forty-eight continental states or territories entitled to eventual admission as states. John Quincy Adams' vision of an America stretching from ocean to ocean had been realized—but at great cost to the aboriginal inhabitants and only after war had forced the dissenting Southern states back into the Union. With the trauma of war and the frustrations of Reconstruction behind them, the United States turned outward seeking new territory, markets, resources, and strategic outposts. The western frontier had ended, and many sought a new frontier. "We are the most advanced and powerful people on earth, and regard to our future welfare demands an abandonment of the doctrines of isolation," Senator Orville Platt asserted in 1893. "It is to the ocean that our children must look as they once looked to the boundless West."[23] Opposition to imperialism was strong in some sectors of the American Congress, public, and press, but during the following decade Platt's views prevailed.

During the 1890s ideals of national mission and economic self-interest propelled America outward. An increasing number of intellectuals, publicists, and politicians like Lodge, Alfred T. Mahan, Walter Hines Page, Theodore Roosevelt, and Albert Shaw urged that new territories be acquired, especially if these lay on the way to new markets abroad. In 1893, for example, the influential Mahan echoed Seward's earlier call for a Central American canal and for annexation of Hawaii. These, he argued, would establish the United States as the dominant commercial and strategic factor in the Pacific and Far East. They would also give the products of Eastern states safe access to vast new markets, and provide naval protection for the Western states.[24] At the same time manufacturers, traders, and entrepreneurs intensified their appeals for new foreign markets, especially in China. While market rewards in Asia ultimately proved illusory, the myth of the vast China market was nonetheless a vital stimulant to expansion.[25] To argue that expansion was fundamentally based on economic incentives, however, is not to suggest that business leaders conspired to lead America into war with Spain. Nor is it to imply that after territories were acquired as springboards to East Asia, the American economy was saved from periodic downturns or major depressions. On the contrary, the rewards of expansion and empire rarely met the grandiose expectations of late-nineteenth-century imperialists.

Although exaggerated, the belief persisted that America must find new markets or risk domestic gluts, recession, and instability. In the 1890s both the industrial and rural sectors of the American economy experienced acute depression. Huge gluts confronted farmers and manufacturers. Prices for farm products were now lower than at any time since the bleak days of the 1840s. Unprecedented industrial efficiency resulted in overproduction for a saturated domestic market. New overseas markets, as well as an expanded local demand through immigration, were viewed increasingly as solutions to this malaise. Abroad, however, access to markets was apparently being stifled by decisions over which no administration in Washington had any control. A wave of protectionism in Europe erected new barriers against American imports. In China possible American markets were threatened as the old European imperialists and Japan attempted to carve the decaying Manchu Empire into spheres of exclusive national influence. Clearly, American expansionists were not alone in thinking that embarrassing domestic surpluses could be absorbed in new overseas markets. Furthermore, the United States viewed the grab for colonies in Africa and Asia by the European states as an additional threat to its own economic expansion. The actions of the Old World imperialists provided a convenient justification for similar American behavior, at least in the Pacific, East Asia, and the Caribbean. Pressure to control Pacific way stations to the allegedly limitless markets of Asia, and later efforts to gain equal access to China through the Open Door policy, signalled America's belated participation in the "new imperialism" which all major industrial states embraced in the late nineteenth century.[26]

For the advocates of expansionism, the Hawaiian islands were ideally situated, both geographically and politically. Since the early 1800s they had served as a vital refuelling and supply station for trade in sandalwood, silks, teas, chinaware, and furs between the West Coast and Canton. American interests, settlement, and investment in the islands had also developed through stages of whaling, missionary activity, sugar planting, and commerce. Anticipating later arguments by expansionists like Mahan, Secretary of State James G. Blaine had advised his minister in Honolulu in 1881 that exclusive control of Hawaii and the proposed Panama Canal were essential for extending America's commercial empire in the Pacific. Hawaii, he asserted, "holds in the western sea much the same position as Cuba in the Atlantic. It is the key to the Gulf trade . . . [U]nder no circumstances can the United States permit any changes in the territorial control of either which would cut it adrift from the American system, whereto they both indispensably belong."[27] Support for this view grew quickly in the years before war with Spain. "We need Hawaii just as much and a great deal more than we did California," William McKinley wrote shortly before he was elected president in 1896. "It is Manifest Destiny."[28] Some of McKinley's advisors shared the view that Hawaii's annexation was an essential element in the drive to secure a share of China. In addition, the president's political mentor, Mark Hanna, suggested that control of the Philippines would also help the United States "take a large slice of the commerce of Asia." After the dust of war with Spain had settled, a leading Republican, Chauncey M. Depew, unambiguously acknowledged the relationship between surplus production at home and colonial adventures abroad when he stated:

> The American people now produced $2 billion worth more than they can consume, and we have met the emergency, and by the providence of God, by the statesmanship of William McKinley, and by the valor of Roosevelt and his associates, we have our market in Cuba . . . in Puerto Rico . . . in Hawaii . . . in the Philippines, and we stand in the presence of 800 million people, with the Pacific as an American lake, and the American artisans producing better and cheaper goods than any country in the world. . . . [T]he world is ours and we have conquered it by Republican principles.[29]

Hawaii, like the Philippines, was considered vital as both a market and a base for wider opportunities. But a broad consensus on Hawaii, the

Philippines, and an isthmian canal did not emerge until war erupted with Spain over Cuba in 1898.

It would be misleading to imply that America's interest in Hawaii simply reflected economic imperatives, recognized and supported by a sympathetic national government. If explicit economic motives were pushing the United States toward overseas commitments by the 1890s, other factors also affected policymakers. Economic factors were fundamental, but they were often rationalized or disguised. As Marilyn B. Young has convincingly argued, the United States went to war with Spain and acquired territories in the Pacific, Asia, and the Caribbean as a result of a range of nationalistic, religious, racist, and political, as well as economic, factors. These merged after about 1895 into a "national neurosis [which] . . . was acted out in the fantastic fervor which preceded the war [with Spain] and perhaps made it inevitable." Certainly by the time Hawaii was annexed many Americans had incorporated (albeit subconsciously) economic aims into a broader perspective "which saw a strong navy, trade, political power and the territory . . . necessary to maintain both trade and power, as complementary factors contributing to the wealth and strength of the nation." Young concludes appropriately that the "economic arguments used by the imperialists were an integral part of a larger complex of nationalist ideals."[30] Certainly there were also times during the debate over imperialism when the rhetoric of marketplace expansion was conveniently invoked to bolster the popular support that vague appeals to prestige, security, and glory sometimes failed to elicit.[31] The very term "manifest destiny" was sufficiently vague and emotive to serve those who sought overseas territory for whatever reason or reasons.

In the 1840s when America was pushing its continental frontiers to their limits, manifest destiny and assumptions of Anglo-Saxon superiority and mission helped stimulate and justify expansion and conquest. In the 1890s these ideas resurfaced; but now, with the addition of social Darwinism, they were more vigorous and "scientific." Writers John Fiske, Josiah Strong, and John W. Burgess were the principal exponents of such views in the later period. Burgess, for example, argued that Teutonic people were "entrusted, in the general economy of history, with the mission of conducting the political civilization of the modern world."[32] Other expansionists, however, were less impressed with appeals to mission than with the possible political consequences of economic dislocation at home. Some pragmatic conservatives argued, for example, that overseas adventures were necessary if the internal division and antagonisms which had attended industrialization, urbanization, and recession in Europe were to be averted in America. "While it might be putting it too strong to say that war is needed in this country now," a Kansas newspaper editorialized, "yet who is there who does not believe, and in fact know, that such a thing would clear the air and stamp out the growth of socialism and anarchy, discontent and sectional prejudices that are gaining a foothold in this nation."[33]

Even among those who argued that an empire was needed there was little agreement on how it might be won. No broad consensus ever existed on the desirability or nature of expansion. Moreover, despite the nationalist hysteria which accompanied the crusade for war with Spain in 1898, opposition to imperialism was very strong in some quarters. Opponents of Hawaii's annexation embraced a wide range of views and interests. The Southern sugar lobby continued to resist closer national ties with an obvious competitor for the limited domestic market. It was also alarmed that annexation of Hawaii would foreshadow acquisition of other territories which could produce sugar relatively cheaply with the help of a compliant non-European work force. Labor interests feared, albeit irrationally, competition from a flood of cheap Asian workers. Anti-imperialists like Senator George Frisbie Hoar, philosopher William James, industrialist Edward Atkinson, labor leader Samuel Gompers, and the *Nation*'s editor E. L. Godkin argued that colonialism was fundamentally undemocratic, inhumane, and immoral. For this group imperialism was an unfortunate departure from traditional American practices. "Most importantly," Thomas Osborne has concluded:

> The anti-imperialists were certain that Hawaii's acquisition constituted the "entering wedge" of a new imperialist policy. For them the annexation of an insular nation symbolized America's loss of innocence. The opponents of empire viewed the United States as the archetype of a virtuous republic—a secularized "City upon a Hill". The possession of Hawaii signified the abandonment of America's time-honored mission of exemplifying the workings of self-government and augured the drift into colonialism with all its attendant embroilments and injustices.

Moreover, Osborne has demonstrated that anti-imperialists were not unanimously and indefinitely opposed to Hawaii's annexation. Some wavered, believing only that territorial expansion was premature, that "Empire Can Wait." Events in Hawaii in 1893 had precipitated America's "Great Debate" over empire, but until 1898 the views of the anti-imperialists generally prevailed in Washington.[34]

Racial arguments and racial fear were also important ingredients in the debate over Hawaii and overseas expansion generally. Ignoring America's substantial black, Indian, and Asian populations, some opponents of annexation argued that incorporation of a so-called mongrel population of detested and dangerous Asiatics would permanently undermine the Anglo-Saxon tradition of the nation. Convinced of the innate inferiority of all who were not derived from Anglo-Saxon or Teutonic stock, these anti-imperialists argued that Asian and Polynesian peoples must be excluded from the political umbrella of the American

Republic. No noncontiguous areas or non-Caucasian peoples should be incorporated, as this would undermine the geographical and racial unity of the Union. The difficulties resulting from emancipation and Reconstruction were sufficient to convince many that America must not embrace new regions populated by people not readily assimilable. If the nation's Constitution was extended to Hawaii or Asia, Congress would confront new dilemmas over race relations: "In the name of the white men of America," Representative Robert F. Broussard of Louisiana argued, "let us not enlarge the scope of this race question." The cultural, racial, and political supremacy of Anglo-Saxons within America would be diluted and perhaps negated by overseas imperialism, Thomas M. Cooley wrote in *Forum* during 1893: "[T]here was an instinctive feeling among American people that protested against the thought . . . that the Constitution of the United States should have capacity for expansion that might extend it over independent states of colored people." If the Constitution permitted the establishment of states consisting of non-whites, he asserted, it might "be extended to cover colonies in Arabia or in Zululand which would eventually become states and send representatives to Washington to assist in governing us." For Cooley, racial issues presented serious impediments to Hawaii's annexation.[35] During the following sixty years most of those opposed to statehood for the islands held a similar view, although their arguments were usually couched in more moderate language.

National opinion in the 1890s was not clearly divided along imperialist versus anti-imperialist lines. Substantial sections of business, Congress, and the informed public differed over specific issues like Hawaii and Cuba, and expressed diverse views on the extent and nature of possible expansion. Some sought colonies in the Pacific but not in Asia or Central America; some promoted informal empire through spheres of influence and the Open Door; others argued conventionally that tougher diplomacy would enable the United States to compete satisfactorily for international markets without acquiring an overseas empire.

However, the opinions of Americans living in the islands were much less divided, at least in relation to the issue of annexation. Their views were shaped by local events which initially had only a limited bearing on the national debate over expansion and empire. Foremost among these was the rebellion against Hawaii's monarchy: in the early 1890s a powerful group of whites abruptly overthrew the old order and immediately asked Washington to annex the islands.

Revolution: End of the Monarchy

The rapid growth of Hawaii's sugar industry and its substantial dependence on American markets after the 1850s provided the foundations on which political union with the United States ultimately rested. When the American Civil War abruptly ended the supply of domestic sugar to the Northern states, the demand for "Sandwich Island sugar" escalated sharply. Capitalizing on this unexpected opportunity island producers boosted production almost tenfold, to about nine thousand tons annually at the end of the Civil War. But with reconstruction of the South's economy came revived competition for Hawaii's growers, who recognized that their long-term prosperity depended on guaranteed access to the American market. Predictably, all efforts to secure formal guarantees were strenuously resisted by representatives of the reemerging South (and for the next one hundred years this pattern was repeated whenever Hawaii sought closer ties with Washington). In an attempt to win permanent duty-free access to the U.S. market, Hawaii was willing to grant the United States exclusive, unrestricted trading rights. But in the decades after the Civil War Washington was less interested in Hawaii's markets than in Pacific security and way stations to Asia. In particular it was anxious to obtain naval station rights at Puuloa (Pearl Harbor), and in return was prepared to grant trading concessions to Hawaii. Ultimately it was the islands' strategic location rather than the promise of immediate commercial advantage which drew the two unequal nations into a special relationship.

The turning point came unexpectedly in 1874, following the death of King Lunalilo. In the elections for a successor, David Kalakaua easily defeated the queen dowager, Emma, the pro-British widow of Kamehameha IV. Later in the year Kalakaua sailed for the United States—the first reigning monarch to make this journey. Meanwhile his representatives pressed for a treaty of reciprocity, although as we have seen, similar initiatives had been rejected during the Civil War and early years of Reconstruction. However, Hawaii's rulers were not anxious to surrender or compromise their nation's sovereignty. Kalakaua was a fervent nationalist and widely regarded as anti-haole. He refused to make unnecessary concessions to any foreign power, but at the same time he appreciated that his vulnerable kingdom could not stand alone. Despite the king's fruitful discussions with President Grant, it was the appeals of Hawaii's increasingly vocal white settlers which ultimately induced Washington to accept a treaty.

The reciprocity arrangements took effect in 1876. They gave Hawaii's sugar duty-free entry into the United States, on condition that the kingdom undertook to make no territorial concessions to any other foreign power. Nor was Hawaii permitted to grant any other nation the privileges of reciprocity. As a concession to mainland sugar interests and to satisfy those congressmen who wanted Pearl Harbor ceded to America, the treaty was to be renegotiated after eight years. In the interval, however, it was an unprecedented victory for Hawaii's white settlers who had anxiously petitioned Washington: "it is on all accounts desirable that our interests should be increasingly and abundantly protected." The treaty served the United States as a signal to all other nations of its special interest in the islands. It was for the United States an unequivocal statement, reiterating that the Monroe Doctrine embraced this distant Pacific outpost, as well as continental America.[36]

The anticipated boom in sugar production immediately followed the new treaty. Hawaii's economy became more closely integrated with, and essentially dependent on, the United States market, capital, and expertise. "The country's economy in effect became mortgaged to the United States," Milton Plesur has observed.[37] For Hawaii's restless planters, however, the treaty did more than provide a guaranteed market and increased profits. Like most haoles, the planters were convinced that Washington was now sympathetic to their pleas for support. Reciprocity was thus interpreted as the first step toward annexation.

The Southern sugar states continued their strong opposition to any form of protection for Hawaii's nascent plantation industries, but by the 1880s principal mainland concern had largely shifted from fear of economic competition to questions of race and immigration control. As Hawaii's planters depended increasingly on Asian labor, alarm was expressed that Hawaii might be transformed into an Asiatic society, controlled perhaps by a rival European power or Japan. By 1881 Secretary Blaine was sufficiently disturbed to instruct his ministers in Paris, Berlin, and London that his government would not tolerate any transfer of Hawaiian territory to another power. He emphasized also that the islands lay within the field of legitimate American commercial domination and must be considered a part of what he suggested vaguely was the American system. Blaine maintained, and his successors implicitly agreed, that in any dispute involving America, Hawaii must maintain "benevolent neutrality" or risk being exposed to an "avowedly American solution." Well before the expansionist surge of 1898, administration officials were prepared to threaten war in order to keep the islands a de facto protectorate of the United States. Such behavior was not without precedent. During the 1880s Washington exploited the terms of its 1878 agreement with Samoa and intervened to ensure Samoa's neutrality, and its own preeminence in the western Pacific. In 1888 these maneuvers resulted in Washington becoming one member of a tripartite protectorate for Samoa. In Samoa, as in Hawaii, America had demonstrated a willingness to confront European states and risk war to promote seemingly minor strategic or trading interests in a remote part of the Pacific. Such behavior foreshadowed stronger initiatives in the 1890s.[38]

The Reciprocity Treaty was renewed and extended in 1884 and 1887, when the United States was granted exclusive access to Pearl Harbor as a naval station. Many newspapers now argued that control of Hawaii was essential if America's commercial and strategic interests were to be protected.[39] A further extension of the treaty was widely anticipated.

Three years later, however, these expectations were suddenly dashed. Congress, through the controversial McKinley Act, abolished all duties on imported raw sugar but at the same time granted local producers a bounty of two cents per pound. Hawaii ceased to receive any tangible benefits from the Reciprocity Treaty. It was lumped with all other foreign producers and placed at a disadvantage relative to domestic producers. More than any single event, the McKinley Act spurred local support for annexation, especially among the dominant white business and sugar groups. The bounty threatened the very livelihood of plantation owners in the islands. Surprisingly, this reversal coincided with other developments which implied that American support for closer formal ties, and eventually annexation, had not waned. In 1891 Secretary Blaine, now a member of President Harrison's administration, advised:

> There are only three places that are of value enough to be taken that are not continental. One is Hawaii and the others are Cuba and Porto Rico. Cuba and Porto Rico are not now imminent and will not be for a generation. Hawaii may come up for decision at any unexpected hour and I hope we shall be prepared to decide in the affirmative.

Harrison was equally convinced of the obvious and urgent need for maintaining and expanding the nation's hold on the islands.[40] But when the "unexpected hour" arrived in January 1893, neither Congress nor the administration acted as Blaine had hoped.

Within Hawaii the tariff dispute confirmed what many whites had long believed—that annexation was essential for the very survival of their wealth and growing political power. In 1887 influential haoles succeeded in bringing the lower house and King Kalakaua under the effective control of the House of Nobles, dominated by propertied and wealthy whites. Unrest among the established plantation owners and their merchant friends led to the formation of a quasi-military organization determined to dictate policy to the extravagant nationalist Kalakaua, now generally referred to as the Merry Monarch. Working through a haole-dominated organization, very inappropriately called the Hawaiian League, opponents of the king pledged to secure a well-run, upright and honest government by whatever means necessary. Under the leadership of the influential attorney and publisher Lórrin A. Thurston, armed members of the league marched on Iolani Palace on June 30, 1887. With the threat of violence they compelled the king to acquiesce to their demands. The so-called Bayonet Constitution they imposed on Kalakaua obliged his once-powerful cabinet favorite, Walter Murray Gibson, to retire. It also weakened the power of Claus Spreckels, an entrepreneur and sugar magnate whose influence threatened the very sovereignty of the small kingdom. More significantly, the new constitution imposed property qualifications which disfranchised about three-quarters of the existing native Hawaiian electorate. It also included a special eligibility clause which permitted any male resident to vote—provided he could read and write in a European language and swore to uphold the new constitution.

The contest over who should govern in the islands was now to be fought according to rules which were heavily biased in favor of the haole minority. Any residual Hawaiian influence which centered on the monarchy was soon extinguished by the very group which had imposed the Bayonet Constitution. If local politics had in the past often resembled a Victorian comic opera, from this point on it became tense and serious. The economic future, social patterns, and political sovereignty of the islands were at stake. The balance of local power now lay with the haole plantation owners and their sympathizers. And this group would not willingly relinquish its new-found authority, which it increasingly sought to bolster with support from Washington.[41]

Hawaiian nationalists, led initially by Robert Wilcox, resisted the changes imposed by the white revolutionaries. Early in 1889 he and a group of native supporters captured Iolani Palace. But their triumph was brief indeed. Under heavy attack they were forced to surrender only hours after seizure of the palace. Although tried for treason, Wilcox was found not guilty by an all-native jury. Wilcox' efforts, and his acquittal, symbolized the resistance of his people. Nonetheless, his efforts failed. In the following decade all other attempts to quash or limit the authority of Hawaii's white elite proved equally futile.

Parties now emerged to fight for the interests of the only ethnic groups not excluded from local politics: a Reform party representing most whites, and a National Reform party representing most still-enfranchised Hawaiians, part-Hawaiians, and a handful of haole sympathizers. Island politics afforded these groups a limited degree of direct representation. But in any contest between them, victory usually went to the predominantly haole group. When Hawaiian nationalists tried to reverse this trend by promoting a revised constitution with a broader franchise, their efforts were quickly aborted.

Queen Liliuokalani succeeded Kalakaua following his death in January 1891. She was determined to assert her sovereignty and promote the rights of her native subjects. But her ambitions merely provided powerful opponents with an ideal opportunity to end the monarchy and concentrate political power even more directly where economic power already lay—in the hands of white settlers. The fact that more than 50 percent of the islands' population was of Japanese extraction and about 20 percent of Chinese origin was essentially irrelevant to the day-to-day working of politics in the islands. Both Asian groups were vital to the economic life of the community; but being foreign-born and denied the vote, neither participated in the political turmoil which brought Hawaii into the United States.

Although Liliuokalani had sworn to uphold the constitution of 1887, she attempted to assert her royal authority over her ministers. Moreover, speculation persisted that she would promulgate a new constitution at the earliest opportunity. These developments compounded the political instability and economic difficulties which characterized the early months of her reign. Predictably, they also gave rise to renewed haole opposition to the monarchy, and encouraged collusion between white settlers and American officials who now tacitly accepted that decisive action must be taken against the old Hawaiian order.

Responsibility for American policy in Hawaii during 1893 rested with Blaine's successor, John W. Foster, and Blaine's close friend, John Stevens, the United States minister in Honolulu. Both officials strongly promoted annexation—albeit with varying degrees of discretion—and local advocates of annexation eagerly attempted to exploit their sympathies.

Late in 1892 Stevens advised that "the facts can hardly fail to lead to the conclusion that the relations and policy of the United States towards Hawaii will soon demand some change, if not decisive measures, with the aim to secure American interests and future supremacy." Hawaii had "reached the parting of the ways," he concluded. "She must now take the road which leads to Asia, or the other which outlets her in America, gives her an American civilization and links her to the care of American Destiny." Foster was confident that incoming president Grover Cleveland would be "if not aggressive, at least positive and active" over Hawaii.[42] Events were to prove Foster's optimism exaggerated. Cleveland's indecision, however, did not delay the collapse of the old Hawaiian order, or undermine the authority of the new haole oligarchy which overthrew the monarchy. Confident that Stevens would sympathetically represent their interests in Washington, Thurston's conspirators moved boldly to wrest control from Liliuokalani.

The crisis over the queen's powers and the deeper conflict over political authority in the islands climaxed dramatically in January 1893. In response to rumors that Liliuokalani intended to promulgate a new constitution which boosted the rights of her native subjects and retrieved some of the monarchy's lost powers, prominent haoles organized to protect their rights and property from royal actions. Led by Thurston, the newly formed Annexation Club (which quickly changed its name to the more euphemistic Committee of Safety) moved to overthrow the queen. Stevens supported this effort with an enthusiasm which exceeded even the wildest expectations of the annexationists.

On January 14 Liliuokalani boldly dissolved the existing legislature and attempted to promulgate a new constitution. Her actions were clearly designed to reverse the changes imposed under the infamous Bayonet Constitution. But two days later, amidst rumblings of rebellion from the haole community, Stevens ordered 150 Marines ashore from the USS *Boston* on the pretext of protecting the United States Legation and Consulate in Honolulu and securing the safety of American citizens. The troops quickly took control of all buildings which the white rebels deemed essential for a successful coup d'etat. With this sudden show of physical strength, the whites deposed the queen and proclaimed a provisional government which was to exist "until terms of union with the United States have been negotiated and agreed upon." This was not the first time American marines had landed in Honolulu. But on the previous occasion, in 1874, they were supported by British troops and acted on behalf of the elected monarch, Kalakaua, against rioters supporting "Queen" Emma. In the coup of 1893, however, American troops acted against the traditional rulers on behalf of a small group of haole insurrectionaries.

The rebels were confident that Washington would soon sanction their actions and embrace their government. Certainly they received some initial encouragement from American officials. Stevens in particular continued to act sympathetically. He hastily recognized the de facto provisional government, declared an American protectorate over the islands, and raised the Stars and Stripes over the old palace in Honolulu. The Cleveland administration officially repudiated the protectorate proclamation but remained silent on all other issues raised by the coup. This did not discourage the rebels. Having wrested control from the old monarchy with unexpected ease, they quickly turned to Washington for sanction and support.[43] While preparations were being made to try the queen and her principal advisers for treason, Thurston set out for Washington with a special mission, which he portrayed as representing a large proportion of the islands' property owners and commercial interests. The composition of the powerful fourteen-member Advisory Council to the provisional government also reflected accurately the interests which the revolution of 1893 served: it contained many owners of substantial sugar stock, but only six Hawaiian citizens, and not one person of native Hawaiian ancestry.[44]

For the representatives of the rebel government, annexation and statehood were separate issues. At no time did they ask for annexation as a state. Indeed, as Charles Hunter has observed: "Over and over the spokesmen for the delegation sent to Washington to seek adoption to the Union let it be known that statehood was precisely what they did not want." Annexation as an American territory was a way of averting possibly insurmountable problems which national independence or, alternatively, statehood might bring for the rebel government. Hawaii was a small, vulnerable outpost in the Pacific and its new rulers doubted their ability to ensure its economic prosperity or physical security without the formal guarantees of American support which would flow automatically from territorial status. In an age of new imperialism in Asia and the Pacific, their insecurity was understandable. "In reality the members of the new Provisional Government in Hawaii hoped for a status somewhat modified from that of the customary American territorial system," Hunter has concluded. "They would have consented to being taken as a protectorate. . . . They knew full well that they could not continue to stand alone." Yet the rebels thought statehood was too high a price to pay for assurances of American support. It was an unattractive option primarily because it necessarily involved unrestricted adult male suffrage under American constitutional requirements and, in the view of the rebel government, this would reverse the gains won by the coup of 1893.[45]

Despite the aims of the new government and the activities of Thurston in Washington, local support for immediate annexation was not uniformly strong, even among whites. Business and commercial interests in Honolulu were essentially united, favoring immediate absorption by the United States. But at the last moment some plantation owners, fearing Congress would legislate to end contract labor, either opposed union or equivocated. Many ardent proponents, however, supported annexation primarily because they opposed further Asian immigration. Many whites were anxious to end contract labor as, in the long-term, it threatened the political, economic, and cultural dominance they had established throughout the nineteenth century. Some Hawaiians, although not enthusiastic about possible annexation, were also anxious to end imported labor and reluctantly accepted annexation as the lesser of two evils. Ironically, among native Hawaiians support for annexation grew as threats against the monarchy materialized. This was largely because many Hawaiians believed annexation meant immediate statehood—and statehood would at least permit the Hawaiians to exert some influence at the polls.[46]

The "Hawaiian pear is now fully ripe, and this is the golden hour for the United States to pluck it," Stevens eagerly told his superiors in Washington immediately after the coup of 1893. Secretary of State Foster apparently shared this view, and argued for a treaty of annexation.[47] But neither the president nor the Senate were yet ready for such decisive action.

Shortly after he was inaugurated for his second term as president, Cleveland withdrew the proposed annexation treaty from the Senate, primarily because it failed to provide for a plebiscite which would test the opinions of all islanders on this question. The president also sent a special commissioner, James H. Blount, to investigate events in the islands. Blount's findings confirmed suspicions that Stevens had colluded with the Annexation Club, that the queen had not surrendered before Stevens had recognized the provisional government, and that the majority of Hawaiian and part-Hawaiian residents did not oppose the queen.[48] The annexation lobby in Washington was unable to counter these damaging, but widely anticipated, findings. When Cleveland announced on December 18, 1893, that his administration opposed annexation, the new white rulers were obliged to accept that national politics was not responsive to the types of pressure they had exploited so effectively in the small island community.

The rebels' defeat in Washington, however, was not without compensation. Although the House of Representatives overwhelmingly agreed that the actions of the so-called new Missionary Monarchy were unjustified and ill-advised, both houses of Congress also promptly passed resolutions warning other nations not to interfere in the affairs of the islands. Washington still jealously sought to exclude other powers from this vital mid-Pacific area. But at the same time, racial fears made many congressmen hostile to a more intimate political relationship with the islands—especially one which implied eventual statehood. "Shall great public issues affecting the vital interests of all our people be submitted for determination to the Senators and Representatives from Hawaii?" Representative Henry Johnson of Indiana later asked rhetorically. Unlike many whites in Hawaii, Johnson deplored any suggestion that nonwhites in the islands should be excluded from political influence in order to overcome this objection against statehood. Such a solution "would impose upon Hawaii . . . by force of positive law the same deprivation of suffrage claimed to exist in the Southern States now, in defiance of law." But the monarchy had been overthrown to enhance the interests of a few, not to bring democracy to the population at large. Hence the rebel government ignored the appeals of congressmen like Johnson and moved quickly to disfranchise virtually all nonwhites and supporters of the former monarch. Voting rights in the new republic were restricted to a mere 2,700 people, almost all of whom were white owners of substantial property. This action did not immediately promote annexation. It did, however, permit the new rulers to launch a concerted drive for closer ties with Washington untroubled by dissenting voices from nationalist Hawaiians who were excluded from the formal political arena. Hawaii's electorate was later enthusiastic about annexation; but this was largely because the electorate, like the small republic's leadership, was narrowly unrepresentative of the islands' diverse community.[49]

While the rebel government was unable to sway events in Washington, it nonetheless had real political authority at home. Acting on Blount's recommendations, Cleveland attempted to induce the rebels to resign and make way for a restoration of the queen. Predictably, the new government resisted. Short of interfering by means of military force, Washington was powerless to reverse events. Moreover, relations between Washington and the provisional government were highly ambivalent. Congress was apparently opposed to annexation, but this did not necessarily mean that it favored restoration. The Cleveland administration took no further action, and on July 4, 1894, the rebels proclaimed the Republic of Hawaii, with Sanford B. Dole as president.

The triumph of the new rulers was completed on January 24, 1895, when Queen Liliuokalani reluctantly renounced all claims to the throne in return for a general amnesty for her defeated supporters.[50] The Hawaiian monarchy had ended, but without annexation its political successors faced an uncertain future.

Annexation

Those who overthrew the old order in Hawaii were dismayed to discover that this action alone did not guarantee annexation by Washington. Ultimately, annexation resulted from national developments which leaders of the island republic could exploit, but over which they exercised no decisive influence. Yet their partially frustrated efforts of 1893–1894 clearly foreshadowed and facilitated annexation five years later. When war erupted with Spain over issues not directly linked to Hawaii, local annexationists and congressional expansionists quickly took advantage of the new circumstances. They doubtless came to share John Hay's famous observation that the Spanish-American conflict was indeed "a splendid little war."

Initially, however, it was Meiji Japan's decision to flex its imperialist muscles in Asia which induced Washington to seek rapproachement with the infant Hawaiian republic. Hawaii's political revolution almost coincided with Japan's easy victory over neighboring China in 1894— an event which many Americans saw as a portent of much broader Japanese military and commercial adventures in the Asian-Pacific region. At the same time, the new government in Hawaii grappled with two related problems resulting from the unwillingness of sugar planters to reduce the level of imported Asian labor. First, the 1890s witnessed an unprecedented influx of Japanese workers. In the fifteen years from 1882 the number of Japanese contracted to plantations rose from a handful to more than thirty thousand. Immigration peaked in 1896–1897, when almost ten thousand Japanese entered Hawaii. Planters found European labor costly and difficult to entice to the harsh, poorly paid work on tropical estates.[51] The new government attempted to sustain white influence by insisting that 10 percent of all immigrants be of European extraction. When this policy failed it took more direct action to restrict the influx of Asian laborers. In 1897 three shiploads of Japanese were refused entry at Honolulu, ostensibly because they had not been processed under the terms of the 1886 Hawaii-Japan immigration agreement. This immediately precipitated a second, acute problem for the rebel government—a confrontation with Japan. The Meiji government protested bitterly, alleged discrimination, halted all contract labor, dispatched its warship *Naniwa* to Honolulu, and threatened war if the issue was not speedily resolved.[52]

Fortunately for the proponents of annexation, 1896 not only brought difficulties with Japan but changes in Washington which quickly paved the way for action to finalize what the coup of 1893 had only foreshadowed. The American elections in November 1896 put a Republican, William McKinley, in the White House and boosted the strength of expansionists in both houses of Congress. The new Republican majorities were also willing to confront Japan, or indeed any other state, which entertained military or commercial designs on Pacific outposts. Two of Hawaii's representatives in Washington, Francis M. Hatch and W. O. Smith, reported ecstatically that the contrast between McKinley and his Democratic predecessor was similar to that between daylight and darkness. They were convinced that the new president would grasp any reasonable opportunity to take the islands.[53] The revived hopes of the rulers of the infant republic were quickly confirmed.

After consulting with Hawaii's officials in Washington, the State Department drafted an annexation treaty which McKinley accepted and sent to the Senate in June 1897. This immediately widened the rift between Hawaii and Japan. However, the United States was now prepared, in effect, to act for Hawaii. The administration was willing to move toward annexation. It was, nevertheless, reluctant to inherit a major dispute with Japan, especially as pressure for intervention in Cuba now threatened to entangle McKinley in overseas difficulties on another front.

Tokyo promptly protested the terms of the draft annexation bill, arguing that it threatened existing Japanese rights in Hawaii and prejudiced claims made by Tokyo in the dispute over immigration. Given the background of bitter congressional debate between imperialists and anti-imperialists, difficulties with Spain over Cuba, and exaggerated popular alarm over Japan's possible ambitions in the Pacific, McKinley's response to Japan was remarkably conciliatory. Secretary of State John Sherman assured Tokyo that annexation would not result in any discrimination against Japanese nationals or commerce, and he induced Hawaii to pay reparations to Japan in connection with the immigration dispute. In return, in December 1897 Japan withdrew its opposition to the proposed treaty.[54]

Secretly, however, through the work of the ebullient under secretary of the Navy, Theodore Roosevelt, the administration took a tougher stand against Japan. It drew up plans to land troops and declare a protectorate over Hawaii should Tokyo prove inflexible on the immigration issue. Such a contingency was anticipated, and perhaps sought, by at least some influential American naval and military officers. Roosevelt, unrepentantly jingoistic, wanted the archipelago annexed "tomorrow," leaving the details of its political status to be dealt with later. "To me this question of possible war with Japan over Hawaii seems of very much more importance than the Spanish one," a prominent member of the Naval War Board advised the secretary of the Navy. "Japan could do

us very much more *permanent* harm on the Pacific Coast than Spain
could do on the Atlantic."[55] In the hysteria which was shortly to accompany war with Spain and the acquisition of an overseas empire, such
exaggerated insecurity was widely shared. By 1898 it had become an
important ingredient in the thrust for new territory.

Congressional debate over annexation was exhaustive, bitter, and
often irrational and exaggerated. In large part it repeated the diverse
views expressed during previous years in the Great Debate over empire.
In tone and substance it also foreshadowed later arguments over statehood. But in the 1890s opposition to closer ties with the multiracial,
noncontiguous islands was proportionately stronger, if not more intense, than during the protracted debate over statehood during 1945–
1959. Moreover, annexation involved wider issues than statehood: it
was an integral factor in the emerging conflict over imperialism, the
nature of the Union, and the future role of the United States in Pacific
and world affairs.

The issues raised by annexation were substantial and enduring. But
too often the debate on this question betrayed a preoccupation with
racial fears and hostilities. The *Honolulu Star* set the unfortunate tone
when it insisted that the central issue was "the white race against
the yellow . . . nothing but annexation can save the islands."[56] Local
whites apparently feared their long-term economic and political survival was threatened by the islands' now predominantly Asian population, which might gain support from an expanding and sympathetic
Japan. Close formal ties with the mainland were viewed as a means of
maintaining white political supremacy in the islands, and of averting
possible future interference by Japan or any other state. Some sugar
planters were prepared to tolerate such risks in order to maintain their
access to contract labor from Asia. But for those whites who supported
the coup of 1893 and anxiously encouraged annexation, the end of contract labor seemed a relatively small price for the guarantees of protection—racial, economic, and military—which would inevitably accompany integration into the United States.

To the dismay of annexationists, the debate over Hawaii's future
could not be isolated from the emotive statehood issue—indeed statehood was the major obstacle to annexation. Throughout 1893–1898 the
leaders of Hawaii's new government firmly rejected all offers of help to
secure statehood. In 1896 they led a move to defeat the first resolution
ever proposed in Congress to grant the islands statehood: "We do not for
a moment anticipate" that the Joint Resolution introduced by Representative George Spalding (Rep., Mich.) "will pass . . . unmodified,"
Hawaii's minister for Foreign Affairs wrote. President McKinley was
left in no doubt as to the attitude of Hawaii's rulers. They wanted
annexation, he was advised, but under terms which gave the islands'
government maximum possible autonomy over home affairs. Statehood

was neither envisaged nor sought. Fortunately for Hawaii's haole rulers, this position was shared by most congressmen and mainland newspapers. Those officials unconvinced of Hawaii's unsuitability for statehood were informed that it "needed the restraining influence of the President of the United States, otherwise it would be subject to all sorts of wild legislation." Statehood would bring with it an elected governor, it was argued, and this would mean handing Hawaii over to the mob. Usually this fear of "mob rule" was expressed in more gentle words, notably in references to the "problems" which would follow if such an "immature" and racially "mixed" electorate was given virtual self-government under statehood.[57]

While Hawaii's lobbyists could apparently separate annexation from statehood, opponents of annexation were convinced that it would inevitably foreshadow statehood. Constitutional precedents certainly added weight to this view. It was the very real possibility of statehood which caused many mainlanders to balk at annexation. For this group, as for later opponents of statehood, Hawaii's people must be permanently disqualified from equality under the American flag because they were overwhelmingly non-Caucasian: "a lot of non-descript Asiatico-Polynesian ignoramuses," a congressman from Missouri described them in the debates of 1898. "How can we endure our shame," he concluded derisively, "when a Chinese senator from Hawaii, with his pig-tail hanging down his back, with his pagan joss in his hand, shall rise from his curule chair and in pidgin English proceed to chop logic with George Frisbie Hoar or Henry Cabot Lodge."[58] Few opponents were prepared to use such derogatory language, but many shared the sentiments it expressed. Opposition to annexation centered on the race-conscious Southern states, although it was never exclusive to this section; and during the sixty years of territorial rule which followed annexation, Southern congressmen dominated all efforts to deny Hawaii's diverse peoples equality under statehood.

Nonetheless, the annexation lobby pushed on. A draft treaty of annexation was approved unanimously by the Hawaii legislature on September 6, 1897. An investigation by Congress, expressions of support from McKinley, discussions between President Dole and administration officials, and a secret Senate debate all followed in late 1897 and early 1898. But the proposed treaty could not muster the two-thirds majority required in both houses of Congress. No consensus had emerged on Hawaii. Friends of the ruling faction in the islands reluctantly accepted that the draft treaty would not pass Congress unless it was converted to a joint resolution requiring only a simple majority in each chamber. A similar strategy had previously brought the short-lived Republic of Texas into the Union.

The sudden outbreak of war with Spain in April 1898 and Commodore George Dewey's victory at Manila Bay on May 1 transformed the debate on Hawaii. Rather than declare neutrality in the conflict, Hawaii acted as an undeclared ally of the United States. Its strategic significance and political sympathies achieved great prominence. It became a vital link in the war with Spain, refuelling and supplying American ships and providing a rest and recreation base for soldiers and sailors en route to the Philippines. "To maintain our flag in the Philippines," a New York newspaper asserted, "we must raise our flag in Hawaii."[59] For expansionists like Mahan, Lodge, and Roosevelt, the logic of this claim was conclusive. The Spanish-American War brought the United States an overseas empire and provoked decisive action on Hawaii.

Three days after Dewey's dramatic victory a new joint resolution to annex Hawaii was introduced into Congress by Representative Francis G. Newlands. In contrast to the unsuccessful treaty of 1897, the Newlands resolution made a major concession to those who feared that annexation would inevitably bring statehood: it deleted the preamble of the treaty which had stipulated that the islands were incorporated into the United States "as an integral part thereof." The omission of this phrase, most constitutional experts believed, removed the implication that the annexed territory was an "inchoate state."[60] This did not stop all of the old arguments, both for and against annexation, from surfacing during debate on the Newlands resolution. But events in the Philippines and feverish demands for an empire were more persuasive than the time-worn assertions about mission, commerce, security, or race. On June 15 the House approved the Newlands resolution by an overwhelming 290 to 91 votes. After fifteen days of intense debate, the Senate on July 6 also approved it. The margin of Senate approval was two to one, 42 votes for, 21 against. In both chambers, voters were aligned essentially along party lines—Republicans in favor, Democrats opposed. The anticipated economic and strategic advantages of expansion clearly appealed more strongly to Northern and Western business interests represented by the Republican party than to the more varied groups represented by the Democrats.[61] For Hawaii, as for the numerous other areas now tied into America's broad empire, 1898 signalled the beginning of a new era when its fortunes would be determined fundamentally by decisions made in Washington.

A century of continental expansion and informal commercial penetration of the Pacific and Central America had, by the start of the twentieth century, induced America to emulate the great powers of the Old World and win an overseas empire. In a sudden burst of imperialist activity it acquired Hawaii, Guam, Wake Island, Puerto Rico, and the Philippines. It also won substantial influence in Cuba and much of Central America, and used the Open Door policy to establish itself as an equal with the numerous other imperialist states seeking to dominate China. Although American goals and policy in all of these areas were linked, the methods of acquisition and types of government imposed on them varied substantially. The dreams of men like Seward, Mahan, Lodge, and Roosevelt for "national expansion and aggrandizement"[62] overriding continental barriers, were suddenly fulfilled. While the decisions for war and territory signalled a departure from continentalism, they were consistent with the form and intention of previous American expansion westward. The roots of the new empire lay in the geographic exhaustion of the old empire, in the transition from an agrarian to an industrial economy, in the demands for new markets and investments abroad, and in the need to protect expanded overseas interests with a navy, bases, an isthmian canal, and political dominion in vital outposts.[63] The material rewards which actually flowed to the United States from its expansionist adventures fell well short of those anticipated by the imperialist lobby. But it was the expectation of gains rather than their realization which propelled America into new imperialism.

These incentives, and the fever for war, were powerful indeed. They submerged the very question of the constitutionality of Hawaii's annexation beneath the allure of nationalism and self-interest. At that time it seemed impertinent for Americans to ask if this initial decision which paved the way for statehood was consistent with the nation's constitutional procedures and principles. In the following decades this question was considered occasionally, but by then it had become a narrow legal issue. "It has long been held in some quarters that the annexation of Hawaii by joint resolution was unconstitutional," William B. Tansill observed in 1954, as "relations between independent Nations can be governed legitimately only by treaties." Tansill concluded, therefore, that a legislative act such as the joint resolution which brought Hawaii under American control could have no extraterritorial impact. Yet this important question has never been considered directly by the U.S. Supreme Court. Rather, the Court has consistently (and perhaps conveniently) "recognised that the methods and means of acquiring territory constitute matters which are within the province exclusively of the political branches of the Government." Nonetheless Westel W. Willoughby's classic study of U.S. constitutional law has argued that

> annexation by legislative act was constitutionally justified upon the same ground that the extension of American sovereignty by statute over the Guano Islands was justified; namely, as an exercise of a right springing from the fact that, in the absence of express constitutional prohibition, the United States as a sovereign nation has all the power that any sovereign nation is recognized by international law and practice to have with reference to such political questions as the annexation of territory. . . .

> It [is] also quite reasonable to argue that the annexation of the Hawaiian Islands by act of Congress was a "necessary and proper" measure for the military defence of the nation, and for the protection and increase of our foreign commerce; for there can be no question but that a conceived military and

commercial need was one of the strongest of the motives that operated to
bring about the annexation.

This was a limp defense indeed. But despite the potential divisiveness of
this question, it never impeded the movement toward statehood.[64]

The ruling white minority in Hawaii welcomed annexation as a guarantee of its political and economic control for at least a generation. Furthermore, in the longer term, annexation made the triumph of white
values and ideology through "Americanization" a formal necessity if the
new territory was ever to achieve statehood. Two years after Hawaii
was annexed, Congress designated it an "incorporated territory." Like
numerous incorporated continental territories before it, this ultimately
entitled the islands to statehood.

For the submerged remnants of Hawaii's once-proud and numerous
native peoples, annexation was a further irreversible indignity. "This
was the ultimate dispossession," Daws has observed poignantly.

> The Hawaiians had lost much of their reason for living long ago, when the
> kapus were abolished; since then a good many of them had lost their lives
> through disease; the survivors lost their land; they lost their leaders, because
> many of the chiefs withdrew from politics in favor of nostalgic self-indul-
> gence; and now at last they lost their independence. Their resistance to all
> this was feeble. It was almost as if they believed what the white man said
> about them, that they had only half learned the lessons of civilization. . . .
> They chose to operate within the conventions laid down by white men, and
> by so doing they put themselves at a disadvantage. They listened to political
> harangues and composed chants to fit the political occasion; they drew up
> petitions and they read the stirring editorials in the Hawaiian language
> newspapers; but beyond that they did not go. And so they became Ameri-
> cans.[65]

Annexation both symbolized and ensured the triumph of foreign influences which had transformed the islands so radically in the preceding
century. The eclipse of Hawaiian culture, traditions, and political authority was also reflected starkly in the fact that less than one in every
four people living in the islands in 1900 was descended from Hawaiian
or part-Hawaiian ancestors. Irrespective of the long-term economic and
social benefits of the changes which accompanied white settlement,
Tom Dinell, Allan Spitz, and others have concluded that "their impact
upon the native Hawaiian population was almost catastrophic." The
once-independent and relatively prosperous native people became an
underprivileged minority. By the time of annexation, the problems of
demoralization and adjustment to imported cultural norms, economic
power, and political authority had so disrupted the native population
that it seemed for a while as if they might die out altogether.[66]

Hawaiian nationalists opposed the various steps which European settlers devised to wrest political power from native rulers and the native electorate. But despite this resistance—which at times included attempts to employ military force—their efforts were ultimately futile. Unable to reverse the coup of 1893, they were powerless to thwart annexation five years later. Indeed, in 1898 Hawaii's native people had to be content with a solemn written protest to the American government against the fact that annexation had taken place "without reference to the consent of the people of the Hawaiian islands."[67] Nearly forty thousand Hawaiians were denied the chance to air their views on annexation. This resulted from the constitution imposed by the coup of 1893, which formally denied the political franchise to those Hawaiian residents who would not renounce their allegiance to the former monarch and who would not pledge to renounce their claim to their native land and accept annexation by the United States.[68] A later report on events in 1898, issued by a dissenting minority of the House Committee on Foreign Affairs, conceded that "the people of Hawaii have not been consulted about the proposed annexation."[69] Not surprisingly, native Hawaiians were conspicuously absent from the public ceremony which officially replaced the Hawaiian flag with the Stars and Stripes in 1898.[70] But for many native Hawaiians the prospect of rule by the United States was less disturbing than the anticipated consequences of Asian immigration and settlement. People of Hawaiian ancestry now constituted barely one-quarter of the total island population. Understandably, many resented foreign influences of all persuasions. Although it was largely a symbolic gesture, some Hawaiians joined secret societies like the Order of Kamehameha which sought to arrest foreign influences and restore indigenous culture and traditions. But the past could not be recaptured. Unable to resist further erosion of their power and traditions, many native Hawaiians and part-Hawaiians tolerated the end of the old order with quiet resignation.

Annexation changed permanently the political options open to Hawaii and its people. Disenchantment with the system of government imposed on the islands persisted long after the events of 1898, and influenced the core of local opposition to both statehood and further Anericanization during more than half a century of territorial rule. It is to this unexpectedly long period of struggle over Hawaii's political future that we now turn. However, in contrast to events in the nineteenth century, after 1898 Hawaii's status and the rights of its people were fundamentally domestic American questions; they were no longer international issues involving the future of a small sovereign nation and its subjects. Annexation ended Hawaii's sovereignty and tied its political future inextricably to the exigences of United States politics and the principles of the United States Constitution.

Chapter 2

Incorporated but Not Equal, 1898–1941

More than a century separated the first tentative references to statehood for Hawaii and its eventual admission. As we have seen, statehood was first discussed in the 1850s. Ironically, it was at this time used by Hawaiian nationalists as a means of defeating possible annexation by Washington. In the following decades Hawaii's haole population anxiously pressed for annexation, but did not seek immediate statehood. Indeed, most of those who helped overthrow the Hawaiian kingdom and to win annexation wanted to avoid statehood—at least until American values were more pervasive and white inhabitants were more numerous.

Hawaii was one of a number of problems which confronted Congress as a result of America's imperialist adventures in the 1890s. Congress had to govern ethnically and geographically diverse colonies in the Pacific, East Asia, and the Caribbean. It was obliged to create an administrative structure, or structures, sufficiently flexible to accommodate the peculiarities of its new possessions. This had to be accomplished without jeopardizing the authority or interests of the metropolitan power. After independence the Northwest Ordinance had guided the forms of government established in numerous sparsely populated continental territories. As Indian tribes were pushed aside, their lands were occupied by white settlers who successfully petitioned for incorporation into the United States as territories. But this pattern of settlement and government did not generally follow the American flag into the overseas possessions it won in the 1890s. Of these possessions, only Hawaii was governed broadly in accordance with precedents growing out of the Northwest Ordinance and a century of territorial settlement. Despite this, Hawaii differed sharply from its continental predecessors. It comprised a collection of mid-Pacific islands, peopled by a unique mixture of native and immigrant groups, which had been annexed by Washington in an unprecedented way.

Annexation was an agonizing question for Congress. No less complex were the resulting issues of Hawaii's political status and the terms under which it should be governed. In part, such problems derived from a belief in Washington that a strategic outpost like Hawaii should be tightly controlled, especially one whose population was primarily "alien." But they were also a product of pressure from white settlers who comprised less than 20 percent of the islands' population and were anxious that territorial status should confirm, not threaten, their established authority. In particular, they wanted territorial rule to ensure physical and economic protection by the United States, even if this brought the islands under immigration laws which restricted the access of planters to Asian labor. The rights and interests of Hawaii's Caucasian minority could be best protected, its members argued, if Washington had ultimate authority over government in the islands. This view subsided very slowly. But by the 1930s, in the face of attacks by Congress against "King Sugar," it was challenged from within the haole group. Many of those who had once championed territorial rule now questioned its capacity to protect their interests. They turned, instead, to statehood. This chapter discusses the patterns of changing support for statehood, both within the islands and in Washington, before war in the Pacific transformed the drive for immediate admission.

Incorporating the Island Territory

In the period between annexation in mid-1898 and the passage of the Organic Act on April 30, 1900, Congress considered the precise form of government to be imposed on Hawaii. Suffrage requirements and immigration laws were vigorously debated. These questions were related to a central preoccupation of most haoles: how to maintain political authority at home within the new framework of the United States Constitution and mounting pressure for a wider franchise in the islands.[1] Fortunately for Hawaii's whites, America's naturalization laws did not extend to immigrants from Asia. In the late nineteenth century Congress was far from anxious to ensure that nonwhites could exercise voting rights equal to those of whites in the various mainland states. It was this reluctance which influenced the voting regulations it eventually established in multiracial Hawaii.

The Organic Act defined franchise restrictions and procedures which excluded all aliens from the right to vote. As Lind has pointed out, this meant that "only a handful of Orientals already citizens of the Republic of Hawaii were granted American citizenship when Hawaii was annexed." Orientals, meaning Chinese and Japanese, constituted almost 60 percent of Hawaii's total population at the turn of the century. Thus, about three-quarters of adult male residents in the islands were permanently excluded from voting by the Organic Act. If born in the islands, however, all children of immigrant parents were automatically citizens and entitled to normal voting rights. By the 1920s children of immigrant laborers began to influence local politics. It was not, however, until the late 1940s, when a large majority of all the Asians in

Hawaii were locally born, that political participation accurately reflected the demographic and ethnic features of the island community.[2]

The most significant provision of the Organic Act was that which, in
effect, repeated part of the draft treaty of annexation and asserted
Hawaii's incorporated status. In June 1898 the Newlands Resolution
had accepted and ratified the "cession" of the islands by the Republican
government of Hawaii. But as indicated previously, the Newlands bill
deleted any reference to that provision of the annexation treaty which
specifically incorporated Hawaii as an integral part of the United
States. This decision was, in effect, reversed by Congress when it
approved Hawaii's Organic Act in 1900. Both the House and Senate
rejected amendments stating that the act should not be interpreted as
implying a congressional promise of future statehood. The defeat of
these amendments helped to establish Hawaii as an incorporated territory. The question of incorporation had far-reaching constitutional and
political implications.

Although the United States Constitution did not distinguish between
incorporated and unincorporated territories, by 1900 the Northwest
Ordinance and a number of important court decisions had established
that Congress could incorporate a territory by declaring the applicabil-
ity of the U.S. Constitution and laws within that territory. Incorporated
status extended to the territory all constitutional and statutory safe-
guards applicable within the states. Section 5 of the Organic Act clearly
made such provisions, stating:

> That the Constitution, and except as herein otherwise provided, all the laws
> of the United States which are not locally applicable, shall have the same
> force and effect within the said territory [Hawaii] as elsewhere in the United
> States.[3]

Implicit in this clause was an assurance of ultimate statehood. A variety
of Supreme Court decisions subsequently acknowledged that the qualified political status of an incorporated territory was an intermediary
step to eventual statehood. In the case of *O'Donoghue v. United States*,
for example, the court's decision stated:

> The impermanent character of these Territorial governments has often been
> noted. Thus it has been said: "The Territorial state is one of pupilage at best.
> . . ." "A Territory, under the Constitution and laws of the United States, is an
> inchoate State."[4]

In 1901 the Supreme Court ruling in the case of *Downes v. Bidwell* stated that Hawaii, although not incorporated through annexation, was
incorporated by the provisions of the Organic Act of 1900. Carl Swisher
has concluded that a series of Supreme Court rulings during 1901–1905
on the political status of America's newly acquired insular possessions

confirmed and defined Hawaii's incorporated status. These decisions stipulated that Hawaii was an "integral part of the United States," and as such "destined for admission as a State" after serving a period of pupilage as a territory. The numerous congressional investigating committees on Hawaiian statehood accepted these decisions and generally referred to the territory as an "inchoate state."[5]

Following the admission of Arizona and New Mexico to the Union as states in 1912, Hawaii and Alaska became the only incorporated territories within the United States. The Philippines, Puerto Rico, Guam, the Virgin Islands, and American Samoa remained unincorporated possessions outside the scope of the U.S. Constitution. Supreme Court decisions in the case *Dorr v. United States* (1904), and *Balzac v. Puerto Rico* (1922), ruled that neither the Philippines nor Puerto Rico had been incorporated, and a distinction between incorporated and unincorporated territories was clearly drawn. Commenting on this question Willoughby wrote in 1910: "If it be that a territory is merely appurtenant to but not 'incorporated' into the United States, Congress in its legislation regarding it is bound by but few of the limitations which apply in the case of incorporated territories." After 1901, United States policy toward unincorporated territories was never premised on an assumption that statehood would ultimately be given to these areas. In contrast, official policy toward Hawaii and Alaska never seriously envisaged an alternative to eventual statehood, although other options were discussed briefly in the 1930s and 1950s. There were many occasions, however, when opponents of statehood attempted to deny this implication of the 1900 act, advocating instead Commonwealth status or even independence. Such solutions were later adopted for Puerto Rico and the Philippines respectively.[6]

Apart from an elected delegate to Congress and elected members of the local legislature, all important posts in the territory's government were filled by appointments determined in Washington. The Organic Act provided a constitution for the new territory, broadly in accordance with provisions previously applied to incorporated territories under the Northwest Ordinance. But the act gave Hawaii's appointed officials greater discretionary powers and wider authority than those afforded officials in any previous territory. It established legislative, judicial, and executive branches of government in Hawaii. A local legislature comprising fifteen elected Senate members and thirty elected members of a House of Representatives was established, but all territorial legislation could be vetoed by the appointed governor or nullified by the U.S. Congress. Nonetheless, an important concession to home rule was also included which permitted the legislature to override a governor's veto on all but money bills. This decision could not be reversed in Washington. The territory's secretary (a position roughly equivalent to that of lieu-

tenant governor), along with judges of the territorial supreme court and
the four major circuit courts, were all appointed by the president. Initially these judicial appointees, unlike the governor, did not have to be
local residents. Hawaii was permitted to elect one delegate to serve in
the national House of Representatives for a two-year term; however, the
delegate had no vote in this body. The territory had neither a voice nor a
vote in the national Senate. Although denied voting representation in
Congress, Hawaii was nonetheless subjected to all taxes, import duties,
and other obligations, such as military service, which were imposed on
existing states. Decisions on such crucial matters as immigration, military or naval uses of the islands, and the political fate of the territory
were all exclusively the preserve of Congress. A number of authors have
commented on the ability of Hawaii's old elite to sustain its unique position and influence despite—or perhaps because of—the requirements of
territorial government through Congress. "No community of comparable size on the mainland was controlled so completely by so few individuals for so long," Lawrence Fuchs has concluded.

> Rarely were political, economic, and social controls simultaneously enforced
> as in Hawaii. Rarely were controls so personal, and rarely were they as
> immune for such counterforces as Eugene Deb's socialism, Woodrow
> Wilson's New Freedom, and Franklin D. Roosevelt's New Deal as in Hawaii.
> For forty years Hawaii's oligarchy skillfully and meticulously spun its web
> of control over the Islands' politics, labor, land, and economic institutions,
> without fundamental challenge.[7]

Alternative pressures did surface, especially around the Hawaiian-
based Home Rule party in the first decade under territorial government, and periodically around labor groups attempting to organize
unions and strikes. The constraints of rule through Congress and presidential appointments were at times insufficient to stifle such pressures.
On these rare occasions, the interests of employers were protected by
the use of co-optation or outright repression.

Prior to World War II economic control in the islands was monopolized by five major sugar corporations, referred to variously (though
seldom affectionately) as the "Big Five," the "hegemony," the "ruling
group," or the "oligarchy." In 1910 this group produced 75 percent of
Hawaii's major commodity, sugar. By 1933 it controlled 96 percent of
the sugar crop. Moreover, as Gavan Daws has concluded, the Big Five
also controlled all sugar-related businesses, including banking, insur-
ance, utilities, wholesale and retail merchandising, and rail and sea
transportation.[8] Through a system of interlocking directorships, thirty
men controlled 116 of the 193 directorships in the Big Five and twenty
other major corporations which dominated the economy of the islands.
All but a few directors of these and sixty-four additional corporations

directly associated with the Big Five were Caucasians.[9] Political power
was also under the centralized control of these related economic corporations. Lind has commented that the Big Five appeared "to constitute
a single monopolistic control over the entire economy and political life
of the islands."[10] The attorney general of Hawaii, Edward P. Dole, a
member of the so-called family compact which exercised immense political and economic influence in the territory, conceded in 1903: "There is
a government in the Territory which is centralized to an extent un-
known in the United States and probably almost as much centralized as
it was in France under Louis XIV."[11] This interest group, through its
lobby in Washington and as a result of general congressional sympathy
for Caucasian interests in the islands, influenced the appointment of
most territorial officials, including governors and judges. Most white
residents had little reason to be dissatisfied with territorial government.

The centralized nature of the territory's government was most clearly
reflected in the wide range of the powers accorded the appointed governor. By stipulating that the governor must be a local resident the act
avoided any suggestion of carpetbag rule. Perhaps because of this safe-
guard, the powers of this office were very broad. Nonetheless, as an
official appointed by the president, the governor might represent the
party which controlled the national executive, and not that which represented the preferences of the local electorate. Unlike officials elected
under the national Constitution, he could not be impeached for miscon-
duct. More importantly perhaps, the appointed governor was in turn
empowered to appoint literally hundreds of local officials. His powers
included the right to invoke martial law, suspend habeas corpus, veto
money bills, and extend legislative sessions to ensure action on appropriations. Finally, matters normally the responsibility of state or local authorities were largely determined by the executive—including health,
education, welfare, and public works.

Despite the political risks which might have flowed from annexation,
the interests of the small group of whites who had overthrown the monarchy were not seriously threatened by the form of government established in 1900. Indeed, their authority was perhaps bolstered, as both
Republican and Democratic administrations in Washington almost without exception appointed governors and top officials from this influential
faction. Changed political circumstances did, however, oblige the kamaaina haoles (whites born or of long residence in the islands) to pursue
new strategies in order to offset the influence of the largest enfranchised
group, the Hawaiians and part-Hawaiians. For the first time since the
Bayonet Constitution of 1887, Polynesians had voting rights equal to
those of whites. While this induced whites to grapple with new challenges, they were seldom forced to make substantial compromises.
As the following pages indicate, the group which Thurston derisively

called the "ignorant majority," was generally unable to translate its numbers into an effective political force.[12] The families and interests which had dominated the short-lived republic maintained effective control of politics, capital, and labor from the early 1900s until after World War II. "I do not think there is any contest as to who shall dominate," a representative of the Hawaiian Sugar Planters' Association confidently asserted in 1920, "the white race, the white people, the Americans in Hawaii are going to dominate and will continue to dominate—there is no question about this."[13] The seeds of future change remained buried, unable to germinate in the unfavorable soil of territorial government.

Early Ambivalence Over Statehood

From 1900 to the early 1930s statehood was the subject of much political rhetoric in the territory; but it was not actively supported by any influential political or economic faction. In his inaugural address as the first territorial governor, Sanford B. Dole spoke of the hope of statehood. Yet during 1901 the legislature declined to petition Congress for it. Residents had little confidence in the prospect of early admission, and little enthusiasm for it. "At best statehood is a long way off," the *Evening Bulletin* commented in 1901 and:

> If it is desired to obtain statehood with a reasonable period of probation it behoves all parties and all factions to be firmly united in each and every appeal made to Congress for an advance toward the goal of independent state. . . . Frequent repetition of the appeal—and the request must be made early and often to be effective—will finally attract interest and attention followed by careful investigation and eventually the prize will be won.

This appeal went unheeded, as did a suggestion made a decade later by the *Friend:*

> The State of Hawaii? It looks well and sounds well. It is time to organize a campaign to secure it.[14]

But another two decades passed before a campaign was inaugurated. Sincere enthusiasm for immediate admission was not openly voiced by any influential individuals or prominent ethnic or political groups until the early 1930s, when haole complacency was disturbed by the impact of the Great Depression on the islands' fragile economy.

Nonetheless, shortly after annexation the territorial legislature initiated a series of formal appeals aimed at promoting eventual statehood. In 1903 it passed a joint resolution requesting Congress to pass "an act enabling the people of this Territory, who are citizens thereby and duly qualified to vote, to meet in Convention and frame a State Constitution whereby and whereunder this Territory may be admitted as a State into the Union." Although similar resolutions were passed in 1911, 1913, 1915, and 1917, it was not until 1919 that Hawaii's delegate, Prince Jonah Kuhio Kalanianaole, introduced the first statehood bill in Congress. This initiative was repeated in 1920. But each bill died quietly in the Committee on Territories. Island politicians accepted these defeats without protest.[15] These initiatives did not reflect widespread enthusiasm for immediate, or indeed eventual, admission. They were, at most, token gestures designed to placate those in the islands and in Congress who rightly viewed territorial rule as a transitory step toward full-fledged democracy and who had supported annexation on this basis. The influential English language newspapers, the *Evening Bulletin* (later the *Honolulu Star-Bulletin*) and the *Honolulu Advertiser,* as well as dominant economic interests in the territory, did not support these modest statehood initiatives. The *Honolulu Star-Bulletin* stated unequivocally in 1920, for example, that "Hawaii is not yet ready for statehood." Nor were the various territorial legislatures genuinely sympathetic. Consistently after 1900 they refused to provide funds to support an organized statehood campaign. Business and community leaders also refused to promote such a drive.[16]

In the aftermath of annexation statehood was not a pressing issue. But the question of who should rule at home under the new constitutional arrangements was of immediate concern, and in the early 1900s it consumed the political energies of both Polynesians and whites. Their conflict was soon submerged beneath a common concern: how to avoid or at least delay the triumph of the non-Caucasian majority in politics, economics, and society. Many haoles and Hawaiians felt that statehood would exacerbate this unwelcome trend—it would necessarily bring with it genuine local democracy, subject to the will of the majority. It appeared inevitable that the descendents of contract laborers from Japan would soon constitute the largest groups of voters. The right to vote could not be denied American citizens, irrespective of their ancestry. By maintaining territorial government, however, the influence of Hawaii's voters could be curtailed and indeed overridden by appointed officials or congressional action. Thus many haoles and Hawaiians were anxious to retain territorial rule and avoid the likely political consequences of statehood.[17]

Formal politics in the early years of the territory was largely a contest involving the two populous enfranchised groups, Caucasians and Hawaiians–part-Hawaiians. Yet it was never a simple contest in which race dictated party preference. The Republican party continued to defend the interests of haoles, while native interests were promoted briefly and somewhat erratically by the Home Rule party. In the first territorial elections, to the alarm of many whites, Hawaiian supporters of the Home Rule party triumphed under the leadership of Robert Wilcox, the

former head of Liliuokalani's nationalist forces. It was indeed ironic
that Wilcox should have been elected as the territory's first delegate to
Congress. The nature of island politics was captured in his party's successful electoral slogan of 1901–*Nana i ka ili*, "Look to the Skin." Predictably the tactics of the Republican party were quickly adjusted to
avert any repetition of their defeat in 1901. In 1902 the GOP candidate
for delegate to Congress was a popular Hawaiian with royal connections, Prince Kuhio, who like Wilcox had been imprisoned for his part
in the abortive uprising of 1895. Following his win in 1902 the prince
served his white political masters well for two decades—so well in fact
that by 1912 the Home Rule party had disintegrated leaving the Republicans in firm control of the territory until after World War II.[18]

Genuine two-party conflict was very short lived. After 1902 a curious
and often uneasy haole-Hawaiian alliance developed under Republican
party authority. The strength of this alliance rested on its ability to
bring immediate rewards to many Hawaiians, especially appointments
to government jobs, without disturbing the property and corporate
bases of white wealth and prestige in the islands. Each faction attempted to exploit the alliance for selfish ends, Fuchs has observed, and "in
some respects mutual benefits were won, but clearly the oligarchy was
more successful in manipulating Hawaiian votes for its purposes than
were Kuhio and his followers in using the oligarchy to restore the Hawaiian people to their former dignity."[19] Skillful maneuvering by the
GOP, effective lobbying in Washington by representatives of the Big
Five, weaknesses within the local Democratic party, growing Hawaiian
disillusionment with formal politics, and increased settlement by whites
helped restore the old elite to a position of unchallenged control. In the
final analysis, however, this authority rested on its overwhelming economic strength and strong social cohesion. As long as territorial government successfully defended the interests of this group, statehood was
never a realistic proposition.

"Hawaii for the Hawaiian" and restoration of the "rights of the Hawaiian people" were the rallying cries of the titular political leader of
the natives, Prince Kuhio. But despite their superior numbers at the
polls, the Polynesians failed to win any enduring victories which might
have advanced Kuhio's stated objectives. The only major material and
cultural concession they were able to wrest from the legislature—the
Hawaiian Homes Act, known as the Hawaii Rehabilitation Act when
passed in 1921—became a poignant symbol of the eclipse of Hawaiian
influence and traditions. This measure ostensibly guaranteed special
homestead leases on pockets of land throughout the island for those
claiming 50 percent or more Hawaiian blood. It was officially welcomed as a victory for the Hawaiians, a triumph of justice for at least
that portion of them which was assumed to be most in need of "rehabili-

tation." However, relatively few native families benefitted from the act, and at the time of statehood only 10 percent of the land originally set aside was being used by Hawaiian or part-Hawaiian families, while about 20 percent was unusable and the remainder was leased to ranches or plantations. As Dinell, Spitz, and others have concluded, its 185,000 acres of generally poor and unused lands did little to restore either the dignity or economic well-being of Hawaii's native population. Rather, the Hawaiian Homes Act and its subsequent failure brought "major victories for Hawaii's political and economic elite," Spitz observed; and plantation owners were "able to exempt sugar lands from homesteading, gain the political allegiance of the Hawaiians, and in the process kill any future homesteading." Like the election of Kuhio, the act was a symbol of Hawaiian influence and survival, but it did little to arrest the declining power or status of the native population.[20]

The restoration of white political authority over the Hawaiian majority shortly after annexation resolved a potential difficulty for the wealthy haole faction. But annexation brought a further major problem, at least for plantation owners. The lucrative system of contract labor was ended abruptly by the Organic Act, and the nation's Chinese Exclusion Act applied equally to the territory, ending a crucial source of labor for Hawaii's planters. Seven years later the gentleman's agreement with Japan further closed the door to cheap Asian labor. But the demand for plantation workers continued unabated. As we have seen, this problem was anticipated by planters, prompting some to oppose annexation. Fortunately, the Philippines were acquired as an American colony at the same time as Hawaii. They promptly became a convenient new source of Asian labor. Filipinos were not restrained by federal laws from entering Hawaii. More than one hundred thousand workers from the provinces of Tagalog, Visayas, and Ilocos arrived in the following thirty years. They comprised more than two-thirds of all plantation laborers by 1932. Like the Japanese and to a lesser extent the Chinese before them, the Filipinos found it difficult to adjust to an alien way of life. They encountered deep hostility from old settlers and recent immigrants alike, and suffered the harsh ghetto existence of the plantations. Many returned home. Those who stayed were assigned to a laboring class made up almost exclusively of men. Unlike other laboring groups who were displaced in part by newer arrivals, the Filipinos were seemingly trapped in a system which afforded them few opportunities for geographic or vocational mobility. Estranged from traditional community and family relationships, Filipinos stayed overwhelmingly on plantations, providing the economic backbone of the fifty-or-so huge plantations which dominated life outside of Honolulu.[21]

Almost 400,000 immigrant workers—mainly southern Chinese, Japanese, and Filipino—arrived in Hawaii from the 1840s to the 1930s.

Ironically, the very workers whose labor had brought immense profits to white sugar interests provided in the long-term the basic threat to the authority of the Caucasian settlers. The level of immigrant labor declined after 1900, and the proportion of island residents of Caucasian ancestry increased. Nevertheless, by 1920 this group still comprised only one-fifth of Hawaii's total population of 255,000. In contrast, there were approximately 110,000 residents of Japanese extraction, more than 40 percent of the population. Chinese, Filipino, Korean, Hawaiian, and part-Hawaiian ethnic groups comprised almost 100,000 residents also.[22]

Most Japanese and Filipinos were resident aliens. Furthermore, many of those born in the territory of Asian parents did not choose to exercise their voting rights. It was estimated that in 1920 less than one-third of all nisei (those born of Japanese immigrants in Hawaii) who were eligible to vote had attempted to register. Nonetheless, on the eve of World War II about one-quarter of Hawaii's registered voters were of Japanese ancestry. Japanese language newspapers, especially the *Hawaii Hochi*, the *Hawaii Asahi*, and the *Kwasan*, often attacked the white oligarchy, and urged nisei to exercise their vote. But in general, until after the Pacific war those Japanese who did vote often supported the dominant, haole-led Republican party. Not until the 1930s were a handful of Japanese elected to office. In this same decade less than 3 percent of appointed positions were given to citizens of Japanese ancestry. The percentage of other nonwhite ethnic groups eligible to vote also increased during these years. Pioneer Hawaiian sociologist Romanzo Adams estimated in 1936 that the percentage of adults of Asian ancestry able to vote had increased to about 40 percent of the enfranchised population. He predicted that by 1944 approximately two-thirds of Hawaii's adult population would have the vote. A significant number of each major ethnic group in the territory would by then exercise full citizenship rights. He concluded prophetically that with an increase in the voting strength of the non-Caucasian majority would come a redistribution of power in the islands.[23]

Many locals had apparently reached a conclusion roughly similar to that advanced by Adams. Certainly an increasing number of Caucasian and Hawaiian citizens identified statehood with possible Japanese control of the local legislature. Writing on *The Human Side of Hawaii* in 1920, Albert Palmer acknowledged that one issue was paramount for whites: "How will it all come out? Will Hawaii at last be American or Japanese? Will it be Christian or Buddhist? East and West are meeting here—which will prevail?" For the Caucasian minority, as Daws has concluded, the answer to such questions was clear: "The important thing was to prevent the Japanese from 'taking over,' whatever that might mean." By maintaining an appointed governor and judges, future

Japanese domination of local politics could be stifled. Territorial status was thus a major vehicle for protecting white interests. Clarence H. Cooke, a wealthy missionary descendent, prominent Republican, and president of the Bank of Hawaii, put this view unambiguously when he wrote during the depression: "through appointment of officers by the President of the United States, such as the governor, secretary of the Territory and judges, we have always had a better class of men in these positions than states enjoyed through their elective systems."[24]

By the 1920s however, some attempts were made to conceal this objective by arguing that the territory's pressing social problems had to be solved before consideration of statehood could be seriously undertaken. The *Honolulu Star-Bulletin* stated, for example:

> The question of future political control is a most vital one, and it is inextricably interwoven with the great problem of Americanization in these islands.

> Hawaii, someday, no doubt will arrive at a status justifying an appeal for statehood, but that day has not yet come. There are too many racial problems waiting on the future for solution.

Usually, however, local English language newspapers were much less polite about the so-called Japanese problem. Paradoxically, the victims of Hawaii's social structure were often blamed for causing discrimination and ethnic antagonism. In the opinion of the *Star-Bulletin*, resentment against the Japanese had been "engendered almost entirely by their temperamental characteristics, their insecurity. . . . Studying deeper into the causes of the feelings entertained against the Japanese we have their insularity, their failure to enter into community life and become part of it, their herding together and aloofness from their occidental neighbours." Some mainland opinions about Hawaii's Japanese were even less tolerant, being notable for explicit racism and hostility. Writing in *Current History* in 1920, for example, Robert Neal suggested that the problem was "how to get rid of the portion of the population, especially the oriental element, which cannot be Americanized, and how to make legal Americans of the portion that cannot be got rid of?" For white supremacists, the political implications of Hawaii's unique racial features were self-evident. "The Americans are being bitterly encysted as a small and dwindling aristocracy," Lothrop Stoddard lamented in *The Rising Tide of Color* (1922). "In 1917 the births of the two races were: Americans, 295; Japanese 5,000! Comment is superfluous." During the 1920s Hawaii's legislature restricted the activities of Japanese language schools and newspapers, and through the Press Regulation Bill permitted the attorney general to censor political literature printed in a foreign language. In the following decade the powerful haole-dominated Taxpayers' League of Honolulu appealed for the introduction of voting restrictions based on racial criteria.[25]

Throughout the interwar years, according to John A. (Jack) Burns, who rose to dominate postwar politics in the islands, the belief was widely held that "certain people are born to rule the lives of others. . . . You had a haole group that believed in the haole-group superiority." Republican authority was synonymous with haole control. Assumptions of racial superiority helped to rationalize the severe inequalities of opportunity and condition experienced by different ethnic groups. These views helped preserve the facade of two-party politics in a community where the Republicans ruled virtually without challenge after 1902. The GOP controlled the legislature until the mid-1950s, except for a split House of Representatives in 1947, usually with majorities of more than four to one over its rivals in both chambers. The fact that governors appointed by the Roosevelt and Truman administrations were nominally Democrats did little to alter this situation. Indeed, many locals saw the hand of the Big Five in these appointments. Moreover, some who won office in the islands as Democrats did so because of Big Five, or occasionally, Dillingham family patronage.[26]

For almost half a century the Republicans held the territorial legislature in an ironclad grip. Daniel Inouye has noted with only slight exaggeration:

> Economic power was still hand-held by the few dominant Caucasian families descended from the missionaries and traders . . . the Castles, Cookes, Baldwins, Damons, Athertons, Robinsons, and most pervasively powerful of all, the Dillinghams. Their economic interests were best defended by the Republican Party and their newspapers diligently preached the Republican message and their plantation supervisors hustled the Republican vote. In 1941 they were still tying the ballot pencil in such a way that, even in the privacy of the curtained booth, a field hand voting for a Democrat might just as well shout it from the top of a palm tree. Not surprisingly, few did.[27]

Commenting on the relationships between the Republican party, kamaaina haoles, and the dominant economic interests, Norman Meller has observed:

> It has been a widely held belief . . . that the leadership of the Republican Party was merely another manifestation in different guise of the same group which enjoyed economic and social dominance in the community. The heavy components of Big Five and plantation administrators in the Republican legislative majorities of the past materially reinforced the belief. This, of course, tended to have ethnic overtones, as Orientals comprised a larger proportion of the lower socio-economic segments of the Island community.[28]

From the early 1930s, when local-born Japanese first won office in the territory, until after World War II, islanders of Asian descent were severely underrepresented in both the House and Senate. Not until 1941 was any nisei legislator elected to the Senate, although in this year six won seats in the House. Daniel Aoki, a Hawaii-born citizen of Japanese extraction who was later prominent in the Democratic party, has observed that the Big Five's economic control was such that individuals who ran as Democrats or did not follow the directives of the Big Five found themselves out of a job. "In other words," he concluded, this group "had a real strong economic stranglehold in the entire community." The hegemony "always talked about *their* two parties," Burns commented in a similar vein. According to him, they could exert their influence and, at will, achieve any desired result at all levels of island politics.[29] This assessment was not confined to disgruntled Democrats. Many younger Republicans—including Hiram Fong, Joseph R. Farrington, and later William Quinn—were disturbed by this sharply concentrated power and appreciated that a close association with the old guard of their party might damage their political careers. Until after the war, however, most members of the legislature were, in Quinn's words, "dictated to by Merchant Street and influential haoles." Fong's early experiences in the legislature illustrate starkly the closed, concentrated nature of political and economic life in the territory. Although he won office in 1938 as a Republican and remained a Republican throughout his long and very distinguished career, Fong was always a political maverick. He quickly came into conflict with leaders of his party, notably the powerful servant of the large sugar corporations clustered around Merchant Street in downtown Honolulu, Royal (Roy) A. Vitousek, whom a colleague in the legislature described as "an agent of the Big Five—their stooge, bought and paid for." Fong was also convinced that Vitousek was in fact the spokesman of the Big Five and that the party was overbalanced in their favor; he withheld support from Vitousek. The reward for acting independently, Fong recalled with surprisingly little bitterness, was constant harrassment from leaders of his own party. This included an attempt to deny him his seat in the legislature. In addition, Fong noted that though not ostracized outright by the party, "I never got any business from the entrenched economic powers here; never any bit of business at all."[30]

Elite control and inequality were not limited to the formal political arena; they penetrated virtually every facet of community life. In the words of the outspoken liberal Democrat Tom Gill the islands were dominated by "a sugar factor hierarchy." "This hierarchy was a closed society. It talked to itself. It spoke to the people through chosen instruments, the principal one being the Republican Party. It enforced its mandates with methods that were often ruthless and always self-serving. It was paternalistic and fundamentally racist."[31] The principal English language newspapers, what's more, unashamedly endorsed the hierarchy's authority and reflected its views—a situation which persisted until after the Pacific war. Ernest Murai, a leader of the Japanese community recalled that the territory was dominated by the Republicans, the Caucasians, with the result that there was a double wage standard based on race, informal but obvious residential segregation along ethnic lines, and the exclusion of many nonwhites from equal participation in community affairs, extending to sports and social clubs. This control also produced unequal educational opportunities, which reflected a combination of socioeconomic and ethnic factors that disadvantaged most severely those nonwhites growing up on the outer islands. Segregation was very real on many plantations, according to Quinn, who commented that the managers "would allow the Japanese to come up the hill only so high." Discrimination against Hawaii's Japanese, he acknowledged, was reflected "in the way they were trained, and in the way they were allowed to take their position in the life of the community."

Understandably, in the interwar years many nonwhites, especially nisei, felt themselves socially ostracized and economically disadvantaged. Recalling his childhood in a Japanese family, Aoki observed: "We were treated fairly in the plantation . . . but still it was not equal treatment with the so-called haole segment of our community." On Maui, for example, the plantations were divided into a "haole camp" occupied exclusively by whites (mainly the bosses), and other areas for nonwhite families. Living in what was in effect a segregated community, Aoki felt excluded. This nurtured feelings of group inferiority—feelings apparently widely shared by others of Oriental descent until after the Second World War. It was difficult to accept their equality with whites, Seichi Hirai later recalled. Under the paternalistic system in prewar Hawaii, nonwhites confronted pervasive (if sometimes subtle) discrimination. As Chuck Mau and most youngsters of Asian parentage found even in the New Deal years, "industry" and the "economic barons" actively discouraged those seeking wider opportunities. For example, youngsters wanting a higher education were often pressured not to leave the islands as this would exacerbate labor shortages. People born of alien parents in Hawaii, an incorporated American territory, were obliged to secure a labor certificate before moving to the mainland for any purpose. Members of the local judiciary responsible for granting these certificates in the late 1930s, Mau observed, were still "indoctrinated" by the "barons" of the Big Five in defining their policies.[32] Many members of Hawaii's Chinese and Japanese communities also believed that kamaaina haoles were consistently given preferences in business and employment at the expense of nonwhites. Haole exclusiveness was economic as well as social.[33]

The economic, social, and even geographic mobility of many ambitious Hawaii-born nonwhites was thwarted by various instruments of social control which penetrated island life. Because of this, Seichi Hirai observed, people from various ethnic groups kept to themselves, except perhaps during school or work. At the very least, many nonwhites felt powerless, believing the haole-dominated political system would not respond sympathetically to their needs.[34] Even if it is conceded that such feelings were sometimes exaggerated or ill founded, they were nonetheless widely shared. And it was these very beliefs which fuelled the drive by many non-Caucasians for equality under statehood. Initially, however, these feelings provided fertile soil for the growth of trade unions.

Those workers who joined infant trade unions were disturbed by the unsympathetic response of plantation owners to demands for improved hours, conditions, and wages. Within a decade of the first substantial organized strike on Oahu in 1909, the largest groups of plantation workers—the Japanese and the Filipinos—had organized separate federations of labor. Major strikes soon followed. The reaction of the *Honolulu Advertiser* to a strike in 1920 waged largely by Japanese workers was typical of the views of property owners. "What we now face is an attempt on the part of an alien race to cripple our principal industry and gain dominance of the American Territory of Hawaii," Thurston's newspaper claimed.[35] But reactions to the demands of labor were not restricted to angry words. Nor were Japanese workers the only problem for the plantation owners. In 1924 the Castle and Cooke plantation at Hanapepe on Kauai was the scene of a bloody conflict between Filipino strikers and police. It left 16 strikers dead, and led to the arrest of 101 strikers, 60 of whom were sentenced to up to four years in prison. Such unfortunate events left hostile memories on all sides, and retarded the growth of unionism. Nonetheless, by the mid-1930s new efforts were being made to organize dock workers along similar lines to those used in waterfront areas of the Pacific coast on the mainland. Yet as the Hilo dock strike of 1938 demonstrated, organized strikers and their picket lines were still deeply resented by business interests. In this strike— which became known as the Hilo Massacre—police fired on picketers, wounding more than 50, some of whom were crippled for life. Protections offered to American workers under New Deal legislation were extended to most mainland areas by the late 1930s. But Hawaii's workers did not reap the benefits of such legislation until after the Pacific War.[36]

Labor unrest provided the most concrete, immediate challenge to the existing economic and political order. Yet, on the eve of the war other pressures surfaced. Cracks appeared in the facade of the Republican party. A handful of independent members began to question its leadership and conservatism. Voices from within the party called for it to be more open and responsive to the wishes of Hawaii's changing electorate. A substantial minority of members of the legislature were now of Asian descent. Moreover, the Democratic party was not totally impotent. Indeed the most important locally elected office, that of mayor of Honolulu, was consistently captured by a very popular part-Hawaiian Democrat, John H. Wilson. At the same time, Roosevelt's Democratic administration proved less responsive than previous administrations to appeals from the territory's legislature, governor, or sugar interests. Indeed the drive for statehood, which began in the mid-1930s, was unmistakable evidence that the customary distribution of power in the islands and between Honolulu and Washington was undergoing unprecedented stress. It suggested that the interests of the old elite could no longer be protected adequately by territorial rule.[37]

Before the mid-1930s, however, statehood was precisely what most influential haoles wished to avoid. Thus the territorial legislature was obliged to tread a delicate political path—it attempted to resist unfavorable congressional interference in island affairs without encouraging demands for full-fledged local autonomy under statehood. Rather than expand on Prince Kuhio's initiatives in Congress and promote enabling bills, Hawaii's political leaders asked Washington to reaffirm Hawaii's rights as an American territory.

Shortly after he became governor in 1921 Wallace R. Farrington recruited a committee to draft legislation which could form the basis of a petition to Congress. It was an indication of the nature of island politics twenty-five years after annexation that the members of this group were all prominent leaders of the Hawaiian republic—Thurston, Edward Dole, and Walter F. Frear. In 1923 their recommendations became a bill of rights, which the legislature and Farrington duly endorsed. Although it protested against political discrimination by Congress, the bill of rights made no explicit reference to statehood (given Thurston's views on the matter, this was a predictable omission). Instead, it attempted to redefine Hawaii's rights within the existing political context of territorial status. The bill of rights asserted Hawaii's right to participate equitably in national measures and requested assurances from Congress that Hawaii would be included "in all acts in aid of good roads, education, farm loans, maternity, home economics, training in agriculture, trade and industry, and other acts of a like nature which apply to the states as a whole." It sought also to clarify Hawaii's status in the Union, and to correct misconceptions in Congress and in some executive departments of the federal government which had in the past led to the territory's exclusion from numerous federal appropriations. The bill emphasized that as an integral part of the Union, Hawaii could not "legally, equitably or morally be discriminated against," and should be included in all financial legislation and appropriations which extended to all states. President Coolidge and Congress formally recognized the bill of rights. Annual appropriations to the territory increased by five hundred thousand dollars immediately, but this was not its principal reward. Most significantly, it confirmed Hawaii's incorporated status. By implication at least, Congress accepted that the territory was entitled to the privileges and benefits of a state wherever its function and responsibilities were those of a state. Although the bill of rights did not end discrimination against the islands, it was viewed by most haoles as a suitable substitute to an appeal for statehood.[38]

By 1927 even the strongly anti-statehood, anti-Japanese *Honolulu Advertiser* conceded that Hawaii exhibited almost all of the attributes which had helped other territories gain statehood. "She has population, wealth, a tradition of political allegiance and loyalty to the United States; pays more taxes to the Federal Treasury than many of the present states; and as a state would lend powerful support to American military and naval defense and to the creation of an appropriate American merchant marine." Such developments, however, did little to convince the powerful Caucasian minority that statehood was necessary. The alternative to territorial government, the *Advertiser* claimed, was "government controlled by an oriental power. . . . such a power is Japan." As late as 1933 a meeting of the Taxpayers League in Honolulu (a predominantly Caucasian body) overwhelmingly endorsed a motion to seek changes in the Organic Act which would restrict the voting rights of non-Caucasians in the territory. Thurston expressed the opinion of most Caucasian inhabitants when he stated in 1927: "Do I object to statehood? Most assuredly not, so long as it remains an ideal, not a reality."[39]

Seeds of the Statehood Drive

Despite occasional unfair treatment at the hands of Congress, during the first three decades as a territory Hawaii's legislature did not act decisively on statehood. Rather it was content to seek more equitable treatment within existing political arrangements. Thus it dutifully sent petitions to Congress, lobbied its friends on Capitol Hill, and supported the efforts of its delegate in the House of Representatives. Not until Congress moved deliberately against Hawaii's sugar producers were these practices seen as ineffectual and statehood accepted as a necessary objective. In the 1920s and 1930s Congress attempted to limit imports of Asian laborers and to reduce Hawaii's access to the sugar markets of the mainland. These threats stung the territory's legislature into uncharacteristically decisive action.

Following decisions by California and some other states to restrict the rights of Japanese residents to own or rent land, Congress moved against Japanese immigration. On July 1, 1924, an immigration act was passed which replaced the earlier gentleman's agreement and in effect ended all further immigration from Japan. Yet mainland pressure against immigrants from any region of Asia—including America's colony in the Philippines—continued unabated. In the late 1920s Filipino laborers became the major focus of hostility. Hawaii's sugar and pineapple plantations now relied heavily on these laborers, demanding a minimum intake of five thousand workers annually. Confronted with Japanese laborers increasingly prepared to organize and seek better conditions and wages, and denied access by the 1924 act to any immigrants from Japan, Hawaii's sugar planters wanted desperately to maintain their access to Filipino workers. The planters supported an organized, influential lobby in Washington for such emergencies, and immediately pressed that Hawaii be exempted from the proposed Filipino exclusion bill. Hawaii's delegate to Congress, Victor S. K. Houston, advised the Planters' Association that statehood was essential if such unfavorable decisions were to be avoided. However, the sugar owners were not yet convinced that such a radical step was appropriate; they were confident their plight would be understood by sympathetic friends on Capitol Hill. Nor was such confidence misplaced. Through its lobby in Washington the Planters' Association was able to incorporate in the subsequent Johnson Immigration Act a provision which permitted Hawaii alone to continue importing Filipino labor.

Despite opposition from sugar interests, Houston continued to press vigorously in Hawaii and Congress for statehood. He argued that equality as a state was essential if further discrimination by Congress was to be avoided. As yet, however, plantation owners were reluctant to jettison their direct access to Washington in return for the very uncertain benefits of democracy at home and popularly elected representatives in Congress. In 1925, for example, the legislature issued a further "Declaration of Rights." This act again redefined the territory's "inalienable rights" as an integrated part of the Union. It was directed ostensibly against federal practices which discriminated against American citizens in the territory, notably Orientals, who were often denied freedom of movement between the islands and the mainland and treated as foreign immigrants when they reached mainland ports. In reality, the declaration was an attempt to strengthen Hawaii's bargaining position during delicate discussions over national immigration laws which threatened its access to Filipino labor.[40]

Nonetheless, local support for statehood continued to grow, and was often expressed openly. The electorate, which now included a substantial number of nisei and second-generation Chinese, was always more sympathetic to this prospect than the powerful Sugar Planters' Association or the Honolulu Chamber of Commerce. Members of the legislature were often caught between these conflicting forces. As a result, the territory's political parties and elected officials generally expressed public support for statehood, but the phrase "immediate statehood" was rarely heard. Conveniently, such pronouncements were not accompanied by plans for achieving this goal in either the immediate or long-term. In 1930, for example, both the Republican and Democratic parties in Hawaii endorsed statehood in their election platforms. The following year a joint resolution seeking statehood passed both houses of the territorial legislature by overwhelming majorities. After 1930 similar resolutions passed most territorial legislatures, but this did not materially advance statehood. Daws has commented aptly that "no one could tell whether a politician was supporting the resolutions because he genuinely wanted something done, or because he knew that nothing would be done." In 1931 the joint resolution was vetoed by the governor, primarily for technical reasons. However, the legislature failed to redraft the bill or to override the veto. This suggested, as C. Nils Tavares observed, that the original favorable vote "was intended more for home consumption and perhaps notice to Congress of future expectations, than for serious consideration then by Congress."[41]

Hawaii was an isolated and relatively insignificant factor in American politics before the depression years. It had rarely gained the attention of the wider American public. But events in the islands in the early 1930s excited real controversy and brought the tropical outpost under national scrutiny. Apart from heightening racial tensions and suspicions, these events suggested that in remote Hawaii whites could commit acts of violence, even murder, with apparent impunity—provided the victims of such attacks were not Caucasians. On September 12, 1931, Thalia Hubbard Massie claimed she had been beaten and criminally assaulted by a group of five Hawaiian and Japanese men (a special enquiry later found that the accused men could not have committed this offense). Shortly afterward the mother and naval-officer husband of Thalia Massie were charged with the murder of one of her alleged attackers, a Hawaiian, Joseph Kahahawai. They were found guilty of manslaughter by a local court and each sentenced to ten years imprisonment. The convicted couple served only one hour of their sentences before they were freed—an executive order by Governor Lawrence M. Judd promptly commuted their sentences. Judd's decision was made after he had talked briefly, in private, with the defendants' celebrated lawyer, Clarence Darrow. It reflected deep, often hysterical white concern for the physical and sexual safety of, in the *Advertiser*'s words, "white women of refinement and culture." This cause célèbre revealed a community subject to racial preoccupations sometimes very similar to those which shaped relations between blacks and whites in mainland states during the 1920s and 1930s. The incident led to charges in Congress that law and order had broken down in the territory. Some mainland opinion was concerned that whites were afforded preferential treatment under the law; but most commentators expressed alarm that the American territory was unsafe for white Americans.[42]

The sequence of events in the Massie case contrasted starkly with those three years earlier when a nisei, Myles Fukunaga, was tried for the murder of Gill Jamieson, the young son of a wealthy haole banker. The trial, conviction, and execution of the mentally unbalanced Fukunaga were all completed within a brief two weeks amid rumors that Honolulu's whites might take matters into their own hands if the law did not quickly deal with him. Viewed together, these two emotive trials doubtless convinced many nonwhites (if there were many not already persuaded) that Hawaii's system of criminal justice was biased by racial stereotyping and prejudice. The divisions and tensions generated by the Massie case helped, as perhaps no other single event had, to expose the nature of white authority in the islands and to stimulate wider opposition to it. The editor of the *Hawaii Hochi*, George Wright, perhaps best summarized the consequences of this miscarriage of justice when he wrote: "More harm has been done the cause of Americanization by recent events than can be remedied in many years. . . . Republican leadership has been discredited and many of the most powerful people in public life stand branded as traitors in the eyes of the common people. . . ." The swing toward the Democrats in Honolulu after this event as well as the election of a Democrat, Lincoln McCandless, as delegate to Congress in 1932 confirmed the growing dissatisfaction with the Republican party. The reaction of Congress to the Massie case also revealed the vulnerability of the islands to outside interference. This further strengthened the demand for full-fledged local autonomy under statehood.[43]

The excited controversy over law and order prompted reactions in Washington which were unacceptable to all sectors of Hawaii. In previous years the Big Five had periodically advocated that a commission government replace territorial rule, assuming of course that it would dictate appointments to this more centralized and "efficient" administration. But in 1932 Congress proposed a form of commission government which was unacceptable to the Big Five, for it recommended that a high commissioner be sent from Washington to direct the affairs of the territory. Realizing that the president, not Merchant Street, would control this appointment, the reaction of Hawaii's Republican and business interests was swift and hostile. They now defended the Organic Act against any threatened violation and criticized the prospect of what they called a carpetbag governor. Commission government had been proposed, but paradoxically in a form unacceptable to its keenest advocates. Local opponents of the haole elite were delighted with its discomfort over this matter. "For years our local leaders in politics and industry have been trying to frighten the people of Hawaii with threats of a

'Commission form of Government,' " "To serve their own selfish ends and whip reluctant citizens into line, they have painted a terrifying picture of this bogey-man," the *Hawaii Hochi* commented with undisguised relish.

> Now the chickens have come home to roost! The imaginary "bogey" has materialised into a vigorous and menacing reality. The amusing feature of the present situation—if there is anything amusing about it—is that the threat is directed against the very ones who have been using it so long as a means of frightening the people of the Territory into doing their bidding. The latest measure introduced in Congress . . . would absolutely prevent the dictation of appointments by the local coterie of "big interests." . . . It would strike a fatal blow at the domination of local governments by our "captains of industry."[44]

Apparently preferring the unfamiliar devils to the ones they knew, a few local opponents of the haole elite were now prepared to risk a commission government.

Immediately upon the Democrats coming to office under Roosevelt, Congress seriously examined possible alternative forms of administration for the territory. With memories of the Massie incidents still fresh, Representative John E. Rankin (Dem., Miss.) introduced into Congress in 1933 a bill to alter the Organic Act and empower the president to appoint nonresidents to the most important positions in the territory—those of governor, secretary, and the judiciary. Many congressmen, especially Southerners, felt this might ensure a pattern of race relations more in keeping with mainland practices (a pattern which presumably would not have permitted white Americans to be sentenced to ten years imprisonment for the manslaughter of a black). Rankin's bill was classified as "must" New Deal legislation by the administration. It was reported favorably by the House Committee on Territories, and passed the House of Representatives, despite protests by some liberals that it would provide a carpetbag governor for the territory. Eventually the legislation was defeated, but only after a protracted filibuster was waged against it by Senators William Borah and Arthur Vandenberg.[45]

In Hawaii, the Rankin bill aroused extreme protests from the delegate to Congress, the Chamber of Commerce, political party executives, and a variety of local business representatives. The legislature passed a resolution opposing it. Governor Judd appointed a three-member Home Rule Commission to protest against the bill in Washington. Local Republican Samuel Wilder King, a member of this commission who protested personally to Roosevelt, returned from Washington in 1933 shocked by the offhand manner with which Hawaii's affairs were managed in Congress. This experience convinced King that statehood was essential. It also prompted him to run as the Republican candidate

for delegate to Congress. After his victory in 1934 King worked con-
scientiously for statehood, although his efforts did not always have the
overwhelming support of party backers. (A popular part-Hawaiian who
had risen to the rank of lieutenant commander of the U.S. Navy, King
resigned his place in Congress in 1942 and rejoined the navy to fight in
the Pacific War.)

The Rankin bill, along with other proposals for forms of commission
government appointed by the president, encouraged a growing number
of islanders to view statehood as a guarantee against the possibility of
severe political discrimination. However, it was the imposition in 1934
of discriminatory economic legislation against "King Sugar" which,
more than any single event, galvanized and broadened support for
statehood. The fact that this action virtually coincided with a brief visit
to the territory by Roosevelt merely underlined Hawaii's unequal status. The president praised the high living standards and educational
achievements of the territory, conceding that they were superior to
those in many areas of the mainland. Nevertheless, such compliments
did not reflect general congressional sympathy for Hawaii and its preca-
riously concentrated economy.[46]

Sugar remained Hawaii's economic backbone. In 1934 it comprised
over 70 percent of total exports to the mainland. Approximately one-
third of the population lived on plantations or were entirely dependent
on plantations for employment. After 1900 the sugar industry was afforded equal treatment with mainland sugar and protected equally by
United States tariff laws. Moreover, the 1924 bill of rights had reassured
local planters that mainland sugar producers would not be given favorable treatment by Congress. But this provided only temporary respite.
A decade later Congress approved the Jones-Costigan Sugar Act, which
seriously reduced Hawaii's sugar quotas in relation to quotas imposed
on mainland states. Mainland sugar producers were given a quota
above their average past production. By contrast, Hawaii's quota was
approximately 10 percent less than its average annual production in
preceding years. Also, Hawaii was permitted to refine locally only 3
percent of its quota of sugar. At the same time Cuba was permitted to
refine 22 percent of its crop, and the Philippines and Puerto Rico to
refine 10 percent of their respective quotas.[47]

The Sugar Act outraged the island community. The Hawaiian Sugar
Planters' Association, English language newspapers, and most political
and commercial groups joined a chorus of opposition against it. A representative of the sugar planters' groups complained because the act
"grossly discriminates against us, not only as compared with the states,
but as compared with the possessions, and even a foreign country."
The *Honolulu Star-Bulletin* protested for identical reasons: "Hawaii is
lumped with foreign countries and possessions, notwithstanding the
fact that Hawaii alone of all non-continental areas pays all federal taxes

and internal revenue to the United States Treasury." The act represented a victory for the mainland sugar producing states of Florida and Louisiana plus the various states which produced sugar beet over the interests of offshore producers.[48]

Hawaii's sugar interests contested the constitutional validity of the Jones-Costigan Act. But this merely brought them greater discomfort. In a case against the secretary of Agriculture the court of the District of Columbia ruled that although provisions of the United States Constitution extended to Hawaii, Congress was at liberty to legislate for the territory and could thus impose limits on the production of sugar in the territory. The implications of this ruling did not go unnoticed in Hawaii. "If Congress has the right to limit the production of sugar," stated a local attorney, "it evidently can limit the production of anything else which may be raised or produced in the territory."[49]

The Sugar Planters' Association was disappointed and dismayed by the Jones-Costigan Act. Without representatives who could vote in Congress, its president suggested, Hawaii could not confidently anticipate equal treatment with the existing states: "Except when it comes to assessing the territory for all federal taxes and compelling us to bear our proportion of the burdens borne by the mainland, we apparently are not to be considered an integral part of the United States."[50] Appeals for political equality quickly followed the realization of economic discrimination. "Taxation without representation was bad enough," stated the vice-president of the Sugar Planters' Association, "but in this instance our own government has denied its own citizens their fair share of their own market."[51] The concrete advantages of immediate statehood were now appreciated by a much wider cross section of business and community leaders. Clearly, a threat to the sugar industry was a threat to the general economy of the islands, especially during the uncertain days of the depression and New Deal. The *Honolulu Star-Bulletin*, which reflected the interests and opinions of most businessmen, was now convinced of the political and economic reasons for statehood.

> Statehood for Hawaii is no longer solely a political aspiration. Bitter experience has shown that as a territory, Hawaii is open to economic attack. . . .
>
> As a territory Hawaii has only one delegate in Congress. He has a seat in the lower house, but no vote on the floor. As a state Hawaii would have two Senators, and with its present population, one representative.
>
> Therefore as a state, Hawaii would have immediately a stronger delegation to uphold its rights than it has as a territory—whether the rights be political, or economic, or both.[52]

Island support for statehood developed quickly in reaction to discrimination by Congress. Even the Sugar Planters' Association recognized that an informal lobby in Washington was an inadequate guarantee against arbitrary, and costly, decisions by Congress or the president. After 1934 Tavares, a prominent early campaigner for statehood observed: "we in Hawaii were by an overwhelming majority . . . converted to the drive for statehood."[53] Developments in Hawaii during 1935–1941 suggest that Tavares' view was, at most, only a slight exaggeration.

Hawaii's sugar interests were finding it harder to live with territorial rule after 1934, but some planters were yet to be convinced that life would be any easier under statehood. The ambivalence of the Big Five, Theon Wright has correctly argued, grew out of a fundamental political dilemma: "if they argued too strongly for statehood they might get it [but] in a form they did not want; and at the same time they realised they needed more political muscle in Washington."[54] Most kamaaina haoles were not yet wholehearted champions of statehood, although they were nonetheless disturbed by the economic consequences of the Jones-Costigan Act. The proportions of nonwhites who were local-born and thus entitled to full political rights grew quickly after the 1920s, threatening to shift the balance of power from the haole-Hawaiian coalition which dominated island politics through the Republican party. The election results of 1932 made this fear more concrete. For many supporters of the old elite the threat to Hawaii's sugar quotas was much less a problem than the danger of Japanese control of elected offices, especially if the power of such offices was increased by statehood.

The support of sugar and business interests in the territory, although at times ambivalent, gave new impetus to the campaign for statehood. King's election as delegate in November 1934 provided an additional boost. He enjoyed strong support from Hawaiians and haoles and was the first prominent elected official from either party to link his political fortunes to those of the statehood cause. He correctly sensed that the events of 1934 had transformed statehood from an empty slogan to a genuine aspiration of many islanders, including some powerful backers of his own party. By 1935 statehood was the announced policy of the Hawaiian Sugar Planters' Association. It donated the services of its public relations experts to the statehood campaign and provided substantial financial support. On June 9 King introduced in Congress "A Bill: To Enable the People of Hawaii to Form a Constitution and State Government and to be Admitted into the Union on an Equal Footing with the Original States." Similar bills had been introduced by previous delegates. However, King's bill was the first to receive serious consideration by either chamber of Congress. King was a sincere and effective champion of statehood, but without supporting pressure from the powerful sugar lobby in Washington, his efforts would have been futile. A six-member subcommittee of the House Committee on Territories was appointed to investigate Hawaii's statehood qualifications. In October it conducted extensive hearings in Hawaii, accepting evidence from 105 witnesses.[55]

Proponents in the territory eagerly grasped the opportunities presented by these unexpected developments. In 1935 an official campaign was organized to promote statehood generally, and to arrange the presentation of favorable testimony at the scheduled congressional investigation. In September a five-member Hawaii Equal Rights Commission was appointed by the governor to provide support for Hawaii's right to equal treatment with the states by the federal government, to prevent discrimination by Congress, and to promote amendments to the Organic Act which would enhance Hawaii's status relative to the states. In part, this mandate simply restated the aims of the petitions sent to Washington a decade earlier. Significantly, however, the Equal Rights Commission was also directed to "make a thorough study of all aspects of statehood for Hawaii and the advisability of submitting the issue to plebiscite at some future date." An appropriation of ten thousand dollars had previously been authorized by the legislature to support the activities of this official statehood body. Its first public act on behalf of statehood was of a kind that would later be seen as a depressing symbol of Hawaii's frustrated ambition—it authorized its ex officio chairman, Governor Joseph B. Poindexter, to present evidence to a visiting team of congressional investigators.[56] Literally hundreds of islanders performed similar rituals, either in Honolulu or Washington, during the next twenty-five years. Nonetheless, in 1935 two unprecedented developments were initiated—an official government-supported campaign was organized and a congressional statehood investigation was undertaken in the island.

Proponents of statehood conceded during the subcommittee investigation that economic motives had provided the immediate impetus for the organization of a formal statehood campaign. They also emphasized, quite legitimately, that Hawaii's campaign rested on other, more basic developments and considerations. By the 1930s population growth and general political and economic conditions in the territory provided a firm basis of support for Hawaii's statehood demands. Hawaii fulfilled many of the traditional conditions necessary for admission. Its population of approximately 180,000 residents exceeded that of many territories at the time of admission, and was greater than the populations of four states, Vermont, Nevada, Delaware, and Wyoming. Slightly less than one-quarter of Hawaii's residents were not American citizens. The overwhelming majority of these 92,000 aliens were first-generation Japanese or Filipino immigrants. Yet this seemingly high proportion of alien residents was lower than the percentage of aliens living in New York or Boston as late as 1930. Hawaii had already served a longer period of territorial pupilage than many territories prior to admission. Its area exceeded that of three of the existing states—Connecticut, Rhode Island, and Delaware—and was almost as large as Vermont, New Hampshire, Massachusetts, or New Jersey. Moreover, Hawaii had an advanced and expanding economy capable of sustaining self-government. It paid more in taxes annually to the federal treasury than fifteen of the states. This sum was five times greater than the amount expended annually by the federal government in the territory for local purposes.[57]

Despite these facts, and favorable testimony from 90 of the 105 witnesses who appeared before the House subcommittee, a majority of the committee did not accept that Hawaii met the conditions necessary for statehood. The committee refused to propose any change in the political status of the territory. Two members recommended that the statehood bill be reported favorably to the House of Representatives. The remaining three found the territory to be "a modern unit of the American Commonwealth, with a political, social and economic structure of the highest type," but recommended that "considerable further study was necessary before a favourable report could be made." Significantly however, all members expressed the opinion that by even a conservative estimate a "comfortable majority" of Hawaii's citizens favored statehood.[58] Most members of the committee rejected immediate statehood, or at least endorsed additional investigation, because they believed "it would be wiser to wait until another generation of American citizens of Oriental ancestry . . . had an opportunity to absorb American ideals and training."[59] The gentle wording of this conclusion could not disguise the widely, if discreetly, acknowledged fact that fear of alien Japanese practices and political weight underpinned most opposition to statehood.

With the support of the sugar lobby in Washington, King continued to press for statehood. In 1937 the House and Senate appointed a joint committee of twelve senators, twelve representatives, and King to investigate the question further.[60] The territorial legislature appropriated twenty thousand dollars to support the activities of the Equal Rights Commission during this investigation.[61] During October 1937 hearings were conducted on the five major islands. The testimony of proponents again emphasized that Hawaii met the traditional conditions necessary for admission. The population size, geographical area, and economic resources of the islands were stressed. Both the willingness and ability of its citizens to maintain an orderly and stable government as well as their desire for statehood were supported with voluminous testimony and statistics compiled by the Equal Rights Commission. The legality of appeals for statehood was supported by frequent references to the Newlands Resolution and the Organic Act, which classified Hawaii as an incorporated territory.[62]

In contrast to the 1935 hearings, opponents also presented exhaustive testimony to the committee. Predictably, most of the arguments against statehood were based, explicitly or implicitly, on appeals to anti-Japanese sentiment. It was argued that Hawaii's population was of predominantly Oriental extraction and could not be classified "as truly thoroughly, fundamentally and unequivocally American." The alleged threat of bloc voting, particularly among the Japanese, and the question of the future loyalty of Japanese residents were sufficient considerations for many to validate their opposition. Some opponents, including a few haoles, were also genuinely alarmed that statehood might consolidate the economic monopoly of the Big Five in the islands. This view had already been expressed forcefully in 1935 by residents who believed that the constraints of decisions imposed by Washington were preferable to a powerful state government dominated and manipulated by the Big Five. The plantations and allied interests like the bar association, interisland transport facilities, and most business enterprises were, Fred W. Beckley told the 1935 subcommittee, "but tentacles of the 'Big Five' octopus of King Sugar's oligarchy." Many nonwhites in particular were alarmed by the concentration of wealth and power in so few hands, but not all accepted that statehood would necessarily accentuate this inequality. Indeed most believed that statehood might help to undermine oligarchic privileges.[63]

In addition to emotive assertions about possible Japanese, or alternatively Big Five, domination of the proposed state, some residents had concrete political reasons for opposing statehood. A few inhabitants of the outer islands believed statehood would reduce their voting representation in the legislature, as statehood legislation included provisions for automatic reapportionment of this body. Under Section 55 of the Organic Act, reapportionment should have occurred after each population census. But outer-island residents, who constituted a majority in each chamber over representatives from Oahu, successfully averted reapportionment after 1900. If introduced on the basis of changes in population distribution, reapportionment would have given Oahu a majority of representatives in the legislature. Investigating committees in 1935 and 1937 found opposition strongest on the outer islands. For example, ten residents of the island of Hawaii testified in 1937, and seven of them strongly opposed statehood. Resistance to the concentration of political power on Oahu and in Honolulu was often fuelled by cultural and ethnic considerations. Many Hawaiian and part-Hawaiian residents of the outer islands viewed reapportionment as but a further formal step toward the triumph of American values and interests, symbolized so acutely by the rapid growth of Honolulu City and the modernization of Oahu.[64]

The findings of the joint committee were influenced substantially by the testimony of opponents. Underlying its recommendations, however, were new factors totally beyond the influence of forces within Hawaii. During the late 1930s relations between the United States and Japan deteriorated sharply. Japan's assault on nationalist China in 1937 and ambitious attempts to develop its Co-prosperity Sphere in Asia gradually drew firm responses from Secretary of State Cordell Hull and President Roosevelt. The joint committee could not have anticipated the shattering consequences of the widening rift between Tokyo and Washington, but its findings were nonetheless determined by what it called "the present disturbed condition of international affairs." Because residents of Japanese ancestry comprised the major single ethnic group in the islands, the committee report implied, the present strained relations with Japan would inevitably induce Congress to reject immediate statehood.[65]

In contrast to the 1935 report, the joint committee did not accept that a majority of Hawaii's citizens wanted statehood. Instead, it requested irrefutable evidence that a substantial majority desired statehood before Congress was again asked to act, and recommended that the territory attempt to determine popular sentiment within the islands on the issue. A minority report issued by a congressman by this time well known to Hawaii, Rankin of Mississippi, was much less ambivalent. It recommended that statehood be postponed indefinitely. As early as 1934 through the Rankin bill, Southern Democrats had assumed the leadership of attempts to frustrate Hawaii's statehood aspirations. Various representatives of the conservative, segregated, race-conscious Southern states willingly performed this function for the next twenty-five years. The report of 1937, however, was not completely negative. The majority opinion conceded that Hawaii had met all the requirements which had previously been set for territories. The apparent contradiction between this finding and the committee's failure to recommend favorable congressional action is difficult to explain. It can only be assumed that the committee recommended additional study because of the strained relations between America and Japan. However, local statehood proponents were able to gain some comfort from the ambiguous findings of the committee. The report emphasized that the disturbed international environment was not a permanent obstacle to Hawaii's aspirations, and concluded that prolonged denial of its valid demands for statehood was unlikely.

> It is obvious that such a community, industrious, prosperous and progressive, will not be content for long to be held in a subordinate position in comparison with other parts of the nation. It is hardly conceivable that the United States, dedicated to the very principle of self-government and equal treatment of all its citizens, should long desire to impose any restrictions upon the full measure of self-government to be accorded Hawaii.[66]

The Long Campaign Begins

Anxious to allay doubts expressed both in Washington and locally that island residents did not solidly favor statehood, local proponents accepted that a vote must be held on the question. As early as 1935, amid the furor generated by the Jones-Costigan Act, the territorial house had approved a joint resolution to hold such a vote. But it was an indication of Hawaii's ambivalence over statehood that this resolution was never even discussed by the Senate. Sam King remained confident that statehood enjoyed strong local support, and introduced in Congress a bill to make a plebiscite mandatory in the elections of 1936. However, this move died in the Committee on Territories.[67]

Undaunted, King worked diligently to convince island politicians that a plebiscite must be conducted. When the joint congressional committee report called for a clear assessment of the electorate's views, King and other statehood advocates immediately interpreted this as a mandate to act. King, in fact, had drafted most of the committee's report. He was the undisputed champion of statehood both in Hawaii and on Capitol Hill, where in the difficult days before Pearl Harbor he had few genuine supporters.[68] "The obvious inference from the report," King informed Vitousek, the most powerful Republican in the legislature and close ally of the Big Five, "is that we should hold a plebiscite on the question of statehood before again asking Congress to pass an enabling act for us."[69] King's persistence was eventually rewarded. In 1938 the local Republican and Democratic parties accepted the proposal. In the following year the legislature agreed to schedule a plebiscite to coincide with the elections of November 1940.[70]

Proponents could scarcely have chosen a less propitious time to conduct such a critical test of local opinion. The years of preparation for the plebiscite coincided with the emergence of a menacing Japanese presence in East Asia and the Pacific. Caught unhappily in the center of the growing storm between Tokyo and Washington, Hawaii's statehood advocates were obliged to modify the wording of the plebiscite question. They recognized that in the face of deteriorating relations with Japan it would be difficult to salvage a favorable result. When initially proposed by territorial Senator Farrington, the bill read: "Are you in favor of immediate statehood for Hawaii?" This was quickly altered to read: "Are you in favor of statehood for Hawaii?" Those answering affirmatively were then to be asked another question: "Are you in favor of statehood for Hawaii NOW?" This wording was also rejected however. Fearing a negative response to any question which embraced the idea of immediate statehood, proponents eventually opted for a deliberately imprecise alternative. When signed into law by Governor Poindexter on May 16, 1939, the plebiscite question asked only: "Do you favor statehood for Hawaii?" The bill was thus ambiguous, designed to avoid the very real possibility that a majority of voters would reject a specific proposal for immediate statehood.[71]

Conscious of the support of the Hawaii Sugar Planters' Association (HSPA) the territorial legislature voted funds to the Equal Rights Commission and gave it responsibility for coordinating the plebiscite campaign. King collaborated with commission members to promote local support. The campaign stressed that statehood was "Hawaii's inherent right as well as its inevitable destiny," and encouraged voters to reject Hawaii's qualified, unequal status. The official, rather cumbersome campaign slogan stated:

> Hawaii, U.S.A.—an integral part of the United States, sharing equally with the forty-eight states the nation's obligations—is entitled to equal rights for her citizens—equal treatment for her industries—equal benefits under national law.[72]

The campaign highlighted equal rights rather than immediate statehood. It was promoted actively by the *Honolulu Star-Bulletin*, but the *Advertiser* remained ambivalent at best. The Pan Pacific Press, publicity agent for the Sugar Planters' Association, was engaged by the Equal Rights Commission to organize publicity. The Sugar Planters' Association donated substantial funds to supplement legislative appropriations and expressed support for the statehood drive.[73] Despite understandable local scepticism over the sincerity of the Big Five's conversion to statehood,[74] influential members of the powerful Hawaiian Sugar Planters' Association were now among its most active proponents. During 1939, for example, the association's president, John Waterhouse, wrote privately that Hawaii should "move heaven and earth" to secure a substantial favorable vote in the plebiscite.[75] During the campaign the vice president of C. Brewer and Company expressed the view of most large corporations when he asked rhetorically, "Is it selfish to desire . . . representation in the Senate of the U.S.? To desire those Senators to protect the economic interests of the territory? To ask that you be accorded the same treatment, more or less, as any other part of the U.S.?" The lessons of 1934 were not forgotten. Predictably, the *Star-Bulletin* agreed that sugar interests had a clear and justifiable interest in statehood as the vehicle for Hawaii's right to self-determination.[76] Most Republicans in the legislature now accepted this view. Moderate republicans like King, Farrington, and Fong did not owe their positions on statehood to pressure from sugar interests. But most conservative Republicans, including legislative leader and attorney to the HSPA Vitousek, only embraced statehood after it became an aspiration of the HSPA.[77]

Unhappily for those committed to statehood, a series of incidents during the plebiscite campaign threw into sharp relief emotion-charged questions concerning the loyalty and Americanization of Hawaii's Japanese. Proponents hoped that the so-called Japanese problem would not form part of the campaign agenda. They were anxious to defuse any controversy which might focus national attention on Hawaii's people of Japanese descent. Early in 1940, for example, the local Democratic and Republican parties had both demurred when residents of Japanese ancestry were fired from jobs on defense projects simply because of their ethnic origin. The parties were nevertheless reluctant to draw attention to this sensitive issue by protesting it in a vigorous way.[78] Such attempts to limit public controversy were eventually undermined. A few weeks before the November elections Kiichi Gunji, a former Japanese consul in Hawaii, commented that the "Japanese in Hawaii are all determined to undergo great sacrifices for Japan during the present uneasy condition" of international relations in the Pacific.[79] Despite substantial evidence that Gunji's words had been misinterpreted by the island press,[80] they confirmed the suspicions of those who viewed Hawaii's Japanese as an immediate security threat.

The alarm sparked by Gunji's statement intensified local opposition to Hawaii's flourishing Japanese language schools, newspapers, and radio stations. Malihini, or newly arrived, haoles, notably those working in defense industries or serving in the military, were especially disturbed by the presence of such foreign institutions on American soil. In 1940 there were 174 Japanese language schools. They were attended, after regular school hours, by more than 40,000 of Hawaii's total public school population of 92,000. Until 1940 noncitizens always comprised a majority of the combined teaching staff of the Japanese schools. These institutions were, as Gunji conceded, a major barrier to statehood. Few islanders were surprised when a convention of the American Legion in Honolulu during 1940 advocated that responsibility for foreign language instruction be transferred to public schools or the university. In recommending that the schools be closed, the American Legion argued that they did not foster Americanization and were often staffed by foreign teachers loyal to their homeland. These proposals were unanimously endorsed by the territory's board of public education.[81]

Japanese language newspapers and radio stations also became targets of this growing intolerance during 1940. The *Star-Bulletin* regularly reprinted articles from the *Hochi* and *Nippu Jiji* under the insensitive heading: "Comment from the Alien Press." At the same time the *Advertiser* seized every opportunity to criticize the alleged willingness of the Japanese language press to defend Tokyo while relations with Washington slid toward war.[82] Pressure from within the islands induced the Japanese language radio stations to cease transmitting the chauvinistic Domei news programs supplied free by the Japanese government.[83] Not all local Japanese were anxious to cut their ties with their native land however. Only a month before the plebiscite was held the Japanese Chamber of Commerce sponsored a shipment of fifty tons of "comfort bags" to soldiers in Japan's army. At the same time an appeal was circulated among prominent Japanese in the islands urging them to support the "holy war" in China by sending donations via the Sumitomo Bank of Honolulu.[84] These were isolated incidents involving only a small fragment of elderly issei (first-generation Japanese) in the territory; but they did irreparable damage to the plebiscite campaign, encouraging rumors about Japanese fifth-column activity and strengthening scepticism about the success of Americanization. Such doubts could not be easily or quickly erased. Rather than highlight particular incidents involving local Japanese, proponents attempted to defend statehood by arguing broadly that all immigrant groups, whether European or Asian, were entitled to freedom of cultural and linguistic expression in their adopted nation.[85] Yet appeals to democratic sentiment and references to America's immigrant origins could not overcome the doubts which fed on emotive incidents involving local Japanese which erupted throughout 1940.

Perhaps the most damaging of these incidents was the heated controversy over dual citizenship sparked by the *Advertiser* on the eve of the November polls. All people born in the territory were American citizens, but before 1924 Japan claimed all people of Japanese ancestry as subjects of the emperor, irrespective of their place of birth. After this date children born abroad of Japanese parents could only acquire Japanese citizenship if they were registered shortly after birth with a Japanese consulate. During the late 1920s large numbers of children born in Hawaii were registered in this way—as many as six thousand annually in 1929. However by 1939 the number of registrations had fallen dramatically to less than one thousand each year.[86] Nonetheless, on the eve of the war forty thousand aliens of Japanese descent lived in the territory, and approximately the same number were dual citizens. Dual citizenship did not necessarily imply dual allegiance. Opponents of statehood argued, however, that if Hawaii's Japanese were committed to their new nation they would immediately end their technical allegiance to Japan by expatriating their Japanese citizenship. Proponents also encouraged expatriation, viewing it as the most effective reply to those anxious about the loyalty of Japanese in the territory. However, expatriation was a complicated and costly procedure. Despite a drive for expatriation led by the *Advertiser*, in 1940 only about one thousand islanders chose to end their dual citizenship. On the other hand, statehood proponents did gain some comfort from the fact that only a handful of infants were registered annually with the Japanese consulate.[87]

The dual citizenship issue simmered until August 1940, when a convention of the American Legion in Honolulu brought it dramatically to the surface. The convention resolved that dual citizens should be excluded from public positions in the territory. In the following elections the Legion attempted to test the loyalty of all candidates who were of Japanese descent by asking them to prove that they were expatriated or had never been dual citizens. One candidate, Sanji Abe, replied that he had initiated, but not yet completed, his expatriation. This was the signal for a vitriolic attack on Hawaii's Japanese by the *Advertiser*—an attack which cut across every facet of the plebiscite campaign and the pending elections. No loyal American could possibly vote for both statehood and a candidate with dual citizenship, the paper claimed. Moreover, the election of Abe would be tantamount to a public admission that his electorate was predominantly un-American. The *Hawaii Hochi* joined the dispute, and attempted to defend Abe's loyalty to America. This simply compounded divisions over the Japanese issue, however, and submerged the plebiscite campaign beneath a public controversy on the very question statehood advocates hoped to ignore.[88] Opponents of statehood, not the Equal Rights Commission, in effect set the agenda of public debate in the final weeks of the campaign. Confronted with this difficulty, the commission was obliged to change its campaign tactics.

The confidence of statehood proponents virtually evaporated during August–September 1940. Yet a wide cross section of islanders continued to endorse the efforts of the Equal Rights Commission. Support came from a majority of the legislature, both political parties, the delegate to Congress, sugar interests, the *Star-Bulletin*, and, significantly, from the two influential Japanese language newspapers, the *Hawaii Hochi* and the *Nippu Jiji*.[89] These supporters accepted the alteration in campaign tactics without dissent. Thus, during its final weeks the campaign conceded openly that the plebiscite was not directly concerned with the question of immediate statehood. A favorable vote, it stressed, would simply imply support for eventual, not immediate, admission. Increasingly, the campaign emphasized that the plebiscite was only an initial step to eventual statehood; that Congress, not Hawaii's voters, would decide when and under what circumstances the territory would be admitted.[90]

This changed strategy was also influenced by the strength of mainland opposition to any proposal for immediate statehood. The 1935 House committee estimated that a comfortable majority supported statehood. By late 1940, however, relations with Japan had deteriorated dramatically. Many Americans, including Hull and Roosevelt, clearly feared that war with Japan was a possibility if not a likelihood in the near future. For proponents of statehood anxious to demonstrate that Hawaii was united and Americanized, developments in East Asia precipitated major new difficulties. Supporters could hardly have chosen a less opportune time to test local convictions about statehood, and by implication the Japanese population of the territory. The Japanese remained the largest single ethnic group, and for many whites and Hawaiians especially statehood still represented the prospect of a state controlled by a Japanese legislature and presided over by a Japanese governor. Some, like John F. G. Stokes, believed that Hawaii had become an instrument of imperial Japanese policy, a base for Japan's ambitions in the Pacific, and an area infiltrated by traitors and corrupted by Japanese values and culture. While few shared such wild conspiratorial and racist views, many felt that it was still too soon to experiment with genuine democracy in the islands. The *Honolulu Advertiser* expressed this view in familiar terms when it argued that statehood was a questionable step which must await an improved international climate and a more mature local electorate.[91]

Despite their determined efforts, statehood supporters were unable to keep racial issues out of public debate on the plebiscite. After the dispute over Abe's citizenship broke, proponents were especially alarmed. Vitousek advised King in Washington of a recent downturn in the enthusiasm for statehood. The campaign committee, desperate to regain the initiative, urged King to return immediately to Honolulu. "We are very anxious to have you participate actively for us," the executive secretary of the Pan Pacific Press wrote King. "We simply must have one or two good personal 'punches' from you." King accepted this request and returned from Congress to campaign during the final days before the plebiscite. King, a part-Hawaiian who enjoyed broad support within the Republican party, confronted the delicate Japanese problem head-on. He argued in particular that opposition to statehood which derived from racial prejudice was itself un-American and a repudiation of the nation's cherished principles.[92]

Proponents gratefully accepted King's timely intervention, but they were not convinced that, by itself, it would be successful. Thus, to coincide with King's appeals, the plebiscite committee used another cornerstone of the local Republican party, the *Honolulu Star-Bulletin*, in a controversial effort to recapture support. Despite the fact that the proportion of islanders of Japanese descent had declined since 1920 from 42 percent to 37 percent, it was still widely believed that as a result of a natural increase in numbers this group would eventually comprise an absolute majority. As we have seen, this view gained wide currency in the early decades of territorial rule; and it did not quickly recede. Those convinced of its validity usually cited a study by the U.S. Bureau of Education completed in 1920 which predicted that by 1940 the Japanese would constitute 47 percent of the local electorate.[93] Yet as the work of Hawaii's respected demographer and sociologist Romanzo Adams demonstrated, these predictions were wildly exaggerated and

based on false premises. As late as 1938 less than 29 percent of the electorate was of Japanese ancestry, and the proportion was never likely to
rise above one-third of the total electorate. In a full-page article in the
Star-Bulletin six days before the plebiscite, the campaign committee
attempted to highlight these figures. Titled "Getting the Facts Straight
about Statehood: The Myth about Japanese Dominance," the article
masqueraded as a normal news story, failing to mention the fact that it
was sponsored by the campaign committee. Such an admission would
have officially linked racial questions to the plebiscite, something which
proponents had studiously sought to avoid. However, King felt no com-
punction about embracing this artificial division of issues, and stated
both privately and publicly that racism was the root cause of hostility to
a "Yes" vote.[94]

Despite the difficulties and diversions which afflicted the official
campaign, the results of the plebiscite offered some comfort to those
who genuinely wanted statehood. It must be conceded, however, that
the returns provided only ambiguous evidence of majority support for
immediate admission. In answer to the question "Do you favor statehood?" 67 percent of citizens answered "Yes." However, slightly more
than 20 percent of those eligible did not vote.[95] Surprisingly Oahu,
which supported 60 percent of the territory's population and was most
exposed to the official campaign, returned the lowest affirmative vote
of any island: only 63 percent of its voters wanted statehood. But on all
other islands the proportion hovered consistently above 70 percent of
those who voted. Only 10 of the territory's 162 precincts recorded a
majority "No" vote, and these precincts were spread throughout all six
representative districts. When interpreting these results some suggested
that the relatively strong outer-island vote for statehood resulted from
the influence of the sugar companies. "King Sugar" could still organize
and deliver the outer islands to the Republican party, they argued, so it
was reasonable to assume it could also deliver an affirmative vote in this
plebiscite.[96] It was also argued that the strength of opposition on Oahu
reflected its larger proportion of malihini haoles, who were most susceptible to arguments emphasizing the "Japanese problem" and the vulnerability of the territory to subversion from within.[97]

The plebiscite question was deliberately imprecise. It did not specify
whether an affirmative vote represented a desire for immediate statehood or admission at a later date, possibly under different local or international circumstances. The result thus indicated only that a two-thirds
majority wanted eventual, but not necessarily immediate, admission.
Undoubtedly, many people voted "Yes" on the clear understanding that
they were not voting for immediate statehood. Indeed, the official campaign encouraged such a view. Because of the ambiguity of the plebiscite question, members of the Equal Rights Commission were obliged

to concede that it had settled very little; statehood remained, as John Snell acknowledged, a hotly debated issue in the territory.[98]

The negative vote was much stronger than proponents originally anticipated. The Pan Pacific Press optimistically aimed to win at least 90 percent endorsement. King, somewhat isolated by his work in Washington, was equally confident, predicting an affirmative vote of 80 percent.[99] These expectations were not realized. Yet proponents were justified in viewing the plebiscite as an overall success. "We think that it was a very good showing in the face of international conditions, petty prejudices and considerable misunderstanding," the executive secretary of the Pan Pacific Press, William Cogswell, wrote privately. King publicly pronounced his satisfaction at the affirmative vote; in private, however, he expressed dismay at the impact of racism on the result.[100]

The plebiscite was a necessary, if unfortunately timed, local initiative. But it could resolve none of the significant national issues which by 1940–1941 impinged directly on Hawaii's statehood aspirations. Even an overwhelming "Yes" vote would have done little to promote early action in Congress. Active public or congressional support for statehood simply did not exist. Indeed opinion polls conducted on the mainland during 1940–1941 indicated that slightly less than half of those interviewed favored eventual statehood. Equally disturbing for local proponents was the fact that only 55 percent of mainland residents believed Hawaii should be defended if it was attacked. In contrast, 74 percent stated that Canada should be defended if it was attacked.[101] War against Japan quickly altered these views, but before Pearl Harbor support for continental security and Anglo-Saxon solidarity generally overrode concern with the security of America's island possessions.

Although military and naval planners in Washington did not share public indifference to Hawaii, their heightened interest in the territory nevertheless served to make the prospects for early admission negligible. While islanders debated the plebiscite issue, the planners examined the possible implications of statehood for national defense policy in the Pacific. By September 1940 Britain's naval strength in East Asia was severely depleted, as it concentrated all possible resources on war against Germany in the Atlantic. Japan eagerly exploited the weakened European presence and interest in East Asia and the Pacific regions. Slowly but firmly the Roosevelt administration attempted to warn Japan that further expansion would not be tolerated, and accepted that Japanese aggression could not be stifled by a policy of conciliation or appeasement. Publicly, America's tougher stance was symbolized in its decision to restrict exports of strategic materials to Japan. Secretly, it resulted in detailed joint defense plans being drawn up with the United Kingdom, the Netherlands, Australia, and New Zealand. Even before Japan commenced its major advance south from China in July 1941, the

United States was preparing for the possibility of war in the Pacific. Indeed, in June 1941 Roosevelt and Hull had indicated privately their receptivity to a joint Anglo-American commitment against Japan should it attack any new areas in Asia.[102]

As American policy hardened, Hawaii's strategic importance increased. Naval planners in Washington were well aware of the implications of war in the Atlantic for European strength in the Pacific, and recognized that the United States must fill the vacuum. When the *New York Times* observed in 1940 that the United States was now the only major Western power whose position in the Pacific was uncompromised,[103] it was simply echoing a view widely shared within the Roosevelt administration and the chiefs of staff. In this context, it was argued, the unprecedented naval and strategic significance of Hawaii dictated that it must remain a territory under the tight control of Washington. Naval and military bases twenty-five hundred miles from continental America in the mid-Pacific were viewed as vital factors in all defense plans. As these plans now explicitly acknowledged Japan as the sole enemy in the Pacific, it followed that Hawaii must remain a territory under the control of a local executive and judiciary appointed by Washington. Indeed, shortly before Pearl Harbor Roosevelt contemplated amending the Organic Act to permit the appointment of a nonresident as governor.[104] On the eve of war with Japan, Caucasians comprised less than one-quarter of Hawaii's population. The implications of this bald fact were, for defense planners in Washington at least, self-evident. In addition, many citizens in Hawaii and on the mainland echoed the *New York Times'* view that, "regardless of the very valid and excellent arguments advanced by Hawaii, this is not the time to give the status of statehood to a territory, the population of which, is over one third Japanese." Doubts about the loyalty of Japanese residents in Hawaii, and the degree to which they had assimilated American ideals and attitudes could not be easily resolved, the *New York Times* observed in September 1940: "Only a crisis could supply proof of the correctness of either view."[105] At Pearl Harbor on December 7, 1941, this crisis erupted.

Chapter 3
The Tests of War

War came abruptly to the Hawaiian islands. On December 7, 1941, Japanese bombs virtually destroyed the United States fleet and installations at Pearl Harbor. America's losses, an official enquiry later acknowledged, marked "the greatest military and naval disaster in our Nation's history."[1] The shock waves from Pearl Harbor and the prolonged conflict with Japan were felt in every sphere of island life. Most significantly, they were a catalyst to Hawaii's statehood ambitions.

During the first twenty-four hours of hostilities the commandant of Hawaii's Department of the U.S. Army, Lieutenant General Walter G. Short, assumed the position of military governor of the territory. Poindexter, the islands' governor, hurriedly acquiesced to the demands of the military, proclaimed martial law, and approved suspension of the writ of habeas corpus. J. Garner Anthony, attorney general of the territory during 1942–1943, was dismayed at Poindexter's virtual abdication.[2] Roosevelt approved these radical changes. Military government was defended as essential for protecting the nation from invasion and possible subversion from within. But it persisted long after the fortunes of war had turned against Japan. It also outlived even the most exaggerated fears of sabotage by Japanese descendents living in the islands. During almost three years of military rule, the Roosevelt administration accepted that Hawaii's constitutional rights as an incorporated American territory must be forfeited to the exigencies of war. Most islanders who were disturbed by Hawaii's unequal status as a territory found military government an additional, severe indignity. In general, the strongest critics of military government were also the most enthusiastic proponents of statehood.[3]

Military government was more severe, arbitrary, and protracted than civil authorities or elected territorial officials had ever imagined possible under the American federal democratic system. Government under these emergency wartime regulations was not unlike that previously reserved for the seceding Southern states under Reconstruction. Like the rebel South in the 1860s and 1870s, Hawaii was exposed to a protracted period of arbitrary military government, and its citizens denied the normal guarantees of the national Constitution and Bill of Rights. Military authorities effectively controlled or supervised virtually every facet of public activity, including public health services, production, wages, prices, and even prostitution. Civil courts were supplanted by military tribunals, and the powers of civilian authorities, including the governor, were consistently overridden. Anthony later concluded: "Thousands of persons were convicted in provost courts, some with trials and some without, and sentences were imposed without regard for the limitations of law in the offenses involved and for offenses unrelated to military security."[4] The press was heavily censored and subject to strict licensing. All but two Japanese language newspapers were closed, and the two permitted to publish, the *Nippu Jiji* and the *Hawaii Hochi*, were obliged to change their names to the apparently less provocative *Hawaii Times* and *Hawaii Herald*. So-called hearings boards were established, comprising representatives of the military, the FBI, and prominent civilians, to "make recommendations as to internment of people who had been taken into custody on suspicion that they were dangerous to the security and defense of the Islands." The severity and unrestrained authority of the military government was reflected unambiguously in the fact that individuals were sometimes convicted for violating the spirit of martial law; plantation laborers could not leave an island without a travel permit from the military; workers could not change jobs without a release from their employers; and individuals could be jailed for absenteeism from work. Harsh constraints applied to all workers, but as one observer noted, plantation laborers, notably the Japanese, were most severely controlled.[5] At the same time, federal laws permitting the seizure of alien property closed three predominantly Japanese banks. Foreign language teaching to children under ten was banned, and steps were taken to exclude people of Japanese ancestry from public employment.[6]

In controlling Hawaii with military government, federal authorities compromised the constitutional and human rights of all citizens, irrespective of their race; but it was Hawaii's Japanese, citizens as well as noncitizens, who suffered most severely.

The Japanese Dilemma

Japan's unprovoked attack on Pearl Harbor realized the worst fears of those who viewed the world simply, in terms of racial loyalties and international conspiracies. It appeared to validate assertions made throughout previous decades by opponents of statehood for Hawaii. Characteristically, this group had accepted that people of Japanese extraction were the "world's most intense nationalists, loyal to the Mikado to the third and fourth generation." In the event of war with the United States, there was allegedly little doubt where the loyalties of these rabid Japanese nationalists would lie. "Every Japanese, born under our

American flag or not, is always a Japanese," Webb Waldron wrote in
American Magazine in 1937. "No matter how much he professes to be
American he is always thinking Japanese thoughts, hoping secretly for
Japanese victory." He concluded with a rhetorical question which con-
cisely expressed the alleged nexus between these racial alarms and possible statehood: "Shall we admit to the dignity and power of statehood a
territory where Japanese, secretly hoping for our overthrow, outnum-
ber mainland Americans 13 to 1?"[7]

Shortly after Pearl Harbor, President Roosevelt initiated a law, which
Congress promptly endorsed, to relocate more than 110,000 Japanese
from the West Coast. Altogether 70,000 American-born citizens and
40,000 Japanese aliens were forcibly moved and incarcerated. Some
remained imprisoned until January 1945. These people were arrested
without warrants, not formally charged, and released only if investigators found them loyal. Yet under the Constitution, sympathy for the
enemy was not an offense. Unlike their mainland counterparts, Hawaii's citizens and residents of Japanese extraction did not suffer mass
arrest or relocation. Nevertheless almost 1,500 were interned, a majority of whom were aliens. Most of the internees were Japanese government representatives, Shinto priests, Japanese language teachers, or
men who had served previously in the Japanese armed forces. Though
few in number, some local leaders of the Japanese community were
picked up, observed a prominent nisei, or AJA (American of Japanese
Ancestry) as those of Japanese descent preferred to be known. When the
war ended in 1945, 277 remained incarcerated. Despite early rumors of
sabotage by Japanese within Hawaii, and some wild suggestions that
Hawaii's 157,000 Japanese be relocated with those from the West Coast,
the overwhelming majority remained free. The economic consequences
for Hawaii of massive relocation and the actual costs of such a procedure encouraged a more sober solution than that adopted in California.
Moreover, Hawaii's island geography and territorial status provided
authorities with options not available on the mainland. Strict military
government over Hawaii's entire population and resources was invoked
immediately after the attack on Pearl Harbor. This made relocation
essentially redundant. In addition it kept Hawaii's Japanese produc-
tively engaged in the nation's war effort.[8]

Anticipating war with Japan, the FBI had established almost twelve
months before Pearl Harbor a special espionage bureau in the Honolulu
Police Department. Headed by Robert Shivers, with John Burns filling
the vital post of liaison officer between the local police and the FBI on
counterespionage matters, this covert branch checked Japanese residents in terms of "background, general reputation and activities, and
anything that might be inimical to the interests of the U.S." Immediately after the Pearl Harbor attack those listed as prime suspects were

promptly incarcerated. This action removed "any chance of them doing any damage," Burns later observed, "even though it might unjustly deprive them of their liberty for a while." Before martial law had been declared Burns was authorized to round up and intern Japanese consular officials, principals and teachers in Japanese language schools, and a few Japanese community leaders. Many of these suspects had not previously been investigated by the espionage branch. Their assumed guilt was a simple function of their common ethnic background. Those captured were taken immediately to the immigration station, by now under military control. Shortly afterward they were interned on Sand Island.[9]

These internment procedures were arbitrary in the extreme. As Burns later conceded, some Japanese "were getting picked-up for having too-much money in their pockets, or having the Japanese flag stored in an old suitcase." One young nisei recalled: "the entire community . . . wanted to squash the so-called Japanese element." It was a period marked by hysteria, according to Dan Aoki, when no Japanese was above suspicion. Even prominent nisei like Mitsuyuki Kido and Ernest Murai, who had worked with the Emergency Service Committee in an attempt to maintain tranquility and productivity among the Japanese populace during the prewar years, felt deeply insecure after their worst fears were realized with the attack on Pearl Harbor. "You can imagine the position of people of Japanese ancestry after December 7th," Murai observed. "They were bewildered, lost, they didn't know where to turn to. They didn't know what was to become of them because they've heard stories." The stories Murai referred to claimed that the U.S. government was planning a mass evacuation of Japanese in the seven Western states. Most AJAs believed the Hawaiian community to be generally hostile and suspicious, Murai recalled. They felt isolated: "we had very few haole friends here." Rumors flourished among the Japanese. There was talk that all those of Japanese ancestry would be shipped to Molokai, and it was widely believed that plans were being drawn up to imprison potentially disloyal able-bodied Japanese in converted school buildings from where they would be released to work during the day. When such plans did not materialize, the explanation offered by many of Japanese descent was simply that the economic situation alone militated against such action. If "they intern all these people, what would happen to the economy?" Murai asked rhetorically. Although exaggerated, the feelings of alarm which generated such rumors were indeed real. And it was the memory of these experiences which shaped the political aspirations of Hawaii's Japanese as the war drew to a close.[10]

The official advice given to the American secretary of War concerning the relocation and internment of mainland Japanese shows clearly the kind of reasoning which lay behind the decision to impose military control on Hawaii's people. "In the war in which we are now engaged," General John L. De Witt advised: "Racial affinities are not severed by migration. The Japanese race is an enemy race and while many . . . have become 'Americanized,' the racial strains are undiluted." Given official policies during 1942–1944, his concluding remarks were apparently persuasive: "There were no grounds for assuming that Japanese-Americans will not turn against the United States." For some, race was apparently sufficient evidence of guilt. Normal citizenship rights were denied and constitutional rights abrogated because a particular ethnic group was assumed guilty of intending to sympathize with, or actually support, an enemy state. Yet as early as 1924 when Japan had instituted a dual citizenship policy which permitted people born abroad of Japanese parentage to register at consulates as subjects of Japan, virtually all such residents in Hawaii had ignored this invitation. Two decades later when war erupted in the Pacific, the ties between Hawaii's Japanese and their ancestral home were even weaker. Despite De Witt's prediction, and the fears of many islanders, no member of Hawaii's Japanese community was ever found guilty of collaborating with the enemy during the Pacific War. At most, as Gwenfread Allen has suggested, only a few thousand older Japanese remained sympathetic to their ancestral homeland. After Pearl Harbor, most of Hawaii's Japanese strove self-consciously to demonstrate their Americanization and their commitment to America's war effort. "Speak American" campaigns were launched, and many Japanese petitioned for permission to anglicize their names. The principal Japanese language school in the islands, the Japanese Central Institute, was liquidated and its assets given to a war memorial fund. Moreover, on one occasion in 1943 almost two thousand Japanese-Americans sent money to Washington expressly for "bombs on Tokyo." Yet for those who shared De Witt's stereotyped views of all Japanese, such actions were unconvincing. As late as 1943 some locals who feared a Japanese presence in Hawaii continued to advocate publicly that no less than one hundred thousand of them should be removed to the mainland and interned.[11]

If the bulk of Hawaii's Japanese escaped forced relocation, they nonetheless encountered considerable hostility and resentment from some sections of the island community. They were exposed to intense social pressure to adopt the dominant social, cultural, and linguistic mores. Some were reluctant to conform, but most younger Japanese citizens accepted that they must adopt and project American customs and values. Ironically, many of those Japanese who were initially assumed to be security risks soon came under strong pressure to demonstrate their loyalty by volunteering for combat duty. "So we were somewhat forced into it; that's how we got into the war," Aoki (who later became president of the famous 442nd Veterans Club) recalled. "All I can say is that

I was fortunate enough to come home." Many nisei who enlisted did so out of a desire to avoid social ostracism and assumed disloyalty. Most were also aware that for the Japanese segment of the islands, Americanization must be demonstrated in an unequivocal, overt way.[12] But as the actions of Hawaii's nisei troops during 1943–1945 suggested, and as the absence of espionage or sabotage in the islands confirmed, legislation to control Hawaii's Japanese was as unnecessary as it was insensitive.

Americans of Japanese ancestry, both in Hawaii and on the West Coast, were painfully aware that their loyalty was widely doubted within the American community. Moreover, in the face of strong but essentially covert racial hostility many Japanese Americans had remained largely separate from white society, an isolated, reserved, and accommodating minority. Pearl Harbor confronted this group with an unprecedented, explicit dilemma. In Hawaii and California, Japanese Americans (most of whom were citizens by birth) were forced to suffer the indignity of unconstitutional restrictions on their movements and rights. At the same time they, more than any other group, were obliged to demonstrate undisputed loyalty to America's war effort and constitutional principles. In the hysteria and recriminations which immediately followed the Pearl Harbor debacle, there were many Americans willing to accept that the Japanese were indeed an enemy within. In the longer term however, war in the Pacific invalidated these irrational suspicions. It provided what many Japanese in Hawaii had long wanted—though obviously in another form—an opportunity to demonstrate conclusively that they were loyal and thoroughly Americanized. "As much as we would hate to see a war between the United States and Japan, and as much as we would hate to see the day come when we would have to participate in such a conflict," a young nisei, Shigeo Yoshida, told the 1937 statehood investigation, "it would be much easier for us I think, if such an emergency should come, to face the enemy than to stand some of the suspicion and criticism, unjust in most cases, levelled against us." His concluding observation undoubtedly reflected the views of many frustrated island-born Japanese citizens: "It is extremely difficult to bear up under the gaff of suspicion and expressions of doubt which have been levelled at us. It would be easier for me to pack a gun and face the enemy."[13]

And when the opportunity to fight for the nation did occur, the behavior and contributions of Hawaii's Japanese were exemplary. The generation for which Yoshida spoke demonstrated an undeviating commitment to America's war effort, and provided unambiguous evidence of the loyalty of all Japanese in the islands. This was at least some consolation for the suffering which war brought to Hawaii.

All ethnic groups in the territory energetically supported the United States war effort. But as a result of the Pearl Harbor attack, a promi-

nent nisei observed, Hawaii's Japanese readily accepted that they had to
demonstrate their national loyalty in a far more concrete manner than
other Americans. The most striking example of this was the combat
record of Hawaii's men of Japanese ancestry who comprised the core of
the volunteer 442nd Regimental Combat Team, and contributed all
1,406 men of the famous 100th Infantry Battalion. Originally called the
Hawaiian Provisional Infantry Battalion, the 100th was formed from
two all-nisei National Guard battalions in the territory. A larger proportion of men of Japanese ancestry volunteered for military service than
from any other ethnic group in the territory. Initially, however, AJAs
wanting to enlist were rejected automatically. Those already enlisted
were barred from receiving additional training and lost the right to bear
arms. They were reduced to the status of laborers in work battalions.
When the War Department finally accepted, in January 1943, that nisei
men could serve in combat, it called for 1,500 volunteers. More than
10,000 Hawaiians of Japanese extraction promptly came forward,
about 40 percent of all those eligible for service. A total of 2,645 were
eventually selected to serve in the 442nd team. Meanwhile, in the 100th
Battalion other nisei troops had undergone training, as a segregated
unit, at Camp McCoy in Wisconsin and Camp Shelby in Mississippi,
where many felt the barbs of racial hostility. In mid-1944 the two AJA
units joined forces in Italy, and their military exploits in the so-called
Go For Broke campaign became a focus of international attention.[14]

In objective terms the wartime contribution made by Hawaii's nisei
population was unsurpassed by that of any comparable number of
Americans. But as Hawaii's statehood proponents reluctantly discovered after the war, racial stereotypes and fears persisted. Although these
views were now expressed less overtly and often disguised by other arguments, they nevertheless proved resilient, despite the unequivocal evidence of nisei loyalty which emerged as a result of Hawaii's energetic
role in the war against Japan. This evidence was unlikely to sway national opinion, the *Honolulu Advertiser* warned soberly a year after
Pearl Harbor, because "an uninformed mainland will not quickly nor
eagerly welcome into the Union of States a new member whose population is largely of Japanese blood." Although the *Advertiser* was still edi-
torially ambivalent over statehood, its belief that racism remained a
major obstacle was well founded. "Regardless of what Hawaii's own
knowledge and experience of its citizens of Japanese ancestry may be," it
concluded, "that knowledge is not shared elsewhere in the nation."[15]
Nevertheless, by the end of the war Americans and their congressional
representatives were better informed about Hawaii than at any previous time.

The combat achievements of Hawaii's troops focused greater national
attention on Hawaii's Japanese than any single event other than the

Pearl Harbor attack. In large part the war record of the nisei soldiers erased the doubts which had understandably surfaced in December 1941. Furthermore, the decisions to let Hawaii's nisei fight in Europe and work as military interpreters in the Pacific helped to remove the early resentment which some AJAs had felt at their exclusion from the war effort. Many of Hawaii's Japanese who did serve felt both "proud and bitter," Murai observed: proud that they were able finally to fight for their country, and bitter because this opportunity was delayed and when it eventually came it involved segregation during training and formation of a distinct, all-AJA battalion. These feelings perhaps intensified the combat determination of Hawaii's nisei volunteers. Members of the 100th Battalion and the 442nd team were awarded more citations for bravery than any other United States infantry units of comparable size during World War II, or indeed any previous war in which America was involved. But their losses were heavy—650 killed and 3,436 wounded in action. This war record, which established the 442nd team as perhaps "the most decorated unit in the entire military history of the United States,"[16] coupled with the overwhelming loyalty of the Hawaiian community during the war, validated statehood proponents' claims that all of Hawaii's people were fundamentally loyal Americans. In the final analysis, this conviction overrode ethnic or community allegiances. The *Honolulu Star-Bulletin* put these views forcefully when it observed at the end of the war: "Our American citizens of Japanese ancestry have acted in uniform and out of uniform, in daily occupation and in the stress and test of battle, just as have our Americans of other ancestries. The basic argument against admission . . . has been answered." War removed the foremost if not the only hindrance to statehood, according to former delegate King, because it negated skepticism about the extent of Americanization of Hawaii's people.[17]

Such skepticism was directed principally at Hawaii's Japanese, but other groups of Asian origin had also been the victims of suspicion. These groups, like the nisei, willingly shouldered the burden of defending their country. The very conspicuous role played by Hawaii's AJAs had tended to obscure the substantial military contributions of Hawaii's other ethnic groups. After Pearl Harbor more than thirty thousand islanders joined the armed forces. In addition to the Japanese, relatively large numbers of Hawaiians, part-Hawaiians, haoles, Chinese, Koreans, and Filipinos also served. Understandably, some later resented the glare of publicity which surrounded nisei veterans while the combat achievements of Hawaiians from other ethnic backgrounds were largely ignored.

Despite this resentment, the war did significantly alter the way in which Hawaii's Japanese were perceived by their fellow citizens. Equally it transformed the self-image and consciousness of this group.

The leaders of Hawaii's Japanese were now determined to expose and confront their people's allegedly second-class status and the subtle discrimination on which it rested. In particular, men like Kido, Murai, Aoki, Robert Oshiro, Sakae Takahashi, and combat hero Inouye developed very similar ideas about Hawaii's society and the future role which Japanese Americans should play in it. "I came to believe with all my heart and soul . . . that the time had come for us to step forward," Inouye later wrote.

> We had fought for that right with all the furious patriotism in our bodies and now we didn't want to go back to the plantations. Times were changing. The old patterns were breaking down. We wanted to take our full place in society, to make the greatest contribution of which we were capable, not for Japanese-Americans, but for Hawaii.

Kido's response to events after 1941 was very similar, although like most nisei leaders he was initially more concerned with his own ethnic group than with the wider island community. "What triggered me into politics," he recalled,

> was the fact that youngsters that were enrolled in the 442nd Combat Team who were then in combat in Italy would write back letters from their hospital beds . . . saying "We were willing to sacrifice our lives and everything, are we coming back to a second class society? What are we going to do when we get back?" We . . . decided that something had to be done, and that . . . one way of bringing about full recognition of the people who made this supreme sacrifice was to get into politics and change the political life of the community and make it more democratic, to bring about—idealistically— . . . equality of opportunity.

The experiences of war, both at home and in combat, stimulated unprecedented pressure from the previously quiescent Japanese community for unqualified political rights. Increasingly statehood was viewed by the leaders of this group as the principal means to this important end.[18] But this view was not restricted to Hawaii's Japanese (although they were perhaps its most vocal and public exponents after 1945). Political leaders of other Asian groups were also anxious to win wider equality through statehood. The contradiction between America's espoused aims in the Second World War and Hawaii's qualified status as an American territory was fully realized by a wide cross section of Hawaii's people only after 1945.

Legacies of War and Military Rule

The question of military government sharply divided the island community after 1941. In particular, it split the influential haole sector, including the Republican party, exposing divisions which never healed completely. Through his newspaper, the *Honolulu Star-Bulletin*, Farrington argued that military rule should be ended as soon as possible, or at least modified. Shortly after he was elected delegate to Congress in 1942 he expressed a similar view in Washington. But relatively few members of the haole minority were initially anxious to fight for civilian rule. Those who did seek to restore full constitutional government—including Attorneys General Anthony and C. Nils Tavares, Judge Delbert Metzger, Farrington, and Poindexter's successor, Governor Ingram Stainback—made little headway until late in the war. In general, Hawaii's business community was delighted with military rule.[19] In the early months of military government, for example, the Honolulu Chamber of Commerce sent a telegram to Roosevelt protesting against efforts to restore civil authority. At least one prominent member of the Roosevelt administration was dismayed "that a large group of American businessmen had so far departed from normal American thinking as to prefer military control of all activities of civilian life [to] the normal processes of American Government."[20] But Hawaii was not a normal part of the American polity, and the Roosevelt administration was apparently in no hurry to restore full constitutional rights to its people.

This reluctance rested on obvious security considerations, but it was compounded by pressure from business interests in the islands. The "hegemony," Burns later claimed, strongly supported the military because it imposed "labor controls that made a man almost a slave." Certainly wages were more tightly controlled than prices, and wage and salary earners made a disproportionately heavy sacrifice to the war effort. The international secretary of the ILWU (International Longshoremen's and Warehousemen's Union), Matthew Meehan, on a visit to the islands early in 1944, likened the extent of controls imposed by the military on workers in Hawaii to that of a concentration camp. While such claims were undoubtedly exaggerated, union organizers argued throughout the war that their activities were subject to constant interference from military authorities. Within a year of Pearl Harbor, union membership had fallen by more than 50 percent, to approximately four thousand members. Understandably, most employers welcomed this trend. Against this background, the efforts of moderates like Farrington and Anthony to curtail military government met strong local resistance from the *Honolulu Advertiser*, powerful business interests, and military officers. Until late in the war the opinions expressed by these vested interest groups prevailed in Washington.[21]

Throughout the war military officials enlisted the support of prominent local conservatives, and appointed them to significant and often lucrative posts in the wartime government. For example, Lorrin P. Thurston, the part owner and manager of the *Honolulu Advertiser*, became the new government's public relations adviser; Walter Dillingham, who amassed a fortune largely from dredging and construction work under government contracts (and maintained a lobbyist in Washington to protect his interests) was made director of food production. Despite the wartime emergency, local businessmen prospered as Hawaii became an important focus of rushed defense expenditure. Not surprisingly, more than a year after Pearl Harbor, the Honolulu Chamber of Commerce again informed Roosevelt that civilian government should not be restored. Many of those who now found military rule so satisfactory were, after the war, to express strong opposition to democratic government under statehood.[22] Short of direct military control through Washington, some continued to favor territorial government, which also stemmed essentially from appointments determined in Washington.

Military rule flatly contradicted America's constitutional principles and could not be sustained indefinitely, despite the support it received from many influential islanders. Gradually martial law was modified and an uneasy system of dual civil and military authority established. Habeas corpus, however, remained suspended and civil authority was subservient to military dictates until military government ended on October 24, 1944.

The formal legal challenge mounted by Anthony, Farrington, and others against military rule was not finally considered by the Supreme Court until December 1945, conveniently after the end of hostilities with Japan. The federal government defended its right to impose martial law on the grounds that full constitutional rights, including provisions of the nation's Bill of Rights, did not extend to outlying territories of the United States, except by specific act of Congress. Territorial citizens protested that military government circumvented Section 5 of the Organic Act, which stated specifically that the Constitution should apply equally in Hawaii as in the rest of the United States. The Supreme Court, in a decision handed down by Justice Hugo Black, ruled in February 1946 that military government was unconstitutional.[23] This vindicated the civil opponents of wartime rule, but it was small compensation for the difficulties experienced by American citizens in Hawaii during the war. Nor was it any real guarantee that Hawaii's rights would not again be abrogated.

The experience of military government prompted many in Hawaii to view statehood as the only vehicle capable of averting a possible recurrence of arbitrary action by the federal government. The desire for equality under statehood was now widely shared by substantial majorities from all ethnic groups. Hawaii's vigorous new attorney general, Tavares, stated during the Supreme Court hearings: "Regardless of the outcome of the Supreme Court case, my sentiments are that Hawaii will never be free from danger and possible contentions like this being made in any case in which civil rights are involved, until and unless it becomes a State." Territorial citizens, especially those who felt additionally vulnerable becaue of their ethnic background, appealed increasingly for full citizenship rights. Many were now convinced that the

liberties ostensibly guaranteed under the national Constitution far out-
weighed any economic disadvantages which would accrue by virtue of
being a territory. In the light of these factors, Tavares argued for the
speedy and vigorous renewal of the struggle for statehood.[24] Some
mainlanders were also convinced that statehood was essential if the
injustices of martial law were to be avoided in the future. George H.
Lehleitner, a very wealthy Louisiana businessman who became Hawaii's most energetic Southern supporter, had witnessed martial law
firsthand as an officer in the U.S. Navy. Disturbed particularly by the
arbitrary and unequal way it was employed against the island's nonwhite community, Lehleitner argued that statehood was essential to
insure that democratic government could never again be denied these
Americans. Burns later credited Lehleitner with spending more time,
energy, and money on the statehood drive than any individual in either
Hawaii or the mainland, although Republican stalwarts understandably accorded Farrington this distinction.[25]

The relaxation of military government over the territory during
1943–1944 and the increasingly secure American position in the Pacific
war encouraged Hawaii to renew its statehood initiatives. In May 1945
the local senate passed a resolution asking Congress to grant immediate
statehood. In the following month, Hawaii's energetic Republican delegate in Washington, Farrington, introduced an enabling bill and
pressed for immediate congressional investigation of Hawaii's qualifications for admission. "The war is not over in the Pacific, but victory is
assured," wrote the *Honolulu Star-Bulletin* in July 1945. "We are now
justified in turning again to active steps for statehood."[26]

By early 1946 national and local support for statehood was unprecedented. In December 1945, Secretary of the Interior Harold S. Ickes
publicly endorsed immediate statehood. Farrington welcomed this as a
milestone, the most important step toward statehood since the 1940
plebiscite. In January 1946 President Truman declared in favor of statehood, the first president to endorse Hawaii's objectives. In this year also
mainland opinion polls indicated that a majority (60 percent) favored
statehood for Hawaii. Only 19 percent opposed it.[27] In January a subcommittee of the House Committee on Interior and Insular Affairs
responded to Farrington's demands in Congress and conducted extensive hearings in Hawaii. The six-member subcommittee under Chairman Henry D. Larcade (Dem., La.) conducted hearings for twelve days
on the five major islands. It accepted testimony from 107 witnesses, 91
of whom favored statehood.[28]

Anxious to demonstrate that Hawaii's people had assimilated into
American society, statehood proponents now frequently used the words
"loyal" and "Americanized" interchangeably. The postwar campaign
for admission relied heavily on the unique achievements of young nisei
soldiers in Europe as evidence that Hawaii had "made its Americanism

work" and "met the test of two world wars with unquestionable loyalty to the flag she served."[29] But the process of Americanization and assimilation was much slower, and less uniform, than statehood proponents were prepared to concede after the Second World War. Certainly the acculturation of an ethnic group comprising almost 40 percent of Hawaii's people could not reasonably be inferred from the heroism displayed in battle by a youthful fragment of this group. The absence of any concrete definition of what constituted an Americanized community, however, permitted proponents to highlight the war record of Hawaii's Japanese in all future debates. The general loyalty and military achievements of Japanese citizens and residents were eagerly grasped by proponents who, until Pearl Harbor, had found it difficult to confront with firm evidence the suspicions and innuendos reserved for Hawaii's Japanese by racially insecure groups both in Hawaii and on the mainland.

The achievements of Hawaii's soldiers in Korea a few years later confirmed their loyalty and Americanism, even in its most explicit anticommunist form. By contrast with 1942–1945, troops from Hawaii were not consigned to separate units in Korea. Nonetheless like America's blacks in World War II, Korea, and Vietnam, and Puerto Ricans in Vietnam, Hawaii's mixed peoples discovered in Korea that nonwhites were not only unequal politically, but were also called upon to make disproportionately heavy sacrifices in war. A total of 426 men from Hawaii were killed in action in Korea, a toll almost five times the national average. The battle casualties of Hawaii's troops totalled more than 1,300—a per-capita rate three times greater than that for the rest of the United States. The Statehood Commission asserted that these sacrifices, and the general commitment of the island community to the war in Asia, negated any arguments which assailed the loyalty of Hawaiians. Such sacrifices also strengthened the conviction that if Hawaii's people were eligible to die for their nation, then surely they should be entitled to participate fully in national politics.[30]

Wars in the Pacific and Asia also underlined Hawaii's crucial strategic significance to the United States. The ideas of Mahan and other expansionists of the late nineteenth century had, it seemed to military authorities at least, been vindicated by events in the 1940s and early 1950s. The cold war tensions which grew out of the uneasy settlements of World War II and Korea further confirmed Hawaii's strategic significance. Its value as America's principal Pacific base was obvious to all those in Washington who viewed Asia's instability and emerging peasant communism as simply an extension of the cold war. After 1945 Farrington attempted to exploit the argument that America should dominate every facet of the postwar Pacific and thus avoid difficulties similar to those which had erupted with the Soviet Union in Europe. He argued that the question of statehood for Hawaii was now an urgent national concern.

> The present is a transitional period. The pattern of American peacetime pol-
> icy is just beginning to take shape. By deciding the Hawaii issue, Congress
> will take an important step in deciding the character and extent of the United
> States policy and influence in the Pacific. . . . American hegemony in the
> Pacific would be confirmed . . . It would serve notice on the world anew
> that the Central and West Pacific constitute a defense zone to the U.S.[31]

There were now many influential Americans who accepted this view. Shortly after Japan's defeat, General Douglas MacArthur, Admiral Chester W. Nimitz, and the secretaries of War and the Navy endorsed statehood because it would integrate Hawaii more effectively and irrevocably into national defense planning. It would also help "extend American democracy" to East Asia, they argued. The Defense Department was no longer perturbed by the peculiar ethnic character of its vital island base. Moreover, Washington now found it embarrassing to have America's stated support for decolonization and democracy abroad compromised so blatantly by Hawaii's semi-colonial status. After the United Nations classified Hawaii as a "non-self-governing" area, this gap between principle and practice was inescapable. Statehood proponents relied heavily on this anomaly in future years. The "United States is striving even at the risk of war to establish the right of self-determination and self-government among the people of the earth," the official statehood campaign later pointed out. "Yet it is denying to a Commonwealth within its own borders the right of self-government in the full measure to which it is entitled. Statehood would undo this paradox."[32]

Other Allied governments encountered similar paradoxes in relation to their colonies in Asia and the Pacific. The war against Japan broke the back of European colonialism, and heralded the gradual retreat of white authority over dependent peoples generally. The demands for decolonization quickly became a chorus after 1945 and, reluctantly, the European powers were obliged to accede to the wishes of their subjects. But America's relations with its "non-self-governing" Pacific territory did not fit this broad pattern. As we have seen, the war heightened the determination of Hawaii's mixed population to demonstrate its loyalty to the metropolitan power. At the same time, war against Japan confirmed the crucial strategic value of the islands to the United States. "If it had not been for the Second World War . . . Hawaii might never have become so deeply integrated with the economic and political mainstream of the country and might never have become a state," Robert Shaplen observed in 1982. "It might have evolved instead from something like a trust territory into an independent or quasi-independent entity, and might by now be looking more eastward than westward and playing a leading role among the Pacific islands, since so many of its people have more in common with these islanders than with the inhabitants of mainland America."[33]

But the war was only one aspect of a process of Americanization which had transformed the allegiances and aspirations of Hawaii's people over more than a century. As the next chapter of this book demonstrates, the diverse population of postwar Hawaii shared very little with any other Polynesian or Asian society. It had become, in ideological terms at least, overwhelmingly and uncritically American. Rather than stimulate demands for a break with Washington, for decolonization, the war strengthened the conviction that Hawaii's future lay within the American system, not outside it. The nationalism of the islands' inhabitants had become a variant of that of the mainland. By contrast, the nationalist movements which surfaced throughout Asia and the Pacific after the war generally rejected the authority and values of metropolitan powers and sought, instead, unqualified national independence.

The United States emphasized in the immediate postwar months that it sought to gain no territory from victory, but wanted to liquidate its existing territories and possessions by granting them self-determination. President Truman asked Congress to consider the possibility of permitting Puerto Rico to conduct a plebiscite to determine its future relationship with the United States, and reaffirmed that the Philippines would be granted independence in 1946.[34] Given Washington's stated policy of granting increased self-government or independence to its territorial possessions, Hawaii's unequal territorial status could not be defended with any degree of consistency. This neocolonial position and the attendant qualified political rights of its citizens were pointedly emphasized in the classification given Hawaii by the United Nations.

Other contradictions between America's principles and practices were also highlighted by the war. Like Hawaii's nisei, black Americans made a disproportionately strong contribution, measured in deaths and casualties, to their nation's combat efforts. Loyalty and sacrifice in war did not guarantee either group genuine equality under the Constitution however. Nonetheless, it became increasingly difficult for Washington to justify or rationalize the continued exclusion of nonwhites from equal access to the vote, education, and work—a situation reflected most starkly in the rigidly segregated Southern states. If discrimination against nonwhites within America was incompatible with espoused American values, so too was discrimination against the mixed population of America's territorial appendages. The new Truman administration argued far more energetically for racial equality than had its New Deal predecessor. It made two important concessions to mounting liberal pressure on racial issues: First, it acknowledged that civil rights and equality at home could not be isolated from the question of equality under the Constitution for residents of incorporated territories. Second, because many territorial citizens were non-Caucasians, it agreed that the issues of statehood and equality for nonwhite Americans were inextricably linked. Thus, after the war Truman lumped these issues together in his tentative legislative program on civil rights. If the Truman administration was to argue before the United Nations that all peoples were entitled to self-determination, and if it was to attack communist states for not guaranteeing the political liberties of their subjects, then clearly it had to remove the gap between theory and practice in its own domain.

By linking Hawaii to other civil rights matters, Truman unwittingly tied it to an issue that was to split Congress for more than two decades. Yet even if the president had excluded statehood from his civil rights program, Southern opponents of racial equality would still have recognized and exploited the links between the two issues. It was widely accepted that the patterns of racial and ethnic relations in the islands were unique and without parallel in any mainland state (certainly not in the segregated South). Unfortunately for statehood enthusiasts, this fact did little to extricate Hawaii from deep-rooted struggles over civil rights.[35]

Although the war in the Pacific did not initiate the campaign for Hawaii's admission, it did give a strong new impetus to such demands. More than any other event, war highlighted and publicized the experiences of Hawaii's mixed population and brought its people for the first time under close national scrutiny. The territory's new national prominence helped to confound and diffuse arguments against statehood which derived from racist premises. At the same time, Hawaii's unfortunate experience of military rule gave unprecedented urgency and strength to demands for constitutional rights equal to those enjoyed by citizens in all states. (With the memory of relocation still painfully fresh, some Japanese Americans on the West Coast undoubtedly found such appeals extremely ironic.) Hawaii emerged from World War II more confident of its Americanization, more prominent in national politics, more convinced of the need for immediate statehood, and more united in the conviction that admission was not only appropriate but imminent. Moreover, war brought new investment, new industries, and new people to the islands from the mainland. Rapid economic, demographic, and social changes in turn helped validate Hawaii's claims that it was now qualified for, and entitled to, immediate admission. But the winds of change which swept across the islands after 1945 also brought unexpected difficulties for the proponents of immediate statehood.

Chapter 4

Postwar Hawaii: An Americanized Community?

It was widely accepted in the decade after the war that Hawaii's people were "thoroughly imbued with American traditions and ideals" and "sympathetic to the principles of democracy as exemplified in the American form of government."[1] Traditionally, these indices of acculturation and ideological uniformity were central guides to the suitability of a territory for statehood. Certainly Hawaii had demonstrated its loyalty to the United States during the war in the Pacific. It had also been integrated into American defense planning, trade, and tourism from the late 1930s, and had sustained representative democratic government throughout its sixty years as a territory. Shortly after the war an investigating committee dispatched from Washington concluded: "the school system of Hawaii has been successful in instilling into the people of many races and backgrounds the objectives and ideals of democracy, and has produced a literate population capable of discharging the duties of citizenship." Island society was consistently described as "loyal," "patriotic," "Americanized," "harmonious," and "democratic." When Lind ended his study of *Hawaii's People* early in the 1960s with the question, "What Are They Becoming?" and answered, "One People Out of Many," he was expressing the popular view of Hawaii as a racial utopia.[2] Certainly most of its peoples accepted American democracy, free enterprise capitalism, and the English language as legitimate and appropriate. Hawaii, it seemed to many observers, was the American melting pot in microcosm—a crucible of immigrant assimilation. Like continental America two and three generations earlier, the Pacific territory was an example of rapid and thorough acculturation of diverse waves of immigrants. There were, however, important distinctions: in Hawaii's case these newcomers were largely Asian, not European; and they moved into a community which had escaped slavery and its unfortunate Southern legacy, segregation. Hawaii's society had no direct parallel on the mainland. In the light of its unique social patterns Lind concluded, "[it] is reasonable to assume that assimilation or the spiritual fusion of Hawaii's people moves more rapidly than [social] or biological amalgamation, but both processes are moving irresistibly forward."[3]

Advocates of statehood had previously expressed similar views, but in more emotive terms. The Statehood Commission, for example, enthusiastically adopted Roosevelt's assertion that "Americanism is a matter of mind and heart; Americanism is not and never was a matter of race and ancestry." Indeed it went so far as to assert that, in terms of its political, educational, and community makeup, Hawaii had become thoroughly imbued with Americanism as early as the 1890s. "Since annexation," it concluded, "Hawaii has made its Americanism work with a high degree of success."[4] If Americanism is defined simply as the internalization of America's political values and nationalism, this claim was not without foundation. Indeed, after World War II most of Hawaii's citizens accepted political democracy under statehood as a legitimate and necessary aspiration. However, in relation to more concrete socioeconomic indices of assimilation, such as employment, housing, property, education, and intermarriage, these claims were less valid. Hawaii's people might have been largely assimilated ideologically and behaviorally (i.e., acculturized) by the 1950s, but not all groups had yet experienced genuine structural assimilation.

Acculturation: Patterns and Processes

It is important, as Talcott Parsons, Milton M. Gordon, Michael Parenti, and others have noted, to distinguish between cultural or ideological assimilation on the one hand, and socioeconomic, institutional, or structural assimilation on the other. Acculturation, which embraces the notion of Americanization, is not synonymous with structural assimilation. Although writing on immigrant experiences in continental America, Gordon's definitions of these terms provide a useful vehicle for analyzing the nature and extent of ethnic assimilation in Hawaii at the time of statehood. Gordon has defined assimilation as "a blanket term which really covers a multitude of subprocesses." He correctly separates ideological factors from social ones, and asserts that:

> The most crucial distinction is one often ignored—the distinction between what I have elsewhere called "behavioral assimilation" and "structural assimilation." The first refers to the absorption of the cultural behavioral patterns of the host society. . . . There is a special term for this process of cultural modification or "behavioral assimilation"—namely "acculturation." "Structural assimilation" on the other hand, refers to the entrance of the immigrants and their descendants into the social cliques, organizations, institutional activities, and general civic life of the receiving society. If this process takes place on a large enough scale, then a high frequency of intermarriage must result.

Like most social scientists, Gordon also made a further distinction between "secondary relationships," involving public, civic, commercial, and political activities in the wider community, and "primary relationships," which embrace friendship patterns, home life, and communal activities. Relationships developed in the secondary area are generally impersonal and segmented. In contrast, primary associations tend to be intimate, warm, and personal.[5] Unfortunately there is not sufficient empirical data to examine thoroughly the types and extent of primary and secondary relationships experienced by Hawaii's various ethnic groups after World War II. However, by using the distinction advanced by Gordon to order the available (if incomplete) evidence, it is possible to reach a reasonably systematic understanding of the nature and patterns of the islands' community on the eve of statehood. In particular, this method permits an assessment of the processes of acculturation and structural assimilation in relation to the assertion, repeated monotonously by statehood proponents, that the island community was thoroughly and uniformly Americanized.

After the war the various congressional reports issued on Hawaii's qualifications for statehood used the terms "Americanized" and "assimilated" in an informal, interchangeable way. Although clearly referring to cultural and ideological factors, these committees attempted to substantiate their confident assertions that Hawaii was thoroughly Americanized by citing what they conceived of as hard evidence. This included the alleged absence of bloc voting, availability of educational and employment opportunities for all groups, the growth of organized labor, and participation by different ethnic groups in the political, commercial, and social life of the islands. This evidence was very selective, and notable primarily for its frequent repetition rather than its breadth or accuracy. It was designed to foster the view that Hawaii, despite its unique immigrant heritage, ethnic patterns, and class cleavages, was fundamentally American in both ideological and socioeconomic terms. After Pearl Harbor, all reports endorsed by majorities of the numerous House and Senate investigating teams accepted these assertions and evidence uncritically. These findings ignored the critical distinction between acculturation and structural assimilation noted above. They also ignored the strong relationship between access to wealth and power on the one hand, and ethnicity and social class on the other—a relationship which remained the fundamental characteristic of Hawaii's community. This is not to deny that some members of all ethnic groups experienced real socioeconomic mobility, or that most residents were incorporated firmly into an "Americanized" value system, by the 1940s. But the distributions of wealth, property, and power remained far from equal, varying dramatically according to settlement patterns and the ethnic backgrounds of each group.

Many of the general findings advanced by sociologists on the experiences of immigrants to continental America and the nature of mainland society after the war might reasonably be applied to Hawaii also, although obviously the social structure of Hawaii was fundamentally dif-

ferent and perhaps more complex than that of mainland America.
Nonetheless, Gordon's conclusion that "while *behavioral assimilation* or
acculturation has taken place in America to a considerable degree,
structural assimilation, with some important exceptions has not been
extensive" describes Hawaii's society on the eve of statehood fairly accurately. Similarly Parenti's finding that acculturation of ethnic groups
throughout America "was most often not followed by social assimilation," is relevant to Hawaii. In America generally, Parenti observed,
though ethnic groups normally became Americanized in their cultural
practices, full social integration did not necessarily follow. "In the face
of widespread acculturation," he concluded, "the minority still maintained a social substructure encompassing primary and secondary group
relations composed essentially of fellow ethnics."[6]

Obviously such generalizations must be qualified when applied to
Hawaii. No one ethnic group comprised a simple majority of the total
island population. Japanese, not whites, were the largest single group.
Curiously, in Hawaii the host, Anglo-American, society never comprised more than one-third of the population from 1900 to the 1950s.
Despite this, the broad patterns of immigrant-group acculturation developed similarly in both the mainland and the islands, although the
rate of acculturation was perhaps more rapid in continental America.
By the late nineteenth century white Anglo-Americans had replaced
native Hawaiians as the host society in the islands. Despite, or perhaps
because of, the numerical strength of other ethnic groups, whites exerted a firm control over virtually every facet of political, economic, educational, and cultural life. Moreover, the very variety of immigrant
groups militated against any one strong countervailing center of influence developing within Hawaii, although eventually the large Japanese
group became a substantial political force and the Chinese experienced
rapid success in business and commerce. Hawaii remained both ethnically and socially pluralistic, but all groups, including most native Hawaiians, were gradually but persistently acculturated to American values and behavioral norms. Neither mainland America nor Hawaii were
genuine melting pots, although each developed its own pervasive myths
in this regard, and each made formal and informal demands on its
immigrant minorities to Americanize and conform to Anglo-American
social and political norms. If Hawaii became "thoroughly Americanized," as various congressional committees asserted, this ironically was
because it had not eliminated ethnicity as a fundamental determinant
of its cultural and community patterns. This paradox was not uniquely
Hawaiian, but was characteristic of American ethnic relations as a
whole.

The pioneering sociological work of Gunnar Myrdal, Robert K. Merton, and others has emphasized that egalitarianism was a fundamental

American ideal. These authors identified a strong theoretical commit-ment to the notions of freedom and equality as defining characteristics of Americanization. Yet such ideals were flatly contradicted by the racial inequalities and prejudices which afflicted American society. In Myrdal's words, this was the *American Dilemma*.[7] By the 1950s most of Hawaii's people shared these national ideals, but in the islands as in the mainland nationalist ideals and social reality did not always coincide. Given the ethnic diversities and socioeconomic inequalities which exist-ed in continental territories when they were granted statehood (espe-cially in areas with slavery or substantial Indian populations), it would be inconsistent to expect Hawaii to have been an essentially egalitarian and homogeneous society before it was qualified for admission. It is arguable that no state had ever met this requirement. Yet as Hawaii's statehood campaign explicitly acknowledged, the islands were a unique case. Not only were they geographically separate from continental America, they were also largely peopled by non-Caucasians, the descen-dents of immigrant laborers from Asia. The only areas previously ac-cepted with substantial nonwhite populations were slave states, and the complex question of statehood for these territories had shaken the Union to its very foundations. Assumptions about race, assimilation, and Anglo-American superiority had changed dramatically in the interven-ing century. Nonetheless, as Richard Meister observed as late as 1974, "The real issue behind much of the turmoil associated with race and ethnic separatism is that most Americans continue to accept without question the ideal of a society based on a 'pleasing uniformity.' "[8] In Hawaii this essential homogeneity was most obviously contradicted by its unique ethnic diversity.

Advocates of statehood for Hawaii accepted that an implicit but per-vasive belief in the need for all groups to assimilate Anglo-American ideals and practices, combined often with explicit racism against all nonwhites, remained the principal obstacle to admission even after World War II. This was a delicate issue which proponents usually con-fronted obliquely with statistics on the rates of intermarriage across racial groups, educational levels and opportunities for various ethnic groups, socioeconomic mobility, trade union and community participa-tion, and the alleged absence of bloc voting along ethnic lines. State-hood proponents argued that Hawaii's society was tolerant, open, and assimilated.[9] They were not, however, disinterested observers. The evi-dence they cited was partial (in both senses of the word): it ignored as much as it revealed. At most it indicated a likely, long-term trend, not a current reality. As evidence that Hawaii's diverse people shared the con-sensus values of mainland Americans, it was reasonably convincing; as evidence of structural assimilation or broad uniformity in social or eco-nomic terms, it left doubt.

Although incomplete and far from uniform, acculturation or "Americanization" of all ethnic groups in Hawaii was substantial by the late 1940s. The experience of war against Japan had both confirmed and accentuated this process. But as a number of historians and social theorists have conceded, it is difficult to identify confidently the means by which minorities incorporate the values of the host society. It is equally difficult to specify the rate and nature of ideological, cultural, or behavioral change in any given society, even in Hawaii with its relatively compressed history of ethnic interaction. America's historians have long grappled with these problems when discussing the experience of immigrants and their descendents in mainland society, which they describe variously as assimilated, integrated, segmented, pluralistic, or stratified.[10] Such problems inevitably confront any student of Hawaiian society also. Yet there can be little doubt that Hawaii became increasingly cohesive and uniform in terms of ideology and values from the 1890s. This transformation coincided with the period of adjustment to the norms of the host society by first and second generations of immigrants. Yet it did not affect all ethnic, regional, or class segments of the island community equally or uniformly. Many residents, especially first-generation immigrants, plantation workers, and native Hawaiians resisted American cultural, social, and linguistic norms, or at least attempted to deflect or modify them. Also, some were effectively excluded from educational, vocational, social, and voting activities open to whites. But other members of all groups, even the once-proud Hawaiians, accommodated fairly quickly (if unenthusiastically) to American values, ideals, and secondary behavioral patterns. The principal vehicles of this change were imported and sustained by white settlers and their descendents. Initially these included Christianity, formal compulsory education in American-style schools, contract labor on plantations owned and managed largely by Americans, use of English as the principal language in public interaction, and the development of commerce and trade with imported American capital and expertise. White European-American dominance in Hawaii shaped the arrangements and values (especially language, religion, law, vocational and housing options) in the formative period around the turn of the century. The impact of this dominance was cumulative. It resulted in a web of interlocking pressures which were both institutional (e.g., education) and informal (e.g., political values). As Hawaii was drawn gradually into the broad historical currents which influenced America generally, the patterns and forms of white influence became less explicit but no less pervasive.

No single criterion is adequate as an index of the decline in ethnic group consciousness or ethnocentrism within a migrant community. Nonetheless, as Lind and a number of other sociologists have suggested, marriage is the best gauge, in the American context at least, of interethnic intimacy. There appears to be a strong positive correlation between the frequency of socially sanctioned marriages between different ethnic groups and the extent of their cultural fusion.[11] From 1912 to 1945 the proportion of interracial marriages in Hawaii is estimated to have increased from about 12 percent to almost 40 percent of all marriages. Within each separate ethnic group, however, the ratio of such marriages did not necessarily increase over time. For the Japanese, at least, the proportion of out-marriages was apparently highest during the years when the influence of single-sex male immigration was most pronounced, and declined slightly as the ratio of the sexes within this group became more equal. Despite such temporary reversals, however, there was a general tendency toward intermarriage.[12] This was relatively common for members of the smaller ethnic groups, notably Hawaiians, part-Hawaiians, Filipinos, Portuguese, Puerto Ricans, and Koreans. Figures compiled by Adams, and later Lind, suggest that the proportion of children of exclusively single-race ancestry also declined—from about 75 percent in 1931 to about 60 percent in the early 1960s. Yet out-marriage was less common for Caucasians and Japanese than for other ethnic groups. These two groups, especially the Japanese, provided a disproportionately small number of children of mixed ancestry. At the time of statehood only 12 percent of children of Japanese ancestry were not exclusively Japanese; only 20 percent of children with Caucasian ancestry had one parent from another ethnic group. In contrast, 76 percent of all children with mixed parentage had one parent of Hawaiian or part-Hawaiian ancestry.[13] To infer from these developments, as Lind and statehood proponents did, that Hawaii had taken a substantial step toward the physical amalgamation of its diverse peoples, is perhaps unwarranted.[14] By the late 1950s the smaller ethnic groups were amalgamating to a considerable degree as a result of intermarriage, but haoles and Japanese remained far more separate and homogeneous community groups.

Some observers of postwar Hawaii maintained that, because of these changing marriage patterns, it was futile, even deceptive, to compile statistics of Hawaii's population by race. As early as 1940 the official census reduced racial types in Hawaii from twelve to eight categories because of the large percentage of marriages "between the two types of part-Hawaiians, and between the Portuguese, Spanish and other Caucasians."[15] Other indices support the view that enthocentrism and racial consciousness had substantially declined by 1946. After 1931 when the first member of Japanese ancestry was elected to the legislature, all major ethnic groups except Filipinos were consistently represented in either the territorial house or senate. Members of Japanese ancestry, however, never comprised more than one-fifth of either chamber.[16] In sharp contrast to many mainland states, no laws promoted racial segregation or formal discrimination. The *Christian Science Monitor* undoubtedly underestimated Hawaii's achievements when it observed: "There is less racial friction and discrimination in Hawaii than in many mainland areas."[17] Lind wrote in 1946 that: "Examination of Hawaii's record of population and vital statistics during the past 25 years reveals a steady trend toward a citizen population of numerous racial antecedents, but unified through their common experience within an American community."[18] Five years later another student of Hawaii's society, Ch'en-K'un Cheng, concluded that all ethnic groups shared "to a very large extent the attitudes, habits and ideas of their fellow Americans in the territory as well as in the continental United States."[19] Not surprisingly such findings were usually repeated before committees investigating Hawaii's bid for statehood.

Writing of the United States as a segmented society, Robert H. Wiebe has argued that the endurance of a unique pattern of relationships between myriad, changing social units had not stifled the growth of a cohesive society in ideological terms. Indeed this unity was essential for social harmony—"a segmented society could not function without it." Wiebe attempts to show how this structurally divided society has avoided fragmentation. "By far the most powerful cement of this new system was consumption," he argues. "Consumption, everybody's stake in society, offered a ready ideological answer to everything from class cleavages to civil rights."[20] It might reasonably be asserted that Wiebe's very general analysis underestimates the significance and permanency of socioeconomic and ethnic divisions in American society. Still, there can be little doubt that a central unity in ideas and values did result from the processes he identifies.

Although geographically remote, Hawaii was nonetheless subject to these processes. Certainly by the 1950s it was an integral part of America's corporate and commercial structures, with a relatively affluent, consumer-oriented local population. Most Chinese, haoles, and Japanese were part of America's "people of plenty" by the 1950s. In 1947, for example, the value of Hawaii's exports to the mainland was $228,353,010. Only three countries exported more to the United States. In the same year Hawaii's 540,000 people purchased $472,241,868 worth of retail goods, most of mainland export. Patterns of advertising and merchandizing increasingly reflected those of West Coast America. Many mainland retailers and businesses established outlets in the islands after the war. Although the Big Five still dominated the islands' economy, business ownership diversified rapidly: thirty-six thousand corporations, firms, and individuals operated in 1945, and the number grew quickly in the next decade. It was usual for Hawaii's executives and businessmen to be educated in mainland universities. During 1900–1960 the proportion of islanders who were Caucasian almost doubled, due largely to increased in-migration from the mainland. At the same time, the proportion of islanders living in Honolulu rose sharply, to about 70 percent. The influx of mainlanders and rapid urbanization consolidated patterns of consumption and economic activity common to modern America.[21] Moreover, improvements in communications, symbolized by the Pacific cable of 1902 and the advent of regular air services after 1936, tied the islands increasingly to the mainland. Radio, and later television, greatly accelerated the impact of American mass culture on the island community and added to the pressures for cultural uniformity and social homogeneity.

The political manifestations of broad acculturation are easier to identify, though no more influential, than the role of mass consumerism and economic change. Despite its peculiar ethnic patterns and island geography, Hawaii was by the late 1950s equally subject to, and fundamentally affected by, the forces which sustained ideological cohesion throughout America generally. For example, political allegiances in the territory closely paralleled those throughout the nation. Public participation in politics, as indicated by voter turnout, was higher in the territory than in virtually any mainland area.[22] Hawaii also shared, and in some respects anticipated, changes in political culture associated with the emergence of anti-communism and McCarthyism throughout America after the war. Whereas the New Deal had affected the islands only marginally, after the war they were not immune to the cold war tensions which fuelled the prolonged and emotive public attacks upon the New Deal and its supporters.

Insofar as acculturation and Americanization were affected by broad processes like the expansion of the middle class, education, the rise of literacy, or mass consumerism, Hawaii was exceptional in an American context largely because such developments came to it relatively late. Although expressed in clichés, the findings of the 1947 investigating team accurately identified the impact of such processes on Hawaii's people. "Distance has never meant a great deal to the American pioneer," it concluded chauvinistically.

> Hardly a century ago California and New York were divided by vast unsettled areas. But it was not many decades before they were welded into one unbroken expanse of national life, with the same customs, the same basic economy, the same standards and ideals.
>
> The pioneer spirit did not stop at the Western seaboard. With a much shorter distance to go than that separating New York and California, it crossed the Pacific and carried the American way of life to Hawaii.[23]

Ernest Gruening, the governor of Alaska and a vigorous champion of statehood for his own territory and Hawaii, studied the impact of "the American way" on the AJAs of Hawaii. He roundly declared: "they are

Americans in every sense of the word just as much as the second or third generations of Americans born of English, Irish, Scotch, Welsh, German, Dutch, French, Italian, Spanish, Slavic, Chinese, or Filipino may be considered Americans." Like President Roosevelt, Gruening defined America as preeminently an idea. He proposed that Hawaii was a unique and stunning incarnation of that idea, "the finest example under the flag of the welding of alien peoples of diverse racial strains into Americans." If few observers could explain how Hawaii had been so quickly Americanized, most were nonetheless convinced that it was. Recalling his visit to Hawaii as a member of the 1937 joint investigating team on statehood, former senator Edward Burke of Nebraska informed Truman: "We mingled with a people whose ideals and institutions are in every respect in accord with the American tradition." Burke supported this assertion by outlining developments in Hawaii's schools, judicial system, mass media, and political leadership. Most members of the investigating committee, he concluded, were convinced as early as 1937 that all of Hawaii's peoples, including the Japanese, were "so imbued with the American ideal that they could be counted upon as loyal citizens in all circumstances." For Burke and others committed to statehood, Hawaii's war record vindicated this early confidence in its Americanization.[24]

Yet there persisted until after the Pacific War a gap between the patterns of culture and living imported from America, and those typical of much of rural nonhaole Hawaii. The latter was generally termed "local culture," but it was more than narrow parochialism. It was a by-product of a number of overlapping factors—difficulties with the English language, immediate social contacts with neighborhood and plantation families, shared economic and work situations, and the relative isolation of plantation or outer-island life. Often manifest in the speaking of pidgin English, the so-called local culture cut across most ethnic divisions, embracing in addition to many Hawaiians and part-Hawaiians, Filipinos, Portuguese, Puerto Ricans, and some rural Japanese. Although seldom explicit it valued informality, egalitarianism, something called aloha spirit, and preservation of traditional norms and arrangements against the inroads of commercialism and Western development. Until perhaps the 1950s local culture symbolized a shared rural past in Hawaii and general exclusion from the institutions and groups which shaped the economic and political life of the islands. Well into the twentieth century, as a number of authors have argued, "intense intercultural contact within the plantation communities provided a more immediate intercultural challenge than the vague pressures for assimilation to a larger American society which existed far away on the mainland."[25] Few of those who journeyed from Washington to investigate statehood were exposed to this essentially rural aspect of Hawaii. In evidence to these investigators, the proponents of statehood, ever anxious to stress the uniformity of Americanization, played down the substantial divisions which local culture symbolized.

The composition and structure of Hawaii's population was changed dramatically by the war. In part it accelerated trends apparent in the prewar years. It hastened participation by Japanese in community affairs, broadened the aspirations of this group, and instilled an unprecedented confidence in at least the younger nisei, convincing them that they could participate fully in the political and commercial life of the territory. Ironically, Hawaii's nonwhite majority, especially the Japanese, became assertive and influential at a time when their relative numerical strength was being eroded. War brought a wave of defense workers from the mainland, and pushed the proportion of whites in the islands to a much higher level than on any previous occasion. The size of the white civilian population more than doubled in only six years. By 1945 over 85 percent of Hawaii's people had been born either in Hawaii or in mainland states. In 1945 Caucasians comprised approximately one-third of the total population, but this figure was inflated by as much as 10 percent as a result of the war. Substantial elements of the Caucasian population were relatively recent arrivals who were stationed on military bases. Because these "new Caucasians" could qualify as territorial citizens after residing permanently in the islands for more than twelve months, they had a significant impact on island politics. These new arrivals were usually unfamiliar with the established haole population of the islands. Some newcomers, especially those from the South, had incorporated the values and practices of the more race-sensitive mainland areas. Most chose to stay aloof from the mixed island society. And unlike many members of the local haole population, the new arrivals were essentially wage and salary earners who were as likely to vote Democratic as Republican.[26]

Statehood proponents eagerly attempted to exploit the increased Caucasian influence, arguing that it was further evidence that the islands were adequately Americanized. At the 1946 congressional hearings, for example, they presented statistics which purported to show that Caucasians now outnumbered people of Japanese ancestry. The fact that these were aberrant figures, based on temporary defense-related employment, was not overlooked by the congressmen. On average, during 1940–1950, Caucasians comprised not more than 25 percent of the total population. In contrast, the proportion of Japanese citizens and residents remained fairly stationary, around 37 percent, while the remainder of the population was made up of Hawaiians and part-Hawaiians (about 15 percent), Filipinos (about 12 percent), Chinese (6 percent), Puerto Ricans (2 percent), and Koreans (less than 2 percent). Unable to argue convincingly that Caucasians comprised a majority in the islands, or indeed that they were the largest single ethnic group, statehood proponents were obliged to argue that Hawaii's diverse peoples were equally imbued with and sympathetic toward the principles of American democracy as exemplified in the nation's Constitution. Some of the more cynical proponents were doubtless tempted to point out to visiting congressmen that many existing mainland states, most notably in the segregated South, were often oblivious to such principles. Usually however, proponents were content to argue patiently that Hawaii was a progressive social laboratory, united fundamentally by common values, racial toleration, and social assimilation. Despite its more complex social and ethnic composition, Hawaii certainly outstripped most mainland regions in these terms. Nonetheless, the claims made about Hawaii's achievements were sometimes exaggerated, and the evidence marshalled to support them was often highly selective. Yet the thrust of arguments advanced by proponents was sound. The acculturation of Hawaii's numerous ethnic groups was persistent and irreversible. Group consciousness had waned, occupational and residential stratification was declining, economic mobility and educational opportunity had improved, and intermarriage across racial lines was fairly common.[27]

Despite the diverse backgrounds and sequential immigration of Hawaii's major ethnic groups, by the late 1940s all had effected a considerable degree of social integration and adjustment to American culture and ideology. Widely available education was partly responsible for the patterns of persistent acculturation. The territory inherited from the kingdom a unique system of government-supported public education. Schooling was compulsory and the attendance law was implemented with reasonable success; after 1900 an estimated 80 percent of all children were exposed to perhaps eight years of formal schooling. The standards and availability of public schooling were very high, comparable with those in mainland states. In 1907 this broadly based school system was complemented by the establishment of the University of Hawaii. The Statehood Commission exaggerated only slightly when, in 1948, it characterized this campus as a unique environment, where growing generations of Hawaiian-born Americans from both Eastern and Western cultures mingled freely and in harmony under the American flag. Measured in terms of general literacy and standards of instruction, the 1947 House investigating committee concluded, Hawaii's educational achievements exceeded those in many states. Predictably, however, the children of the most recent immigrant groups, notably the Filipinos, were least likely to attend school. Outer-island institutions, which the children of plantation workers were most likely to attend, were generally inferior to those on the more populous and urban Oahu. Haole children were more likely to attend private schools and mainland universities than their Oriental counterparts. The public school system, however, exposed a substantial proportion of children from all ethnic groups to educational programs of a uniformly high standard. Moreover, these programs incorporated very self-conscious attempts to instill American ideas and values in the young. The 1947 congressional team lauded Hawaii for its outstanding efforts in its successful campaign to institute Americanization in its schools.[28]

Although there persisted until long after World War II considerable variation in the amount of schooling the various groups received, education transformed the values and aspirations of all sectors of island society. From the late 1920s, as the proportion of teachers trained in mainland institutions rose sharply, schools and curricula were increasingly free of elite haole influence. Many teachers from the mainland were young. "They came with this fresh, unbiased, idealistic concept untouched by the local hegemony," Oshiro recalled. "They had a tremendous impact, I think, on all of us." Working with the influential principal of McKinley High School, Dr. Miles Carey, a champion of open and progressive education, many teachers in the territory's public schools felt free to underscore inconsistencies between American ideals as they were professed and practiced in the islands. These specific influences, along with the general impact of the idealism of the New Deal in the 1930s, helped to undermine the authority of the old order and further eroded the strength of ethnic customs and the use of languages other than English. The experiences of Mitsuyuki Kido, one of the first teachers of Japanese descent, typify such changes. "I identified myself as a Democrat—I was enamored of FDR and his idealism," Kido recalled, and as a teacher, "I tried to point out to my students some of the inequalities in Hawaiian society—the political, economic and social structure was so controlled by a small group that I felt that the American dream of a free, democratic society was the thing we should try to achieve in Hawaii." Like Fuchs and other commentators, Kido agreed that for the old order at least, education was a Trojan horse. He observed that although the business elite recognized the perils of his type of teaching, they could hardly interfere, given the value they themselves placed on education. Much of this education stressed the fundamental significance of democracy, economic and social as well as political.[29]

Education could not be controlled, even if its fruits were at times unpalatable to some. Before the war some haoles had lamented the costs and consequences of public education, viewing it at worst as a menace and at best an unnecessary extravagance. Even after the war some in Hawaii remained anxious to limit the social and political consequences of broad public education, especially as pressure for the redistribution of power and wealth surfaced. But for many Caucasians, parents and teachers, events up to 1945 had confirmed the value of education as a homogenizing agent and a vehicle for monitoring and moulding social change. "In a degree astonishing to those who note it for the first time," a private committee on Postwar Needs of Hawaiian Education reported with evident relief, "there has been a welding of this social miscellany [the perceived extremity of Hawaii's ethnic complexity] with all its abrupt differences, into a democratic community." Anticipating the concern of those who sought to stifle or direct the forces of change unleashed by the war and the arrival of New Dealism in the islands, this group asked: "How shall we go about controlling social change?" Its answer perhaps overestimated the power of schooling, but it nonetheless reflected a clear perception of the relationship which existed between formal learning and social change. Its reply was unequivocal. "In a democratic community, by definition, the method of control is always *education*." Certainly the role of education as an agent of acculturation cannot be dismissed, and many doubtless shared this group's view that in postwar Hawaii education was a means to avert social instability as well as to illuminate and assist in the achievement of democratic ideals.[30] Ironically, the seeds sown by educators and teachers in prewar Hawaii later gave rise to the very pressures this predominantly Caucasian group wished to contain.

If acculturation through education was a broad often imperceptible process, it could also be an explicit, self-conscious movement. During World War I and throughout the 1920s, intolerant nativist groups throughout the United States had attempted to impose total, unqualified Americanization on recent arrivals from Europe. Assimilation through education and acceptance of Anglo-American customs and ideals was the central thrust of this powerful, organized movement. In Hawaii such pressures were less formal or overt, being most pronounced in the years surrounding the war against Japan. Yet from the time of their arrival as contract laborers, Hawaii's various Asian minorities, especially the large Japanese group, found that the practice of American customs and ideals was a necessary precondition to social and vocational acceptance by the dominant white society. Americanization, as we have seen, was a central aim of the islands' educational system. Moreover, military rule indicated firmly that in a time of stress Hawaii's Japanese, and to a lesser extent other Asian groups, were acutely vulnerable to white suspicions and insecurities—fears similar to those which had motivated the national Americanization movement a generation earlier. The Japanese had been obliged to demonstrate their loyalty unequivocally during the war. In the postwar years too they anxiously, and at times self-consciously, attempted to demonstrate that they were Americanized beyond question. As Gruening observed in 1947, "the loyalty of the Americans of Japanese descent in Hawaii has not only been normal, it has been conspicuous, exceptional and outstanding."

By the 1950s the chauvinistic concern with Americanization might more appropriately have been directed against smaller groups, especially the Filipinos and Hawaiians. The disadvantaged Filipino group was, as late as the 1940s and 1950s, experiencing patterns of settlement and incorporation common to first- or second-generation immigrant groups. Many Hawaiians and part-Hawaiians were reluctant to accommodate themselves fully to imported public norms and withdrew from or resisted haole dominance. Edwin Burrows noted in 1947, for example, that "recreation reversion" was increasingly common among native Hawaiian groups, and was manifest in the revival of traditional pageantry and folklore. Alienation and demoralization, as expressed in alcoholism and absenteeism from work or school, also remained a feature of some native communities.[31]

The Limits of Structural Assimilation

Supporters of statehood were understandably anxious to place confident generalizations about Hawaii's Americanization before investigators, and they conveniently ignored evidence which might have contradicted these generalizations. Fifteen percent of Hawaii's people were born outside Hawaii or the mainland—one-quarter of all Koreans and more than half of all Filipinos were still within this so-called alien category. Moreover, as late as 1950 30 percent of Hawaii's adult Japanese and almost 20 percent of its adult Chinese did not qualify for territorial citizenship. Only 65 percent of its adult population had qualified for territorial citizenship (this figure was perhaps artificially low, as all Americans who had not resided in the territory for at least a year were excluded from citizenship). When the last official survey of literacy was made in 1930, 15 percent were judged to be illiterate (although almost without exception this group comprised older people brought originally to the islands from Asia before the end of contract labor). Approximately one-quarter of the population surveyed could not speak English.[32] Moreover, pidgin English was still used widely, especially in rural areas. Such information later provided valuable ammunition to those who wished to defeat statehood.

Even some of Hawaii's most ardent statehood supporters acknowledged privately, if not publicly, that the degree of assimilation of various ethnic groups, and of different generations within each group, was not uniform. Quite appropriately, many in Hawaii felt that thorough assimilation was a high price to pay for statehood. However, by focusing exclusively on those trends in interethnic relations which would be viewed favorably by congressional investigators, and by constantly asserting that all groups had assimilated satisfactorily, proponents glossed over the serious strains, divisions, and inequalities which still characterized Hawaii's social, economic, and political structures. The war record of Hawaii's mixed races and the influx of more white citizens could not camouflage these realities nor quickly eradicate the legacy of more than half a century of control by a relatively small group of haoles.

The war did not initiate fundamental social or political changes in the islands. It did, however, dramatically accentuate developments which had their roots in the peculiar labor and immigrant patterns fostered by the powerful white minority late in the nineteenth century. Second- and third-generation descendents of imported Asian laborers were responsible for the changes which surfaced tentatively in the 1930s, and which reached fruition in the decade after World War II. The consequences of these developments had been anticipated, and resisted, by the old order. But while they could be delayed they could not be permanently avoided. The children and grandchildren of Chinese contract laborers were the first Asians to seek the rewards which had previously been reserved largely for haoles and a few part-Hawaiians. However, the Chinese made only a limited impact on existing social and political arrangements, largely because by 1940 they comprised less than 8 percent of Hawaii's population. Initially their achievements were commercial and vocational rather than political. Moreover, as later and numerically stronger laboring groups arrived, many mobile Chinese identified increasingly with haole aspirations and willingly supported the Republican party's attempts to preserve the political and economic status quo.

The large, increasingly visible Japanese American sector of Hawaii was less affluent or mobile than the Chinese, but it was numerically much stronger. The nisei had followed the Chinese in grasping available educational opportunities and moving from agricultural work to urban pursuits and small businesses. It has been estimated that in the decade before Pearl Harbor the Japanese operated more than 40 percent of all retail outlets in the islands. A larger proportion of Japanese than Hawaiians, Filipinos, or Koreans were also occupied in managerial and professional positions. Nevertheless haoles and Chinese still dominated virtually all avenues of commerce and big business. As we have seen, the war heightened Japanese awareness of the social divisions and economic inequalities within Hawaii, but virtually all had long understood the hierarchical nature of the island community. Of all immigrant groups, only the Filipinos had suffered more. The problems confronting Filipinos stemmed largely from economic disadvantages and political neglect. The Japanese experienced unequal opportunities in social, vocational, and cultural fields. Their numbers, cohesion, and aspirations were sufficient to threaten many whites, Chinese, and Hawaiians, especially after they began to exercise the vote in substantial numbers during the 1930s. The reaction against the Japanese exacerbated social tensions, but could not ultimately thwart their legitimate aspirations for equal citizenship rights.[33] Nonetheless, the decades which saw their emergence were characterized by allegations that they threatened the physical security and American values of Hawaii, voted as a bloc along racial lines, and conspired through organized political and trade union activities to translate their numerical superiority into political and economic supremacy.[34]

Such charges betrayed fears of the consequences of genuine political and industrial democracy, which before World War II remained a distant prospect. Not until the late 1940s were the votes of Hawaii's Japanese a decisive factor in island politics. Similarly, in the industrial arena their influence came relatively late. In the same year that Congress passed Roosevelt's Magna Carta for labor, the Wagner Act of 1935, total union membership in Hawaii stood at only five hundred. New Deal legislation encouraged rapid growth after this date. By 1940 ten thousand Hawaiian workers, mostly Japanese, were unionized. Controls imposed by the military government temporarily reversed this trend, halving membership in less than two years. But by 1947 the unions had mushroomed, and now embraced about sixty thousand workers.[35] Despite the postwar growth of trade unions and the disproportionately heavy influence of nisei in most unions, Japanese Americans still exerted only marginal influence on Hawaii's political and economic life. Certainly, their power never mirrored their numerical strength.

After the 1920s and early 1930s second- and third-generation descendents of immigrant laborers moved increasingly from plantations to towns and cities, most notably Hilo and Honolulu. As defense spending increased, tertiary industry grew and employment opportunities widened for most groups with reasonable levels of education. Virtually all Chinese and most Japanese had grasped these new opportunities by the mid-1950s and had migrated to new jobs and new, essentially segmented neighborhoods in Honolulu or larger towns. The process of acculturation accelerated substantially during and after World War II. Urbanization, more varied employment, longer periods of education and job training, and the growth of a large, reasonably affluent middle class all boosted this change. New systems of mass communication and advertising, most notably radio and television, allied to the growth of modern patterns of consumerism which closely mirrored developments on the mainland, made the processes of Americanization and acculturation even more pervasive. Other factors reinforced this inexorable trend. Foremost among these were: the expansion of expendable incomes associated with improved living standards for all groups; more frequent geographic and social mobility, which blurred class and ethnic divisions; and the tourist boom, which had been so confidently anticipated in the decade before statehood.[36]

Occupational opportunities expanded for all groups after 1945, but in the face of declining haole paternalism and rising Japanese influence, many Hawaiians and part-Hawaiians found relatively good jobs more difficult to win. At the same time, income differentials between the various ethnic groups declined substantially. Yet professional and technical jobs were still dominated disproportionately by Caucasians and Chinese, while Filipinos and Puerto Ricans filled very few such positions. Inequalities in employee incomes reflected the persistence of economic and social stratification. At the top were the Caucasians, followed by Chinese, Koreans, and Japanese, who all enjoyed substantial advantages over Hawaiians, Portuguese, Puerto Ricans, and Filipinos. In 1950 the percentages of each major group in professional occupations were estimated to be: Caucasians, 16.9; Chinese, 10.7; Koreans, 8.5; Japanese, 5.5; Hawaiians, 3.3; and Filipinos a mere 1.2. (Data for racially mixed groups is not available, although in general it seems that the family incomes of non-mixed households were higher than those of mixed families.) Residential patterns, revealed most clearly in Honolulu, also indicated as late as 1950 that ethnicity remained a basic factor determining access to housing as well as employment. Although many Chinese and some Koreans and Japanese had moved into predominantly white residential neighborhoods, most descendents of contract laborers lived in middle- or low-status areas.[37] Residential and vocational inequalities were reflected in and confirmed by informal patterns of ethnic and class discrimination. While always more subtle and less pervasive than that confronted by black Americans in most mainland states, informal discrimination and prejudice did exist. The findings of a series of independent studies on conditions in business, employment, the law courts, and housing revealed discrimination against nonhaole groups, and a feeling among haoles that they were inherently entitled to higher positions and better treatment than others. Discrimination against Chinese and Japanese groups, however, was often mitigated by the relatively high economic and social position of the Chinese, or by the support given to Japanese by other members of their numerically strong and now modestly mobile group.[38]

According to Harry V. Ball and Douglas S. Yamamura, economic factors alone rarely affected the patterns of discrimination. To the extent that economic or class factors could be isolated from ethnic ones, they concluded, discrimination appeared to derive essentially from racial considerations. When Robert Oshiro returned to Hawaii in 1954 with a master of law degree from Duke University, he confronted a situation all too common to educated nonwhites—his application for a position with a Big Five firm was rejected with the phrase, "We never hire a local." In the decade after the war many of Hawaii's Japanese still felt themselves the victims of unequal opportunities resulting from discrimination, both conscious and unconscious, by the haole establishment. A series of recent interviews with the men who led attempts by the AJAs to reshape island politics after 1945 are dotted with references to such discrimination. Examples discussed range from differential wages, unwritten rules that AJAs not be hired by the legislature, clear restrictions against Japanese living in some residential areas, exclusion from social and sporting clubs and business organizations, and a general belief that local politics was under the control, for the most part, of the Caucasians. William Richardson, a Burns supporter of mixed Hawaiian, Chinese, and English ancestry, was no less disturbed than his nisei friends by this concentration of power and privilege. The Japanese had numerical superiority, he observed, but that was all. In reaction, AJAs formed their own clubs and organizations. Murai commented in reference to one such association, the Japanese Chamber of Commerce, that it was a necessary measure, to provide an economic defense. Significantly, the Japanese Chamber of Commerce was widely known as the Kenjinkai, a name which implied that its intended function was as a means to help Japanese children better themselves occupationally or socially. Yet if unequal treatment nurtured a desire for change, very few nisei reacted with bitterness or overt hostility. Despite Theon Wright's exaggerated claim that deep resentment had been building and festering among the Japanese, especially the second generation, since the early plantation days and that it erupted dramatically after World War II, most AJAs were content to work patiently through established political channels in a society which they were apparently confident would eventually respond to their needs.[39]

Haoles enjoyed unique privileges and advantages in virtually every aspect of life. This favorable position had emerged in the late nineteenth century and was deeply embedded in the institutional and social structure of the islands. As late as 1950, for example, Stainback reported privately to Washington: "I am the first Governor that ever appointed a single citizen of Japanese ancestry to any position whatsoever in the Territory." (Given the governor's unrelenting hostility to Hawaii's Japanese community, the irony of this claim could scarcely have escaped officials of Truman's administration.) Filipinos and Japanese remained largely excluded from political office, landownership, and high-status jobs until the late 1940s. Some Chinese and Hawaiians who supported the oligarchy expressed concern that even within the Republican party haoles enjoyed special advantages. Race preferences and racial ideas inevitably developed to sustain and protect these unequal privileges. Suspicions voiced against the Japanese can only be understood in this light. Various studies have concluded that ethnocentrism, racial stereotyping, and high levels of social distance between groups persisted in Hawaii throughout the 1950s, and indeed long after statehood.[40] Obviously, expressed racial prejudice was not restricted to whites against Japanese, but this antipathy was the most widespread. In contrast, white-Hawaiian relations were still often broadly paternalistic, although in the decade before statehood an increased proportion of Hawaiians and part-Hawaiians found greater independence and joined labor unions or the Democratic party.

The protection of existing privileges for whites and a few others, mainly Chinese, demanded that patterns of political domination be sustained if possible. Robin M. Williams, Jr., has written that "whenever a number of persons within a society have enjoyed for a considerable period of time certain opportunities for getting wealth, for exercising power and authority, and for successfully claiming prestige and social deference, there is a strong tendency for these people to feel that these benefits are theirs 'by right.' " The conflicts which surfaced in Hawaii between unions (largely Japanese) and business groups (largely white) in the decade after the war symbolized the vigorous defense of what Williams calls "an established system of vested interests" by a long-dominant group against an unprecedented challenge from other groups. In identifying both the industrial and political wings of this threat as Communist led or dominated, the old order in Hawaii grasped hopefully at an issue calculated to rally broader resistance.[41] But the unequal allocation and control of political and economic resources in the islands could no longer be sustained with customary assurance. It began to crack in the face of a rising middle class, greater mobility and assertiveness by all non-Caucasian groups, organized labor, and the growth of a determined young Democratic party. But as late as the 1950s these cracks were still relatively narrow.

Ownership of real property was more concentrated in Hawaii than in any mainland state. This unequal situation was a legacy of haole domination at the time of annexation, and it persisted throughout the six decades of territorial rule. In 1959 eleven families controlled more than half of all private land in Hawaii (or expressed another way, 30 percent of all available land). It was estimated that not more than one hundred families still owned about 90 percent of all privately owned land. Only 2.5 percent of land (two hundred thousand acres) was set aside for ownership by native Hawaiians under the provisions of the Hawaiian Homes Commission Act of 1921, an act designed, in its own words, "not only to put the Hawaiians back onto the land but by doing so to place them in more healthful surroundings, withdrawing them from crowded city tenements, and in this way to rehabilitate the race." The native population also benefitted from the activities of the largest single landholder, the Bishop Estate. Established following a bequest from Princess Bernice Pauahi in 1884, this charitable trust controlled 22 percent of nongovernment land on Oahu and about 16 percent of all such land throughout the islands. The estate was dedicated to providing access to land and education for Hawaiians which, it was anticipated, would enable them to "compete with other nationalities in the struggle for national existence."[42] Despite these important concessions to native Hawaiians, a postwar congressional team correctly pointed out that land remained concentrated in the hands of a few individuals, companies, or estates, a situation without parallel in any mainland state.[43]

The distribution of wealth was substantially more equitable than the distribution of land, but Hawaii remained deeply stratified in income terms. Moreover wealth and ethnic background were still closely correlated, despite the increased socioeconomic mobility which characterized many areas of postwar life. Certainly Hawaii's Chinese and Japanese made substantial gains after 1945. As measured in per capita terms, the Chinese had by 1959 replaced haoles as the wealthiest ethnic group. This change was influenced by two important factors: the immense wealth of a small number of new Chinese millionaire businessmen like Chinn Ho and Hiram Fong, and the influx of large numbers of mainland white wage and salary earners in defense and service industries, especially tourism, which substantially reduced the average per capita income of whites. Wen Lang Li has generalized on the impressiveness of the upward social mobility of Chinese Americans throughout the United States within the previous two decades. Li's observation might reasonably be applied to Hawaii's Chinese in an earlier period, immediately after the war. Certainly island Chinese were even more successful, more assimilated, better educated, and less divided along vocational lines than were their mainland counterparts. Yet as Li cautions, assimilation is not the same thing as integration. Hawaii's Chinese may have been less isolated than mainland Chinese from primary contacts with their host society, but by the 1950s neither Chinese group was substantially integrated. Writing of Hawaii's Chinese more than a decade after statehood, Nancy Young argued that postwar predictions of the total assimilation of this group were inaccurate. She observed that, for a large proportion of Hawaii's Chinese, their most meaningful nonoccupational activities took place within an exclusively Chinese social environment. She further concluded that a strong ethnic identification persisted among the Chinese in Hawaii.[44]

The remarkable material success of Hawaii's Chinese was not duplicated by any other ethnic group. It reflected both their social cohesion and relatively early arrival in the islands. However, later arrivals also improved their own material conditions. But as the Japanese and Filipino experiences suggest, these groups rarely changed their economic situation relative to that of other groups. Moreover, the first settlers, the Hawaiians, were by the 1950s last in socioeconomic terms. Median income distribution in the decade 1949–1959 suggested the persistence of class divisions which generally coincided with ethnic divisions. Caucasians and Chinese were in the top bracket, Japanese occupied the middle range, and Filipinos, Hawaiians, and part-Hawaiians were the poorest. Such figures, however, do not indicate the substantial inequalities which existed within each group, although they do suggest a general correlation between class and ethnicity.[45]

The large Japanese group now occupied a lower middle position in economic terms, but Japanese access to real property was limited. Despite increased political, commercial, and educational participation, most Japanese remained socially, and to a lesser extent economically, separate. Certainly in terms of primary relationships they were at most only marginally assimilated. Japanese was the most widely used language after English and pidgin. Buddhism remained a substantial religious alternative to Christianity. It was estimated that 70 percent of Hawaii's Japanese were nominal Buddhists in the 1950s. Private education and managerial positions were less available to nisei than to whites. Japanese businessmen maintained a separate Japanese Chamber of Commerce in Honolulu. As late as 1960 approximately 12 percent of Hawaii's Japanese were foreign-born. The last available data on the proportion of Japanese who were citizens, that for 1950, indicated that one-quarter of adult Japanese did not meet this formal criterion of Americanization. After the war Hawaii's Japanese were far more assertive politically than their counterparts on the West Coast. The relative numerical strength of island Japanese was largely responsible for this. But both groups were now located essentially within middle vocational and educational ranges. Indeed, at the time of statehood, the median income of Hawaii's Japanese exceeded that of its whites. However, this upward economic mobility did not quickly translate into definite patterns of assimilation in primary terms. Erosion of ethnic cohesion and separation was fairly slow in both Japanese American groups, although gradual and uneven changes were taking place. By the late 1950s very few nisei or sansei (third-generation AJAs) did not endorse publicly dominant American values or patterns of secondary behavior. Yet most of Hawaii's Japanese still identified with, and lived within, a fairly viable ethnic community—even if this community was less separate or clearly defined in the late 1950s than at any time before the war.

Evidence available on the degree and nature of assimilation and integration by Hawaii's Japanese in the 1950s is essentially ambiguous and incomplete. But recent studies have conceded that considerable acculturation had taken place. Despite this homogenizing trend, however, ethnic group solidarity persisted, and the primary relationships enjoyed by Japanese Americans remained fairly distinct from those of the wider community. Like Hawaii's Chinese, or Asian groups throughout the nation, the substantial Americanization or assimilation of Hawaii's Japanese did not necessarily imply rapid or thorough integration in structural terms. Indeed, more than a decade after statehood a number of authors continued to draw attention to the persistence of ethnic social cohesion, the strength of extended family ties, and the tendency among various ethnic groups to cling to cultural practices transported by their ancestors from Asia. Michael Haas and Peter Resurrection observed in 1976, for example, that "social life tends to focus around members of extended families, which usually share a common ethnic identity, with the result that members of diverse groups who work side by side in the daytime may be unaware of the home life of their co-workers in the evenings and weekends." "In this respect," they concluded, "Hawaii's social patterns are segregated along racial and class lines."[46]

If by the late 1950s Hawaii's Japanese were marginally assimilated in secondary terms only, the Filipino, Hawaiian, and part-Hawaiian groups were even more separate and acutely disadvantaged. They had the lowest per capita incomes, the highest infant mortality rates, the least education, and were the least urbanized. As late as 1950 less than 15 percent of adult Filipinos were citizens, while more than 40 percent of all Filipinos were born outside the United States. The unemployment rate among Filipino aliens was so high in 1950 that the territorial government investigated ways of transporting six thousand of them to California, where it was hoped they could find work as farm laborers. The chairman of Stainback's Full Employment Committee was among those who thought this a convenient way to reduce unemployment and the drain on the territory's welfare funds. Despite Hawaii's high average living standards, and in the words of the Statehood Commission a "notable health record," native Hawaiians and many Filipinos had access only to an inferior health delivery service. Stainback acknowledged privately in 1950 that, "Our tuberculosis rate is one of the highest in the nation, and the rate among the native Hawaiians is appalling." Many members of these groups may have shared ideals and nationalist values with other citizens of Hawaii, but in social and economic terms they were still undeniably disadvantaged. David Trask, Jr., a prominent part-Hawaiian, detected racial and class distinctions in island society more than a generation after the war. His observation was applicable, at the very least, to those of Hawaiian or Filipino extraction. The persistence of local culture, referred to earlier in this chapter, both reflected and compounded these socioeconomic and status divisions.[47]

Postwar Hawaii was an increasingly open and mobile society. Nevertheless, not all groups shared equally in this change. Writing shortly after statehood, Lind, while subscribing to the belief that broad opportunities existed for all groups, still cautioned: "we must recognize that not all of the immigrant groups have availed themselves of the opportunities for economic and social advancement to the same degree and that the more recently arrived immigrant groups necessarily operate at a disadvantage as compared to the earlier arrivals."[48] However, despite their early special relationship with white society, by the 1940s and 1950s the descendents of Hawaii's native population were increasingly exposed to disadvantages not unlike those experienced by the newest nonwhite arrivals. The rapid growth of Chinese and Japanese influence was accompanied by a relative loss of status and influence for native Hawaiians. They now gained fewer and fewer tangible rewards from the paternalism which had characterized prewar society. Moreover, they were too weak economically and still too few in number to compete effectively with the larger Oriental groups.

Typical of many white liberal assessments of the way native Hawaiians had responded to the loss of land, authority, and culture was Burns' comment: "I don't think they allowed themselves to brood on it too much. That was the way it was—Take it, enjoy life while you can enjoy it, go ahead." The belief that accommodation was an appropriate response to subjugation permeated white thinking long after World War II. Haoles "always wanted to keep the vast and unruly mass of natives from the ballot," Burns recalled, and Hawaiians and part-Hawaiians often accepted this as they accepted other changes, because they knew resistance would be futile. Like many dispossessed aboriginal peoples in other parts of the Pacific, native Hawaiians tended to internalize the very assumption of inferiority used by white settlers to rationalize colonization. Powerlessness, paternalism, and inequality gradually inculcated what Burns and other locals referred to as "a subtle inferiority of spirit"—feelings of incompetence and separateness bred of domination by other cultures. And the haole paternalism which had helped nurture these feelings dissipated very slowly. For example, Elizabeth Farrington observed with unintended irony many years after statehood, that "everything" the Hawaiians have "progressed towards has been because of the education they've gotten from us." She further suggested that if the native population had been left to run Hawaii it might not be far removed from the Stone Age.[49]

If many Hawaiians and part-Hawaiians experienced a loss of pride and self-confidence, some other groups shared this problem, although to a substantially lesser degree. Burns noted that, like Hawaiians, many local Japanese simply accepted their unequal position in society. Almost a generation after statehood, a prominent member of Hawaii's Japanese community commented on the largely undiluted pervasiveness of haole mores and institutions, and concluded sadly: "Now, even today, the thing to be is a Haole, you know what I mean? To acculimate [sic] yourself to our society is to act like a Haole and Haoles—so-called Haoles—from the good old days when they were always the better bred people and so forth. . . . it was never good to be on the other side of the fence." The descendents of some of Hawaii's native peoples were afforded mi-

nority influence within the very paternalistic apparatus of the local
Republican party after annexation. In the face of expanding Asian immigration Hawaiians sided with the Republicans. The more numerous
descendents of Hawaii's Japanese, however, experienced no real political compensations for their general social exclusion until after the
Pacific War.[50]

Hawaiians and part-Hawaiians were more likely to oppose statehood
than were members of other ethnic groups. Their hostility was nurtured
by concerns more substantial than racial animosity toward the Japanese, or understandable alarm that demographic and voting changes
would quickly erode native political influence. Statehood undoubtedly
symbolized to some descendents of the indigenous population the total
demise of traditional culture and social patterns. It signalled the victory
of foreign practices and values, whether they be of occidental or oriental origin, over those which characterized the islands before missionaries arrived in the 1820s. "Something indefinable would be lost," Alice
Kamokila Campbell, a very wealthy part-Hawaiian territorial senator
who claimed Hawaiian royalty as her immediate ancestors, observed
sadly. "I do not feel . . . that we should forfeit the traditional rights
and privileges of the natives of our islands for a mere thimbleful of votes
in Congress, that we, the lovers of Hawaii from long association with it,
should sacrifice our birthright for the greed of alien desires to remain on
our shores." Alice Campbell's views were not necessarily those of all or
even most islanders of Hawaiian ancestry; but she was the most prominent, and certainly the most outspoken, representative of her people.
During the war she championed martial law and assailed Hawaii's Japanese, although her hostility to statehood did not derive simply from her
feelings about the local Japanese community. She was a genuine conservative and a fervent, if sometimes eccentric, Hawaiian nationalist. If
old Hawaii could not be revived, she felt, then certainly nothing should
be done which might further distance the patterns of island life from
those of the nineteenth century. Statehood would simply compound the
indignities of territorial rule, unleash new changes, and quicken the end
of traditional Hawaii.[51]

The number of pure Hawaiians had declined to only ten thousand by
1945. About sixty-one thousand, 12 percent of Hawaii's total population, were of part-Hawaiian extraction. Disturbed by their loss of numbers, land, and influence, some Hawaiians resisted statehood. In part,
this was simply a gesture of hostility; but some believed statehood
would confirm the political and economic power of the overwhelming
non-Hawaiian majority. The total number of Hawaiians and part-Hawaiians in 1940 was substantially less than the number of either the Japanese or Caucasians, and only marginally greater than the number of
Filipinos. Statehood, they believed, would accentuate the influence of

this alien majority which was both unsympathetic toward and unfamiliar with the customs and feelings of native Hawaiians, whom Senator
Campbell called "the real people of Hawaii."[52] Understandably, a resi-
due of native resentment remained against changes imposed by immigration over which they had exercised no real control after 1893. But
belated verbal protests could not stifle further change or recapture a
past now submerged beneath more than a century of foreign penetration and settlement.

Status distinctions both reflected and reinforced class and ethnic divisions. The material success of many Chinese and the political assertiveness of many Japanese meant that by the mid-1950s haole dominance
was under strong challenge for the first time since the late nineteenth
century. But the status patterns which Jitsuichi Matsuoka and others
had identified before the war remained largely intact. On the basis of a
study of race preferences among Hawaii's Japanese, Matsuoka argued
that status reflected socioeconomic factors rather than physiognomy.
The order of preference expressed by Japanese was: other Japanese,
Caucasians, Chinese, white-Hawaiians, Korean, Hawaiian, Portuguese, Filipino, and Puerto Rican. Moreover, within each group significant status differences persisted. For example, Hawaiians descended
from chiefs were viewed as superior to commoners; Hakka Chinese
were considered inferior to Punti; and Okinawans were the least respected Japanese. In general, studies of island society from the 1930s to
the 1950s agree that substantial status divisions persisted, and identify
the gradient of social preferences as haole - Chinese - Japanese - Filipino, with native Hawaiians interspersed throughout the lower end of
the continuum. Non-Caucasian groups, Burrows observed in 1947, invariably discovered that "the tolerance and friendliness among races,
for which Hawaii has been justly celebrated, prevailed only within
limits, and at a price." He concluded that in postwar Hawaii "the price
demanded by the dominant haoles—never in so many words, but nevertheless insistent—has been cheerful acceptance by other peoples of a
subordinate place."[53]

This pattern of substantial ethnic segmentation, in primary terms at
least, was compounded and complicated by socioeconomic divisions.
Moreover, it was prolonged, in part, by subtle forms of discrimination
as well as the persistence of paternalism, especially by whites toward
Hawaiians. Studies undertaken in the decade before statehood revealed
considerable resentment among non-Caucasians against unequal opportunities in employment, the administration of justice, and housing.
Many educated nonhaoles, in particular, felt frustrated by what they
saw as economic and social discrimination against them, and criticized
the importation of whites to fill managerial or skilled positions. Despite
"its unique degree of racial heterogeneity and overt norms of racial tol-

erance," Graham Kinloch and Geoffrey Borders concluded a generation after the war, "racial tension and conflict is far from being entirely absent." In contrast to many mainland areas, severe ethnic conflict and explicit racism rarely disrupted life in Hawaii. Serious racial tensions surfaced only occasionally after World War II, most notably in the form of resentment against the increasingly visible presence of Japanese in trade unions, jobs, and politics.[54]

Like most immigrant-receiving regions throughout the United States, Hawaii had experienced only limited and uneven structural assimilation by the 1950s, although acculturation was well developed if less pervasive than in mainland communities. In general, class and ethnicity overlapped in the island community. Some members of all immigrant groups had experienced substantial socioeconomic mobility. Most shared common secondary relationships in such areas as public education, political participation, and consumerism. Still, there were only partial similarities in the primary relationships and experiences of most groups, including those descended from immigrant Asian labor, notably the Chinese, Japanese, and Filipinos. Haoles and Hawaiians, for very different reasons and in very different ways, shared few primary experiences with each other or with Asian minorities. Like most descendents of mainland immigrants who arrived after the Civil War, minorities in the islands maintained social substructures which largely embraced fellow ethnics. "In Hawaii it was not so much income or occupation that determined one's friends, voting affiliations, or prospects for power and prestige," Fuchs has written. "In the forty years that followed Annexation, the people of Hawaii thought of themselves not primarily as doctors, lawyers, druggists or field hands—or even as Americans—but as *haoles*, Hawaiians, Portuguese, Chinese, Japanese or Filipinos." This social pattern broke down only slowly after the war.[55] Given Hawaii's relatively compressed history as an immigrant-receiving, white-dominated society, the persistence of such divisions is not unexpected. It is perhaps more difficult to explain the substantial acculturation of Hawaii's mixed peoples to Anglo-American values than it is to understand why primary-group cohesion remained a fundamental characteristic of the various ethnic minorities.

Given the patterns of acculturation discussed here, it is not surprising that support for statehood transcended racial, economic, and political divisions within Hawaiian society. All postwar congressional investigations acknowledged this fact, and as a corollary, accepted that all segments of the island community were fundamentally Americanized. Nonetheless, in 1947 an investigating team cautioned: "With so many children of alien parentage among them, a definite program of Americanization is necessary."[56] Americanization had developed rapidly but, this observation implied, it was not yet complete. In the years after the war local opponents of statehood clung to the view that Hawaii's predominantly nonwhite peoples were not sufficiently Americanized to warrant statehood. A few argued that such racially diverse people could never become truly American, that ideological assimilation could never overcome racial and ethnic group consciousness. Nevertheless, the evidence of growing acculturation persuaded every team of congressional investigators after the war that Hawaii was equipped for statehood.

Racial fears and antagonism were deep-rooted and seldom amenable to rational argument. Opposition to statehood based on fear of Japanese political influence, Louis Cain noted in the late 1930s, "presupposes disloyalty of citizens of alien parentage, presumes that a minority voting as a racial bloc would prevail, and that traitors would be elected." In objective terms, the years 1941–1945 had invalidated such suspicions. But those preoccupied with questions of race were seldom affected by the evidence of Japanese loyalty and sacrifice in the war. Cain warned congressional investigators before the war of the danger of setting up race as an obstacle to statehood. Such a stance, he proposed, was not only irrational but un-American, and threatened to disrupt the atmosphere of racial tolerance which characterized Hawaii. "I submit to you that you cannot breed loyalty with suspicion. To raise embargoes on citizenship because of ancestry would tend to force the people so accused into racial blocs for self-protection."[57] These were fine sentiments, and they were even more appropriate after Pearl Harbor than before. Yet in both Hawaii and in Congress, substantial numbers remained unimpressed by the view that Hawaii's Japanese were thoroughly Americanized and entitled to full citizenship under statehood. As the possibility of action by Congress improved after the war, opposition to statehood became more explicit, forceful, and overt. It remained very much a minority sentiment, but it was no longer confined to the private whisperings of a few.

Debate over the Americanization of Hawaii's people became more public and more ideological as it was affected by the growing national controversy over internal subversion and un-American activities in the early years of the cold war. Ultimately, the wild charges made during the McCarthy era against the island community were exposed as irrelevant to statehood and without foundation. The exaggerated charges made by statehood opponents were contradicted at every turn by the deep-rooted Americanization of the islands which had begun more than a century earlier. Nonetheless, during the late 1940s and early 1950s the nature of Hawaii's Americanization was again the subject of bitter national debate.

Chapter 5

Issues Confused, 1946–1950: Civil Rights, Party Politics, and Communism

Hawaii remained essentially isolated from the economic and social forces which shaped change in mainland America before World War II. But new energies and pressures were released immediately after hostilities ended. These rapidly transformed existing social and political arrangements in the territory, and precipitated intense conflicts in virtually every sphere of community life. In large part the seeds of change had lain dormant in prewar Hawaii, unable to flower in the tightly controlled, uniquely complex island environment. After 1945, however, the ethnic and class tensions which cut across all aspects of community and politics quickly surfaced. Initially, the most apparent postwar development was the emergence of a strong, organized, allegedly Communist-controlled labor movement. The reaction of the old order to this new symbol of industrial and social confrontation was harsh and exceedingly determined. The ensuing conflict between labor and management, between wage earners and the owners of property, had an indirect but decisive bearing on Hawaii's statehood aspirations. Political and ideological struggles in Hawaii during 1946–1950 anticipated and in some ways foreshadowed disputes focused nationally by McCarthyism. After the war the question of statehood was inextricably confused with the issues of communist subversion and internal security. The alleged relationship between statehood for a vulnerable Pacific territory and the internal security of the nation became the principal explicit objection voiced against statehood both locally and in Congress. Hawaii's record during the Pacific War had made it difficult to portray the Japanese per se as the enemy within. But the cold war made it possible to level this emotive charge against allegedly Communist-led unions which were supported overwhelmingly by workers of Asian extraction. Thus, conveniently, opposition to trade unions and anti-Japanese sentiment converged. This curious amalgam of anti-communism and racism was to prove a frustrating new obstacle to statehood.

The statehood issue was not only confused by the crusade against communism, it was also enmeshed in the bitter sectional conflicts over the related issues of civil rights for ethnic minorities, the limits of state control over racial practices within their borders, and the ongoing contest for power in Congress between the two major political parties and factions within these parties. Hawaii's admission threatened to disrupt the political and sectional status quo in Congress. Statehood was an explicit challenge to the power and interests of a conservative coalition of old guard Republicans and Southern Democrats. This group fought vigorously against any erosion of its influence, and in so doing it resisted Hawaii's bid for statehood. After 1945 congressional action was determined much less by the validity of Hawaii's appeals for entry than by the anticipated effects this might have on civil rights legislation and sectional and political strength in Washington.

An Optimistic Campaign

Hawaii's formal statehood campaign was revived and restructured shortly after the war. The early enthusiasm which promoted these initiatives soon evaporated, however, as local proponents accepted reluctantly that a forceful and expensive campaign could only exert modest influence in Washington. In May 1946 a Citizens' Statehood Committee replaced the old Equal Rights Commission.[1] The new committee was financed from the governor's contingency fund—an arrangement later found to be unsatisfactory because it relied on the sympathy of an official appointed by Washington. The Citizens' Committee was headed by an executive board of 15 members, and supported by a general committee of 230 with representatives from all the major islands. The executive board was appointed by the governor, but a majority of its members was drawn from the local legislature. The general committee included all members of the legislature and the former Equal Rights Commission, the mayor of Honolulu, and representatives of business, academic, and civic groups. An initial fund of ten thousand dollars was allocated to support the new organization, and additional grants were to be given when required.[2]

Joseph Farrington, the wealthy son of a former governor of the territory and Republican delegate to Congress until his sudden death in 1954, gave firm guidance to the early postwar drive for eventual admission. He was actively supported by another Republican, former delegate Sam King, whom Eisenhower later appointed governor of the territory. Both men had sat patiently in Congress as virtual observers, denied the right to vote. Both were keenly aware that minority opinion often prevailed in Congress, as procedural obstacles could negate or at least delay legislation which might have commanded majority support on the floors of each chamber. Other proponents gradually learned what Farrington and King were doubtless conscious of in 1946–1947— that committee maneuvering and back room strategies were often decisive in Congress. They also learned, along with many liberals and blacks from mainland states, not to underestimate the entrenched con-

servatism or tactical ability of old guard Republicans and Southern
Democrats.

In the early postwar years, however, most statehood proponents optimistically felt that popular democratic pressure would overcome the
hostility of an apparently small faction of congressmen determined to
defeat Hawaii. Farrington, it seems, was somewhat more realistic. He
asked members of the territory's legislature to establish a permanent
office in Washington as a vehicle for lobbying Congress. However,
Democratic appointee Governor Stainback was unimpressed by this
view. He rejected Farrington's request, claiming that the use of territorial funds to support the delegate in Washington would involve partisan
politics, and would undermine the existing unity which the drive for
statehood had forged between diverse political parties and factions.
Stainback also refused to call a special session of the legislature to consider the type of campaign most appropriate for the islands. The governor had previously supported statehood and was a member of the Equal
Rights Commission; but by mid-1946 local Democrats as well as Republicans like King openly criticized his new ambivalence on this issue. A
few months earlier the central committee of Hawaii's Democratic party
had recommended successfully to Truman that Stainback be reappoint-
ed. This was an action which all progressive local Democrats and sincere statehood proponents later regretted.[3]

The activities of the Statehood Committee during 1946 typified the
sort of campaign pursued by local proponents until 1959. It distributed
more than thirty-eight thousand items of statehood data in Hawaii and
the mainland, and sent fifteen hundred lengthy statements of Hawaii's
qualifications for statehood to congressmen, newspapers, and a variety
of national organizations.[4] Estimates made shortly after the war indicated that more than 90 percent of all mainland newspapers supported
immediate statehood. It was also endorsed by such diverse organizations as the Disabled American Veterans, the National Education Association, the National Association for the Advancement of Colored People, more than two thousand Chambers of Commerce, and the House
Committee on Territories.[5]

Dissatisfied with the existing organizational base of the campaign,
but delighted with the massive national support statehood had now
received, the territorial legislature took firm control of the campaign.
On February 24, 1947, the president of the local senate, Eugene S.
Capellas, introduced a bill to set up a statehood body supported by
appropriations granted by the legislature rather than the governor's
contingency fund. This body was designed to replace the loosely organized citizens' group which had established temporary offices in Honolulu and Washington, but lacked adequate financial support. Propo-

nents were convinced by early 1947 that Stainback was reluctant to either support immediate statehood or provide sufficient funds for this purpose to the committee. Thus in May 1947, members of the legislature overcame the governor's ambivalence by establishing a permanent eight-member Statehood Commission with a budget of two hundred thousand dollars for 1947–1948. At the same time, a resolution supporting immediate admission unanimously passed the local house and senate.[6]

The bipartisan commission was appointed in June. Its original members were: A. T. Longley, chairman; King, Metzger, and Trask, members at large; Gavien Bush, county of Hawaii; Charles A. Rice, county of Kauai; F. W. Broadbent, county of Maui; and Lorrin P. Thurston, county of Oahu. (Thurston was a surprise choice, as the influential *Advertiser*, which he partly owned, was unsympathetic to statehood, and many islanders felt he shared this opinion.) George W. McLane was appointed full-time executive secretary of the commission. An additional committee comprising six senators and six members of the House of Representatives was appointed to advise the commission.[7] Responsibility for conducting the statehood campaign was thereby made a de facto function of the territorial legislature.

From mid-1947 until statehood was finally achieved, the commission conducted an expensive and necessarily protracted campaign for immediate admission. However, its responsibilities were broadly defined and included tasks not directly related to statehood as such. The commission was instructed to:

(a) support the movement for admission of the territory to statehood; (b) until such admission is granted, advocate and support the rights and claims of the territory and its inhabitants to treatment or usage, the same as, or equal to, that received by the several states of the United States Union from the Federal Government; (c) oppose and attempt to defeat or prevent federal and state legislation discriminatory against the territory and its inhabitants; and (d) assist the legislature in attaining such amendments to the Organic Act as are duly requested by the legislature.

The commission was directed to correct any misinformation or refute any false statements made about the territory, and to provide members of staff to testify before congressional investigating committees. Provision was made for it to carry on advertising and publicity campaigns on a national or regional scale and to perform any functions it considered "necessary or advisable" to promote the interests of the territory.[8] Despite constant setbacks in Washington and periodic criticism at home, the commission met its obligations enthusiastically and effectively during its unexpectedly long life. Short of actually gaining statehood, however, the commission was powerless to ensure that the territory and its citizens be granted equality with the existing states, and unable to insist that Congress not discriminate against the territory.

The commission maintained offices in Honolulu and Washington. After mid-1947 it published folders, pamphlets, and books on statehood, and intermittently, the *Hawaii Statehood News*. It regularly submitted details of Hawaii's statehood qualifications to members of Congress, government offices and departments, mainland newspapers and magazines, business and community organizations, schools and universities. Its office maintained contact with more than seventeen hundred daily newspaper editors, and in the first decade of its operations the number of editorials favoring statehood grew from a modest five hundred to about three thousand annually. It distributed up to forty thousand pamphlets and other literature on statehood each year. In addition it lobbied all representatives and senators in Washington by periodically bombarding them with a blizzard of private letters. More significantly, members of the commission lobbied energetically on Capitol Hill, giving special attention to committee members and floor leaders. Farrington, King, McLane, and McLane's successors Jack M. Fox and Jan Jabulka were the most effective lobbyists in Washington until Burns arrived as the new delegate to Congress in 1956.[9] After 1946 the commission's Washington office supplied a prodigious amount of material to congressmen of all political persuasions. Virtually all the information used by supporters of statehood in subsequent debate in Congress, as well as much of the basic information cited by opponents (such as that on Hawaii's mixed population), was supplied through the Washington office, although it was usually collected and organized by supporters in Honolulu.[10] This exhaustive campaign promoted strong public and newspaper support throughout most mainland states, and helped to convince a growing number of congressmen that Hawaii was theoretically entitled to statehood. These developments alone were no guarantee that Congress would act favorably and decisively, but they were indispensable preliminary steps to eventual action.

The first postwar Congress, the Seventy-ninth (1945–1946), refused to debate statehood legislation on the floor of either chamber. The favorable report issued by the House subcommittee which had investigated the issue under Chairman Larcade was not endorsed by the full House Committee on Territories. Farrington, with the support of Larcade, attempted to move the report forward, but failed.[11] There was virtually no chance of affirmative action by both chambers, as the Senate had not yet examined the question in committee. Senator William F. Knowland (Rep., Calif.), who proved to be one of Hawaii's most active supporters on Capitol Hill, had introduced a statehood bill in the Senate, but it was not taken up by the committee.[12] Hawaii was not yet classified as a high priority in the Truman administration's legislative program. And although statehood enjoyed at least tacit majority support throughout the nation and was endorsed by most newspapers, as well as the Democratic administration and the Republican party, Congress was essentially uninterested in the statehood issue during the prelude to the mid-term elections of 1946. It was not an issue in the campaign.

The results of the 1946 elections shocked the Democrats. For the first time since 1938 the GOP gained majorities in both chambers and won governorships in more than half the states. For Hawaii, which had been virtually a one-party, Republican territory for almost half a century, the sweeping GOP victories of 1946 were indeed good news. Farrington, along with most local proponents, confidently assumed that a Republican Congress would quickly admit the Republican-controlled islands to statehood.[13]

Their optimism appeared well-founded when the new Congress met. An unprecedented number of statehood bills were introduced in the House during the opening of the Eightieth Congress (1947–1948). Eleven representatives introduced bills identical to the legislation introduced by Farrington. But only one Southern representative, Larcade, introduced a statehood bill. Most were presented by Republicans from Western states. Statehood legislation was quickly taken up by Republican leaders in the House. In March the Committee on Public Lands (formerly the House Committee on Territories), under Chairman Richard J. Welch (Rep., Calif.), conducted its first hearings on Hawaiian statehood in Washington.[14]

In contrast to previous investigations, these hearings related primarily to national aspects of the issue, particularly the possible impact of statehood on national defense, trade, and United States foreign policy in Asia and the Pacific. The committee heard evidence from thirty-five witnesses over thirteen days. Secretary of the Interior Julius A. Krug best summarized the opinions of those who testified when he stated:

> There is no room in our scheme of government for holding an incorporated territory in a perpetual state of "tutelage." . . . I do not care what standard you apply: whether it is population, devotion to American ideals, the effect upon the nation in foreign affairs, wealth, ability for self government, loyalty, competence in business or government, or social consciousness; Hawaii passes the test. If we have any faith that "Governments are instituted among men deriving their just powers from the consent of the governed," we should keep faith. . . . [15]

Witnesses gave voluminous favorable testimony on all aspects of statehood. Farrington and two members of the territory's senate, Thelma M. Akana (Rep.) and William Heen (Dem.), reiterated that Hawaii was qualified for admission. Stainback also gave supportive testimony, perhaps because his reappointment had not yet been confirmed and he did not wish to appear unsympathetic to the wishes of most islanders. Representatives of the Hawaiian Sugar Planters' Association and the Honolulu Chamber of Commerce repeated testimony presented to the Larcade subcommittee which stressed that equal representation in Congress was essential if Hawaii was to gain an equal footing with the mainland states.[16] Generally, testimony emphasized that Hawaii was entitled to and desired immediate statehood. In the following years proponents were obliged to present such arguments ad nauseum.

The appearance of a host of eager statehood proponents before congressional investigating teams became an annual ritual after the war. Unavoidably, the statements which they dutifully made became tiresome and predictable. Their arguments were essentially irrelevant to the selfish interests and prejudices which increasingly shaped the reaction of Congress. Yet in the absence of affirmative action by both chambers of Congress, statehood proponents had no alternative but to sustain an active public campaign, lobby energetically in Washington, and volunteer evidence before seemingly interminable committee hearings in both Washington and the islands. Only occasionally, in response to specific objections raised by opponents after 1947, did the thrust of testimony given by proponents change. Usually, these objections were irrelevant, exaggerated, and beyond rational debate. Supporters confronted such arguments patiently and firmly. But by the early 1950s most accepted reluctantly that a formal statehood campaign could not alone overcome either the prejudices or tactics of those determined to deny Hawaii equality with mainland states. The fears which preoccupied these opponents, and the tactics they were prepared to exploit, were revealed as the statehood question was periodically debated by Congress after 1946. In the face of these developments Hawaii's vigorous campaign and valid arguments became increasingly meaningless. Sectional self-interest and cynical partisan politics determined Hawaii's fate on Capitol Hill.

The Conservative Coalition Surfaces: Eightieth Congress

In March 1947 the House Public Lands Committee recommended for the first time that the House immediately approve statehood. No member of the committee opposed this instruction. "If any doubt concerning the readiness of Hawaii to assume the responsibilities of statehood existed . . . prior to the recent hearing," the report concluded, "they were dispelled by the experts, both civilian and military." The Rules Committee promptly scheduled Hawaii for consideration on the floor of the House. No one opposed the bill when it came before this powerful committee. Its chairman, Leo E. Allen (Rep., Ill.), thus suggested naively that Hawaii remain a nonpartisan issue. The full House debate commenced on June 30, 1947. A bipartisan group of proponents reiterated Hawaii's qualifications and desire for admission. Passage of statehood legislation would not be the signal that the United States had taken up a new policy, Farrington contended, but would simply represent the fulfillment of a policy initiated by annexation of the islands.[17] Mike Mansfield (Dem., Mont.) argued that statehood could not be denied, because the citizens of Hawaii were "asking with an overwhelming voice for normal absorption into the body politic of the United States with all the privileges and obligations of American citizenship." Those who spoke forcefully against the bill were either Democrats from Southern states (like E. E. Cox of Georgia and W. R. Poage of Texas) or Republicans representing large states (like Frederic Coudert of New York). After debate lasting only four hours, the Republican majority leadership brought the statehood bill (symbolically numbered H.R. 49) to a vote. It passed, but only by a modest margin, 196 votes to 133.[18] Significantly, almost one-quarter of all representatives abstained from voting. This was the first occasion that either chamber of Congress had approved statehood for an offshore territory.

Although the vote did not conform rigidly to party divisions, it did reflect narrow party and sectional interests. Republicans supported Hawaii by a margin of almost three to one (141 votes to 56). In contrast, only fifty-five Democrats voted yes, while seventy-seven voted no. Formal endorsement of statehood by the Democratic administration did not sway a majority of House Democrats. Given this voting pattern it is impossible to agree with the *New York Times* when it stated that it could detect no partisanship in the outcome of the vote. The *Honolulu Star-Bulletin*'s suggestion that the vote did not reflect partisan or sectional considerations was equally inaccurate.[19]

Sectional division was clearly evidenced in the House debate and vote. Principal support came from the smaller New England states, the Western states, Mountain states, and the large Far Western state, California. Opposition derived almost exclusively from the eleven Southern states, the border states of Missouri and Maryland, and some large Northern states, notably Pennsylvania, New York, Illinois, Ohio, and New Jersey. Most of the ninety-four representatives who abstained from voting were representatives of large Northern states. However, a majority in only one Northern state, Pennsylvania, voted against admission. Four former Confederate states—Alabama, Arkansas, Virginia, and Texas—voted unanimously against statehood. A majority of representatives from the Southern states of Georgia, Mississippi, North Carolina, South Carolina, Tennessee, and the border states of Missouri and Maryland opposed statehood. A majority of representatives from only two

Southern states, Louisiana and Florida, favored Hawaii. The eleven
former Confederate states provided only fifteen affirmative votes while
sixty-three votes opposed. All but two Southern opponents were members of the Democratic party. In contrast, all the representatives of large
Northern states who opposed statehood were Republican.[20]

The proportion of congressmen prepared to support Hawaii increased
throughout the next twelve years; but the pronounced voting pattern of
1947 was duplicated whenever the issue was actually put to a vote in the
House. On no occasion during 1947–1959 did a majority of representatives actually oppose statehood, although in 1947 a substantial number
abstained from voting. The alignments which emerged in the first
House vote reflected political and sectional factors that subsequently
complicated and delayed all future attempts to push a statehood bill
through both the House and the Senate.

The strong support given Hawaii by House Republicans was influenced, in part at least, by the simple fact that the islands were a traditional Republican stronghold. Most observers anticipated that statehood would place two additional loyal Republicans in the United States
Senate. From 1902 to 1946 both houses of the territorial legislature had
consistently been controlled by substantial Republican majorities. With
one brief exception, all delegates to Congress had been Republicans.
The days of GOP ascendancy were about to end, but in 1946 this was
not anticipated. In the territorial elections of 1946, half of the thirty
House members elected were Democrats; Republicans kept a majority
in the Senate. This was the best result ever by the local Democrats, but
most observers thought it was simply a temporary reversal for the GOP.
Nor could the Democrats yet muster a serious challenge to Farrington's
secure position as delegate to Congress.

Both sides of national politics found it difficult to resist narrow partisan pressures. In general, Democrats were reluctant to elevate strongly
Republican Hawaii and thereby help to undermine their own party's
power in Congress. In the Senate, where the two parties were usually
quite evenly balanced, this was a critical issue. Two additional assured
votes for either side might make the difference between majority or
minority status in this chamber. After the 1946 elections, for example,
the Republican majority was only six; after 1952 party numbers were
equal and the vote of Vice President Richard Nixon was necessary to
permit the Republicans to organize the Senate. Some Democrats opposed Hawaii's admission during the Eightieth Congress because it
would complicate their task of regaining control of the Senate. A number of Democrats wanted to delay Hawaii's admission until Alaska
could be simultaneously admitted. Alaska was traditionally a Democratic territory. Thus some Democrats wanted Congress to consider
both territories concurrently as they thought this strategy would nullify

unilateral gains by the GOP.[21] In antebellum America the critical problem of admitting new states without disrupting sectional or party balance in Congress had usually been resolved (in the short-term at least) by expedient procedures which admitted new states in pairs. Given such significant precedents, it was hardly surprising that the questions of statehood for Hawaii and Alaska were immediately fused when they came before Congress.

In contrast to Hawaii, Alaska's claims were based less on its ability to meet the traditional preconditions for admission than on assertions that statehood was necessary to ensure the satisfactory economic development of the territory. Alaska was certainly less qualified than Hawaii. Its population was approximately two hundred thousand, about half that of Hawaii. These people were sparsely scattered over an area twice the size of Texas, and were neither numerically nor financially capable of supporting a state government. More than 90 percent of all land was owned by the federal government, largely for defense purposes. Opponents thus argued that the vast northern area should remain a territory under firm federal control. However, the relatively small population of Alaska, its inability to develop its natural resources without federal aid, and its importance in national defense planning were not considered by a 1947 House subcommittee as sufficient reason to deny it immediate statehood. Moreover, Truman had endorsed Alaska's admission.

But during 1946–1947 the Republican-controlled House of Representatives refused to consider Alaska, despite the unanimously positive report of its subcommittee and its favorable vote on Hawaii.[22] Some members sincerely believed that Alaska was not yet qualified, but party politics was perhaps the major factor averting House action. Certainly, most Republicans were unenthusiastic about Alaska because they had no desire to add to the Democrats' power in Congress, especially in the Senate. Predictably, after 1947 many Democrats stressed that if Alaska was not admitted at the same time as Hawaii, then both should be denied entry. Truman apparently shared this view. Reporters on Capitol Hill wrote confidently that he would veto a separate Hawaii bill in the unlikely event that it passed the Senate as well as the House in 1947–1948. "Unless he can get statehood for Democratic Alaska at the same time and offset the Republican gains from Hawaii," the *Star-Bulletin* claimed, "Truman is sure to veto the bill." "On the other hand," it asserted, "a Republican controlled Congress is just as sure not to give Alaska a chance to add to the Democrats in the legislature." Truman carefully endorsed statehood for both territories in 1947; but the Republican party wanted Congress to consider only Hawaii.[23]

In the months following the favorable House vote proponents learned some bitter lessons about the nature of politics on Capitol Hill. They also came to accept, however reluctantly, that real power in Congress rested in the Senate and that victory in the House was not necessarily a precursor of success in the Senate.

The *Christian Science Monitor* proclaimed that statehood for Hawaii was closer than ever after the House had shown its approval in June 1947.[24] Proponents anticipated that the Senate would act favorably, if not in 1947 then certainly in 1948.[25] The political, sectional, and racial issues introduced by opponents in the House debate had not averted, or indeed delayed, the vote in this chamber. These issues nevertheless had a decisive negative impact on Hawaii's prospects when the statehood bill was considered by the Senate.

Under the chairmanship of Senator Guy Cordon (Rep., Calif.), the Senate subcommittee on Territories and Insular Affairs conducted extensive investigations in Hawaii in January 1948. Testimony was accepted from 231 witnesses during eleven days of hearings on all major islands. Only 16 witnesses opposed immediate statehood. Previous committees dispatched by the House had heard all of these arguments during 1935–1947, but senators, particularly those opposed to statehood, willingly authorized a fresh investigation. After 1948 this became a convenient tactic of delay. Predictably, there was never any shortage of congressmen eager to volunteer for a free trip to the exotic Pacific islands as members of investigating teams. (Disgruntled islanders later protested that these pilgrimages were blatant political junkets which did little to broaden support for statehood in Washington.) Cordon's subcommittee heard exhaustive supporting testimony from representatives of business and labor groups, the Hawaii Statehood Commission, community service organizations, academics, members of the Republican and Democratic parties, and citizens from all major ethnic groups in the islands.[26] His findings reflected the opinions of the overwhelming majority of witnesses. He reported in March that Hawaii "met the requirements for statehood" and was "able and ready to accept the social, political and economic responsibilities of State government."

It was widely expected that this action would pave the way for debate of the House-approved bill on the floor of the Senate. Instead of sending the bill on, however, the chairman of the committee to which Cordon reported, the old guard conservative Hugh Butler (Rep., Nebr.), scheduled additional hearings. These began in Washington in April under a new subcommittee which this time included Butler. No testimony was given which opposed statehood, but numerous letters and statements were submitted in opposition.[27] "It was indicative of the lack of any real opposition to statehood for Hawaii, or sound argument against it," the *New York Times* observed, "that not a single witness appeared in opposition."[28] Yet the Senate Committee on Public Lands again refused to send the bill on. Senator Eugene D. Millikin (Rep., Colo.) moved on May 9 that action on the subcommittee reports be deferred indefinitely. After a "furious fight" the committee agreed by a margin of seven votes to five to accept Millikin's motion. This abrupt decision was tantamount to defeat of the bill in the Eightieth Congress. Identical bills must pass both chambers during one Congress, or subsequently be reintroduced in both chambers. Thus, the Millikin resolution nullified the favorable House action of 1947. Ironically, the committee's decision was made the day after Robert A. Taft (Ohio), chairman of the Republican Policy Committee, had placed it on the proposed agenda for Senate action.[29]

Farrington was reportedly very dejected after the Millikin motion had won. He attributed the decision to the prejudice and isolationism of the likes of Butler, and privately referred to it as a "damned outrage." Truman's White House staff viewed Farrington's position sympathetically, and suggested that some senators wanted to delay Hawaii in order to justify yet another junket to the islands. Led by Farrington, Hawaii's Republicans had lobbied energetically but ineffectually in Washington. The statehood bill was now "deader than a doornail," one of Truman's aides conceded privately on May 10.[30]

Most supporters of the Millikin resolution were conservative Republicans who sometimes voted with the Southern faction in Congress and opposed liberal domestic legislation. There were no Southern Democrats on the committee.[31] This vote clearly indicated that Republican opposition was stronger in the Senate than in the House. Writing in the *New York Times*, Arthur Krock suggested that Senate Republicans were apprehensive about the influence Hawaii would exercise in the Senate. They feared, Krock suggested, that Hawaii's senators might be the decisive factor in controversial issues, such as labor legislation. Krock noted that many Republican senators were privately alarmed that Hawaii's votes would increase liberal strength in Congress. The dramatic Democratic gains in the territorial elections of 1946, and the growth of organized labor were accepted by some Republicans as permanent, threatening trends. Thus, many Republicans believed that Hawaii might send at least one Democratic senator to Congress. In addition, some senators from both parties privately expressed alarm that congressional representatives would not be Caucasians.[32]

Yet Hawaii did have some dedicated supporters in the Senate. The influential Republicans Knowland and Cordon refused to accept the committee decision as final. During May 1948 they led a vigorous attempt to bring H.R. 49 to the Senate floor. Knowland moved to discharge the Public Lands Committee of responsibility for the statehood bill and thus place it on the Senate calendar. Although the *Washington Evening Star* stated that it failed to see any legitimate reason for delaying consideration of the bill or opposing Knowland's resolution, the Senate rejected the resolution by a decisive margin of fifty-one votes to twenty after only one hour of debate.[33]

This defeat resulted from a combination of influences which reflected conservative versus liberal cleavages in the Senate, as well as party preferences. One-third of all Senate Democrats abstained from voting, but more than 70 percent of those who did participate recorded a "No" vote. With only three exceptions all of the Democrats who voted negatively were from the eleven former Confederate states. They were joined by a majority of Republicans. This voting alignment conformed closely to the conservative-liberal split which emerged whenever the Senate debated civil rights or related legislation.[34]

Filibustering by conservative senators helped to defeat Truman's civil rights program during 1947–1948. Most senators who supported statehood also consistently backed civil rights measures. In addition, they wanted to pass cloture legislation that would limit debate and permit votes to be taken on controversial issues. The positions adopted by individual senators on cloture were thus fairly accurate barometers of their liberalism, especially on racial matters. All Democrats and all but two Republicans who voted for the Knowland resolution and retained their Senate seats also voted for cloture legislation in 1949.[35] Opposition to the Knowland resolution derived almost exclusively from conservative Republicans and Southern Democrats. "The list of opposing Republicans reads like a roll-call of the Old Guard," observed William H. Ewing, Washington correspondent of the *Honolulu Star-Bulletin*.[36] This voting alignment was very similar to that on Hawaii in the House the previous year. But as proponents discovered in the following decade, conservative strength was relatively much stronger in the Senate than in the House. At the same time, senators could employ a range of procedural tactics which were calculated to cripple legislation to which they objected.

The Senate vote in 1948 did not relate exclusively to the question of statehood for Hawaii. It also involved the important issue of support for procedural rules. Many senators apparently wanted statehood but would not support Knowland's move. Some voted negatively because the resolution sought to circumvent normal committee functions, not because they opposed statehood. Larcade pointed out that "unfortunate circumstances . . . resulted in the resolution being placed in a legislative position where it was impossible to vote on the main issue rather than the motion to discharge the Committee." However, this influence should not be overestimated. Knowland correctly commented that his resolution would have passed had a majority of senators been genuinely "enthusiastic" about statehood. Moreover, the brief Senate debate focused on statehood rather than procedural matters. Cordon's admission of his inability to thoroughly investigate Hawaii's political or economic situation was eagerly exploited by opponents. They argued that further investigations were obviously necessary. Knowland replied that Hawaii had been adequately investigated. As he and other supporters doggedly pointed out, by 1948 Congress had completed seventy days of hearings on this question. Almost five hundred witnesses had testified in favor of statehood; only sixty-six had opposed it. More than three thousand pages of testimony had already been taken. "The record of testimony and information built up around the question of [Hawaii's] statehood," Knowland remarked, "is more voluminous and complete than was the case for any other state prior to its admission."[37] Even the most pessimistic proponent could hardly have imagined in 1948 that it would take another ten years of exhaustive, repetitive investigations before resistance in Congress was finally overcome.

Real Obstacles: The South, Civil Rights, and Statehood

Despite the periodic intervention of party politics, this was not the major reason for the alignments evidenced in the first or subsequent congressional votes on Hawaii. The core of resistance derived from a combination of racial and sectional influences. This resistance exploited the issues of party power and state representation in Congress, but it derived from much stronger ideas and prejudices than simple party affiliations. And it was supported by representatives of a cohesive, determined, and substantial section of mainland America—the South.

After 1945 an overwhelming majority of Southern congressmen opposed Hawaii's admission. They were adamant that Congress should not acquire power to legislate in areas over which individual states assumed control after Reconstruction. The Civil War had brought the rebel South back into the Union, but almost a century later Southern states remained unrepentant upholders of states' rights. They had once defended states' rights in order to sanction their peculiar institution, slavery, and now they championed them to protect their unique segregated social practices and laws. To guard their sectional interests Southern representatives determined to resist all attempts to dilute the power of their section in Congress, especially in the Senate. Statehood for Hawaii was perceived as a direct threat to existing Southern authority on Capitol Hill. One Mississippi newspaper cautioned that Hawaii's two senators might command the key vote on major legislation involving racial issues on the mainland United States.[38] Similarly, a Texas newspaper argued that statehood would "give Hawaii the right to exercise two Senators' worth of self-determination" on the South.[39] Any doubts which might have existed over the South's position on statehood were quickly dispelled when the issue came before Congress after the war.[40] For more than a decade opposition from the South, especially in House committees and on the floor of the Senate, was the decisive factor contributing to the perennial defeat of statehood legislation.

Southern resistance was also influenced by racism directed against all nonwhites. Publicly, this was expressed in the timeworn argument that Hawaii's mixed population of natives and Asians could never be assimilated into American society. Racial fears were compounded by the belief that Hawaii's congressmen would probably be non-Caucasians, and would certainly be liberal on questions of racial equality and civil rights. Larcade, one of the few Southerners who supported statehood, conceded the importance of this concern when he stated in the House debate:

> . . . my people, the South, and myself have definite opinions in regard to the racial question; however, on my visit to Hawaii I observed men and women of all races intermingling and assimilating in perfect . . . harmony. If that is their way of life, that is their business, and they are entitled to their way of life. In the South we do not approve of this way of life, and this should be our business; and like Hawaii all that we ask is that we be given the same privileges to make our own determination in this respect.

Most Southerners were convinced, however, that the ability of states to determine domestic racial policies would be eroded by Hawaii's admission; two new, liberal senators might give the pro-civil rights factions a majority in the Senate. Certainly they would not boost the power of the Southern bloc. In the words of the powerful Mississippi Democrat Senator James Eastland, senators from Hawaii would mean "two votes for socialized medicine, . . . two votes for Government ownership of industry, two votes against all racial segregation and two votes against the South on all social matters." Statehood for the Pacific islands would contribute to the destruction of "our dual schools, our social institutions and harmonious racial relations," Eastland claimed.[41]

Southern opponents were seldom embarrassed by the racist character of their arguments. In the 1947 debate, for example, Prince Preston, Jr., (Dem., Ga.) stated:

> What does it [the Hawaii bill] do? It makes citizens with equal rights with you and me of 180,000 Japanese. . . . It gives these people the same rights you and I have; we, the descendants of those who created, fought and maintained this country. Who are those people? . . . descendants of the recently deposed [sic] Emperor of Japan. . . . When you give these people the same rights we have today, you will have two Senators speaking for these 180,000 Japanese.[42]

Supporters were generally reluctant to denounce explicitly the racist bias of such resistance. However, Robert Hale (Rep., Maine) made the point late in the House debate that the fundamental justification for serious opposition to statehood was the mixed racial population of the islands. He attempted to expose the assumptions of racial superiority by arguing:

Let us be frank about it. The opposition to this measure arises primarily from
the fact that the racial strains in Hawaii are more Asiatic than European.
This opposition springs from a dangerous form of racism. . . . I tremble to
think what the American future will be if we predicate any national policy
on an assumption of inferiority in Asiatic peoples.[43]

This "dangerous form of racism" was not restricted to a few congressmen. Indeed their views reflected a substantial body of mainland opinion. In letters to congressmen demanding that Hawaii be rejected,
various mainland groups and individuals expressed alarm that whites
comprised only a minority of the proposed state's population. Not all
such views came from the South.[44] Racial fears provided the foundation
for most mainland opposition to Hawaii until 1959.

A small minority of newspapers from various geographical areas of
the United States advocated that Hawaii be denied statehood. "Opponents, though in the minority, have a strong case," the *Portland Press
Herald* (Maine) remarked. It then analyzed the racial composition of
the territory and expressed consternation at the "thought of two Japanese Senators and two Japanese Representatives in Congress." The *Portland Evening Express* was even more explicit when it claimed that statehood should be denied because citizens of Japanese ancestry practiced
bloc voting: "The Japanese in the Hawaiian islands have reached high
subordinate positions, but so long as Hawaii is a territory they can reach
no higher. . . . In the Hawaiian islands the Japanese are still Japanese.
Their voting power is a bloc. . . . They vote as Japanese to strengthen
their tribal position."[45] The *Topeka Daily Capital* (Kans.) expressed fear
that Hawaii's admission would permit "a new influx of Japs into the
islands" and result in "a heavy infiltration of Orientals into our citizenship." Predictably, some Southern newspapers also argued strenuously
against Hawaii. After comparing Hawaii's position with that of the
Philippines prior to 1946, the *Jackson Clarion-Ledger* (Miss.) concluded
that independence would be the wisest political status for Hawaii, and
certainly in the best interests of the nation. The *Houston Post* (Tex.)
remarked that the advisability of admitting new states depended not on
physical size, population, or level of civilization, but rather on the
impact of new congressmen on the political strength of existing states. It
concluded that statehood should be denied because Hawaii's representatives in Congress might not support the interests of Texas.[46]

A preoccupation with states' rights was not restricted exclusively to
the old Confederacy. Some conservative Republicans from the more
populous Northern states were anxious that membership of the Senate
should not be extended. Along with many Southerners they argued that
Hawaii's admission would establish a dangerous precedent. Ignoring
the fact that Alaska was the only other incorporated territory, opponents maintained that Puerto Rico and the Virgin Islands as well as

Alaska would inevitably be admitted after Hawaii. Coudert, a lead-ing conservative Republican opponent and anti-communist crusader, stated:

> What we do on this bill is bound to . . . set a precedent for Alaska and Puerto Rico and such other insular territories as we now possess . . . [I]n considering the position we take on this bill we must consider all three of these dependencies and determine whether or not we are about to admit them to statehood with the two Senators that go with statehood, and the resultant further distortion of popular representation in Congress.

Many congressmen were determined to preserve the existing voting strength of their particular state in Congress. Coudert unashamedly expressed this position. He protested that the Hawaii bill would in effect grant Hawaii one senator for every 35,000 island citizens. In contrast, one senator from New York State represented at least 2,500,000 citizens. "My complaint is constitutional," Coudert stated.[47] Similar arguments had been levelled against the structure of the Senate when the Constitu-tion was originally drafted in the late eighteenth century, and they resurfaced whenever Congress debated the entry of new states.

Most opponents were far less concerned with constitutional principles than with the immediate political realities involved in protecting the existing social order of the South. During the Senate debate in 1948 the real obstacles to Hawaii's ambitions emerged as participants acknowl-edged openly that statehood for either Hawaii or Alaska was a central issue in the broader liberal-conservative battle over civil rights and desegregation. Hawaii was thus enmeshed in the most pervasive and bitterly contested aspect of American domestic politics after World War II. It is not possible to understand the delays and reversals which con-fronted Hawaii without appreciating this relationship.

In his state of the Union message in January 1948 Truman stressed that his desire was to insure that basic human rights were extended to all citizens. Acting on the advice of a Committee on Civil Rights which he had appointed twelve months earlier, Truman acknowledged that equal political, educational, and economic opportunities were not available to all citizens. He recommended a comprehensive policy aimed at eliminating discrimination based on "race, or creed, or color, or land, or origin."[48] His ten-point program included anti-lynching laws, abolition of poll taxes, equal voting rights, and an attack on dis-crimination in employment. New enforcement agencies were also rec-ommended, most notably a permanent Fair Employment Practices Commission, a Civil Rights Division in the Department of Justice, and a Civil Rights Commission. Truman undoubtedly had black Americans in mind when he made these proposals, but his program was not limited to this most oppressed group. "There still are examples—flagrant examples—of discrimination which are utterly contrary to our ideals," Truman proclaimed. "Not all groups enjoy full privileges of citizenship and participate in the government under which they live." An assault on these inequalities demanded full citizenship rights for all minorities, including the inhabitants of America's territories. Statehood for Hawaii was thus included as one part of Truman's comprehensive civil rights program.[49]

Given the conservative nature of Congress, the program was most ambitious. It was, however, more a statement of principles and intention than a confident legislative agenda: "I sent the Congress a Civil Rights message," Truman recorded in his diary. "They no doubt will receive it as coldly as they did my state of the Union message. But it needs to be said." When he left office five years later the legal structures of discrimination had scarcely been touched, let alone dismantled. But in the interval the proposition that blacks should be entitled to full equality had gained much wider support, and civil rights had emerged as a burning issue in virtually all facets of domestic politics. Truman was convinced that segregation, discrimination, and racial violence must be eliminated from the South, that "equality of opportunity for all human beings" must replace such a "radically wrong" system.[50] Cold war crises and McCarthyism diverted his second administration from civil rights questions, but these did not weaken his personal conviction nor reduce the determination of blacks and liberals to overthrow discriminatory practices based on race. The South, however, resisted vehemently all aspects of the civil rights program. The only part which actually came before Congress for serious debate during Truman's terms of office was statehood for the territories. Yet even this mild civil rights proposal confronted determined opposition from those who viewed it as a threat to their power in the Senate and an affront to their notions of white superiority. Even if Truman had not classified Hawaii as an explicit civil rights issue, it still would not have escaped the strategy of resistance adopted by Southern Democrats against any legislation which challenged their political power.

Southern representatives were less united in their opposition to Hawaii than were Southern senators. V. O. Key, Jr., observed in 1949 a fundamental similarity in the voting behavior of Southerners in both the House and Senate. However, Southern representatives spoke for smaller constituencies than senators, and often represented predominantly urban or black electorates. Thus, there was a tendency in the voting behavior of some Southern representatives to deviate from the voting pattern exhibited by most Southern senators.[51] Virtually all Southern senators opposed the admission of Hawaii because they believed Hawaii's Senate delegation would support the liberal Senate faction on civil rights, cloture, and labor legislation.[52] For some Southern members of the House, however, these considerations were not of over-riding importance. Hence a slightly smaller proportion of Southern representatives than Southern senators opposed Hawaii.

No part of Truman's optimistic program to end, or at least limit, discrimination was approved by the Senate during 1947–1948. Conservative Republicans and Southern Democrats easily defeated legislation on the floor, filibustered against it, or used procedural strategies in committee to stop it from reaching the floor of the Senate. Indeed, liberal proposals suffered defeat or emasculation in both chambers of Congress. The Alaska bill was unanimously reported by a subcommittee of the House, but it was not debated in either the House or the Senate during the Eightieth Congress. Legislation to establish a Fair Employment Practices Act, a major aspect of Truman's program on civil rights, was not debated in the Senate. The Republican leadership was not committed to this legislation, and Southern Democrats were expected to filibuster to defeat it. The House and Senate Judiciary Committees reported anti-lynching bills, but these were never voted on. Anti-poll tax legislation, which might have improved the voting opportunities of poor Southern blacks, managed to pass the House during 1945 and 1947. But the Dixiecrats easily averted a Senate vote on it. Liberals and civil rights supporters also failed to establish an effective cloture rule in the Senate.[53] In the following years Truman referred to his intransigent Southern colleagues variously, but privately, as "Dixiecrats," "Republicats" ("helpers" of the GOP who were nominally Democrats), or "Southern 'Democrats'—who are not Democrats." But they could not be dismissed as merely a disruptive minority faction of his party, for they effectively dictated the fortunes of the Democrats' legislative programs during Truman's two terms as president.[54]

"The informal conservative coalition of Southern Democrats and Northern Republicans," William C. Berman has observed, "remained powerful enough to hamstring and block all efforts to put new civil laws on the statute books."[55] The fact that the Senate refused to liberalize its rules governing filibusters both symbolized and confirmed the strength of conservatives. Key's pioneering studies have demonstrated that during 1933–1945, an odd confluence of circumstances sometimes compelled nearly three-quarters of the Southerners to join the Republicans in a coalition against non-Southern Democrats. After the New Deal and Roosevelt's death, Republican strength in Congress grew, while Southern Democrats sustained their strong minority influence. Southern Democrats strongly resisted civil rights, progressive labor legislation, and any extension of federal power at the expense of states' rights. Conservative large-state Republicans usually opposed labor interests and sought to minimize possible federal encroachments on states' rights.[56] To protect these interests effectively, conservatives had to maintain at least a veto power in the Senate. This was possible while the conservative coalition could sustain reasonable numbers in the Senate and rely on their existing right to invoke a filibuster or threat of filibuster against what they perceived as liberal proposals. Statehood for Hawaii thus had important implications for the future of national politics.

Southern opposition to Truman's civil rights program and related measures was intense and uncompromising. During 1948 an anti-civil rights faction bolted the Democratic party and established the Dixiecrat party. The Dixiecrats unsuccessfully contested the 1948 elections on a platform which called on all loyal Americans to support segregation and states' rights. Dixiecrat presidential candidate Strom Thurmond (S. C.) won a majority in four Southern states—Alabama, Louisiana, Mississippi, and South Carolina. But not all Southern Democrats were prepared to leave the party. Moreover, progressives under the leadership of Henry Wallace also split with Truman. Despite defections from the right and left, Truman won a substantial if unexpected victory over the very confident Republican candidate, Thomas E. Dewey. Black voters, encouraged by Truman's stand on civil rights, helped boost his margin of victory. The Democrats also gained control of both houses of Congress by large majorities.[57] But increased liberal strength on Capitol Hill during 1949–1950 could not salvage Truman's civil rights program—and hence statehood for Hawaii—from humiliating defeat at the hands of its intransigent opponents. Moreover, before any part of this program could be addressed by the new Congress, Hawaii was obliged to confront another emotive obstacle to admission—the charge that the island community was Communist controlled. This development linked Hawaii to another central aspect of the liberal versus conservative conflict in national politics during the late 1940s and early 1950s—the battle over McCarthyism and un-American activities.

Red Herrings: The Communist Issue and Statehood

Resistance to statehood within Hawaii did not derive exclusively from anxiety over growing Asian influences. It was also fed by anti-labor and anti-communist passions, feelings which were animated after 1945 by the cold war abroad and the growth of vigorous trade unions at home. Prior to World War II, as John Shoemaker observed, management in Hawaii equated unionism with radicalism and successfully exploited all its influence to restrict the organization of labor.[58] As we have seen, wartime conditions and martial law also stifled union growth. In January 1944 the only large union in the islands, the International Longshoremen's and Warehousemen's Union (ILWU) had only nine hundred members. Two years later, however, its membership had climbed to thirty-three thousand. Wage contracts negotiated by the ILWU during 1945–1946 increased the total wages of its members by $10 million.[59]

Labor's new authority resulted in part from the Hawaii Employment

Relations Act (the Little Wagner Act), passed in 1945, which extended the rights of collective organization and bargaining to agricultural workers. Large numbers of Japanese and Filipino laborers on sugar and pineapple plantations joined unions for the first time. Leaders of the ILWU, notably Jack Kawano and its regional director, Jack Hall, quickly recruited the majority of Hawaii's plantation workers and stevedores into this union. When the opportunity for labor to escape the tight controls of owners and managers finally arrived after the war, most unskilled workers eagerly joined the unions. War had helped weaken the grip of plantation owners and big business on labor. It also stimulated demands for a larger, more varied work force. These circumstances gave unions a unique opportunity to bargain effectively for increased wages and improved conditions. If management proved intractable, unions were willing to strike and hold out for a reasonable response. Not surprisingly, many planters, property owners, and businessmen found this new situation extremely unpalatable. At the same time, some were disturbed by the very fact that the Little Wagner Act had been approved by a legislature which the Republican party controlled. Fong has observed that this unexpected action implied that moderate elements now had real influence in the party and might no longer be subservient to wishes of those who had dominated island politics before the war.[60]

Immediately after Hawaii reverted to a peacetime economy, organized labor was prepared to challenge entrenched economic and political forces in the territory. Hall predicted early in 1946 that relations between employers and unions in Hawaii could not be forever harmonious. He anticipated that disagreements would develop between labor and employers, and warned of organized strikes.[61] According to Edward Johannessen, labor had acquired a new significance in the territory; almost everywhere in the economic, political, and social life of Hawaii its effects were evident.[62]

Before Pearl Harbor, as we have seen, it was labor that lost ground in strike situations; often strikes brought about the collapse of the union.[63] But the first major strike after the war, the sugar strike of 1946, suggested that relations between employers and employees had indeed entered a new phase. On September 1, 1946, twenty-one thousand sugar plantation workers, members of the ILWU, went on strike. Their action closed down thirty-three of the thirty-four plantations for seventy-four days.[64] Although the strike was led by Hall, a Caucasian, most of the workers involved were of Asian ancestry, principally Japanese or Filipinos (the latter comprised the largest single ethnic group on the plantations after the early 1930s). Non-Caucasian ethnic groups tended to sympathize with the strikers and supported the strike with financial contributions. By contrast, Caucasians tended to identify with and support the employer interests.[65] The unionists were successful in gaining increased wages and better working conditions. "The victory was a tremendous one," Hall claimed. "The interracial unity and determination of the workers to end for all time dictatorial control over their lives and destinies is the outstanding feature of the strike."[66]

Organized labor also made a successful bid for influence in the territory's legislature. Through its Political Action Committee the ILWU endorsed sympathetic candidates in the elections of November 1945. Most of these were members of the Democratic party, which won more seats at this election than on any occasion previously. But Farrington, a Republican, also accepted endorsement, as did a few other more liberal members of his party. Labor endorsed twenty-one candidates for the thirty-seat lower house. Sixteen of these were elected. In the Senate there were nine seats vacant. Labor endorsed seven candidates, six of whom were elected. Two ILWU officials, Joseph Alapai Kaholokula and Amos Ignacio, were elected to the House.[67] It should not be inferred that labor's support was an essential ingredient in the victories of all endorsed candidates however. Most of the majority Republican party won without it. What's more, Farrington and many other candidates would certainly have won irrespective of endorsement.

The growing political influence now exercised by labor and non-Caucasian citizens was, however, reflected in political gains made by the Democratic party. In the 1946–1947 session of the territorial legislature the Democratic party gained unprecedented support. Half of the members of the House of Representatives were Democrats. In the Senate, the Republicans maintained only a one vote majority. In contrast to the Caucasian-dominated Republican party, nonwhites comprised a majority of the Democratic party. It should be emphasized that all major ethnic groups were represented in each party. Nonetheless, as late as 1954 it was found that two-thirds of the members of the Democratic party were of Japanese or mixed ancestry. Republican party membership was two-thirds Caucasian, with the remainder largely of Hawaiian or Chinese extraction.[68] In the immediate postwar years these racial alignments were even more pronounced than in 1954.

Along with the many changes which transformed island life after 1945, war had a critical bearing on the fortunes of both organized labor and the Democratic party. One returned nisei veteran recalled the dissatisfaction of AJA soldiers even before going off to war, and explained their determination upon their return to change Hawaii's social structure. Murai, another influential nisei explained that during 1945–1946 all minority groups knew they were politically disadvantaged, and that in some way race was the causal factor. Politics, Murai said, appeared to be the most efficacious means to alter this situation. This conviction was not restricted to those of Japanese descent. The informal coalition largely responsible for rejuvenating the Democratic party comprised Burns, Hall, David Benz, Murai, Kido, Aoki, and Kawano, along with a prominent member of Hawaii's Chinese community, Chuck Mau. These allies were later referred to as the Burns faction or group; nevertheless in the immediate postwar months Mau was the group's unofficial political leader and Kawano its most successful union organizer. While based largely on the support of Japanese, Filipino, and to a limited extent Hawaiian and Chinese groups, public leadership of both labor and the new Democrats soon rested with two Caucasians, Hall and Burns. The two men very early reached an understanding that labor activities be reserved for Hall and party activities left to Burns.[69]

Building on contacts established with Japanese community leaders and members of the Emergency Service Committee during the war, Burns and his supporters began to build a new Democratic party through precinct and grass roots organization. Realizing that it would be impossible to infiltrate and transform the local Republican party, the Burns group focused exclusively on the disorganized Democratic party, which was run by a relatively small group of haoles. According to Kido, "[We] felt that if we got into the Democratic party we would be able to control it, set up a machinery and offer the people of Hawaii an alternative."[70]

Later, after memories of the bitterness of postwar politics had been dulled by time and success, Burns recalled the relative ease with which his so-called Young Turks had taken control of the Democratic party. In fact, it had been a divisive and protracted struggle for control, spanning the years 1946–1956. And it was a contest not only between old and new Democrats, but also an increasingly bitter struggle between the Burns group and a range of other independent and ambitious young liberals equally anxious to build and lead a revived party. Foremost among these were local lawyers Tom Gill and Vincent Esposito, and a controversial malihini and former marine by the name of Frank Fasi. If these men shared with Burns a desire to defeat the old order and transform island society, the deep divisions within the Democratic party during the next two decades suggested they had very little else in common.

It was the Burns faction that was largely responsible for challenging and gradually defeating the old guard Democrats, represented by Stainback, Charles and Harold Rice, and various members of the Heen, Trask, and Holt families. "I was called some pretty rugged names [by the old guard]," Burns recalled, "the least of which was 'communist.' " Largely untouched by the liberalism of the New Deal, both major parties in the islands remained fundamentally conservative, with those in authority still deeply suspicious of reform and reformers. There were perhaps many wealthy Caucasians who, like Elizabeth Farrington, found it difficult to understand Burns and his pragmatic brand of liberalism. "He was a haole, but he was against the haoles, some how," she recalled with dismay: "he was getting even with them." Local-born Caucasians were not expected to identify with, and certainly not champion, the underdog in society.[71]

In general, the Burns group was united by a common desire to create equality of opportunity and to get their fair share of power. Rather than being radicals, Communists, or fellow travellers, as they were so often portrayed, the leaders of this group were pragmatic, fairly cautious liberals, anxious to establish a genuine two-party system of government. While the individual political ambitions of the group's leaders, especially Burns and Inouye, cannot be ignored, it was united initially by a desire to help those who as yet had no spokesmen in government. Mau (one of the few prominent postwar Democrats of Chinese parentage), who later drifted away from the Burns faction, acknowledged that the early goals of his party were essentially limited to "getting good and fair employment—better wages, better working conditions for the ordinary working people" along with "more participation in government . . . for the working classes, the poor people." "We had a philosophy of government which [was] much more liberal [than old guard Democrats]," he observed. "They were more conservative. They were older. They had been in government for a long time. They of course knew the ropes and occasionally I guess they played around with the Republican gang." If old guard Democrats were disturbed by the challenge from within their party after 1945, the traditional backers of the Republican party were even more alarmed when this same challenge threatened their authority a few years later.[72]

After 1948 the strength of the Burns faction was further boosted as a large number of prominent veterans, notably Inouye and Spark Matsunaga, returned to the islands and joined the Democrats. Educated under the GI Bill, many of these veterans were of Japanese parentage. They were confident of their Americanism and eager to wrest power from the haole-dominated Republican party. Burns and his friends patiently cultivated their support. In contrast, Quinn has conceded, the Republicans ignored, even rejected them. Complacency and entrenched conservatism in the Republican party made the task of the young Democrats relatively easy. Even in the 1950s, Quinn recalled, most Republicans were complacent, believing their political preeminence was inviolable and eternal. Consequently, organization at precinct level was often neglected and campaigns were conducted in a very relaxed way. The party's hierarchy acted in the 1940s much as it had before the war: candidates were usually nominated and accepted without debate or an open contest; organizational support given to candidates was generally very poor, and the party remained biased against people of Asian descent, especially the AJAs. In the late 1940s only about 15 percent of Hawaii's electorate were registered members of either party. Despite this, the Republican legislature approved a "closed" primary bill in 1949. Fong recalled that this greatly inhibited his party's electoral fortunes, as it had the effect of reinforcing Merchant Street's authority over party organization and selection of candidates, and Merchant Street was largely unaware of the nature and aspirations of Hawaii's electorate. In general, traditional practices and traditional associations weighed heavily on the Republican party after the war. It failed to meet the challenges of a rapidly changing society and itself became a victim of these changes.[73]

The Young Turks of the Democratic party eagerly recruited new members. Oshiro's explanation of why he joined the Burns group typified the motives of many of its supporters, especially those of Japanese ancestry. "I don't like to say it this way but I identified myself with the working class, the have-nots and the ones who felt that they had not been treated fairly," he stated. "We were trying to improve the working conditions of the laboring people here," Murai, an established dentist, later explained. "Of course the majority of these were of Japanese ancestry, but it wasn't only them; it was the Filipinos, and the Chinese, and the rest of them." Those who identified with the Burns group accepted, albeit unofficially, a common program which, according to Kido, embraced the following aims: (1) assistance to returning veterans; (2) pursuit of equality of opportunity; (3) free public education and an expanded role for education in the lives of the people; (4) the achievement of improved standards of living via political strategies such as a minimum wage, better unemployment benefits, and the like; and (5) progressive taxation assessed, first, according to ability to pay, and, second, on real property. While most members of the group accepted that the land being monopolized by the few should be turned over to the many, they rejected the use of direct expropriation by legislative acts as a means to this end. Rather, "we wanted real property taxes based on highest and best use," Kido concluded. "Using that principle we could unfreeze a lot of land for residential purposes." In the context of island politics in the 1940s this was an ambitious program. And when viewed in conjunction with the demands then being made by a militant labor movement, it foreshadowed a period of uncertainty and dislocation in political and industrial life.[74]

As we have seen, war politicized Hawaii's Japanese, challenging them to reject the paternalism and exclusion of prewar life. But old political habits and attitudes, the results of a lifetime of indoctrination, died hard among local Japanese, Aoki recalled a generation later, "coming from the plantation community where all your life they have been telling you: 'Stay away from politics; leave politics alone; politics is dirty; we'll handle politics and we'll take care of these things for you.' "

More than any other experience, combat as an American soldier helped counter this conditioning. "When they throw you [into combat] . . . and you see your buddy getting killed right next to you and somebody gets maimed then you begin to wonder 'What the Hell am I doing here?' " Aoki commented. "And our attitude was that if we were good enough to be sent off to be killed and go to war, certainly we had a place for ourselves in our community in peace time." The impact of the war on nisei Americans, captured so forcefully by Aoki's comments, closely paralleled its impact on Afro-Americans throughout the nation. War highlighted a fundamental double standard in American life which meant that many minority Americans, while excluded from normal political and social equality, had nonetheless to be prepared to risk their lives for the nation. This gap between rhetoric and reality in national life was no longer accepted passively by Hawaii's Japanese. The benefits of organizing, of forming a cohesive and powerful political base from which to press for change became apparent to some, Aoki observed. Increasingly, the ILWU, the fledgling reformist arm of the Democratic party, and in an informal way the 442nd Veterans' Club provided this base. Immediate statehood was now a primary aim of these groups. More than any other event, statehood would symbolize and confirm the equality of Hawaii's nonwhites under the American Constitution. Throughout the postwar years statehood enjoyed more united support from local Japanese than from any other ethnic group.[75]

Organized labor was now confident, aggressive, and broad based; the Democratic party had emerged as a genuine alternative to the long-dominant Republicans; and Hawaii's Japanese were now politically active and self-assured. These were related aspects of underlying social, economic, and political changes which threatened the power and perhaps ultimately the wealth and status of the old, predominantly haole elite. These changes had a profound impact on every facet of the statehood campaign.

Resistance to these developments influenced the core of all local opposition to statehood. Very few residents were prepared to voice public hostility to statehood; but a much larger number uttered this sentiment in private. Opponents argued with some validity that people who resisted statehood, for whatever reason, would not declare their position publicly.[76] Stokes exaggerated greatly when he suggested that "implied threats and pressure tactics" or "fear . . . prevented many from expressing their opposition."[77] But it was clearly not expedient for business or community leaders to object. Sociologist Bernard Hormann observed that those who did not want statehood for racial reasons rarely dared to publicize this opposition.[78] Some businessmen, and perhaps some politicians, were reluctant to oppose it publicly because this might alienate the large Japanese ethnic group. Significantly, only one of the residents who presented negative testimony at the 1946 hearings had substantial business or political associations in the islands.[79] It was neither intelligent politics nor sound business practice to publicly oppose statehood after 1945.[80] The results of a ballot on immediate statehood conducted by the Honolulu Chamber of Commerce early in 1946 support this contention. Almost two-thirds of the 1,307 members of the chamber were Caucasians and part-Hawaiians.[81] Only 42 percent of the membership returned ballots, with 170 opposing immediate statehood. A majority of the negative returns were unsigned.[82] Although the Honolulu Chamber of Commerce was not a representative sample of the general population of Hawaii, these returns suggest that there was considerable minority opposition from business interests and whites in Honolulu at least. They also indicate that most opponents preferred to express their opinion anonymously or privately. Moreover, within this particular segment of Honolulu citizens, approximately one-third opposed immediate admission. Although only about 10 percent of the testimony presented to the 1946 subcommittee was negative, local opposition was possibly more widespread than was apparent during these hearings. The *Honolulu Advertiser,* which had never given unqualified support to immediate statehood, remarked after the 1946 hearings had ended: "It was unfortunate that opposing testimony was not better documented and more forcefully delivered. The underground of opposition confined itself to whisperings, and failed to make its point." An outspoken member of the territory's senate, William C. ("Doc") Hill (Rep., Hawaii), claimed that the majority was reluctant to express its true opinion on statehood. He alleged that thousands of local residents did "not voice their sentiments openly because of fear of political and economic retaliation at the hands of certain racial groups and certain politicians seeking to use the statehood issue for their own glory and political advantage." No evidence of such reprisals was ever uncovered. Nonetheless as William Quinn, the territory's last governor, later observed, until 1959 "the articulated opposition and the real opposition were two different things." Few people were prepared to acknowledge openly their belief that statehood would "turn Hawaii over to the Japanese."[83]

Concern with possible Japanese influence in the proposed state was generally expressed in an indirect, covert form. Opponents maintained that Hawaii was not sufficiently Americanized, and its various ethnic groups not adequately assimilated to warrant statehood. Almost invariably this view was supported by claims that citizens of Japanese extraction voted overwhelmingly along racial lines. In view of the political control exercised by the cohesive haole elite through the Republican party before the war, it was indeed ironic that the Japanese were now condemned for allegedly voting as a bloc. Charges of bloc voting by the Japanese were never substantiated. The 1946 subcommittee concluded that, at worst, some ambiguous evidence of bloc voting did exist, but that this had not assumed serious proportions. Patterns of voting behavior were generally consistent with those for mainland areas like New York or Chicago, which also had very mixed ethnic populations.[84]

After the war, as before, opposition to statehood was also linked to the issue of reapportionment. But only a minority of outer-island residents now felt strongly about the fact that statehood would guarantee new, more equitable electoral boundaries throughout the islands. By 1945 Oahu supported more than 60 percent of all registered voters, but elected less than half of the territory's legislature. Statehood would immediately remove this electoral bias. Hence the outer islands remained generally less enthusiastic than Oahu about statehood. Two senators from the outer islands—Harold M. Rice and Clarence Crozier —spoke against the resolution before the legislature in 1945. In the following years, the Senator from the Big Island, the island of Hawaii, Doc Hill, was the only outer-island representative to oppose statehood consistently in the legislature.[85] Overt local opposition increased considerably as soon as martial law ended, but it related primarily to particular ethnic, social, and economic groupings in the territory, not to any one geographic region. (In 1956, three years before statehood, those opposed to reapportionment finally lost their fight and the Democrat-controlled legislature instituted the first redistribution of electoral districts since the Organic Act of 1900.)

Local opposition to statehood was restricted almost exclusively to a small minority of only two groups, Hawaiians and Caucasians, who equated majority rule with domination by an alien, Asian population. Alice Campbell expressed this view rigidly and frequently in the following years. During the 1946 subcommittee hearings she stated forcefully that she opposed statehood "in any form and at any time." The 37 percent of Hawaii's population of Japanese descent, Campbell argued, represented a "menace" which was already apparent in every aspect of private and public life in the territory. "It is obvious," she concluded, "that in due time they will get a definite hold of the islands politically and economically." John Stokes, who had presented a similar view to the 1935 hearings, again echoed this argument in 1946. But he expressed the opinions of only a small fragment of local whites when he asserted emotionally that, under statehood, Caucasians in the territory "would be endlessly enslaved because the control by our Japanese overlords would be complete and permanent." He presented statistics which allegedly demonstrated that descendents of Japanese immigrants would control the proposed state: "it is the children and grandchildren of these enemy aliens who are about to dominate Hawaii's electorate." This reflexive hostility to full citizenship for Hawaii's Japanese was not widespread, but it was tenacious.[86]

Typical of this intolerant attitude was the opinion expressed by a former Republican committeewoman, Mrs. F. Bolte, to the 1948 House investigation. Her disjointed, emotive testimony alleged that statehood would permit the laboring class of Orientals to triumph politically and culturally in the islands. Alarmed by the fact that some Japanese communities remained separate from mainstream Hawaiian society, that many schools were attended largely by students of Japanese parentage, and that Japanese language radio broadcasts were still made, Mrs. Bolte suggested to visiting congressmen that they were ignorant of the true nature of Hawaii's society. Finally, she projected her racism onto the investigators, claiming that, "The Negroes to you people are not any worse than the Japanese to a lot of us people in the islands."[87]

Local statehood advocates claimed optimistically that 90 percent of Hawaii's people now favored immediate admission. But the House subcommittee was undoubtedly more accurate when it estimated that a majority of at least two to one wanted statehood.[88] Nonetheless this support was sufficient to convince Truman's secretary of the Interior that Congress should quickly admit Hawaii. "The period of apprenticeship served by the people of Hawaii should now be brought to a close," Krug stated, "and on the basis of the amply demonstrated readiness of Hawaii for statehood, the Congress should fulfill its early and reiterated pledges to admit the territory to the Union when it was qualified."[89] Statehood proponents were strongly encouraged by support from the Truman administration, and were no longer constrained by doubts previously expressed about the loyalty and Americanization of Hawaii's Japanese. "If the prerequisites for statehood have already been met in all other respects, and if the doubt as to the loyalty of a portion of our population has been allayed by the war," King asked a House investigating team, "then what remaining condition must we fulfill before we take our rightful place as the forty-ninth state?"[90] This question, in various forms, was repeated persistently during the following fifteen years. Yet those who felt threatened by Hawaii's so-called Japanese problem were not easily persuaded that war had demonstrated Hawaii's right to statehood.

Charges of future Japanese control were undemocratic, unfashionable, and impossible to substantiate. Hence many opponents preferred to argue, as they had before the war, that the unchecked economic power of the Big Five made statehood inappropriate. Certainly, as the House subcommittee acknowledged in 1946, the five major sugar agencies continued to dominate a substantial portion of the islands' economy. In addition, landholdings remained concentrated in the hands of a few.[91] Some protested that statehood would confirm the centralized economic and land control of these huge companies, and argued that it should be delayed until the economic fabric of the islands became more open and equal.[92] Yet as the *Advertiser* commented, for virtually all opponents "the financial superiority" of the Big Five "was of secondary importance to the numerical superiority of the Japanese."[93] Leading opponents ingeniously tried to attribute the economic supremacy of the white oligopoly to the support given it by local Japanese. Not surprisingly, they failed to identify the precise relationship which purportedly existed between these two very disparate groups.[94]

As we have seen, the Big Five did wield enormous power over Hawaii's economy and, to a lesser extent, its politics. Even in the late 1940s as Kido and many others have observed, Hawaii's social, economic, and political climate was distinct from that of the mainland: "it was a conservative community dominated by the oligarchy and anybody who spoke against it was ostracized and even penalized."[95] This assessment was not confined to Democrats or disgruntled nisei. It was certainly shared by some moderate Republicans, including Fong and at times Farrington, although those who aspired to office as Republicans were understandably reluctant to express such sentiments publicly. But as the Statehood Commission pointed out, questions of monopoly or elite control were not directly relevant to the statehood issue.[96] Certainly, the concentration of wealth and power in various mainland territories had not affected their demands for statehood in the nineteenth century. Indeed, in Hawaii's case it might reasonably have been expected that the increased local authority of a new state legislature would help to undermine the power of the few large corporations. Even if it is conceded that the influence of the Big Five was a legitimate issue in the statehood debate, the war had initiated changes which quickly challenged its traditional authority.[97]

The two major arguments made against Hawaii immediately after the war were fundamentally contradictory. Allegations that Japanese citizens would control the proposed state were clearly inconsistent with the contention that statehood should be denied because the Caucasian-owned sugar corporations exercised monopolistic economic control and undue political influence in the islands. Hostility to the alleged economic monopoly of the sugar corporations, however, was not a genuine preoccupation of many opponents. This was demonstrated conclusively when, after the outbreak of severe labor unrest, opponents suddenly ignored the alleged threat of big business and grasped instead onto a new issue calculated to appeal more effectively to influential haoles. It was now argued that the real threat to the islands came from the left, not the right. Against a background of growing cold war suspicions and national insecurity, opponents asserted that statehood would consolidate the economic and political control of the islands by militant left-wing, allegedly Communist-controlled labor unions.

Early in 1947 the commanding general of the Army in Hawaii presented Governor Stainback with a list of alleged Communists. (Just six years before, Army and FBI lists had resulted in the internment of locals allegedly sympathetic to Japan. Now the enemy within was Soviet communism and there were doubtless some in Hawaii who wished suspected Communists could be dealt with as promptly and simply as were the earlier Japanese suspects.) Among those nominated as Communists were Hall and Kawano, both close political associates of Burns and Mau. In April, Hugh Butler, the chairman of the crucial Senate Public Lands Committee, claimed that entry would be delayed until labor interests stopped controlling the territory's government. The following month he suggested that Hawaii be incorporated as a county of California.[98] During the House debate in June, some opponents argued that statehood should be denied until the influence of labor unions in the territory was reduced. Yet opposition based ostensibly on concern with the political and economic influence of labor was of little consequence during the first House debate. Indeed many opponents still argued that the Big Five exercised decisive power over the islands' economy and politics, and that statehood would simply consolidate this monopoly control of "labor, agriculture, manufacturing, banking, transport and public services."[99]

Consistency and understatement were never the hallmarks of arguments advanced by opponents. By late 1947 local and congressional opponents were asserting that communist influences in the territory should be removed before its relationship with Washington was changed.[100] After the House had passed the Hawaii bill in mid-1947, Governor Stainback apparently accepted this view and refused to endorse statehood. He now pledged to "unearth" the "dangers of Communism" in Hawaii and requested an investigation of the problem by the U.S. Department of Justice. (Old guard Democrats were no more sympathetic to the growing militancy of labor in the islands than were their counterparts in the Republican party.) At the same time some community leaders who had previously supported admission changed their public attitude. The "irresponsible actions of Union leadership," warned A. G. Budge, president of Castle and Cooke, would undermine Senate action. Others who had never embraced statehood were quick to exploit the growing furor over strikes and communism. For example, Campbell formed an Anti-Statehood Committee with an office in Honolulu. This organization was established, she claimed, in response to "many requests from Congressmen who opposed statehood and wanted detailed evidence to support their opinion."[101]

Caught between a personal commitment to statehood and mounting pressure from old guard Democrats as well as Republicans to expose communist and labor power in the islands, Farrington chose a compromise path. He requested a limited investigation of the issue, and suggested that the FBI make all records of Communists in the territory available to a local investigation committee.[102] Farrington was not anxious to alienate labor groups, as their support might later help him stem the tide of support for his Democratic rivals. Moreover, he recognized correctly that the communist issue could not be ignored or pushed aside, but had to be confronted openly if statehood was not to be further jeopardized.

Ever since he was first elected delegate in 1942, Farrington enjoyed wide popular support. He appealed not only to traditional GOP voters, but also to moderate labor groups and many newly mobile Asian voters. Unless the Democrats could make substantial inroads into this support they were condemned to the political wilderness, except in Honolulu City. When the communist issue surfaced dramatically after the war, some local conservatives felt betrayed by Farrington and the *Star-Bulletin*, claiming that Farrington and Allen had allied with the Communist dissidents within the Democratic party. Another islander, Joe Keenan, observed privately: "There is a weird combination between the owner and publisher of a newspaper, Farrington, who is a reactionary Republican," joining with the ILWU and Harry Bridges' "left-wing crowd for popular elections to attract the Japanese (almost 50% of the voters), the Chinese, and others of the yellow race." Such comments were racially as well as politically inspired. They were also wildly exaggerated, although Farrington did enjoy wide popularity and initially vacillated over the communist question. Unlike many fellow Republicans, Farrington was generally disturbed by the frequent accusations of communist which were levelled against labor organizers by big business interests. As a result, Elizabeth Farrington observed, he was "called a communist and everything else" by these very interests. Conscious of the likely adverse effects the highly volatile communist issue might have on the statehood drive and his own political survival, Farrington's *Star-Bulletin* cautioned local citizens against reacting hysterically to the real or fancied dangers of communism in Hawaii.[103] Later however, as support for the Democrats grew, his paper succumbed to these very pressures.

The infusion of the communist issue into the national debate on statehood did not create new resistance to admission. It did, however, make existing arguments against entry more effective and difficult to combat. It also made local opposition far more overt and confident. During subsequent years opponents emphasized that the question of statehood could not be viewed in isolation from the question of communist influence in the islands. Equal status in the Union and the right to influence national domestic or foreign policy, they argued, should be denied a territory dominated by un-American, subversive, communist interests. The effectiveness of this argument derived less from the actual extent of the influence of communism in Hawaii than from the anti-communist hysteria which poisoned the national political climate during the early years of the cold war and which reached its climax during the McCarthy era of the early 1950s.

Attempts to impose ideological consensus and expose activities perceived as disloyal or subversive predated America's entry into the war against Japan and the other Axis states. They also predated difficulties with the Soviet Union in Eastern Europe. In America, Louis Hartz has observed, socialism was a "national heresy." Certainly, the phenomenon now generally referred to as McCarthyism was not a brief aberration of the early cold war. Rather, as Robert Griffith and others have argued, "it was a natural expression of America's political culture and a logical though extreme product of its political machinery." The anti-communist persuasion and preoccupation with internal subversion reflected entrenched hostility to radicalism from the left, an irrational identification of all social change with communism, and a general susceptibility to conspiracy theories. The formal precursor of McCarthyism, the Dies Committee on Un-American activities was established late in the New Deal years, in 1938. It enjoyed strong support and adequate congressional funding in its attempt to expose groups and individuals "sympathetic with totalitarian ideology." In 1940 Congress passed the Alien Registration Act (or Smith Act) which prohibited the teaching or advocacy of the violent overthrow of the United States government, thereby establishing guilt by intent or association. The Un-American Activities Committee was made a standing committee of the House of Representatives shortly after the war.[104]

Cold war tensions quickly exacerbated distrust of communism and helped condition a widely held belief that Communists had infiltrated government, labor unions, and schools in the United States. The Mundt-Nixon bill of 1947 was perhaps the first decisive indication of the extent of anti-communist sentiment. Intended to secure swift prosecution of Communists and so-called subversives, this bill passed the House but was defeated in the Senate. In this year Truman established an order which permitted investigation of the loyalty of civil servants. As a result of these investigations 212 people were dismissed, but none was prosecuted immediately. Many Americans were apparently prepared to abandon parts of the nation's Constitution and deny full citizenship rights to those who espoused a conflicting ideology or supported a fringe political group like the Communist party. Well before Senator Joe McCarthy had begun his public crusade against "Communists," "liberals," and "subversives," Congress and the administration had moved to expose those who supported un-American causes. Conservatives like Democrat Pat McCarran, chairman of the Senate Judiciary Committee, did not need any prompting from McCarthy. Nor did they have to await the groundswell of anti-communism which accompanied the "loss" of China late in 1949 or the frustrations of Korea in the early 1950s. Truman's election victory of 1948, along with growing liberal support for civil rights and Soviet gains in Eastern Europe, had convinced many conservatives by 1947–1948 that America was being eroded from within. McCarran, for example, was anxious to stamp out the "Communist-liberal heresy of racial equality," and to expose those officials who had allegedly appeased communism in Europe and Asia.[105]

Hawaii was isolated geographically, but not ideologically. Certainly, it was sufficiently Americanized to share fully in the surge of anti-communism which affected the nation beginning in the late 1940s. Indeed in some respects Hawaii's experience was a prelude to events in the United States generally. Anti-communist sentiment and arguments were important ingredients in the strategy invoked against Hawaiian statehood, especially in the Senate.

As we have seen, the House approved Hawaii in mid-1947. The Senate, however, did not begin preliminary committee hearings on the bill until early the following year. The Statehood Commission attempted to exploit this new situation. It engaged the Holst and Cummings advertising agency, at a cost of three thousand dollars per month, to direct publicity in Washington during the first months of 1948. New campaign material was collected and distributed. Three local Republicans were sent to Washington to urge national Republican support "strictly on a party line." In addition, on September 25, 1947, the commission had appointed six subcommittees to draft various sections of a proposed state constitution. Local proponents were confident that these initiatives would ensure favorable action by the Senate in 1948. But the *Hilo Tribune Herald* was more realistic. It acknowledged that major obstacles remained and warned that deliberations on statehood might hinge on considerations of political pragmatism rather than on the merits of statehood itself.[106]

Conducted against a background of growing concern over internal subversion and the cold war, the Senate investigations of Hawaii in early 1948 could not avoid the deep conflicts between labor and capital or charges that Hawaii was Communist controlled and a threat to national security. Less than 10 percent of the evidence taken by Cordon's committee was negative. But a larger number opposed admission before this Senate hearing than during the previous two House investigations conducted after the war. To assess more accurately the state of private opinion in the islands, Cordon requested that citizens submit their views in writing to him. He gave an assurance that names would not be made public unless otherwise stipulated by correspondents. According to Cordon, his appeals inspired a substantial influx of letters. His survey revealed that 58 percent favored immediate statehood, 40 percent were opposed. Almost half of the correspondents who opposed statehood cited the racial character of the territory as the reason for their position. In addition, some objected to statehood because the Japanese allegedly practiced bloc voting. The communist problem in Hawaii was cited by approximately one-quarter of those against statehood.[107] If this evidence is accepted as representative, then clearly racial considerations remained the basic reason for local opposition.

After the war, however, opponents increasingly argued that their position derived from fear of communism in the islands. The *Houston Post* predicted in 1947 that this issue did not promise to enhance the chances of statehood in Congress.[108] Communism provided a convenient new focus for opponents in both Hawaii and Washington. For example, Hill informed Cordon that statehood should be delayed until the extent of communist influence in the islands could be more clearly assessed. "There is a sort of tradition here that if you are not in favor of statehood immediately . . . you are more or less a traitor and disloyal," he claimed. "That has been worked up by Delegate Farrington mostly. I think that some day we should have statehood, but I do not think we should have it now. My main reason is the I.L.W.U. and the Communist situation." In a letter to Butler, Hill asserted that the Federal Bureau of Investigation, Stainback, and Army and Navy intelligence were familiar with the "dangerous inroads" made by communism in the territory. Hill contended that statehood would give a subversive element an opportunity to dominate the proposed state government.[109] Previously, however, Hill had commented that, "A Jap is a Jap even after a thousand years and can't become Americanized."[110] While Hill later regretted this indiscretion, there can be little doubt that many haoles still shared his opinion of the Japanese, or that some accepted his view that un-American ethnic and communist groups were inseparable elements of one general problem.

Hill's views were supported in public by a small minority of local citizens. For example, Walter Dillingham, president of the Hawaiian Dredging and Construction Company and possibly the richest Hawaii-born citizen in the territory, argued that maintenance of territorial status was necessary to stop labor leaders from gaining "economic, political and social control of the islands." For him, the only valid interests in the territory were employer interests, and he opposed statehood because it would possibly reduce the influence of business interests in Hawaii's government. According to Elizabeth Farrington, Dillingham and other wealthy residents were comfortable with territorial rule because it enabled them to strike bargains directly with officials in Washington and bypass interference from elected representatives in either Honolulu or Washington. In a similar vein, Samuel P. King has commented: "Walter Dillingham had better connections in Washington than most States: and he could see that statehood would decrease his influence, rather dramatically." Fuchs has inferred that Dillingham also opposed statehood because he believed it would strengthen Oriental influence in local government.[111] Hawaiian Airlines employee Larry Powell argued that statehood should be opposed simply because "every one of those who have been accused of being Communists or subversives and every 'liberal' is radically in favor of statehood." Campbell attempted to correlate the growth of labor unions with the increased political and economic influence exercised by citizens of Japanese ancestry. Ignoring his previous opposition to the Big Five, Stokes informed Cordon that statehood should not be granted because the Communist-controlled ILWU had all but taken over the Democratic party, and had insinuated itself into the Republican party. Such assertions gained at least oblique support in the influential *Honolulu Advertiser*, which was partly owned by Lorrin P. Thurston. Incensed by the *Advertiser*'s position on statehood, Honolulu's Democratic mayor John Wilson purchased space in other island newspapers to denounce Thurston as "Public Enemy No. 2" of statehood—second only to Butler, the unofficial leader of opponents in the nation's Senate.[112] Locally, the communist issue stimulated fresh debate over who would control the future state and permitted opponents to focus on more palatable arguments than those relating exclusively to the political and economic power of the islands' Japanese. Nationally, allegations of communist subversion provided a convenient rationalization for self-interested opposition based on party affiliations, racial prejudices, or states' rights considerations.

The small number of witnesses who informed Cordon that communism was "threatening Hawaii's economic structure and future welfare" failed to document precisely the extent of communist influence. Cordon reported early in 1948 that although there were active Communist organizers in Hawaii, as throughout the nation, the evidence did not support the allegations that communism exerted extreme influence in the islands. As far as Cordon could determine, there were less than one hundred Communists in Hawaii. No evidence was presented to Cordon proving the infiltration of Communists into the legislature or any elective office in the territory.[113] Even Thomas O'Brien, author of *The Plot to Sovietize Hawaii* (1948), conceded: "There are probably comparatively few Communist agents in the Territory."[114]

Nonetheless, statehood opponents and anti-labor factions maintained that communism constituted a real threat to the political and economic security of the islands. Stainback, a conservative Democrat who had reputedly appointed more Republicans than Democrats to high posts and through whose long service to the interests of the Big Five, some said, the Democratic party had nearly been extinguished,[115] now charged that communism was rampant in Hawaii:

> The I.L.W.U. Union which controls the labor in the production of sugar, pineapples and our marine transportation system, is completely dominated

by Communists. All their leaders are actively enrolled Communists, most of them from the Mainland, with a number of local lieutenants. We also have some in our University and among our school teachers.

O'Brien contended that although true card-carrying Communists constituted a small minority in the territory, these few Communists had been able to seduce both the professional liberals and a number of discontented workers.[116] If actual Communists couldn't be found they were simply invented by those determined to unearth a threat from the left. The tactics of smear, exaggeration, and unsubstantiated accusation later identified with McCarthyism were introduced into Hawaii during 1948–1949.

The tenacity and frequency of these accusations reflected deep tensions within the local Democratic party and growing hostility from a majority of Democrats to their titular leader in the islands, Stainback. These strains emerged as labor groups and Japanese Americans began to use the Democratic party as a vehicle for progressive industrial and social change. By 1948, however, this new liberal faction met open resistance from an entrenched, conservative, and largely haole minority within the party. This conflict remained unresolved until Stainback was replaced in 1951. In the interval, the Central Committee of the Democratic party, which was now dominated by Burns' Young Turks, urged Truman to dismiss the governor whom Roosevelt had appointed in 1942. The charges laid against Stainback in petitions to the president, secretary of the Interior, and Democratic National Committee were very serious. But most focused on his political activities in relation to the fortunes of the Democratic party, not administrative inefficiency or impropriety. Among the charges made were allegations that he had failed to give active support to local Democrats; appointed mainly Republicans to high offices; supported efforts to destroy labor unionism; blatantly encouraged untrue and imagined allegations of Communist infiltration in the Democratic party; and undermined Hawaii's statehood prospects through his refusal to back appeals for statehood to Congress. The Truman administration was initially unimpressed by these charges. It remained sympathetic to Stainback's private reports which played up the threat of communism to the islands and the local Democratic party. In May 1948, for example, he wrote Undersecretary of the Interior Oscar Chapman: "As feared, the communists have taken over the so-called 'Democratic' Party organization in Hawaii—lock, stock and barrel." Stainback was adamant that the recent convention of his party had been controlled by Hall, who was supported by "enrolled communists, the fellow travellers, the sympathisers, the members of the I.L.W.U. who were controlled by communist leaders, and those joining up with these leaders through ignorance or political ambition."[117]

While unaware of the actual contents of Stainback's reports to Washington, liberal Democrats correctly suspected that they gave a very biased view of local events, and an unsympathetic picture of those younger party members anxious to wrest power from the conservatives. In an attempt to counter Stainback's influence (particularly over appointments), Burns and Mau travelled to Washington to meet with and lobby administration officials and leading Democrats in Congress. It was their hope that they could demonstrate that the local party was viable and vital, Burns recalled. Apart from a meeting with Truman, Burns established direct and lasting contacts with various White House aides and labor union leaders. Building on these during 1948–1950, the Burns faction gradually came to control Democratic party patronage in the islands.[118]

If Stainback—along with other local conservatives from both parties —was disturbed by an alleged threat from the left, he was equally alarmed by the spectre of growing Japanese political influence in the islands. During 1947 he had warned Washington confidentially that "the communist drive . . . is making great headway, particularly among the Japanese." He identified as the most ominous development in local politics, "the inroads of communism upon the Japanese of the community, particularly those connected with labor organizations." This was a wild assertion indeed. It confused the new political and industrial assertiveness of Hawaii's nisei population with radical socialism. Yet when the FBI finally identified a handful of islanders as Communists, Japanese Americans were conspicuously underrepresented in the list, while haoles were overrepresented. Stainback, like many defenders of the old order in Hawaii, was convinced that the Japanese were a particularly vulnerable and embittered group. He asserted the extreme susceptibility of the Japanese to communism, and informed the Truman administration:

> Because the early Japanese here, who were plantation laborers, lived pretty much under a feudal system and since the younger generation has become educated and their scale of life has risen, they are considerably embittered, many of them connecting the white race and its government with tyranny and oppression. Moreover, the communists are using as propaganda the appeal to race prejudice, strenuously contending that the Japanese are discriminated against in the employment of labor on the plantations and elsewhere, that they are not given the better paid positions even though qualified therefore. *Whatever the reason*, the Japanese have proved very susceptible to the communistic propaganda and, as one communist stated, Hawaii is the "most fertile field for communism in the whole nation."

When complaining about Communist domination of the local Democratic party convention a year later, Stainback again betrayed his preoccupation with the racial characteristics of those on the left. "Incidently," he told Chapman, "practically no white men were elected to any positions, as the whole communist appeal to race hatred was very effectively used."[119]

At most, only limited and sometimes contradictory evidence existed to support the charge that Hawaii was heavily influenced by Communists. Even if such evidence had existed, it should have been immaterial in a society ostensibly wedded to principles of free speech and free association. Nonetheless, in late 1947 Dr. and Mrs. John Reinecke were suspended from their teaching positions by the Territorial Board of Commissioners of Public Instruction because of their alleged associations with the Communist party. Some members of the Hawaiian Civil Liberties Committee, formed to defend the Reineckes, were later also identified as Communists. The House Un-American Activities Committee unanimously agreed in 1950 that the Civil Liberties Committee was "a subversive organization initiated and operated by communists for the sole purpose of expanding the influence of the small communist minority in the Territory of Hawaii." Leadership of the powerful ILWU was also widely assumed to be Communist. In 1944 the ILWU was cited by a special Congressional Committee on Un-American Activities as having a solidly entrenched Communist leadership. Harry Bridges, national president of the ILWU-CIO, was classified by anti-statehood and anti-labor factions as a Communist. The United States Supreme Court, however, later ruled that the charge that Bridges was a Communist had not been substantiated. Hall and other union leaders were also classified as Communists by local Army intelligence sources, and usually identified with the Communist party by statehood opponents, the local press, and later by the House Un-American Activities Committee. Indeed, during 1948 O'Brien and a former Communist Ichiro Izuka independently claimed that a majority of ILWU officials were members of the Communist party. Hall, Charles Fujimoto, Dwight Freeman, Ralph Vossbrink, and Robert McElrath were among the labor leaders named by Izuka and O'Brien.[120]

Allegations that the Democratic party was dominated by Communists or sympathizers of communism were never substantiated. In May 1948 the Democratic Party Convention repudiated the anti-labor strategy promoted by a conservative faction of Democrats led by Stainback, Heen, and Chief Justice James L. Coke. But an attempt by the ILWU to gain control of the party failed. Independent Democrats won most of the critical votes taken at the convention. The influence of organized labor within the Democratic party was strong, but not dominant. Former Communist Kawano stated that only eight delegates seated at the convention were Communists. Thus Communists constituted less than 5 percent of all delegates seated. (In contrast, Stainback informed Washington that ninety-one of the five hundred delegates were Communists, and that, in league with those sympathetic to them, they had a two-to-one margin of control at the convention.) Liberal Democrats were now well aware that communism had become their party's Achilles heel, and they grasped every opportunity to discredit it. "The Democrats made a point throughout the Convention of denouncing Communism and also the Republicans for 'smearing' the Democratic Party with a communist taint," Riley H. Allen, editor of the *Star-Bulletin* wrote Farrington in Washington. "In view of the Democrats' utterances," Allen concluded, "the Republicans are not going to find it easy to identify the Democratic Party with the Communist Party."[121]

Yet the extent of alleged communist influence in the Democratic party remained a major issue in Hawaiian politics. Statehood opponents, anti-labor interests, and opponents of the Democratic party relied heavily upon this issue to avert statehood, defend the interests of employers, and retard the appeal of the Democratic party to the local electorate. Republicans certainly felt that the communist issue could be used to electoral advantage; but it was a double-edged sword. By exaggerating the menace of communism many Republicans and old guard Democrats gave credence to the anti-statehood campaign and risked losing the electoral support of sincere statehood proponents. Hence Farrington and some pro-statehood Republicans were ambivalent over the issue. Most Democrats, like Honolulu's outspoken Mayor Wilson, identified all those who exaggerated the threat of subversion from within as opponents of statehood. A trenchant critic of Stainback's "indifference and neglect" of his party, Wilson asserted that a majority of people who express "fear of growing Communist activities in the territory as a basis of their opposition" to statehood "do not honestly believe in any Communist menace here but are using this red herring in their actual fear of a curtailment of the present political power of big-business."[122] Representatives of labor asserted that attempts to identify unions with communism were calculated to engender a generalized atmosphere of hysteria, and thus undermine the interests of labor organizations and the Democratic party.[123]

During elections for the territory's legislature in 1948 the communist bogey was exploited with some effect by elements of the Republican party. More damaging than GOP tactics, however, were the internal divisions within Democratic ranks over the extent and nature of communist influence in their own party. Stainback led the conservative faction. Prominent Democrats like Wilson and Mau were, he alleged, communist sympathizers. In the same unsubstantiated way he charged the Democrats' new national committeeman, Charles E. Kauhane, with being "completely subservient to Hall and his communist gang."[124] If the governor was alarmed by the strength of the left in his party, he was, as indicated earlier, also concerned that few "white men" held influential posts within it.[125] There were many who shared Stainback's exaggerated views. The *Honolulu Advertiser*, which generally reflected the attitudes of conservative Republican party and business interests, stated early in 1948 that "left-wing democracy" was being perpetrated on the people of Hawaii:

> . . . we dislike Harry Bridges so roundly and distrust him so deeply that we want no part of him or his stooges controlling our political life. Harry and his nefarious C.I.O. are interlopers in these fair islands, preaching an alien ideology, to wit, class consciousness, class hatred and class strife, stirring up trouble by needless and disruptive strikes with a view to ruining private enterprise and setting up state socialism, with a dictatorship of the proletariat.[126]

Organized labor had arrived late in the territory. Nevertheless the reaction to it, in terms of the slogans and tactics of McCarthyism, took root relatively early in the fertile soil provided by bitter conflict between big business and newly emergent working groups. Despite the strong national trend toward the Democratic party, in the elections of late 1948 island Democrats suffered severe losses. The gains made in 1946 were reversed as the GOP won a House majority of ten and a Senate majority of three. In addition, Farrington won a landslide victory over his rival Burns, winning more than two-thirds of the vote.[127] As mainland liberals were shortly to learn, communism was a damaging electoral issue for the Democratic party. Allegations that the territory's Democrats were sympathetic to and influenced by communism were the major issues in the election campaign of 1948. As indicated previously in this chapter, the Republicans exploited communism, while the Democrats split over it. After their election defeat some Democrats charged Stainback with openly supporting fabrications of communist infiltration of the party.[128] Farrington, ever eager to promote statehood, interpreted his massive victory as a clear and enthusiastic endorsement of immediate statehood, and proof that communist influence in the territory posed no threat to its government.[129] Yet the fact that Republicans had partly based their election campaigns on opposition to communist and left-wing labor influence in the territory gave some credence to the arguments advanced by opponents of statehood.

It should be emphasized, however, that many local residents who opposed the so-called subversive communistic influence in labor unions also supported statehood. Farrington's *Honolulu Star-Bulletin*, for example, simultaneously promoted statehood and denounced left-wing influence in local unions.[130] Nonetheless during 1948 and after, local and congressional opponents of statehood attempted to equate support for statehood with tacit sympathy for the interests of labor and communism in Hawaii.[131] As previously indicated, local opponents were determined to preserve the political, economic, and racial status quo. The question of who should rule at home was more important to opponents than the issue of self-government and equal citizenship for Hawaii's people. Similarly, congressional opponents were much more concerned with political and sectional control in Congress than with granting full democratic rights to Hawaii. Both groups seized enthusiastically on any issue which might delay change. Available evidence suggests that the problem of communism in Hawaii was comparatively no greater than in any other part of the United States. Nonetheless, during 1948 the communist issue became the dominant, overt argument employed both locally and in Congress against Hawaii's efforts to gain statehood.

Cynical Politics: Eighty-first Congress

The Democrats dominated both chambers of the Eighty-first Congress, 1949–1950. In contrast, Hawaii's political complexion was again over-whelmingly Republican. Nonetheless, when Truman reiterated his ten-point civil rights package early in 1949 he included statehood for Hawaii and Alaska. Early in the new session seven Hawaii statehood bills were introduced in the House and two in the Senate. Farrington and Senator Estes Kefauver (Dem., Tenn.), one of the few Southerners committed to statehood, introduced identical bills in the House and Senate. A protracted legislative battle was foreshadowed, however, when a leading opponent, Senator Butler, introduced a bill to grant Hawaii only one voting member in the House of Representatives and the right to elect its own governor.[132] Opponents were clearly deter-mined not to add any new members to the Senate. Communism, it seems, was only a threat if Hawaii sent senators to Washington.

Mau claimed that he and Burns were responsible for the politically astute choice of Kefauver, a prominent Southerner, as leader of the Democratic supporters in the Senate. Island Democrats were anxious indeed to be identified with statehood and to reap the electoral harvest which might accrue if they could break the congressional deadlock over the issue. Farrington's position was perhaps more delicate. He was obliged to initiate or accept tactics involving Democrats, as his fellow Republicans did not control Congress. But he was anxious that progress on statehood be seen to be a result of his endeavors and Republican sup-port, not Democratic initiatives. In the short-term, however, neither party was able to exploit statehood successfully. Democrats were em-barrassed by the intransigence and overt racism of most Southern repre-sentatives of their party. Republicans were equally disturbed by the inflexibility and narrowness of their party's old guard.

Those Republicans opposed to or ambivalent about immediate state-hood conveniently blamed "lousy goddam Dixiecrats" for defeat in

Congress. In response, island Democrats charged local Republicans, including Farrington and King, with insincerity because they only supported enabling legislation in Congress. Unlike an admission bill (which Burns later successfully introduced), enabling legislation required approval by the infamous Rules Committee before it could be debated. During 1947–1948, Farrington had rejected suggestions that he introduce an admission bill, believing that it was a questionable procedure which would simply be interpreted on Capitol Hill as a subterfuge. In the absence of a drafted and approved constitution for the proposed state, Farrington was correct to maintain that Hawaii was not yet in a position to justify an admission bill. After the Constitutional Convention of 1950 this situation no longer applied. Local Democrats from the Burns camp argued that Farrington's position betrayed the ambivalence of many island Republicans on statehood: it reflected a pattern which persisted until the Republicans lost office. Anxious to avoid the charge that the Southern racist wing of their own party had perennially delayed statehood, local Democrats later claimed that many powerful members of the GOP in Hawaii were for statehood in public, but against it in private. It was also alleged that while in Washington the Farringtons and their aides had totally ignored the Southern bloc. This alleged reluctance to cultivate broad regional and bipartisan support had little actual bearing on the fate of statehood legislation. It did, however, provide the Democrats with additional ammunition in the debates over congressional strategy. Farrington also refused to amend the statehood bill to give Hawaii one (not two) members in the House of Representatives. Democrat opponents immediately claimed that this inflexibility was another deliberate, if subtle, device for galvanizing opposition to the legislation in Congress. At worst, Democrats charged, Farrington and his wealthy GOP backers were opposed to immediate statehood. At best, the Republican delegate was a poor strategist and ineffectual lobbyist. While some local newspapermen privately endorsed this assessment, the heavily pro-Republican island press largely ignored the whole issue.[133]

Before late 1948 both national parties had accepted only eventual statehood planks in their platforms. As a delegate to the 1948 Democratic National Convention, however, Mau managed (after an exhaustive struggle) to have his party adopt an immediate statehood plank. "We felt it was very important," he later observed. "Because if the Democrats were to build their political strength in Hawaii we should be the first of the political parties to get that plank in. . . . It showed the ordinary people in Hawaii that the Democrats in Hawaii at least cared for them." Acceptance of this plank helped vindicate the activities of the Young Turks, and further boosted membership of their party.[134] But Farrington's hold on the position as delegate to Congress remained fast.

Most electors accepted that he was a sincere advocate of statehood and believed his moderate tactics would quickly win admission.

If most young island Democrats were anxious to use statehood as a vehicle for equalizing their society, they were also determined to exploit the issue electorally. To achieve this it was essential that the national Democratic party not be identified, through its reactionary Southern faction, as the principal opponent of Hawaii. The day after Truman's second inauguration, Burns and Mau again made personal contact with political influentials in Washington. Aware that statehood was a civil rights issue, they concentrated initially on liberals, beginning with Hubert Humphrey. Humphrey advised them that statehood was contingent upon winning over the Southern intransigents who had recently walked out of the national convention: "Without their support, it's dead." In the following decade Burns and other local Democrats followed this advice religiously. "We took that cue" and "remembered it well," Mau recalled. "And that is why [Burns] . . . made friends with speaker Rayburn and Lyndon Johnson and other Southern Senators. And he concentrated on them." These lobbying activities were further expanded after Burns became Hawaii's delegate to Congress in 1957.[135]

By early 1949 the Statehood Commission accepted that publicity alone could not guarantee action in Congress. It eagerly supported the lobbying activities of Democrats, especially Burns and Mau, as well as those of prominent Republicans like Farrington and the new chairman of the commission, King. Also, McLane had by now developed many influential contacts. Despite growing frustration with the cynicism of politics on Capitol Hill, he pursued his lobbying activities with commendable enthusiasm. During the Eighty-first Congress the commission received $136,000 from the legislature, maintained its offices in Honolulu and Washington, and flooded Capitol Hill and newspaper offices with information. The territory's legislature again passed resolutions asking Congress for immediate statehood. The only dissenting vote in either chamber was cast by Doc Hill.[136] Again the Statehood Commission expressed confidence that Hawaii was nearer than ever to statehood. In March 1949 separate Hawaii and Alaska bills reached the powerful House Rules Committee. The *New York Times* immediately observed that there was no justification for the House and the Senate to delay in accepting Hawaii as a state.[137]

However, the statehood bill made no further progress in either chamber of Congress in 1949.[138] A poll conducted by the Hearst newspaper group in August 1949 indicated that a solid majority of the House not only favored statehood for Hawaii, but was amenable to voting on it in the current session. McLane estimated that 244 members of the 435-member House would vote for statehood in 1949.[139] Yet a majority of the Rules Committee refused to report Hawaii. Republican members of the committee decided to block any action on Alaska until Hawaii was reported separately. But Democrats comprised a majority of the committee and they united to promote Alaska before Hawaii. A further barrier resulted from the fact that the committee chairman, Adolph J. Sabath (Dem., Ill.), and four of its Southern Democrat members—Cox (Ga.), Howard Smith (Va.), William Colmer (Miss.), and John Lyle (Tex.)—implacably opposed the admission of either territory.[140] However, some House Democrats, even a few from Southern states, supported the separate admission of Republican-dominated Hawaii. The chairman of the House Public Lands Committee, J. Hardin Peterson (Dem., Fla.), attempted to discharge the bill from further consideration by the Rules Committee. "Though there is considerable support in the House for action . . . to get the Hawaii statehood bill to the House floor where it is quite certain of passage," McLane informed the Hawaii Statehood Commission, "it is apparent that many House members are reluctant to invoke discharge petitions." In July Peterson conceded that there was no prospect of action during the first session of the Eighty-first Congress.[141]

The Democratic House leadership was reluctant to promote the immediate separate admission of Hawaii. House Speaker Sam Rayburn (Dem., Tex.) indicated to the Hearst poll that he was undecided on statehood. The *Washington Post*, however, reported that Rayburn was definitely opposed. Majority Leader John McCormack (Dem., Mass.) supported statehood but was undecided about bringing it to a vote in 1949. Partisan politics doubtless induced this convenient ambivalence, which now afflicted most liberal Democrats.[142] Hawaii enjoyed stronger backing from Republicans than from Democrats. Most Democrats endorsed the joint admission of Alaska and Hawaii, or opposed the entry of either territory. A few only supported Democrat-dominated Alaska. Southern Democrats, of course, overwhelmingly opposed both territories. Early in 1949 the Democratic administration pressed for consideration of Alaska before Hawaii. Combined Republican and Southern Democratic opposition nullified this strategy. The Rules Committee took no action on Alaskan statehood during 1949.[143] Opponents of both territories combined with a majority of Democrats who opposed the separate admission of Hawaii and with a majority of Republicans who opposed the separate admission of Alaska to avert House debate on either territory.

In the Senate, the Democrats refused to schedule debate on Hawaii until the House had acted. Nonetheless, Senate opponents were not inactive. While the Hawaii bill was before the House Rules Committee, Butler reported to the Senate Interior and Insular Affairs Committee on an investigation he had conveniently undertaken in Hawaii late the previous year. His investigation began shortly after the Alger Hiss case

broke in August 1948. This protracted, celebrated episode brought the
New Deal liberal into disrepute as an alleged spy and communist sym-
pathizer. More than any single event, the Hiss affair focused national
attention on internal security. The fact that this preoccupation was
exaggerated and largely without foundation did not in any way retard
its influence on the nation's mood. Amid mounting controversy fanned
by the Hiss case, Butler began the third Senate investigation of statehood for Hawaii. He was implacably opposed to statehood and, as
chairman of the Interior and Insular Affairs Committee, was determined to exploit the emotive internal subversion issue for cynical political ends. Conservative Republicans in the islands were doubtless delighted when Butler scheduled his investigation to coincide with the
campaign for the local elections of 1948. During November he conducted seventy-seven confidential interviews in Hawaii and accepted
public testimony from more than one hundred additional witnesses. But
his investigation did not focus on statehood per se. As the title of his
subsequent report suggested, its central concern was "Communist Penetration of the Hawaiian Islands." Butler's visit and enquiries were front-
page news. Few local proponents doubted that he would unearth sufficient people concerned about Japanese or union influences to justify a
negative report. Predictably, however, Butler's report was not made
public until June 1949, a few days before Congress was again due to
consider statehood legislation.

Butler recommended without equivocation that statehood for Hawaii
be "indefinitely deferred."[144] A few weeks previously the House Public
Lands Committee had also, if unwittingly, fuelled the controversy on
internal subversion. Its report conceded that the extent of communist
influence in the territory had not been fully ascertained, but concluded
that "the people of the territory were alert to the problem and would be
better able to cope with it as a State than as a Territory."[145] Butler's findings could clearly not have been issued at a more opportune time for
those determined to defeat Hawaii.

In seven thousand words of unrelenting hyperbole, Butler charged
that "international revolutionary communism has a firm grip on the
economic, political and social life in the Territory." The Japanese might
not have sabotaged the United States at Pearl Harbor, but foreign influences were clearly undermining internal security and threatening
America's position in the cold war against the USSR. "Since VJ-day, in
September 1945," Butler charged,

> the Hawaiian Islands have become one of the central operations bases and a
> strategic clearing house for the Communist campaign against the United
> States of America. By the well known infiltration tactics of world Commu-
> nism, a relative handful of Moscow adherents in the islands, operating

chiefly through the International Longshoremen's and Warehousemen's
Union, has persistently sabotaged the economic life of the Territory. This pre-
meditated campaign of stoppages, and violent racial agitation, is inspired,
managed, directed and financed largely through the international headquar-
ters of the I.L.W.U. in San Francisco.

The president of the ILWU, Bridges, was classified as the "unseen Communist." Primarily through the activities of Bridges and Hall, communism had "penetrated every aspect of life in the Territory—business,
labor, transportation, agriculture, education, publishing, radio enter-
tainment, and, in lesser degree even the religious life of the community."
To support these wild charges, Butler offered a variety of what he represented as evidence. By 1947, he claimed, there were eleven branches of
the Communist party in Hawaii, controlled by a ten-member executive
committee which included Hall, Jack Kimoto, Robert and Ah Quon
McElrath, Charles and Eileen Fujimoto, Ralph Vossbrink, and David
Hyun. Butler was keen to identify local Japanese as Communists. Party
activities, he asserted, were promoted by a "Communist-line Japanese
newspaper," the *Hawaii Star*, and a secret educational group comprising
Hall, Freeman, and John Reinecke. Through the Political Action Committee, the Communist party had gained control of the local Democratic party. Communists also controlled the Hawaii Civil Liberties
Union. Using these organizations and the ILWU, he alleged, party
members attempted to implement programs and policies outlined by
the Communist party in Moscow. These demanded strikes, sabotage of
legitimate business activity, and disruption within the community "at a
time," Butler argued, "when every consideration of patriotism and national welfare demands peace, harmony and constructive co-operation
for the general welfare." In particular, he maintained, Communists
were directed to disrupt wharf activities and shipping between Hawaii
and the mainland, for in this way they could paralyze the island
economy.[146]

At the same time as he asserted that Hawaii was in the grip of communism, Butler also emphasized the numerical supremacy of residents
of Japanese ancestry in the territory. A preoccupation with the racial
complexion of the islands was by no means confined to representatives
of the deep South. Privately Butler argued against the possibility that
crucial national questions might be determined by "Hawaiian Representatives and Senators, perhaps of some Oriental nationality." He was
adamant that he did not want to see "two Japs in the United States Senate." Four years later he was equally concerned that the island state
might be under the control of Orientals. The "alien backgrounds" of
many citizens in the territory, Butler wrote with characteristic insen-
sitivity, meant that they were "unusually susceptible to appeals to racial
hatred or to Communism or other alien creeds." Butler was strongly

influenced by the racial fears which motivated many statehood opponents, and was prepared to exploit racial prejudice as well as political
intolerance. His findings were based largely on anonymous testimony
and reflected the timeworn bias of many of the old, die-hard opponents
of statehood, the *Honolulu Star-Bulletin* suggested bitterly.[147] It was
certainly more than coincidental that Butler's purported findings echoed the assertions of local opponents like Hill, Campbell, O'Brien,
Stainback, and Dillingham. His claims were also influenced substantially by a pamphlet published earlier by Izuka which allegedly told the
"Truth About Communism in Hawaii."[148] Izuka, a disgruntled former
member of the ILWU who had established a rival but ultimately unsuccessful union of plantation workers on Hawaii and Kauai, provided
much of the fuel for the local un-American campaign after 1946.

Butler concluded adamantly that the issues of statehood and internal
subversion were inextricably linked. "Statehood for Hawaii is a primary
objective of the Communist Party in the Territory," his report stated.

> It is my opinion that the immediate objectives of the I.L.W.U. Communist
> Party conspirators in Hawaii are:
> (1) Statehood, with a State constitution to be dictated by the tools of
>   Moscow in Honolulu.
> (2) Removal of Gov. Ingram M. Stainback to be replaced by a Governor
>   named by the Communist High command in Hawaii;
> (3) A general strike to paralyze all business activities in the islands.

Moreover, Butler argued, the admission of Hawaii was contrary to the
national interest because it would place the American people in a "permanent league with Communism within the structure of the Federal
Union."[149] Such assertions were highly fanciful, but they were calculated to exploit an unprecedented development in the islands—the maritime strike of 1949.

Butler released his report in June 1949, almost two months after the
beginning of the most serious industrial dispute in Hawaii's history. On
May 1 about two thousand dock workers, members of the ILWU, went
out on strike. This action crippled Hawaii's waterfront and disrupted
the entire island economy for more than six months. The strike was
directed by Bridges, Hall, and McElrath—a fact not lost on those who
viewed union activity as synonymous with communist subversion.[150] It
was now ten years since a group of organized waterfront workers in
Hilo had first tested the resolve of the Big Five. This early strike, as we
have seen in chapter 2, provoked angry retaliation and was a disaster
for the unionists. Two years later, on Kauai, another union strike was
easily beaten.[151] Things were very different by 1949 however.

The dock workers held out for 157 days in a dispute which cost the
territory an estimated $100 million. Supporters of the strike, including

most of the Burns faction of the Democratic party, were convinced that
a truly secret polling of opinion throughout the islands would have
revealed overwhelming support for the strikers. Newspapers and elite
opinion, on the other hand, bitterly opposed the disruption, viewing it
as firm evidence of left-wing and Communist control of the once-pas-
sive island community. The strike brought the simmering conflict between capital and labor into the open. No maritime strike of this magni-
tude had ever been waged in the United States. Unemployment in the
territory increased from nineteen thousand to thirty-four thousand during the conflict. When it finally ended, almost one person in every five
was unemployed. Yet the strike was more a symbol of Hawaii's pecu-
liarly concentrated patterns of ownership under the Big Five than a
cause of economic difficulties. Moreover, its effects were aggravated by
decisions made in Washington. During 1945–1950, annual military expenditure in Hawaii declined from about $800 million to less than $150
million. This, combined with the effects of the strike, produced perhaps
the most serious depression Hawaii had experienced. Hawaii's island
geography and essentially undiversified economic base made it uniquely
vulnerable to this unhappy combination of circumstances. During the
early days of the strike Stainback claimed that the "economic strangula-
tion" being imposed by the unions was more serious than the effects of
World War II on the islands. But the Truman administration was apparently unconvinced, and refused to intervene in the dispute. Hawaii had
to find its own solution. A compromise settlement was eventually se-
cured, but only after protracted and bitter negotiations between the
ILWU and employer representatives and passage of an act by a special
session of the legislature which permitted the government to seize and
operate the crippled stevedoring companies.[152] The formal ending of the
strike did little to reduce tensions between labor and management. Predictably, and as the tone of Butler's report implied, the strike became a
propaganda weapon for those determined to resist statehood.

Claude Jagger registered profound surprise at the change in public
attitudes in Hawaii as a result of the dock problems. He advised the
White House: "The feeling that we are the victims of a communist plot
is widespread among the people generally." Jagger was president of the
influential Hawaiian Economic Foundation, an organization supported
by the larger corporations in an effort to break down residual community suspicion of big business in the islands. Jagger claimed to be a self-
confessed champion of unionism who had "not infrequently been called
a radical" for maintaining this attitude. He was doubtless more liberal
than his backers and emphatic that he was not a red-baiter. Nonetheless, he advised Truman to check the FBI dossiers on union leaders in the
islands. Like many statehood supporters, especially those with business
interests, Jagger was alarmed that Washington had refused to invoke

the national emergency section of the labor-management act against the dock strikers. Equally, he was concerned about possible communist influence in the islands. Initially Hawaii's legislature had resisted federal intervention, fearing that it would confirm mainland suspicions that the islands were unstable politically and vulnerable economically. If Hawaii could not manage its own affairs as a territory, some implied, why should it be permitted greater self-government as a state? Jagger conceded that the territory had been reluctant to highlight its difficulties for two understandable reasons: "First, those of us who are firmly devoted to Statehood for Hawaii know that senators are sensitive to reports of radicalism in Hawaii"; and, "Second, we need mainland capital down here." Even if immediate statehood was not crucial to the economic survival of Hawaii, mainland capital and investment confidence were. Hawaii's high level of unemployment underscored this fact. Despite a decline of almost fifteen thousand in Hawaii's civilian population after the war, by 1949 more than 17 percent of the work force was unemployed. War in Korea reversed this trend dramatically during 1951–1952.[153] But in the aftermath of the dock strike, confidence in Hawaii's economic survival was shaken. Economic insecurity compounded irrational fears of internal subversion, and accentuated the tensions over unionism and suspected communism which now sharply divided the island community.

Supported by substantial business interests, the *Honolulu Advertiser* increased its criticism of labor activities and refused to give unequivocal support to immediate statehood. It commented in September 1949 that immediate statehood would provide the powerful communist elements with a vehicle whereby they could grab key positions and power in the proposed state government. The *Advertiser* consistently argued that communist influence and a left-wing takeover, using communist strategies, of the Democratic party machine were tangible barriers to statehood.[154] (The conservative nature of Hawaii's nonlaboring community can clearly be gauged from the opinions expressed by two dominant newspapers, the *Advertiser* and the *Star-Bulletin*. The *Bulletin* was the mouthpiece of Farrington and moderate Republicans, and its influence was challenged not from the left, but from the right, in the form of the *Advertiser*, which reflected reactionary white opinion and conservative Republican party views in terms rarely used in any mainland papers after the New Deal.) But the *Advertiser* was not alone in suggesting that the maritime strike made statehood inadvisable. For example, a special report sent to Truman and congressional leaders by the Bar Association of Hawaii warned that Communists—"a subversive group serving the ends of a foreign power"—were attempting to control the islands.[155] Some businessmen would only support statehood, the *New York Times* observed, when there was no prospect that leftists or Communists would control the legislature of the new state. The opinion of this group was perhaps best expressed by Dillingham. "I don't think we should be admitted until we're perfectly sure that through the vote we could control these islands according to the American way of life," he stated. "We're subject out here to Union dictators who want to get control of this important spot politically, economically and militarily." King was obliged to concede during the strike that concern over the potential of leftist labor elements to control state politics was eroding enthusiasm for statehood in some quarters. White House officials and some of Hawaii's friends in Congress also were said to view the strike as detrimental to statehood.[156]

Farrington, as well as members of the islands' legislature, attempted to demonstrate that opposition to communism was consistent with support for statehood. They asserted that the strike simply pointed up Hawaii's political isolation and unequal status. The federal government's prompt action in comparable situations on the mainland had helped to end dock strikes.[157] But Washington did not invoke the Taft-Hartley law against the ILWU in 1949. Had Hawaii been a state, Farrington argued, it might have quickly gained federal assistance to end the strike. Stainback, aware of his delicate position as an appointee of the Democratic administration, made only mild criticism of its failure to intervene decisively to end the strike. He was apparently confident that the dock seizure law passed by the territorial legislature would be effective, despite the efforts of Bridges and his so-called cohorts.[158]

While Hawaii had been sensitive to the charge that it was controlled by un-American ethnic elements before Pearl Harbor, it was also sensitive to the charge that it was controlled by un-American political and industrial groups during the cold war. A series of measures passed by an emergency session of the territory's legislature immediately after the 1949 strike began were explicitly designed to demonstrate that subversive elements were totally ineffectual in the islands. Despite strong opposition from the ILWU and the stevedoring companies, these measures included legislation which authorized the territory to seize and operate the docks until a settlement was reached. Fong attempted to turn this "most drastic legislation" to the advantage of statehood by arguing that it proved the integrity of the legislature in resisting pressure from any and all special interests. Also included in the measures was an anti-subversives act which required people working in the stevedoring industry to stipulate on oath that they were not Communists. Three days after the dock strike began, a compulsory non-communist oath for all public employees in the territory was instituted. Although membership in the Communist party was not illegal in the United States, territorial employees and prospective employees were required to state on oath that they were not and had not been during the preceding five years members of the Communist party. An appropriation of seventy-five thousand dollars was made by the territorial legislature to support the activities of a seven-member commission on subversive activities. Moreover, in response to Butler's report, the legislature by joint resolution requested the House Un-American Activities Committee to investigate communist activities in Hawaii. These actions were designed partly to refute allegations of communist influence in Hawaii and thereby support statehood.[159] They reflected both the strength of anti-communist sentiment in the territory, and the determination of some statehood proponents to negate Butler's charges.

Proponents denied that the communist issue was related to the question of statehood, and attempted to expose the contradictions contained in Butler's report. "I do not wish to minimize the menace of Communism," Farrington informed Congress, but "I cannot agree that the issue is pertinent to our just claims to statehood."[160] In fact, Butler's report conceded that the vast majority of Hawaii's citizens were loyal advocates of self-government as defined by American tradition. He also acknowledged that a majority in Hawaii sought to defeat communism. Proponents emphasized that these observations contradicted his conclusion that the Communist party would influence the new state constitution through its control of a majority of the delegates chosen to draft it. Moreover, they argued that, as any proposed state constitution would be subject to approval by plebiscite in the territory and by Congress, subversive influences could not conceivably dictate the structure of the constitution.[161] Exposure of the inconsistencies in Butler's report did not, however, lessen the appeal of the communist argument to opponents after 1949. Nor did Butler's failure to name more than ten Communists deter the House Un-American Activities Committee from conducting investigations in Hawaii.

The dock strike and Butler's report also led to the establishment of a local citizens' committee determined to oppose and expose communism in the territory. On June 14, 1949, a public meeting of approximately three hundred residents formed the Hawaii Residents' Association (Imua). Initially set up to battle the effects of the waterfront strike, the group remained a permanent anti-communist association. Conveniently, it confused communism with trade unionism generally, attacking fellow travellers in both the ILWU and Democratic party. Burns, for example, was portrayed publicly as "the man in red socks." Membership of Imua climbed to about one thousand within three weeks of its formation. Its members were almost exclusively Caucasians from the conservative Republican-employer faction in the community, or were military officers. Imua was initiated and partly financed by the Dillingham family. Its primary explicit function was to uphold the United States Constitution and to maintain freedom of private enterprise in the com-

munity. To achieve these objectives Imua pledged to "combat Communism and other subversive elements" and to "oppose individuals or
groups who plot to destroy the right of individual enterprise."[162] Imua
adopted no official policy on statehood, but its subsequent activities
demonstrated that a majority of its members sought to delay or defeat
statehood. They clearly believed that white interests, and unrestrained
capitalism, could be best protected by territorial government and
would be threatened by full-fledged democracy under a state constitution.

Truman urged immediate concurrent action on both Hawaii and
Alaska when the second session of the Eighty-first Congress convened in
1950. He also met personally with the chairman of the House Rules
Committee in an effort to dislodge the bills from this traditionally obstructionist group. This initiative was unsuccessful.[163] However, after
the requisite twenty-one days the chairman of the Public Lands Committee, Peterson, discharged the bills from the grip of the Rules Committee. A discharge petition was also used to bring another part of Truman's civil rights program to the floor—a bill to establish a Committee
on Fair Employment Practices. This bill had priority over Hawaii and
Alaska;[164] but Democrat and Republican House leaders agreed that the
fair employment bill would be followed by Alaska and Hawaii. The
Democrats now firmly controlled Congress and Democratic Alaska had
priority over Republican Hawaii. This strategy was portrayed as a sincere and reasonable device for extricating statehood from party politics
by balancing the likely gains by each party in Congress. In addition,
Democrats believed that this procedure would induce more Republicans to vote for Alaska, as Hawaii would not be considered if Alaska
was defeated.[165]

The House passed a weakened Fair Employment Act in February.
Shortly afterward, on March 3, it approved statehood for Alaska by a
fairly close margin, 186 votes to 146. Alaska received considerable bipartisan support, but a majority of Southern Democrats and some
large-state Republicans voted against it. In addition, one hundred
members abstained from voting. Some opponents of Alaska sincerely
believed that it was not qualified for immediate admission. Most, however, viewed the admission of Alaska as a threat to their states' existing
influence in the Senate, claiming that under statehood Alaska's citizens
would exercise approximately "200 times the representation" of a citizen of New York State in the national Senate.[166] States' rights champions
feared the admission of any new senators, whether they be from Alaska
or Hawaii. Most Republicans, however, were more enthusiastic about
Hawaii than Alaska. Nonetheless the general liberal-conservative House
division on the Alaska issue in 1950 closely resembled the voting pattern
on Hawaii in 1947.

Hawaii was debated thoroughly by the House during March 6–7, 1950. In contrast to the debate in 1947, opponents now focused on the question of internal subversion. Butler's alarmist report was quoted and paraphrased extensively. Cox, for example, used it when he told the House that by admitting Hawaii "we are creating a state that we know is Communist controlled. . . . When you admit Hawaii you will have accepted into the sisterhood of States a community that Harry Bridges dominates." Proponents replied that communism constituted no more grave a threat in Hawaii than in the nation in general. Others rightly pointed out that internal security was not a genuine concern of most opponents. Hale again charged, as he had in 1947, that "a fairly low form of racism" based on hostility to Hawaii's mixed population, motivated most opponents.[167] With the exception of the wild charges of communist influence, no significant new arguments were introduced into the House debate.

On March 7 the House again voted to admit Hawaii. The margin of victory was much greater than in 1947—262 votes to only 110—in part because fewer Representatives abstained.[168] The vote in 1950 did not conform rigidly to party lines, but as with the previous House vote a larger proportion of Republicans than Democrats voted affirmatively. Republicans voted 120 for statehood and 32 against; Democrats voted 141 for and 71 against. Predictably, opposition again derived largely from Democratic representatives of Southern states and Republican representatives of large Northern states. Southern Democrats provided slightly more than 80 percent of all negative Democratic votes. Republican representatives from the large Northern states—New York, Pennsylvania, Michigan, Ohio, and Illinois—provided more than 90 percent of all Republican opposition.[169]

The favorable House action coincided with preparations for the constitutional convention in Honolulu. Proponents, like McLane, were now confident that the Senate would follow the example of the House in voting emphatically for statehood. To prompt the Senate, the Statehood Commission sent seventy-five citizens to Washington, and the territory's legislature appropriated an additional twenty-five thousand dollars for its campaign. Joseph C. O'Mahoney (Dem., Wyo.), the new chairman of the powerful Senate Committee on Interior and Insular Affairs, assured these visitors to Capitol Hill that his committee would not "evade or avoid the issue."[170]

Nevertheless, O'Mahoney refused to schedule hearings on statehood until after the House Un-American Activities Committee had completed its study of communism in the islands. Shortly before this investigation opened in Honolulu on April 9, 1950, a court in San Francisco made a controversial ruling which statehood opponents eagerly exploited. The court ruled that Harry Bridges, president of the eighty-thousand-strong West Coast ILWU and organizer of the union's protracted dock strike in Hawaii, was guilty of perjury for falsely denying previous membership in the Communist party. Bridges, an Australian, had not acknowledged membership when he became a naturalized American citizen in 1945. Following the court's ruling in 1950, Bridges' American citizenship was revoked and he was sentenced to five years in prison. He immediately appealed against his conviction. Four years later, when McCarthyism had been largely discredited, the U.S. Supreme Court upheld Bridges' appeal, albeit on a technicality. In the meantime, however, the verdict of the San Francisco court was sweet music for statehood opponents. They cited it as further proof that the ILWU, and by implication Hawaii, were controlled by Communists.[171] Commenting on Bridges' conviction, Jack Hall stated bitterly: "If President Roosevelt were alive today he would be convicted as a communist under the hysteria that is rampant in our nation." Hall's comment, and developments before the House Un-American Activities Committee in Honolulu during the following few weeks, gave new substance to the fears of that insecure minority in Hawaii who apparently believed their community was so fragile it could be subverted by a handful of radicals.[172]

The anti-communist committee subpoenaed sixty-eight witnesses to appear before it. Among these were Hall, McElrath, Kimoto, Fujimoto, and Reinecke. Thirty-nine witnesses invoked the Fifth Amendment of the United States Constitution, and refused to answer the question of whether they were, or ever had been, members of the Communist party. Their refusals were based on the grounds that answers to this question might be self-incriminating. Former affiliations with the Communist party were admitted by seventeen witnesses.[173] The evidence presented by those who did not invoke the Fifth Amendment indicated that local Communist party membership was greatest during 1946–1949, and even then did not exceed about 130 members. Chairman Francis E. Walter (Dem., Pa.) subsequently informed a Senate committee investigating statehood that there were never more than 160 Communists in Hawaii, and by 1950 there were less than 100. Independent Federal Bureau of Investigation estimates agreed. Most people identified as Communists were members of the ILWU or the Hawaii Civil Liberties Union. Yet a small number had been active in the Democratic party, most notably Kawano. These revelations temporarily slowed the growth of the Burns faction within the party, and influenced at least one of its principal figures, Mau, to reduce his ties with the group. The Kawano incident was an acute embarrassment for progressive local Democrats, but they successfully denied any knowledge of Kawano's secret affiliations. "None of us knew that he was connected with the Communist party at the time," his close friend Mau stated. "It never dawned on me that he was a Communist."[174]

However, the efforts of local Communists to influence the Democratic party during 1946–1950 were abortive. Communists also failed to infiltrate local unions affiliated with the American Federation of Labor.[175] Even J. Edgar Hoover, an official not noted for sympathy to the left in any form, conceded that communism was less of a problem in Hawaii than in the nation generally by 1950.[176] This information, coupled with the evidence given to the House Un-American Activities Committee, as Robert Carr has concluded, demonstrated unequivocally the feebleness and impotence of the communist movement in Hawaii then and at any time in the past.[177] But at the height of the red scare not many islanders were prepared to argue publicly that existing fears of subversion from within were alarmist or exaggerated.

At the opening session of the investigation into subversive activities, Chairman Walter denied charges that the intent of the hearings was to damage the statehood campaign.[178] California's redoubtable anti-communist member of this committee, Richard Nixon, also claimed that regardless of its findings, communism was not an appropriate issue for the statehood debate in Congress.[179] Yet the hearings on statehood conducted by the Senate Insular Affairs Committee in May of that year focused almost exclusively on the communist issue.[180] Given the hysterical national debate over internal subversion, and recent incidents in Hawaii, it would have been surprising if the hearings had been restricted to questions genuinely relevant to statehood.

If the Senate committee's hearings were largely sidetracked by the House un-American inquiry, its report was not. On June 29 a bipartisan group of nine senators from the Insular Affairs Committee reported the Hawaii bill to the Senate floor. It took similar action on an Alaska bill. The responsible committee in the Senate had never before taken such a decisive step on statehood. Butler was the only member to vote against the Hawaii bill in committee.[181] He inserted a dissenting minority opinion in the report which betrayed his preoccupation with red herrings rather than substantive issues. Citing the refusal of the 1950 Hawaii Democratic Party Convention to expel fifteen delegates who had invoked the Fifth Amendment during the recent un-American Activities hearings, Butler contended that the Democratic party was Communist controlled. He again asserted that if statehood was granted, Communists might have a "decisive voice in selecting the Governor, the judiciary, the police and other officials of importance." However, the energetic Republican senator did not focus exclusively on this question. Presumably to demonstrate that his argument was not primarily one of race, Butler conceded that there was "no reason why a man of Japanese or other Oriental extraction should not be as loyal a citizen and as good an American as a man of any other racial extraction." Paradoxically, he then implied that he opposed statehood because a majority of Hawaii's residents were non-Caucasians. Most of Hawaii's people had "traditions, customs and outlooks" that were Asian rather than American. Butler predicted that before long residents of Asian ancestry would achieve total ascendency in all aspects of island life. Had Hawaii "been settled and primarily populated by Americans from the mainland," he concluded, "there might be no great problem about admitting it as a state." Butler recommended that Hawaii be granted a political status similar to that granted the unincorporated territory of Puerto Rico.[182]

Truman strongly encouraged the Senate committee to report both statehood bills. In evidence placed before its hearings Truman concluded that the case for statehood rested on both "moral and legal grounds." More importantly, the president also stated that he would attempt to bring both bills to a vote in the Senate before the Eighty-first Congress ended late in 1950. However, Truman's intentions far outstripped his influence. The Senate was expected to adjourn in late August. Senators were anxious to leave Washington to campaign in the mid-term elections of 1950. The statehood bills thus had less than eight weeks—from early July to late August—in which to pass the Senate. In early July, however, the Democratic Senate Policy Committee, with the concurrence of the Senate minority leadership, reduced its proposed legislative program to a few major bills. The Hawaii and Alaska bills were omitted from this list of so-called must legislation. Majority Leader Scott Lucas (Dem., Ill.) stated that consideration depended upon the length of time the Senate remained in session. The *New York Times* concluded that if the Hawaii bill could be brought to a vote in the Senate before adjournment, it would have the support necessary for its passage.[183]

Having failed to defeat Hawaii in the House or in the Senate committee, statehood opponents had only one effective tactical option open to them—the filibuster. Rarely, however, was it necessary for senators determined to defeat legislation to actually stand and speak on the floor of the Senate for long periods. The mere threat of such behavior was usually sufficient to induce a change in the Senate's agenda. Between 1917 and 1964 only six filibusters or threatened filibusters were actually defeated by cloture.[184] During the 1950s members of the conservative coalition were rightly confident that, as a last resort, they could block a vote on legislation which they opposed by filibuster. Liberal civil rights initiatives bore the brunt of such tactics, and statehood was a civil rights issue. In July 1950 a vigorous advocate of white supremacy, Senator James O. Eastland (Dem., Miss.), implied that he and like-minded senators would filibuster if necessary against statehood. If either the Hawaii or Alaska bill was called up for debate, he advised, the Mundt-Ferguson anti-communist bill would be substituted for them. This blatantly discriminatory bill would have prohibited Communists from holding public office and made the registration of all individual Communists compulsory. It would thus have complemented the Alien Registration Act (the Smith Act) of 1940 and the Internal Security Act of 1950 (the McCarran Act) which made it unlawful to advocate the violent overthrow of the government and compelled all organizations designated as subversive to register with the attorney general. Debate on the Mundt-Ferguson proposals would have reopened sensitive wounds within the Democratic party in an election year. Liberal Democrats were already electorally vulnerable on the communist issue and anxious to deny conservatives another chance to exploit it. The anti-statehood faction fully appreciated also that debate on the Mundt-Ferguson bill would be bitter and perhaps inconclusive. It would not only aggravate tensions within the Democratic party but also delay adjournment of the Senate. Rather than confront these possibilities, the Democratic leadership acquiesced. Early in August it withdrew plans to schedule debate on statehood before the November elections.[185] Although the Senate did not finally adjourn until September, statehood was not debated. The threat of obstruction, it seems, was sufficient to defeat Hawaii in 1950.

The election results of that year had a direct bearing on Hawaii's future. The Democratic party retained control of both chambers of Congress. But in the Senate it ruled with a slender two-seat majority. More important was the impact of the election on liberal-conservative cleavages in Congress. Opponents of Truman's modest Fair Deal and civil rights program made important gains and the surprise 1948 upsurge in support for liberal Democrats was reversed abruptly in 1950. The *New York Times* estimated that conservative Republicans and anti-administration Democrats would now control 54 seats in the Senate, and 237 in the House—a clear majority in each chamber. Almost half of the Democrats elected to the House and Senate were from eleven former Confederate states.[186] Liberal measures had little chance of success in this Congress. Equally significant, however, was the failure of either party to gain a decisive majority in the Senate. Thus, four new senators might tip the scales of power either way. In the Eighty-second Congress Democrats determined to maintain their slim majority in the Senate and refused to promote Republican Hawaii[187] unless Democratic Alaska was first admitted. To complicate matters further, many Republicans refused to give priority to an Alaska bill because they had no guarantee that the Democratic administration would immediately bring the Hawaii bill to a favorable vote. The national political implications of statehood legislation thus acquired new significance.

However, before the Eighty-second Congress actually convened, Truman made a sincere attempt to break the impasse in the Senate. Congress was reconvened on November 27, 1950. On the opening day of this special lame duck session, Vice President Alben Barkley (Ky.) placed before the Senate a letter from Truman urging the immediate admission of Hawaii and Alaska. Debate began on Alaska the following day. It lasted three days.[188] Those senators who later led the fight against Hawaii were also intransigent opponents of Alaska. Included in this energetic group were Butler, Eastland, John Stennis (Dem., Miss.), Richard Russell (Dem., Ga.), John McClennan (Dem., Ark.), and Kenneth McKellar (Dem., Tenn.). An attempt by proponents to bring the bill to a vote by a unanimous consent motion was blocked by Eastland. On December 5, 1950, liberals acknowledged that statehood opponents were prepared to filibuster to defeat the Alaska bill. The Democrat leadership thus deferred further consideration of either statehood bill during 1950.[189] O'Mahoney correctly charged that the Southern Democrat-led resistance represented a full-blown filibuster.[190] Truman was bitterly disappointed, observing privately that the Dixiecrats were obsessed with two things—"color and power." Many Southerners "still have that antebellum proslavery outlook," he wrote confidentially. "The main difficulty with the South is that they are living eighty years behind the times and the sooner they come out of it the better it will be for the country and themselves." Looking back on the failure of his moderate legislative program the president commented dejectedly: "I suppose the Presidents in the past have had hostile Congresses—but they were frankly of the opposition. This one—the 81st—happens to be of my own party on the surface. But the majority is made up of Republicans and recalcitrant Southern 'Democrats'—who are not Democrats. So I get the responsibility and the blame."[191]

It was no coincidence that civil rights legislation was also defeated during 1950 by Southern-led filibusters. The fair employment act was never voted on in the Senate, as Eastland successfully invoked a filibuster against it.[192] Similarly, an attempt by liberals (with the explicit support of Truman) to establish an effective cloture rule was also defeated. As originally adopted, the cloture rule permitted a two-thirds majority in the Senate to terminate or limit debate; but after its inception in 1917 a series of precedents and rulings made it ineffective. In 1949 the Senate accepted a compromise which slightly altered the cloture rule. However, this change was essentially cosmetic. Indeed it was so ineffectual that Southern Democrats actually voted for the new rule, and continued to exploit the filibuster after it was approved.[193] Certainly the changed cloture rule did little to limit the obstructionist power of a determined conservative minority in the Senate. Hawaii and Alaska, as well as other aspects of Truman's civil rights program, could not overcome this tactical veto. Few congressmen privately doubted the real reasons why the Southerners had invoked this strategy against Hawaii and Alaska. Confident that he knew what had frustrated the drive for statehood, Senator Clinton Anderson (Dem., N. M.), one of its strongest advocates later wrote confidentially:

> The Southern Democratic Senators who are greatly concerned about civil rights are not enthusiastic about statehood for either Hawaii or Alaska or both because they do not want to add two or four Senators who might not support them in keeping their filibuster going against civil rights laws. It is pretty close right now. There are plenty of votes in the Senate to pass civil rights legislation but under our present Senate rules 32 Senators can filibuster forever and we cannot close debate. If you add four more Senators they would have to find some new allies and they have just barely enough now, so they have been a little slow about adding additional Senators.[194]

"There is no valid reason of justice or even of expediency for withholding 'statehood' any longer," the Statehood Commission proclaimed in late 1948.[195] Such a view was politically naive. It ignored the impact of important changes in Hawaii and Congress after the war. Statehood legislation became an integral factor in the heated, largely sectional dispute over civil rights during 1947–1950. The debates in Congress also revealed strong, if scattered, hostility to the admission of a state which was not overwhelmingly Caucasian. Explicit racism was not amenable to reasoned argument, but it remained a core factor behind the obstructionist tactics employed by many opponents—especially those from Southern states. Moreover, Hawaii's entry as a state would inevitably affect the political, as well as sectional, composition of Congress. Republican Hawaii was thus increasingly linked with Democratic Alaska as the Truman administration attempted to counter possible GOP gains from the separate admission of Hawaii. The related issues of communist influence in Hawaii and internal security further confused the debate in Congress. Within the context of these divisive and emotive national questions the objective validity of Hawaii's appeal for statehood was of little significance. Party strength in Congress and preservation of states' rights were fundamental issues; the status of Hawaii's relatively small population was not. The interaction of these political and sectional factors in Congress was to deny Hawaii's admission for ten frustrating years.

Chapter 6

A Constitution in Search
of a State

Fifteen of the twenty-nine former territories entered the Union by drafting and adopting state constitutions before Congress finally accepted them as states. Confronted with a "lethargic Congress,"[1] Hawaii's decision to draft a constitution before Congress passed enabling legislation was based on long-established precedent. In 1791 Vermont was admitted as a state without prior approval of an enabling bill. Seven of the states admitted by this procedure had their constitutions approved unconditionally by Congress at the same time as it passed their admission bills. By first adopting "state" constitutions most territories had been able to encourage favorable action by Congress.[2] Hawaii expected a similar result. But by 1949–1950 it also confronted unique obstacles which it hoped a constitutional convention might help to overcome. "Should Hawaii's State Constitution be announced by prominent constitutional authorities to be an eminently satisfactory document," McLane observed, "it would refute charges that the islands were being subverted internally by un-American elements."[3] Significantly, the decision to schedule a convention for 1950 was taken in mid-1949, against a background of bitter local divisions over the dock strike and Butler's allegations that Communists and fellow travellers controlled the territory. Although the Statehood Commission had previously called for a constitutional convention, it was not until the communist issue erupted that money was actually allocated for this purpose. In July 1949 the legislature appropriated $295,000 for the anticipated convention. However, this decision was not merely an attempt to demonstrate that Hawaii was sympathetic to American political ideals and capable of framing a constitution appropriate for an American state. The laborious and expensive steps involved in electing delegates and in drafting and ratifying a constitution were also taken to confirm that immediate statehood was overwhelmingly supported by Hawaii's electorate.[4] Local opinion had not been tested since the ambiguous and inconclusive plebiscite of 1940, although nearly all those elected to the legislature after the war wanted statehood.

Early in 1948 the Statehood Commission accepted responsibility for drafting a tentative state constitution. A State Constitution Committee with authority to submit its proposals directly to a convention was appointed by the commission. The recommendations of the Constitution Committee derived largely from the work of various subcommittees of the New York State Constitutional Committee of 1938. In addition, Hawaii's Constitution Committee, and later all delegates to the convention, were helped by the Territorial Legislative Reference Bureau. It collected manuals and relevant data from previous state constitution committees, compiled comparative data on existing state constitutions, and requested information from "groups interested in constitutional revision in California, Florida, Kentucky, Louisiana, Minnesota, New Jersey and Tennessee." Further guidance was obtained from the Legislative Reference Bureau of the Library of Congress, the model constitution of the National Municipal League, the American Political Science Association, The American Bar Association, and the Council of State Governments.[5]

On March 21, 1950, sixty-three delegates were elected to a constitutional convention. Any qualified voter was entitled to be a candidate for a position as delegate. In an attempt to divorce convention decisions from partisan political issues, candidates were not permitted to designate party affiliations when campaigning. Nevertheless, both major political parties attempted to gain a majority at the convention.[6] Republicans gained twenty-nine seats; recognized Democrats won twenty-three seats. The remaining eleven candidates were not specifically identified with either major party. Thus neither Republicans nor Democrats dominated the convention.[7] But as labor interests and some liberal Democrats later discovered with dismay, they were consistently outvoted by conservative elements throughout the convention. The result, as we shall see, was a constitution which incorporated some of the excesses associated with McCarthyism: it compromised the rights of free speech and free association which the nation's Constitution and Bill of Rights were designed to guarantee.

The sixty-three-member convention was elected by ninety-seven thousand citizens, almost 80 percent of those entitled to vote. Statehood proponents eagerly interpreted this as evidence that eight out of every ten islanders wanted immediate statehood. Yet as critics pointed out, it did not follow that a willingness to vote for these delegates necessarily indicated support for immediate admission. The convention was broadly based, but citizens of Japanese and Filipino extraction were underrepresented. On the other hand (as had so often been the case in the past), whites and to a lesser extent Chinese were overrepresented. Twenty-seven delegates were Caucasians, twenty were of Japanese descent, eleven were Hawaiians or part-Hawaiians, and five were of Chinese descent. No ethnic group constituted an absolute majority in the convention.[8] However, no delegates of Filipino ancestry were elected, although Filipinos comprised approximately 12 percent of the popula-

tion of Hawaii (however, only slightly more than 50 percent of this ethnic group was naturalized and thus eligible to vote).[9] Some found this
imbalance unfortunate. Others argued that it was further proof that
Asian groups did not bloc vote. Oahu, which supported more than 60
percent of Hawaii's five hundred thousand people, elected a majority
(thirty-six) of convention delegates. The county of Hawaii elected
twelve delegates, the county of Maui nine, and the county of Kauai
six.[10] Although many delegates were lawyers, a variety of occupational
interests were represented. Most, however, were drawn from the old
haole business elite or from the small, if expanding, middle class.[11]
Twenty-two members of the legislature were nominated for the convention, but only twelve won seats. The ILWU endorsed fourteen candidates, but two alone were successful. Only five women won seats at the
convention.[12]

Delegates convened at Iolani Palace on April 4, 1950, to draft the
proposed state constitution. Farrington told an early session that an
acceptable constitution would offer "a complete and final answer to
charges discrediting, prejudicing, and bringing into doubt the character" of Hawaii's people.[13] Conscious of the need to establish conclusively
the loyalty of delegates and thereby refute Butler's charge that left-wing
influences would dictate the state's constitution, the convention stipulated that all delegates must make an oath of loyalty. This was in part
an overreaction by a community which felt particularly vulnerable on
the issues of internal security, but it was a position supported enthusiastically by all factions of the local Republican party. A motion moved by
the Republicans' rising star, Fong, stipulated that all delegates must
state on oath that they were not members of the Communist party and
had not been members of the Communist party during the preceding
five years. Fong's proposal was based on the loyalty oath added to the
Organic Act shortly before the dock strike of 1949, and it was promptly
accepted. All convention members took the oath. The *Honolulu Star-
Bulletin* stated confidently that this action would demonstrate the
Americanism of all delegates. But the suspicions and tensions raised by
McCarthyism and Mao Tse-tung's recent victory in China could not easily be subdued. The convention coincided with McCarthy's wild assertions that members of the State Department, especially Owen Lattimore, were communist sympathizers who had contributed to the "loss"
of China.[14] Not surprisingly, statehood proponents were anxious that a
consensus against communism be seen to emerge from the convention—
even if this unity had to be imposed by loyalty oaths and the expulsion
of delegates suspected of being sympathetic to America's cold war enemy. Some members of the convention were reluctant to join a witch
hunt against fellow delegates who had been elected democratically to
their posts. But McCarthyite congressmen and mainland opponents of

statehood had conveniently arranged that the House Un-American Activities Committee (HUAC) should hold hearings in Honolulu just as the constitutional convention began. The presence of this single-minded committee was calculated to highlight the alleged connection between internal subversion and statehood for the territory. Confronted with the public and press furor stirred up by the HUAC, even some of the more liberal delegates were persuaded that the convention must not be seen to be soft on communism and internal security.

The convention could scarcely have begun at a worse moment for statehood proponents. On April 10, Richard Kageyama, Democratic member of the Honolulu Board of Supervision and a convention delegate, stated before the Un-American Activities Committee that he had been a member of the Communist party during 1947. The following day, Kageyama resigned from the convention. Kageyama conceded that his testimony to the HUAC contradicted his oath of loyalty, but indicated in his defense that his membership in the Communist party in 1947 had been a brief, disillusioning experience. Convention delegates accepted his resignation unanimously. But on a split vote they also agreed to a resolution which recognized that his cooperation with the HUAC in "testifying before and otherwise assisting it in the exposure of Communists and Communist activities in Hawaii has been of distinct service to this country." Given the strength of McCarthyism in mid-1950 it is not surprising that Kageyama's testimony rather than the actions of the constitutional convention made front-page news in the *New York Times* and other mainland newspapers.[15] What is more, to the dismay of statehood proponents, the Kageyama incident was but one of a series of exposures about communism which hung over the convention.

Another convention delegate was also caught in the net cast by the Un-American Activities Committee in Honolulu. Frank G. Silva, business agent for the ILWU on Kauai, was identified as a former Communist on April 11 in testimony by Ichiro Izuka.[16] When subpoenaed to testify before this committee, Silva "declined to answer any questions regarding his membership of the Communist Party on the ground of self-incrimination."[17] Unlike Kageyama, Silva refused to resign from the convention. In reply, forty-eight delegates signed a resolution which argued that he should be ejected because of his contempt of the Congressional Committee on Un-American Activities. This resolution was soon modified, as Silva was legally not in contempt of Congress. Instead, delegates voted by a margin of fifty-three to seven to expel him from the convention on the grounds of "contumacious conduct" before the congressional committee. Silva's cause was certainly not advanced by his fiery charge that delegates of the convention ranged from "tools of the big five" to moral "cowards."[18] Kageyama and Silva were dealt with decisively, but the broader questions raised by their associations with the Communist party could not be dismissed as easily or swiftly. The communist issue would simply not go away. Out of sixty-six residents subpoenaed to testify before the House committee, thirty-nine responded in the same way as Silva. As the next chapter of this book demonstrates, the actions of the so-called reluctant 39 provided new ammunition for Hawaii's implacable opponents on Capitol Hill.

The constitutional convention met on seventy-eight working days. Those who naively believed that the official nonpartisan convention would not become a heated political arena were soon disillusioned. Republicans won control of virtually all important posts. The chairman of the Statehood Commission, former delegate to Congress King, was unanimously elected temporary president of the convention. He was later elected permanent chairman. Three of the four vice presidents and the secretary of the convention were also Republicans. One vice president was drawn from each of the four counties: Fong won office from Oahu; Arthur Woolaway was elected from Maui; Thomas Sakakihara won from the Big Island; and the lone Democrat Charles Rice (a committed if somewhat independent member of the old guard who had little in common with members of the emerging Democratic party) was elected from Kauai. The office of secretary went to a Republican, Hebden Porteus. Predictably, Democrats promptly charged their opponents with exploiting the convention for partisan advantage. However, various political and geographic interests were also strongly represented on other committees and fairly prominent during general debate.

The draft constitution was based largely on recommendations made by the Hawaii State Constitution Committee and studies compiled by the Legislative Reference Bureau in a four-hundred-page book, *Manual of State Constitutional Provisions.* This information was made available to all delegates and served as a preliminary guide for committee decisions and general debate. The convention divided into twenty committees which were directed to make specific recommendations on aspects of the constitution such as a bill of rights, education, labor, executive functions, or the Hawaiian Homes Commission Act. Committee memberships varied, but all committees comprised between seven and fifteen delegates. Recommendations of the various committees formed the basis of subsequent debate by the committee of the whole. Thus the convention debated each article of the draft. When agreed upon, the specific wording of each clause was finalized by the Styles Committee and then submitted for final reading and vote by the committee of the whole.[19]

The draft constitution was finally approved on July 22, 1950. Only one delegate voted against it. Marguerite K. Ashford, a Statehood Commission member from Molokai, objected to the article on the Hawaiian Homes Commission which required that Congress consent to any decisions by the state government on matters relating to the management and disposal of lands under the Hawaiian Rehabilitation Act of 1921. In her view, any exceptional provisions for native Hawaiians constituted racial discrimination, which Congress could reject as unconstitutional. A small number of legislators from the neighbor islands, including Harold Rice of Maui and William Nobriga of the Big Island, joined the attack on the Hawaiian Homes Act, advocating its repeal and the substitution of fee simple title for lands currently occupied by Hawaiians under this act. At the same time, some native Hawaiians were reluctant to embrace a state constitution which gave distant officials in Washington joint authority over the future of their unique homesteading lands.[20] But unlike Ashford, most delegates with reservations about the draft hoped to amend it in the legislature rather than defeat it in the convention.

A special session of the territorial legislature was convened on September 29, 1950, to consider the draft constitution. By a unanimous vote the House of Representatives agreed to submit it to the electorate without alteration. In the Senate, however, Nobriga, Ben F. Dillingham (Rep., Oahu), and J. B. Fernandez (Dem., Kauai) expressed opposition to some of its provisions. All three argued that the proposed seventy-six-member legislature was too large. Nobriga, an outspoken critic of the Hawaiian Rehabilitation Act, was adamant that Hawaiian Home Lands provisions should be omitted from the constitution and from all statehood bills. Dillingham's opposition was in part a reaction to the fact that the proposed constitution did not limit the taxing power of the state.[21] Predictably, Stainback was out of step with both his party and the electorate at large over the constitution. He advised the special session of the legislature that the draft proposal should be amended. In his view it was "too unwieldly, cumbersome and expensive." Stainback also argued that the draft be changed because it did not completely correct the disproportionately heavy representation accorded to the outer islands. There were many in Hawaii who portrayed such arguments as another unsubtle attempt by their appointed governor to jeopardize or at least delay statehood. However, the governor did not flatly oppose the constitution. Indeed, he conceded it to be generally excellent.[22] Moreover, his concern with the excessive power it gave the outer islands was shared by many people from Oahu who understandably felt that reapportionment was long overdue.

Despite this opposition, the Senate passed the constitution without amendment by a decisive thirteen-to-one vote on October 11, 1950. Nobriga cast the only dissenting vote.[23] Neither chamber of the local legislature amended the draft. Thus it was submitted to the territorial electorate for ratification exactly as written by the constitutional convention.

A campaign for ratification was conducted jointly by the Statehood Commission and a special committee formed by the constitutional convention. More than two hundred thousand information folders were distributed in Hawaii. Both the Republican and Democratic parties (with the important exception of Stainback) actively supported the proposed constitution. McLane returned to Honolulu from Washington late in September to direct the affirmative campaign.[24]

Statehood proponents were adamant that those who expressed dissatisfaction with the draft constitution did so simply to defeat statehood. For example, Randolph Crossley, chairman of the Republican party, charged that the Democratic governor was attempting to undermine the statehood campaign by opposing the constitution. Despite Stainback's position on statehood, he did have genuine reservations about certain aspects of the constitution. A substantial minority of citizens also opposed the constitution—albeit for a variety of reasons. The most sustained objections were mounted by the powerful ILWU. It was not opposed to statehood per se, but bitterly resented some of the clauses of the proposed constitution.[25] Ironically, by adopting this position the union unwittingly strengthened the position of the small but determined group of anti-statehood, anti-labor conservatives. As late as May 1950, the ILWU had publicly endorsed immediate statehood. Nonetheless it was disturbed by the proposed constitution and conducted a vigorous campaign against its ratification.

Union spokesmen argued that the constitution did not permit adequate direct public participation in government. This view was shared by many nonunionists, especially from within the Japanese and Chinese communities. Opposition centered on the clauses which called for the election of only two statewide officials—the governor and lieutenant governor—and provided for executive appointment of all other judicial and administrative positions in the proposed state. The powers of the territory's governor were a central issue in the local contest over statehood. Predictably they were also the most keenly disputed issues during the convention. The appointment of officials and judges would be more efficient, Fong argued, but direct election would be more democratic. In the final analysis, most delegates favored efficiency over increased democracy. It was widely believed that appointments made by Hawaii's governors, especially Stainback, had been heavily biased in favor of haoles. Many felt that direct election of all prominent officials in the new state would ensure that all ethnic groups were fairly represented in political life. However, the convention did not accept this view. A motion moved by Yasutaka Fukushima to provide for the election of all local supreme court justices and judges of the circuit courts was squashed, fifty votes to eleven. A compromise moved by Fong to elect the chief justice and empower him to appoint all other judges also failed —although by a reduced margin of thirty-seven to twenty. A related move to permit direct election of the state's attorney general was also defeated, although by a relatively narrow margin of thirty-five to twenty-five. Efforts to have education controlled by elected officials were also rejected. However, the convention did establish a relatively large house (fifty-one members) and Senate (twenty-five members). This increased the likelihood that all ethnic groups would be directly represented in the legislature.[26]

In general labor leaders argued that the proposed executive was much too powerful and the influence permitted the outer islands too great. They also resented the fact that the constitution did not permit the use of initiative, referendum, and recall—procedures, adopted by many states during the Progressive Era, which boosted the direct role of the public in government. These were all substantial criticisms. The constitution could certainly have been less centralized and reserved fewer powers to the executive branch. Still, some found the arguments of the ILWU less than genuine, and suggested that the union's opposition to the constitution derived simply from the fact that it made compulsory a loyalty oath for all government employees and elected representatives.[27]

Local statehood proponents were determined to establish Hawaii's anti-communist credentials, even if this meant that basic democratic rights of citizens might be compromised. They reacted to the charges of Butler and other McCarthyite conservatives in a way which tacitly endorsed the view that internal subversion was a real not an imagined threat. The loyalty oath incorporated into Hawaii's draft constitution closely resembled the infamous 1940 federal anti-subversive act—the Smith Act. Article 14, Section 3 stated: "No person who advocates, or who aids or belongs to any party, organization, or association which advocates the overthrow by force or violence of the government of this State or of the United States shall be qualified to hold any public office or employment." All elected representatives and prospective government employees were also compelled to state on oath that they would "defend the Constitution of the United States and the Constitution of the State of Hawaii." Hawaii's constitution was the first "state" constitution to incorporate such provisions.[28]

Despite opposition from the ILWU on the left, and the Dillingham anti-statehood faction on the right, the electorate ratified the draft constitution. It was submitted to the people at the general election on November 7, 1950, and approved by slightly more than a three-to-one majority of voters. The constitution was endorsed by 82,788 votes, and rejected by 27,109. It gained majority support in all precincts.[29] The substantial negative vote did not accurately represent the strength of opposition to statehood per se, as the campaign against ratification was organized and largely supported by the pro-statehood ILWU. Yet the strength of dissatisfaction with the constitution was much stronger than statehood proponents had anticipated or desired. A substantial minority —almost a third of those who voted—was apparently not prepared to accept statehood on the terms written into the constitution.

In 1940 the plebiscite had indicated only that a majority of citizens

favored eventual statehood. The evidence presented by the 1950 vote
was less ambiguous. It suggested that a substantial majority wanted
statehood under the constitution drafted earlier in 1950. But opponents
could still argue that Hawaii's people had never actually voted on the
separate question of immediate statehood.

Hawaii's constitution incorporated many of the usual provisions of
existing state constitutions, but it also reflected the peculiar demands
and needs of the unique island community. It included the traditional
bill of rights guaranteeing trial by jury in civil and criminal cases, as
well as freedom of religion, speech, and the press. The right of assembly
and redress of grievances was assured. However, the bill of rights also
included two unique provisions which were influenced by Hawaii's
wartime experience and a desire to preserve its relatively harmonious
multiracial society. Article 1, Section 13, stipulated that the writ of
habeas corpus could be suspended by the legislature alone. Moreover,
the supremacy of civil authority was clearly defined. Article 1, Section
14, stated simply: "The military shall be held in strict subordination to
the civil power." The bill of rights also explicitly prohibited segregation
or discrimination in public schools and other institutions, and guaranteed equal protection under the law and full civil rights to all citizens,
regardless of race, religion, sex, or ancestry.[30] These substantial guarantees were qualified, however, by the loyalty oath which directly challenged the democratic right of all citizens to associate freely in the political arena without fear of penalty by the state. The fact that this clause
mirrored federal loyalty oaths was small comfort to its critics.

Although generally a conservative document, the constitution nonetheless made an important concession to employee interests. It specifically guaranteed the right of persons privately employed to organize
themselves into a collective bargaining unit, and the right of public
employees to organize for the purpose of presenting their grievances and
proposals to the state. Only three states—New York, New Jersey, and
Missouri—had revised their constitutions and included similar provisions.[31]

The most significant feature of the constitution concerned the governor: it provided for a very strong executive branch. The governor was to
be elected to the usual four-year term of office. He was responsible for
the traditional duties ascribed to state governors, namely, the carrying
out of the laws, the right to recommend legislation, and command of
the armed forces of the state. In addition, however, the governor of the
proposed state of Hawaii was given power to appoint the heads of the
various administrative departments established by the legislature. Executive departments were reduced from thirty-two under the Organic Act
to a maximum of twenty under the new constitution. To facilitate greater administrative coordination in executive departments, provision was

made for an "administrative director to serve at the pleasure of the Governor." Moreover, as James M. Burns and John W. Peltason have pointed out, legislative reapportionment whereby population changes were registered in the House—a seemingly insoluble problem in many states—was left to the executive and the courts rather than the legislature.[32] As noted above, another feature of the constitution, which also broadened the functions of the executive, established the judiciary on an appointed rather than an elected basis. This had been the practice under territorial rule, but it was exceptional for a state constitution to include such a provision. The constitution set up one supreme court and various circuit courts and inferior courts. Provision was made for the governor, "with the advice and consent of the Senate," to appoint "the justices of the supreme court and the judges of the circuit courts."[33] Through the articles of "Taxation and Finance" the governor controlled the purse strings and thereby, according to S. Gale Lowrie, was in a position to exert decisive influence on state activities. It was the duty of the governor to submit a complete budget to the legislature, but at the same time he was authorized to veto or reduce proposed legislative appropriations.[34] He was also granted power to veto legislation within a ten-day period following final passage by the legislature. The governor and the lieutenant governor were the only two officials elected directly by all citizens of the state.[35] By these provisions, Lowrie has concluded, the drafters of Hawaii's constitution had essentially established "one of the most powerful executive offices in the United States."[36]

The state legislature was to comprise two houses: a Senate with twenty-five members and a House of Representatives with fifty-one members. House members were elected for two-year terms; senators for four years. The proposed legislature was smaller than the legislatures of most of the existing states. Only five states had a Senate comprising less than twenty-five members. Only eight states had a House of Representatives with less than fifty-one seats. Because Hawaii had a population of less than half a million, this comparatively small seventy-six-member legislature would nonetheless have provided one legislative representative for every 1,760 registered voters in 1950.[37]

The organization of the legislature was influenced by Hawaii's unique island geography. The six senatorial districts represented areas which did not necessarily support approximately equal populations. Each Senate district included either part of a major island or a group of islands. Representation in the lower house was apportioned on the basis of population. In the Senate, representatives from outer islands, which supported less than half of Hawaii's population, comprised a majority. In the House most representatives were from Oahu. This was a compromise solution to the controversial question of reapportionment. Sectional division over the issue of reapportionment was further dissipated

by the inclusion of a provision for automatic reapportionment of the
House in accordance with population changes every ten years. However, a constitutional amendment was necessary to authorize reapportionment of the Senate.[38]

The minimum age for voting in state or local elections was twenty
years under the new constitution. This continued a practice established
under territorial rule. Only Georgia permitted citizens less than twenty-
one years of age to vote in such elections before 1950.[39]

Hawaii's proposed constitution was a brief document of less than
fourteen thousand words. John Bebout, assistant secretary of the Council of the National Municipal League, observed that its drafters had
resisted "virtually all temptations and pressures to include the kind of
restrictive and legislative details that . . . so encumbered most of the
constitutions of the older states."[40] By excluding all statutory material
and superfluities, the legislature of the proposed state was left reasonably free to respond flexibly and effectively to the changing needs of the
state.[41] Rather than "outline constitutional procedures for the state to
follow," Lowrie commented, the constitution simply asserted "the basic
duties of the state, leaving it to the legislature of the future to devise
appropriate means of meeting these obligations."[42]

"The Constitution as drawn up by the Constitutional Convention has
been hailed as perhaps the best state constitution in existence," the *Star-
Bulletin* claimed enthusiastically in September 1950.[43] This view was
not wholly without foundation. Despite the restrictions it imposed on
civil liberties through the mandatory loyalty oath, and the concentrated
power of the executive notwithstanding, the constitution was generally
acclaimed as an excellent, flexible document. Bebout emphasized, for
example, that Hawaii's constitution "demonstrated that it is perfectly
possible in the 20th century, as it was in the 18th, to write a Constitution that is confined to fundamentals." Political scientists Burns and
Peltason praised it for avoiding many of the flaws and frailties of other
state constitutions, and for incorporating fresh ideas and the recommendations of contemporary experts for improving the organization of the
executive and judicial branches of state government. Lowrie, in 1951,
complimented its stylistic and organizational excellence.[44]

The events of 1950 clearly demonstrated Hawaii's ability to organize
a state government and its desire to gain immediate admission. They
also refuted Senator Butler's allegation that Hawaii's constitution
would be "dictated by the tools of Moscow in Honolulu."[45] Ratification
of the constitution in the face of strong ILWU opposition, inclusion of a
loyalty oath, and the prompt expulsion of Silva from the convention
invalidated statehood opponents' claims that the territory was Communist controlled. In 1951 a U.S. Senate investigating committee correctly
concluded that "the prophesy that the State constitution of Hawaii

would reflect Communist influence has not been even remotely fulfilled."[46]

Other developments in Hawaii during 1950 also refuted the contention that labor interests or Communists dominated the political life of
the territory. The 1950–1951 territorial legislature, like the constitutional convention, included representatives of virtually all major political and economic interests, as well as social and ethnic groups. Ethnically, for example, the House of Representatives comprised fourteen
Caucasians or part-Hawaiians, ten members of Japanese ancestry, three
of Chinese-Hawaiian extraction, two of Hawaiian ancestry, and one of
Chinese ancestry. Politically, labor interests were represented, but the
strongly anti-labor Republican party held thirty of the forty-five seats in
the legislature. During 1950 also, the House Un-American Activities
Committee found that the ILWU was Communist led, but failed to confirm Butler's suggestion that the Democratic party and the territory's
economy were Communist controlled.[47]

"The framing of a Hawaii State Constitution," McLane advised the
Statehood Commission, "would soon make Hawaii the 49th State."[48]
The constitution was used deliberately as a tool in the statehood drive.
It was cited consistently as evidence that Hawaii, despite its uniquely
mixed peoples and its radical labor movement, was an unexceptional
American community. As Meller has correctly pointed out, the constitution "showed and was meant to demonstrate how thoroughly the people
of the Islands were imbued with American political and cultural traditions."[49] Even before the convention ended, a large delegation of its
members visited Washington to lobby Senate investigators and point out
the territory's success in containing so-called un-American elements.
"Great interest was expressed in Washington in our constitutional convention," Fong reported. "The constitution we present to congress will
in no small measure determine the outcome of the statehood campaign.
Congressmen are impressed, too, with the action of the Hawaii legislature in handling the long waterfront strike here, and in the action of the
constitutional convention in expelling two delegates."[50] By drafting and
ratifying its proposed state constitution the territory reaffirmed its capacity and desire for self-government. It was not only qualified for
statehood, but now for the first time was fully prepared for immediate
admission. No longer would approval by Congress merely enable Hawaii to take the steps, such as drafting an appropriate constitution, necessary to become a state. Now congressional approval would guarantee
prompt admission. The new constitution was thus potentially a decisive
initiative. In practice, however, it had little direct impact on the wider
forces which shaped congressional action, or inaction, on statehood.

Chapter 7
Politics of Nonaction, 1951–1956

The procedures and arrangements under which Congress operates, like all institutional processes, are not neutral. Both implicit inertia and explicit manipulation determine what Congress does and does not decide. The agenda adopted by Congress essentially decides the fate of legislation. Only a small proportion of the bills introduced ever receive serious consideration by relevant committees. Few bills escape the barriers which opponents of legislation in House or Senate committees can invoke to prevent a debate on the floor of either chamber. As political scientists have long acknowledged, it is the numerous committees and subcommittees which mould, promote, or bury legislation. Although the combined number of House and Senate committees is less than 40, there are more than 250 subcommittees. The significance of these small, unrepresentative groups can scarcely be overstated. They have, in effect, veto power over most bills. Woodrow Wilson once observed that "Congress, in its Committee rooms, is Congress at work."[1] But he could not have anticipated that the power of these committees would perhaps rival that of Congress itself as the amount and complexity of legislation increased. Nor did he appreciate sufficiently that committees are select groups which do not necessarily reflect the views of a majority of representatives or senators on a particular issue. Legislation is often defeated, delayed, or amended by committees, although it might have the support of a majority on the floor of either or both chambers. From 1950 statehood proponents learned with dismay that the Congress they so eagerly wished to join could have its legislation vetoed or obstructed by a small minority of its members.

In recent years congressional procedures have been reformed and streamlined, but such changes came too late to help Hawaii. Before 1960 a majority in committee was given to the party which had a majority in the chamber to which the committee was responsible. The most powerful member of any committee was the chairman. Even without the support of a majority of the committee, he could block or modify legislation. A chairman could arrange the agenda, schedule (or not schedule) meetings or hearings, or appoint a subcommittee comprising members sympathetic to his views and direct controversial legislation to this group. Chairs were usually held by a member of the majority party, but like committee membership in general, they were determined on the basis of seniority. The majority party in Congress, however, was sometimes hostile to the administration. Thus in many vital committees, control of procedure and voting power lay with elderly, conservative members who were not necessarily from the same party as the president. "The population of the United States as a whole is increasingly young, geographically mobile and urban," Ira Katznelson and Mark Kesselman have pointed out, but "Committee chairmen tend to be old, rural and Southern."[2] Representatives from solidly Democratic Southern electorates generally enjoyed much longer tenure of office than representatives elected by other, more volatile sections of the country. The seniority system thereby permitted the South to exercise disproportionately strong influence in Congress. The consequences of these arrangements were most obviously and most decisively illustrated in the work of the powerful House Rules Committee, which in effect had the power to determine the agenda of the House. During 1937, for example, three Democratic and four Republican members of this committee blocked much New Deal legislation. In the following decade the conservative coalition of Southern Democrats and old guard Republicans thwarted liberal legislation sponsored by Roosevelt and Truman in committees rather than on the floors of Congress. And if other tactics failed, the filibuster remained a potent device for defeating the will of Congress.

The power of the Rules Committee was restricted temporarily during 1949–1950. Liberal Democrats, with the support of urban Republicans, overrode the conservative coalition and instituted a discharge rule. This permitted the chairman of a standing committee to call up his legislation if the Rules Committee refused to sanction it within a twenty-one-day period. Legislation on Hawaii and Alaska, as well as an anti-poll tax bill and minimum wage legislation, was brought to a floor vote in 1950 as a result of this new procedure. But after conservative strength had been bolstered by the mid-term elections in November 1950, the coalition quickly repealed the discharge rule. The Rules Committee immediately resumed its traditional, obstructionist role. Fred Greenstein has pointed out that the American political process allows various individuals and groups, through their veto power, to delay or stall policymaking. Congress, he correctly concluded, is a prime example of that process. "The checkmating possibilities are so substantial that one wonders how any policy—especially on controversial issues—ever emerged from the Washington labyrinth."[3] By manipulating committee procedures and the filibuster, opponents in Congress were able to block the controversial statehood question during 1950–1958. The strategies they adopted were transparently cynical, but extremely effective.

Eighty-second Congress, 1951–1952

The Senate defeat of 1950 was a bitter reversal for all those in Honolulu who were working so optimistically and energetically to shape the proposed state's constitution. While conceding its disappointment and frustration, the Statehood Commission was nonetheless firmly resolved to carry on with the campaign. Republicans still dominated the commission and gave Farrington every possible support, although many Democrats continued to mutter privately that the GOP still looked forward to statehood in the eventual, not immediate, future. The official campaign lost further momentum in mid-1951 when McLane returned to Honolulu to work in the governor's office. He was replaced as executive secretary to the Statehood Commission by Jabulka, who had previously been on the staff of the *Honolulu Advertiser*.[4] McLane had worked closely with Farrington and members of the commission, helping both to advance the statehood cause in Washington and to organize the constitutional convention in Honolulu. They had given the campaign continuity, efficiency, and a solid foundation. They had found, however, that hard work and enthusiasm often went unrewarded on Capitol Hill.

Local Democrats were no less determined than their political opponents to be identified with the statehood drive. But their efforts were frustrated by Stainback's vigorous opposition to statehood. They were also angered by his (usually veiled) suggestions that Hawaii's Japanese were a racial and political threat to the islands. In April 1951 Truman made a decision which most island Democrats thought was long overdue: he belatedly replaced Stainback with a nominee who was more sympathetic to the mainstream of his party and genuinely enthusiastic about immediate admission. Oren E. Long was appointed governor, although some Democrats felt that Honolulu's energetic seventy-nine-year-old Mayor, Wilson, or Ernest Kai were the local Democrats most entitled to fulfill this powerful post. Nonetheless, the young Democrats had now proved their political muscle against the old guard. Still, it was a qualified victory.

"One of the gripes we had as Democrats in those early days was that the national appointing authority and the national Democratic party did not consider the wishes and aspirations of the people of Hawaii, of the Democrats of Hawaii," Kido stated. "They appointed governors, . . . judges, . . . customs officials, district attorneys—without consultation with local officials. . . . [If] we wanted to develop a strong Democratic party in Hawaii, the party had to be consulted." Appointments made previously by Roosevelt and Truman had so seldom advantaged the local party that, indeed, Mau, Burns, and others wryly questioned whether or not the appointees were Democrats. Their conclusion was that many were pro-Republican. They were often referred to as "pseu-

do-Democrats" or "so-called Democrats," and were viewed as the pup-
pets of elite business interests. It was obvious to Richardson "that the
appointments were being dictated by the Big Five and the appointees
were going to those who had friends in the U.S. Senate." "I couldn't live
my life under this kind of set-up," Richardson stated. Certainly many
were convinced that the Big Five's privileged connection with Capitol
Hill had to be summarily dismantled and along with it the misconception that local candidates were inept or unqualified. Led by Burns, the
young Democrats thus lobbied strongly in Washington against Stainback and the so-called old guard. Truman and Interior Secretary Chapman were the principal targets of their activities. Burns and Kido in
particular were determined that a new Democratic governor should
agree in advance to make appointments which would consolidate the
local arm of the party, a practice which had served the GOP well in previous decades. But the first choice of the Young Turks, Kai, a part-
Hawaiian who had graduated from Yale Law School and served as secretary and attorney general of the territory, rejected these conditions.
Long, a native of Kansas who had lived in the territory since 1917 and
had exhibited some liberal inclinations as head of the Schools Department, was then selected. He was a compromise candidate. No people of
Oriental descent were considered as it was felt this would retard the
growth of the party by alienating local haole, Hawaiian, and part-
Hawaiian voters. Moreover, as Mau acknowledged, the Southern Democrat bloc in Congress was expected to veto any such nomination. Race
was a central factor in both island and mainland politics. The fact that
Long was a Caucasian with a mainland background made him a very
safe choice. He replaced another Caucasian originally from the South.[5]

While the Burns faction had successfully backed Long, its recommendations that Kido be made secretary of Hawaii (a position equivalent to
lieutenant governor) and Mau be appointed attorney general were rejected by Washington. Being non-Caucasian and identified as pro-labor,
Kido later claimed, both he and Mau were unacceptable to the Southern Democrats in Congress; Long was induced to find other candidates.
This lesson was not lost on Burns supporters, who pushed hard and with
eventual success to have Sakae Takahashi made treasurer under Long.
The nature of local politics and patronage was gradually changing.
"Our Democratic governors previously didn't owe the local party any
obligation, and never dealt with the local party," Kido commented.
"But with the coming of Oren Long . . . governors . . . had to play
with the party."[6]

Confident that statehood now enjoyed the support of a majority in
the House, proponents realistically focused their campaign on the Senate after 1950. This strategy met with some initial success as the Senate
Interior Committee reported favorably on both Hawaii and Alaska dur-

ing 1951. However, support for Hawaii was much stronger than for Alaska. Hawaii won a five-vote margin, while Alaska gained a slim one-vote majority.[7] Led by Butler, opponents signed a dissenting report which charged that Communists still held a tight grip on the economy, politics, and social life of Hawaii. Given Hoover's comment in March that there were only thirty-six Communist party members in Hawaii, this dissenting opinion was clearly without substance. Moreover, Hoover conceded that forty of the existing states had more Communists than Hawaii.[8] The majority report cited this information and dismissed the communist issue as irrelevant and highly exaggerated. It also refuted the suggestion ᵗʰat Hawaii was unqualified for statehood because most of its people were aliens. Hawaii's residents were true Americans, the report suggested, and could not justifiably be denied complete political parity with other Americans simply because they were largely of Asiatic ancestry. The Statehood Commission welcomed this majority opinion as the most forceful report yet issued by Congress. The fact that it came from the Senate rather than the House was especially encouraging. Local proponents were convinced Hawaii's statehood bill would be brought to the Senate before the year (1951) was out.[9] Despite the optimism, however, the Senate took no further action on either territory during 1951. A threat by conservatives to filibuster was sufficient to avert a debate.[10]

When Congress resumed in January 1952 this threat was repeated. Opponents focused on the Alaska bill, as it apparently enjoyed less support in the Senate than Hawaii. If Alaska was defeated or interminably delayed, it was considered most unlikely that the Democrats would push forward with separate legislation to admit Republican Hawaii. Farrington was confident Hawaii could muster fifty-five votes in the Senate, if it could ever be brought to an actual vote. But potential majority support was irrelevant unless the threat of a filibuster could be overcome. And in January 1952 leading Senate opponents met and devised a detailed filibuster strategy. At the same time Farrington convened a meeting of proponents. It included Democratic and Republican leaders, Interior Secretary Chapman, and officials from both Hawaii and Alaska. With the support of the White House, agreement was reached on a new strategy aimed at bringing both territories into the Union simultaneously. Under this arrangement, Democratic Alaska was to be debated before Hawaii. The Truman administration would support no alternative procedure.[11]

On February 3, 1952, the Alaska bill was again debated by the Senate. An attempt to substitute Alaska with a Hawaii bill was defeated. The debate on Alaska was vigorous and protracted, consuming eleven days of debate over a four-week period. It had all the hallmarks of a filibuster and was cut short only when the Senate voted to recommit

Alaska to the relevant committee for further consideration. This action was tantamount to the defeat of both Alaska and Hawaii during the Eighty-second Congress.[12]

The recommital motion, moved by George Smathers (Dem., Fla.), provided that the Senate committee conduct additional hearings on Alaska, and consider granting Commonwealth status as an alternative to statehood. Although passed during debate which was technically restricted to Alaska, Smathers' motion stipulated that the Senate committee consider an alternative status to statehood for "the territories," not Alaska per se. It thus constituted an attempt to grant Commonwealth status to both Alaska and Hawaii. Commonwealth status would give each territory the right to elect its own governor, legislature, and executive officials, vote in presidential elections, and elect a voting delegation to the House of Representatives plus a nonvoting delegate to the Senate. It would take a constitutional amendment, however, for Commonwealth status to be granted to Hawaii or Alaska.[13] Smathers' motion was a convenient alternative tactic to the exhaustive filibuster which would have been necessary to avert a Senate vote during the remainder of 1952.

Increasingly during the 1950s, local and mainland opponents attempted to delay or avert statehood by promoting an alternative political status for Hawaii. In 1952, after fifty-three years as an unincorporated territory, Puerto Rico was made a Commonwealth under a unique arrangement accepted by Congress, the president, and its own electorate. The U.S. Constitution did not specifically provide for such a status. Under the Commonwealth Act of 1952 Puerto Rico's residents were granted American citizenship but denied voting representation in Congress or the right to vote in national presidential elections. While this decision did not give Puerto Ricans equal political rights with other American citizens, it did give them unique economic benefits. As a Commonwealth, Puerto Rico was entitled to generous grants-in-aid from the U.S. government. In addition, Puerto Rico's residents were exempted from payment of all federal U.S. taxes.[14] Some observers suggested that by this action Washington had purchased control of Puerto Rico, and averted any potential challenge to the political and ethnic composition of Congress which might have come had Puerto Rico sought to follow the statehood example presented by Hawaii. During 1953 and after, more opponents of Hawaii pushed the idea of Commonwealth status as a substitute for statehood.

The Commonwealth idea was first suggested by Butler in his anti-statehood report of 1949. A year after Smathers' motion had been passed by the Senate, opponents introduced a bill to grant Hawaii increased self-government under a political status very similar to that accorded Puerto Rico. During the Senate hearings of mid-1953, Smathers suggested that another plebiscite be held to determine whether Hawaii's citizens desired Commonwealth status or statehood.[15]

These moves were transparent designs to obstruct statehood, but they also reflected the growth of a determined pro-Commonwealth minority within Hawaii. Significantly, virtually all those who wanted this new status also opposed statehood. Stainback, Campbell, and O'Brien, for example, all proposed Commonwealth status during the 1953 Senate hearings. Stainback suggested that one attractive feature of Commonwealth status was the exemption from federal taxes which it gave to Hawaii's residents. During 1952 Hawaii paid $140 million in federal taxes. Commonwealth supporters argued that if this money were paid to the local legislature or if taxes were reduced, the territory would undergo unprecedented economic growth. Moreover, the abolition of federal taxes would negate statehood proponents' claims that as a territory Hawaii was subject to taxation without representation. O'Brien informed the Senate Insular Affairs Committee that if given the choice between statehood, with all the additional obligations it entailed, and Commonwealth status, with the federal tax exemption, Hawaii's people would vote emphatically in favor of Commonwealth status.[16] O'Brien grossly exaggerated. Nonetheless, during 1953–1954 unprecedented local support for Commonwealth status—either as a permanent alternative to statehood or a temporary means toward increased home rule —developed. In March 1954 J. Harold Hughes, with the support of Campbell and Stainback, formed the Commonwealth for Hawaii organization. Hughes claimed that "several hundred business people" were interested in Commonwealth status.[17] Growing support for Commonwealth status reflected the belief that all federal taxes paid by Hawaii's residents and all customs duties collected in Hawaii would be remitted by the federal government. Commonwealth advocates estimated that this would save Hawaii between $135 million and $185 million per annum, and permit a significant decrease in income tax payments by island residents. Despite a reduction in the individual's tax burden, the Commonwealth government would collect greater revenue per capita than the proposed state government, and could thus foster rapid economic development in Hawaii. According to Stainback, this political system would ensure the continued development of local industry and business and encourage a marked increase in the level of mainland investment. Although denied voting representation in Congress, Hawaii, like Puerto Rico, would constitute a self-governing state. Its citizens would be protected by the United States Constitution. "We do not have to stay in our present situation, neither is statehood necessary," Stainback argued in 1954. "We can have all our freedom and independence under Commonwealth status."[18]

These claims were vehemently refuted by local statehood supporters.

King pointed out that advocates of Commonwealth status were attempting to utilize this issue to conceal their real opposition to statehood. He charged that Commonwealth proposals were based on fal-
lacious arguments and motivated by "race prejudice and distrust of
democracy." King correctly emphasized that Commonwealth status did
not necessarily guarantee that taxes would be remitted. In contrast to
Hawaii, Puerto Rico was never an incorporated territory. It was thus
never legally entitled to statehood. Puerto Rico did not at any time pay
federal taxes. Thus the exemption of Puerto Rico from such taxes was
not directly a result of its Commonwealth status. Although federal taxes
might be reduced or abolished under a Commonwealth government,
King argued, such economic advantages were not necessarily permanent. Moreover, rejection of incorporated status and acceptance of
Commonwealth status might lessen Hawaii's share of federal appropriations and possibly reduce Hawaii's sugar quota. Finally, King stressed,
Commonwealth status would deny Hawaii's citizens the right to send
voting representatives to Congress or participate in national presidential elections.[19]

As Commonwealth status was promoted essentially by statehood opponents it was largely supported by Caucasians and a few part-Hawaiian or Hawaiian citizens. Hughes claimed that Commonwealth status
enjoyed considerable private support from businessmen who found it
"necessary to remain inarticulate" because of "the fear of boycott of
their business by the Japanese population."[20] Influential Democrats,
most notably Burns, alleged that some prominent businessmen still privately opposed statehood. Yet not all Commonwealth supporters opposed statehood. Some former statehood proponents suggested that acceptance of Commonwealth status might be a necessary intermediary
step to statehood, and a means of increasing local taxation revenue and
curbing rising unemployment. Harold W. Rice, a former Democratic
senator and a vice president of the constitutional convention, was perhaps the most influential citizen apart from Stainback to offer at least
tentative support to the Commonwealth proposal.[21]

Ironically many of those who had previously attacked unions and liberal Democrats as threats to American democracy in the islands, now
supported a plan which would deny Hawaii's people their legitimate
democratic rights as American citizens. Those who wanted Hawaii to
join Puerto Rico as a Commonwealth tax haven were apparently prepared to sacrifice democracy at home for uncertain economic gains.
Significantly, those who paid the most tax expected to benefit most from
Commonwealth status. Not surprisingly, many wealthy islanders, including Campbell and Dillingham, found the Commonwealth proposal
very appealing. Those who had never wanted political equality under
statehood found in Commonwealth status a convenient means of pre-

serving, and perhaps extending, their political and economic privileges. Throughout the 1950s they supplied voluminous material on the alleged advantages of Commonwealth status to various congressmen and statehood hearings, and attempted to foster wider local enthusiasm for this alternative to statehood.[22] The Commonwealth proposal was actively supported—but only by a small minority of local citizens. At most the Commonwealth issue complicated but did not seriously delay action on statehood in either chamber of Congress.

The majority support given in the Senate to Smathers' motion to reconsider Alaska and investigate Commonwealth status for both Alaska and Hawaii did not necessarily imply that a majority favored this alternative status for either territory. Approved by the narrowest possible margin, the recommital vote did indicate however, that the Senate was evenly divided over statehood. As with previous House votes, this division reflected conservative-liberal cleavages rather than party affiliations. Voting for recommittal, and thus against statehood, were twenty-five Democrats and twenty Republicans. Voting against recommital, and thus for statehood, were twenty-four Democrats and twenty Republicans. The strongest support for statehood derived from representatives of Western and Mountain states. By contrast, Southern Democrats voted overwhelmingly for recommittal, as did conservative "Taft Republicans."[23] The strength of the conservatives on this bill was slightly inflated as a result of bargains struck with moderate and undecided GOP senators. Southern opponents of Hawaii lobbied furiously, offering those who supported Smathers' motion a quid pro quo of Southern votes on legislation which they considered vital. The conservative coalition could still muster, at a price, majority support in the Senate. Nonetheless the filibuster remained the least costly and most effective device for the conservatives, as it could be invoked without majority support.

The confusion surrounding the Smathers motion brought into high relief the fact that while Hawaii and Alaska were technically separate legislative measures, they were always lumped together when considered by the Senate. Bipartisan Senate supporters of both territories agreed to promote debate on Alaska immediately before Hawaii. If effective, this strategy would have admitted both territories simultaneously. Some Republicans agreed to support Democratic Alaska in return for the support of liberal Democrats on Hawaii.[24] If successful, this strategy would not disturb the strength of each party in the Senate. By reviving this device, which had proved so popular with other territories throughout the nineteenth century, proponents hoped to eliminate partisan politics from the debates over statehood. But the decision to recommit Alaska undermined this bipartisan approach. Once Alaska was rejected, members of the Democratic party effectively withdrew their support from Hawaii. Thus, party politics now cut across every facet of the statehood question.

Immediately after Alaska was recommitted, the Democratic leader in the Senate, Ernest W. McFarland (Ariz.), refused to schedule a debate on Hawaii. In reply a prominent Republican friend of Hawaii, Knowland, attempted to bring the bill to the floor for debate. But on March 3, 1952, the Senate voted forty-seven to thirty-two to substitute the controversial submerged oil lands bill for the Hawaii bill. In contrast to the previous Senate vote on Alaska, Hawaii did not receive strong bipartisan support. Twenty-six Republicans and only six Democrats favored consideration of the separate Hawaii bill.[25] Significantly, Hawaii was supported by more Republican senators than Alaska, and was opposed by more Democrats who withdrew their support because the Alaska measure had previously been defeated. In the narrowly controlled Democratic Senate, defeat of Democratic Alaska inevitably resulted in simultaneous defeat of Republican Hawaii. The Democratic majority refused to permit Senate debate on a separate Hawaii bill during 1952.[26]

Eighty-third Congress, 1953–1954

A swing toward the Republicans in the national elections of November 1952 did little to extricate Hawaii from narrow partisan conflicts. However, the successful Republican platform included a commitment to immediate statehood, and Republicans sympathetic to Hawaii controlled key positions in the new Senate; Taft was the majority leader, Knowland chaired the party's Policy Committee, and the subcommittee on Territories was presided over by Cordon. Statehood was ranked third on the Republicans' list of eleven "musts" for action by Congress. Also, a significant number of new senators were elected in 1952 who had previously supported statehood legislation in the House. Republicans controlled the House and Senate during 1953–1954, although they maintained only a one-seat majority in the Senate. The new Republican president, Eisenhower, with the backing of the Republican majorities in both houses, was expected to schedule Hawaii for debate ahead of Alaska. But in 1952 Alaska unexpectedly went Republican, giving Eisenhower's party power in both territories. These results added new confidence to the statehood drive. Political partisanship suggested that the new Republican administration would welcome new states if they were likely to bolster GOP strength, especially in the Senate.[27]

The changed mood on Capitol Hill was expressed most surprisingly in the conversion of Hawaii's inveterate critic Senator Butler. As late as May 1952 he was still opposed to immediate admission. But in June he wrote Farrington to the effect that he would do his best to have a plank favoring immediate statehood adopted at the forthcoming national convention. In private Butler continued to harbor doubts about the wisdom of such a pledge, but political ambition and party loyalty induced his new public attitude. Like Farrington, Butler was a supporter of Senator

Taft in the contest for the party's presidential candidate. And in the
prelude to the Republican National Convention Taft insisted that Butler
change his position and embrace immediate action on Hawaii. "Just
what was said between Senator Taft and Senator Butler, I do not know,"
Elizabeth Farrington later commented, "but we were confident that
Senator Taft had put Senator Butler into a situation that if he wanted to
continue in the prestige positions he held in the Senate, he would have
to go along with statehood for Hawaii." Despite Taft's defeat by Eisenhower, Butler was committed to his party's platform and the president's
pledges on statehood. Thus in early 1953, as the new chairman of the
Senate Committee on Interior and Insular Affairs, Butler dutifully gave
public approval to Hawaii. He acknowledged the political expediency
of his stated position in a private letter. Since statehood seemed now to
be an inevitable eventuality, he wrote: "I would rather that they be
admitted under a Republican administration with the prospects of two
Republican Senators than sometime when their [sic] might be a Democratic administration and we might lose control of the Islands."[28]

Eisenhower's victory gave the Republicans power over appointments
in the territory, but the local party could not agree on a candidate for
the vital post of governor. To the chagrin of some party faithfuls in
Honolulu, Farrington used his association with "Taft Republicans" in
Washington to win the governorship for his old friend King. The Republican hierarchy in Honolulu had encouraged Eisenhower to appoint
the local party chairman, Randolf Crossley. However, Taft had served
in Congress with King and accepted the argument that the former delegate and Statehood Commission chairman was an ideal choice, one who
would boost the fortunes of the local party, especially among Hawaiians
and part-Hawaiians. King was appointed over Eisenhower's objections,
his successor claimed, because Taft warned Eisenhower that were King
not appointed the administration might lose the support of Taft's influential faction in the Senate. Farrington's initiatives were motivated
partly by friendship and partly by a realistic appreciation of King's popularity in the islands. King's sincerity on statehood was beyond question, and this fact also influenced Farrington's preference.[29] The new
governor took office on February 28, 1953. He was the first person of
Hawaiian descent to occupy Iolani Palace since the ill-fated Queen
Liliuokalani in the early 1890s. His appointment was greeted with the
words *Ka Mo-i Iloko o ka Halealii*, "There's a King in the Palace."

The Republican victories of 1952 were interpreted by the Statehood
Commission as "substantial reasons for the belief that few times in the
history of our long campaign have so many new and favorable factors
combined to lend strength to our cause."[30] However, this further example of the commission's perennial optimism was soon punctured by
events in Washington.

The departure of Truman and many liberals from Washington permitted civil rights legislation to be pushed to the periphery of national politics. The new Republican administration was not expected to promote progressive legislation aimed at ending segregation or lessening discrimination. Nor was it anxious to establish an effective cloture rule. Thus some observers suggested that Southern hostility to Hawaii's admission would lessen during 1953–1954. If civil rights legislation was not actually before Congress then it was assumed Hawaii's liberal position on racial issues would not be a direct threat to the Southern faction. Hence the former Democratic governor of Alaska, Gruening, commented optimistically in 1953 that "opposition will no doubt be recorded against the Hawaii bill . . . , but will scarcely go to the lengths of a filibuster." And in January 1953 leading Southern Democrat opponents of civil rights legislation stated that while they remained opposed they would not wage a filibuster to defeat Hawaii in the Senate.[31]

In his first state of the Union message, February 2, 1953, Eisenhower urged that statehood be granted Hawaii at the first possible electoral opportunity in 1954. But if the new Republican president wanted Hawaii admitted, he was not similarly disposed toward Alaska. "The silence of Republican leaders on Alaska leaves one plain conclusion," the *Louisville Courier-Journal* correctly pointed out. "They want traditionally Republican Hawaii in the Union, but not traditionally Democratic Alaska." The Republican party was clearly anxious to increase its slender one-seat majority in the Senate by admitting Hawaii separately. Liberal Democrats criticized this bias as blatant partisanship. Moreover, witbout the unanimous support of Republicans in the Senate this partisan strategy could not triumph. Some conservative Republicans, most notably Butler, accepted Eisenhower's strategy and expediently changed their opinion on Hawaii. However, other old guard Republicans, as well as their erstwhile Democratic allies from the South, continued to oppose both territories.[32] Eisenhower's strategy was thus unlikely to succeed. It could only be saved by defections from the Democratic party, an unlikely prospect in view of the cynical Republican position on Alaska.

The Eisenhower administration defended its opposition to Alaska on the grounds that the territory's population was too small and scattered, and its economic development too limited to justify admission. Certainly the vast northern territory was less qualified than Hawaii. And yet the Republican election platform of 1952 had endorsed "statehood for Alaska under an equitable enabling act." When he was chief of staff of the Army, Eisenhower had supported statehood for both territories as an important defense measure. In 1950 Eisenhower had also stated that Alaska and Hawaii should soon be granted self-government and equal participation in the affairs of the nation. The *New York Times* correctly observed early in 1953 that the reversal of Republican policy on Alaska was fundamentally attributable to partisan politics.[33]

Island Republicans were seemingly unworried by Eisenhower's inconsistent behavior over statehood. The legislature duly allocated another $140,000 for the campaign. It also sent its new governor, King, the new Statehood Commission chairman, Tavares, and former governor Long to Washington to help Farrington lobby uncommitted senators from both parties. When the House Insular Affairs Committee began yet another hearing on Hawaii in February 1953 the *Star-Bulletin* observed confidently that this would be the final investigation of Hawaii's bid for statehood. Such optimism was again premature, although in March 1953 the Senate also began extensive new committee hearings on Hawaii. Tavares observed that these were the most important ever undertaken on Hawaii.[34] They resulted in important changes to the provisions of the statehood bill.

If the issue of communism in the islands was largely a smoke screen for states' rights opposition to statehood, the growth of communism abroad was certainly a serious matter for Washington's cold war warriors. Hawaii was America's principal Pacific base and the Pentagon was adamant that statehood must not compromise Washington's control of all base facilities or limit Washington's access to land which might be used for defense or communication purposes. The Korean War compounded this determination. Events in Asia and the Pacific in the decade after Pearl Harbor had seemingly validated Alfred Mahan's belief that the islands were vital stepping stones to Asia. Mahan could hardly have anticipated, however, that the expansion which he so strongly favored in the 1890s might in the very long-term embroil his nation in massive land wars to defend unspecified American interests in distant areas like South Korea and Vietnam. By the early 1950s the Pentagon was anxious to strengthen Hawaii. Defense expenditure rose sharply from less than $150 million in 1950 to about $340 million in 1959. Military spending now earned Hawaii greater revenue than the export of sugar and pineapples combined. In 1935 it totalled less than 10 percent of the value of these staple exports. By 1958–1959 approximately one person in every four derived their livelihood directly from defense expenditure.[35] Hawaii's economic survival depended upon decisions made in Washington. Local representatives and officials were sensitive to this fact. But they were also determined that the Pentagon should not exploit Hawaii's vulnerable economic circumstances and ride roughshod over the islands' vital interests. During 1953 Washington and Hawaii clashed heatedly over the nature and scope of Defense Department influence in the proposed new Pacific state.

The Defense Department argued that the Hawaii statehood bill must be amended to give the federal government exclusive control, rather than concurrent jurisdiction, over all lands which might be used for defense purposes. The amendment provided "that exclusive jurisdiction be reserved to the United States in those lands now held by the United States and held for military, naval and coast guard purposes for the exercise by Congress of exclusive legislation as provided by Article 1, Section 8, Clause 17 of the U.S. Constitution." Previously, the Pentagon had not found any fault with legislation to admit Hawaii. The proposed amendment contradicted the provisions of the Organic Act and the Newlands Resolution. These stipulated that public lands in the territory were held for the benefit of the people of Hawaii, except sections temporarily set aside for federal use. The Organic Act also gave the territorial legislature "*concurrent* jurisdiction over *all* lands in the territory, *including* military reservations." The Defense Department amendment would have established throughout the islands many small areas of land over which the federal government had exclusive jurisdiction. "This was an intolerable prospect," Tavares has written. Statehood proponents immediately objected to the proposed amendment. With the support of proponents in the Senate and House, Farrington and Tavares agreed "to fight the Pentagon on this issue in the Committee and on the floor of the House and risk delaying statehood rather than agree to the Pentagon's demands." Tavares, a most able former attorney general of the territory, conferred with a delegation of Pentagon officials and a compromise was accepted by both sides. It permitted the federal government to exercise exclusive jurisdiction over the disputed areas, provided the proposed state retained civil and criminal jurisdiction within these areas. With the memory of martial law and the long eclipse of civil authority still fresh, the issue of civil versus military authority remained a sensitive question for most island residents. The terms of the compromise permitted the federal government to maintain exclusive jurisdiction over disputed areas only while the various portions of land were deemed to be "critical areas" by the president of the United States, or the secretary of Defense. Tavares thus won an important concession which ensured further negotiation on all disputed areas and denied the Pentagon permanent unilateral control of these areas. This compromise was incorporated into the Hawaii bill. It later influenced settlement of the bitter controversy over the vast tracts of land owned by the federal government in Alaska.[36]

When the statehood bill came before the relevant Senate committee it was further amended. In response to a request from the U.S. Navy, the island of Palmyra and a number of other small islands were excluded from the boundaries of the proposed state. The Newlands Resolution and the Organic Act referred generally to "the Hawaiian Islands and Their Dependencies" as constituting the territory of Hawaii, but did not specifically delineate the boundaries of the territory. In 1953, following extensive consultation with Tavares and Farrington, the Senate committee defined new, reduced geographical limits for the proposed state. The Navy was less concerned with Palmyra than with the possibility that Midway and Johnson Islands might be considered also as dependencies of Hawaii. Subsequent Hawaii statehood bills, including the one finally approved in 1959, thus provided that as a condition of statehood Hawaii's citizens must ratify by plebiscite the provision for the new state boundaries, which stipulated:

> The State of Hawaii shall consist of all the islands together with their appurtenant reefs and territorial waters, included in the Territory of Hawaii on the date of enactment of this Act, except the atoll known as Palmyra, together with its appurtenant reefs and territorial waters, but the said State shall not be deemed to include the Midway Islands, Johnson Island, Sand Island (offshore from Johnson Island) or Kingman Reef, together with their appurtenant reefs and territorial waters.[37]

During 1953 resistance to Hawaii was by no means restricted to these specific clauses of the statehood bill. In the House and Senate committees, and on the floors of both chambers, opponents employed complex obstructionist tactics which ultimately defeated statehood again. In the House Committee on Interior and Insular Affairs, for example, James A. Haley (Dem., Fla.) moved that Hawaii's proposed strength in the House of Representatives be reduced from two members to one. This motion was rejected by seventeen votes to eight. In the House, Coudert and John Pillion (Rep., N.Y.) introduced legislation to amend the nation's Constitution. They proposed

> that any state hereafter admitted shall be entitled to one Senate seat only when it attains a population of one half of the average population represented by each Senator of all the other states, and shall be entitled to two Senators only if it attains a population of one and a half times the average population represented by each Senator of all the other states.

Pillion suggested that admission be deferred until this amendment was approved.[38]

Committee Democrats, many of whom supported the immediate admission of both Hawaii and Alaska, also sought to amend the Hawaii bill. Clair Engle (Dem., Calif.) moved that the Alaska bill be added so that both territories could be considered concurrently by the House. This motion was defeated by a one-vote margin, fourteen votes to thirteen. Thirteen Republicans and only one Democrat voted against Engle's motion. Eleven of the thirteen affirmative votes were supplied by Democrats. Most Democrats supported this motion in the hope of ensuring concurrent admission of Hawaii and Alaska. A minority of committee Democrats, those from the South, wanted it because they believed there would be much stronger congressional opposition to a combined bill than to a separate Hawaii bill. Despite the defeat of this Democrat-sponsored amendment, eight of the twelve Democrats on the committee subsequently supported the separate Hawaii bill.[39]

The House Committee was less divided than its Senate counterpart. It favorably reported the Hawaii bill on March 3, 1953, by an over-whelming twenty-one votes to five.[40] Two days later the Republican-controlled House Rules Committee approved a rule granting the bill four hours of floor debate. Opposition to granting this rule was led by the intractable Virginian Smith, who protested that "the vote of one Chinaman in Hawaii would be worth as much as votes of 31 citizens of New York state when it came to electing Senators."[41] Hawaii was debated on March 9, 1953. Opponents again contended that the admission of Hawaii would foreshadow statehood for Alaska, Puerto Rico, Guam, and the Virgin Islands and thus further reduce the influence of large states in the Senate. Predictably they also alleged that Hawaii's admission threatened the security of the nation, as the territory was Communist dominated.[42] Some Southern Democrats argued that Hawaii should be denied entry as a state because the United States had never granted statehood to an area where Caucasians were a minority.[43] Party politics, however, were now of more immediate significance than the underlying racial or sectional arguments.

Hostility to a separate Hawaii bill was much stronger in the House during 1953–1954 than previously. Most Democrats were now prepared to reject Hawaii in the hope that this tactic would force Eisenhower to schedule debate on both territories. Northern and Southern Democrats thus combined in an effort to recommit Hawaii to committee. McCormack stated that many Democrats who supported Hawaii could not accept a separate Hawaii bill because the Eisenhower administration had broken a "clear understanding" between the parties that both territories would be considered at or about the same time. He expressed the views of virtually all non-Southern Democrats when he stated: "I am deeply concerned . . . that we are not going to be given an opportunity at this time to consider the admission of Alaska to the Union." Engle, a vigorous statehood supporter, also agreed that Hawaii should be recommitted "because . . . it is the only practical way to get any assurance at all that Alaskan statehood will be brought to the floor." Democrat supporters of both territories charged the administration with bald partisanship in promoting Hawaii while ignoring Alaska.[44]

Southern Democrats who opposed the admission of either territory exploited these new circumstances most adroitly in the Senate. But they narrowly lost their major battles with the Republican majority in the House. The first test of strength came when Dwight Rogers (Dem., Fla.) moved that the House recommit Hawaii to committee. This was rejected by 227 votes to 182. Democrats voted overwhelmingly for recommital. They were joined by only a few Republicans from states with large populations. This unusual Republican unity reflected the new majority party's determination to defeat the Democratic party on what John Saylor (Rep., Pa.) stated was "the first major test of the Eisenhower Administration."[45]

Despite this setback, Southern opponents pressed on. Rogers proposed two amendments to the Hawaii bill. The first stipulated that Congress, not the president, be authorized to approve the new states' constitutions. This proposal was obviously designed to make Hawaii's admission virtually impossible, as it also stipulated that a two-thirds majority must approve the constitution in both the House and the Senate. Most observers agreed that it would be a very long time indeed before Hawaii could muster such support in the Senate. However, Saylor moved a substitute amendment which stipulated only that simple majorities in both chambers must approve the constitution. This motion was passed. A second amendment proposed by Rogers was approved. This reduced Hawaii's proposed strength in the House of Representatives from two seats to one. It was a small concession to statehood opponents' claims that as a state Hawaii's representation would be disproportionately large.[46]

The House again voted on a separate Hawaii bill on March 10, 1953. It was approved for the third time. The vote was 274 for, 138 against.[47] Hawaii again enjoyed considerable bipartisan support. But opposition from Democrats was stronger in 1953 than in 1947 or 1950.[48] Only 37 Republicans voted "No," but they were joined by 100 Democrats. In contrast, 177 Republicans and 97 Democrats voted "Yes." Again virtually all opponents were Southern Democrats or Republicans from large states. They were joined by a few Democrats who would normally have supported Hawaii but were now dissatisfied with the partisan strategy adopted by Eisenhower. Earlier in the session, many Northern and Western Democrats had expressed this concern by supporting recommittal of the separate Hawaii bill. Nonetheless, when the vote on statehood was finally taken most non-Southern Democrats relented and voted affirmatively.[49] This concession resulted from a belief that many Republicans would abandon the Eisenhower strategy once Hawaii was approved by the House. Some naively expected that Alaska would be considered later in 1953. Such confidence was misplaced.

The Alaska bill was reported favorably by the House Insular Affairs Committee during 1953. Nevertheless, it could not overcome conservative Republican opposition in the powerful House Rules Committee, and never reached the floor of the House. Democrats then determined to defeat the Eisenhower strategy in the Senate.

House Democrats had failed to get concurrent action on the two territories, but their Senate colleagues were more successful. The Senate

Interior and Insular Affairs Committee combined the Hawaii and Alaska bills. Senator Anderson moved on May 12, 1953, that the Senate conduct concurrent hearings on the two bills and report them simultaneously. This motion passed by eight votes to seven. All seven Democrats and one Republican supported Anderson's motion.[50] But Eisenhower's party was determined to accept only Hawaii.[51] The resulting impasse was not broken during 1953. The *New York Times* concluded that Senate inaction was the lamentable result of political considerations which were totally unrelated to the statehood question.[52] Such assessments ignored the persistent and decisive opposition to both territories which derived not from a concern with party strength in Congress, but from a much deeper determination to preserve the South's peculiar sectional interests.

Hawaii was not debated in the Senate during 1953, but it was examined thoroughly by the relevant Senate committee in July. At all previous investigations an overwhelming majority of witnesses had endorsed immediate statehood. By contrast, opinions were evenly divided during the 1953 hearings—almost half of the 682 pages of testimony opposed Hawaii's entry.

The communist bogey remained the most convenient argument for those who did not want statehood. Former Governor Stainback, O'Brien, Dillingham, former Hawaii Chief Justice James Coke, Campbell, and former Hawaii Taxation Commissioner William Borthwick presented exhaustive testimony or inserted evidence which emphasized the supposed threat of communism to Hawaii.[53] This evidence largely repeated the allegations made by Butler in 1949 and by the HUAC in 1950; it also highlighted other developments in Hawaii during 1951–1953. Late in 1951 seven purported leaders of the Hawaii Communist party were arrested by the Federal Bureau of Investigation. Hall and Reinecke were among those detained. All were charged with violating the Alien Registration Act of 1940 (the Smith Act), which prohibited teaching or advocating the violent overthrow of the United States government. A few days before the Senate hearings began in Washington, these seven people were found guilty by a court in Hawaii. The six male defendants were each sentenced to five years imprisonment and fined five thousand dollars. Given the earlier conviction of Bridges, these sentences were hardly unexpected. The Hawaii court's decision was immediately greeted by a strike of twenty thousand members of the ILWU. Approximately two thousand dock workers refused to load military cargo for the Korean War. More than 80 percent of all ILWU members employed by sugar and pineapple corporations also joined the strike.

The strike lasted only a few days, but it provided statehood opponents with additional evidence of communist influence in the islands. The kamaaina haole elite had not yet accommodated itself to the industrial and political forces that were redistributing power, and to a lesser extent wealth, in the once-stable island community. For many members of this group, disruption, instability, and uncertainty were obviously the result of the un-American and conspiratorial activities of subversive communist elements. The "Hawaii seven" had their convictions under the Smith Act overturned by an appeals court five years later. Nevertheless, in the meantime the convictions provided apparently tangible evidence that the ILWU was controlled by communist subversives. Moreover during the trial of the "Hawaii seven," local Democratic party leaders appeared as character witnesses for Hall and several other defendants. Mayor Wilson and the Democrats' 1952 candidate for delegate to Congress, Delbert Metzger, were among those citizens prepared to defend Hall's honesty and loyalty.[54] Statehood opponents, and conservative Republicans, immediately seized upon this as additional evidence that Communists and communist sympathizers dominated the local Democratic party. The action of Wilson and Metzger was a small victory for principle over cynical politics, but both men were nonetheless attacked vehemently for their personal and ideological loyalties. Burns claimed that he offered to testify on behalf of his friend Hall, who he described privately as "one helluva American," but because this action might have meant political suicide for the aspiring Democratic county chairman, Hall rejected the offer. "He didn't wanta throw me to the wolves," Burns commented. Those who did testify for members of the "Hawaii seven," Burns later observed, were subsequently closed out of important positions in local politics.[55]

Hawaii's Republican-controlled legislature and the strongly anti-labor *Star-Bulletin* and *Advertiser* waged a bitter propaganda war on unions and liberal Democrats. On July 7, 1953, for example, the Hawaii Territorial Commission on Subversive Activities published a three-hundred-page report which concluded that though the Communist party had been forced underground, it remained a "dangerous influence in the islands." It predicted that, "continuing Communist control of the I.L.W.U. . . . will endanger the national security of the United States in the event of war between this country and the Soviet Union."[56] During the early 1950s Farrington's *Star-Bulletin* and the conservative, pro-Republican *Advertiser* both launched frequent attacks on communist and leftist elements in the ILWU and the Democratic party.[57] Farrington, for example, called for the resignation of Judge Metzger from the Statehood Commission, presumably because Metzger had reduced the bail imposed originally on the seven persons convicted under the Smith Act, given a favorable character reference for Hall, and publicly denounced the "suppressive measures" adopted by Congress to prosecute alleged Communists. Governor King endorsed Farrington's request, charging that with respect to communism, Metzger did "not appear to acknowledge or appreciate the conspiratorial nature of the forces that are at work against our country." Farrington warned Hawaii's people that tolerance of communism in the islands was a threat to Hawaii's statehood prospects.[58] Yet such exaggerated warnings merely served to exacerbate the negative influence of this issue on statehood. For anti-labor extremists, like the predominantly white and wealthy members of the anti-communist organization Imua, Farrington's statements were a welcome implicit vindication of their McCarthyist activities. The fact that Imua's principal backers were also opposed to statehood was widely recognized in Honolulu. When local Republicans sought to exploit the communist issue they perhaps unwittingly gave credence to the allegations of the small but vigorous anti-statehood faction centered on Imua.[59] Statehood opponents in Congress also exploited the statements of local Republicans and Honolulu's major newspapers. Eastland and Smathers, for example, quoted these sources at length in the Senate debates.[60]

Despite these developments, the negative impact of the communist issue should not be exaggerated. It was, as the San Francisco Examiner remarked, at most "a convenient argument for stalling off a decision on the statehood question."[61] If the communist issue hadn't existed, it would have been invented. Indeed, in large measure it was a fabrication of statehood opponents and those anxious to retain the political and economic status quo in Hawaii. For this group any threat to the established order from organized labor, the Democratic party, or local Japanese was a consequence of communist influence and un-American sympathies. As McCarthyism was discredited nationally and the Korean War wound down to a stalemate, the appeal of hysterical anti-communism receded both in Hawaii and on the mainland. After 1953 statehood opponents were obliged to prop up their arguments with issues more substantive than simple anti-communism. But as is obvious throughout this study, changes in the argument over Hawaii did not really affect its fortunes in Congress. This was demonstrated starkly by events in 1954.

"The political complexions of the two Territories and of the present Congress," Senator Anderson observed, "make it virtually impossible to push Hawaii statehood through in 1954 unless Alaska is granted the same status."[62] This prediction gained even greater weight when in his state of the Union message on January 7, 1954, Eisenhower endorsed only Hawaii and ignored Alaska.[63] Republican partisanship had alienated moderate Democrats during 1953 and was likely to have the same effect during 1954. Yet it was not the only major barrier to Hawaii. "It might be necessary to talk for days," Eastland stated, "and this the South must do" to defeat all statehood legislation.[64] Eastland had emerged as the unofficial leader of Southern tactics and debate against both territories. However, no Southern-led filibuster was actually required. Procedural maneuvers were sufficient to keep the separate Hawaii bill from the floor of the Senate during 1954.

Southern Democrats failed to stop the Senate Insular Affairs Committee from endorsing Hawaii early in 1954.[65] But on January 19 the committee again voted eight to seven to combine the Hawaii and Alaska bills. Republicans confidently expected to report Hawaii separately. While one conservative GOP member, George N. Malone (Nev.) was expected to defect, at least one Democrat, Russell B. Long (La.) was induced to vote with the Republicans. Long's sudden willingness to desert his Southern friends resulted from some fairly public and unsubtle horse trading with GOP leaders over the offshore oil bill during 1953. Louisiana gained concessions from this legislation, and as the quid pro quo, Long agreed to support the Republicans' partisan strategy on Hawaii. However, Henry C. Dworshak, a Republican committeeman from Idaho, unexpectedly deserted the GOP and voted with committee Democrats. Dworshak genuinely wanted to ensure that the Senate had the option to vote on either Hawaii or Alaska separately, or both at once. However, his action gave the Democrats a one-vote majority in committee and resulted in the Hawaii and Alaska bills being joined. Some liberal Democrats again supported this move because they believed it would force the Eisenhower administration to change its position on Alaska. Southern Democrats, however, supported this tactic because they believed it would defeat both territories. Like the *New York Times*, all members were aware "that substantial opposition to each proposal, while not strong enough to defeat either separately, would be more than enough in combination" to defeat a one-package bill.[66]

The Senate committee's decision forced Eisenhower's hand. The administration now assured Democrats that if Hawaii was reported separately Alaska would be debated in the Senate not later than thirty days after debate ended on Hawaii. Committee Chairman Butler, who had conveniently changed his opinion about Hawaii, also had second thoughts on Alaska. He now supported immediate statehood for the northern territory, provided it was admitted after Hawaii. Butler's quick conversion on Alaska, like that of the GOP generally, was widely interpreted as yet another exercise in cheap politics. Even if both statehood bills passed both chambers of Congress in 1954, only Hawaii could vote in the national elections of that year. In contrast to Hawaii, Alaska had not yet drafted or adopted its "state" constitution. Thus Alaska could not be admitted in time for its citizens to vote in the November elections.[67]

Despite such complications the Senate committee (or at least Dworshak) was induced to reconsider its position. On January 27, in response to a motion by Dworshak, it voted eight to seven to report separate statehood bills. Hawaii was then reported by a decisive twelve votes to three. Smathers conceded that Hawaii's prospects in the Senate were excellent. Seven days after the Hawaii bill was reported, the Senate committee, by fourteen votes to one, also reported Alaska to the Senate floor.[68]

On March 4, 1954, the Senate began its first debate ever on a separate Hawaii statehood bill. Republican leaders again claimed that Alaska would be debated immediately after Hawaii. But Senate Democrats and a few anti-statehood Republicans united against this tactic. Smathers successfully lobbied these factions, gaining strong support for uniting the two bills.[69] Southern Democrats were now in an unassailable position within their own party. Many of these conservatives had stood by passively as McCarthyite Republicans had assaulted and undermined the Truman administration. Few were anxious to defend their nominal national leader, the liberal Adlai Stevenson. "The South has the bit in its teeth," Stevenson complained after the 1952 elections, "and will bite the harder if it has anything to bite."[70] Southerners were perhaps more pragmatic than previously, as the appointment of the relatively young Lyndon Johnson as minority Senate leader testified. But they remained united on such fundamental questions as race and states' rights, and essentially unperturbed by the passivity and conservatism of the Eisenhower administration. Understandably, this ascendent faction of the Democratic party was not going to support initiatives which might erode its newfound strength in Congress.

At their first party conference in 1954 only two Democrats indicated support for a separate Hawaii bill. Johnson spoke for most of his party when he stated that the two statehood bills must be combined in order to negate Republican partisanship. This charge against the GOP was easy to substantiate as the Republican-controlled House Rules Committee refused to report Alaska in any form throughout 1953–1954. Moreover Johnson stated that in the unlikely event of separate bills passing both the House and Senate, Eisenhower could veto the Alaska bill while accepting Hawaii.[71] It is worth repeating that while some Democrats wanted the statehood bills combined so that both territories would be admitted, others wanted a combined bill because they believed it would never pass the Senate.

Against this background, Anderson moved that the Senate amend the Hawaii bill and provide for the simultaneous admission of Alaska. On March 11, 1954, the Senate passed Anderson's motion by a narrow margin of forty-six votes to forty-three. Only five senators failed to vote with the majority of their respective parties on the motion. Support for combining the bills came from forty-two Democrats, three Republicans, and the independent senator Wayne Morse (Oreg.). Forty-one

Republicans and two Democrats voted negatively. GOP leaders appealed for party unity, but three Republicans crossed the floor. Only two senators (Long and Spessard L. Holland) deserted the Democratic ranks to support a separate Hawaii bill.[72] As was predicted, support for the Anderson amendment came from an incongruous alliance of those adamantly opposed to statehood and those strongly in favor of it.[73] The vote was roundly judged to be the Eisenhower administration's first serious setback in 1954.[74] Certainly the Democrats had achieved on the Senate floor what they had narrowly failed to establish in committee. They had united to combine the statehood bills, but they remained deeply divided over the ultimate fate of either territory.

The combined bill was debated intermittently in the Senate for almost three weeks in March 1954 while Southern Democrats predictably threatened to wage a filibuster against it. Eastland stated on March 16, after speaking for four hours against the measure, that he had barely reached the "preface" of his remarks. He suggested he would take three or four days to complete his statement.[75] Before a Senate attended by only a few senators, Eastland, Stennis, Smathers, and Price Daniel (Dem., Tex.) spoke exhaustively against any expansion of the Union, and supported the granting of Commonwealth status to both Hawaii and Alaska. "Whether a filibuster or not," the *Star-Bulletin* commented, "the 'long talk' on statehood is obviously a device to kill the bill."[76]

However, it was unnecessary to sustain a protracted filibuster. Opponents did not stop the Senate from voting on a combined bill because they knew it would not pass the House. Before this vote was taken, however, opponents made a last-ditch effort to grant the territories a status similar to that recently given Puerto Rico. A Commonwealth amendment supported largely by Southerners hostile to Hawaii was defeated by sixty votes to twenty-four on April 1, 1954. Opponents also offered an amendment which provided for a plebiscite in each territory on the question of Commonwealth status. However this was rejected by fifty-nine votes to twenty-six.[77]

Finally, on April 1, 1954, the Senate passed the Hawaii-Alaska bill. The margin of victory was decisive—fifty-seven votes to twenty-eight. Thirty-three Republicans, twenty-three Democrats, and Morse voted affirmatively. Nineteen Democrats and nine Republicans voted negatively. Only three Southern Democrats did not oppose the bill.[78] This Senate vote, like previous House votes on the separate Hawaii bill, reflected a liberal-conservative division. It also suggested that, when isolated from partisan politics, Hawaii enjoyed majority bipartisan support in the Senate as well as in the House.

However, the anti-statehood faction permitted this Senate action only because it was convinced the House would not pass the combined bill in 1954. William Fulbright (Dem., Ark.) acknowledged shortly before the debate ended: "We are told definitely that the House will never pass a bill granting statehood to Alaska." Indeed it appears the Republican leadership assured anti-statehood senators that the combined bill would not be brought to the House floor before the Eighty-third Congress adjourned.[79] A filibuster was thus unnecessary.

Three alternative legislative procedures were available to ensure that the House considered the combined legislation: it could have been brought to the floor of the House by a unanimous consent motion; it could have been placed before the House Rules Committee and debated by the House following the granting of a favorable rule by this committee; or a conference of interested senior members of both chambers could have been appointed to resolve the differences between the House and Senate versions of the statehood legislation. In the case of this third alternative both the House and Senate had to approve the legislation as reported from such a conference before it could be forwarded to the president for approval or rejection. Without substantial support from members of the majority party in Congress or endorsement by the administration, none of these procedures had a reasonable chance of success. Conscious of this, and aware of Eisenhower's hostility to Alaska, the anti-statehood faction was understandably confident that a combined bill would never become law. Few observers were surprised when the House Rules Committee refused to report the bill. Neither the president nor House Majority Leader Joseph Martin (Mass.) attempted to lever the bill out of the Rules Committee.[80]

Nevertheless, individual supporters attempted to bring the Hawaii-Alaska bill to the House floor during April 1954 by initiating a petition against the Rules Committee. Democrats supplied half of the 218 signatures necessary to pass the petition. But pressure from the Eisenhower administration promptly collapsed Republican support for this tactic.[81]

Supporters also made a unanimous consent motion to establish a conference of House and Senate members to resolve differences in the statehood bills. An objection by Democrat House Leader Rayburn killed this motion. They then introduced a resolution requesting a ruling from the House Rules Committee to send the combined bill to a joint House-Senate conference. Opposition from the Republican administration defeated this move. The Republican-controlled Rules Committee refused to authorize a joint conference, and on July 26, 1954, after prolonged debate, the committee voted to end consideration of the resolution.[82]

During the summer of 1954 leading Republicans, including Vice President Nixon, indicated publicly that the administration was making a sincere attempt to disengage Hawaii from the combined bill. The separate bill was then to be resubmitted to the Senate. In addition, Knowland promised that, if necessary, he would see to it that both statehood bills would be separately scheduled in the Senate.[83] These GOP claims were viewed as cynical and insincere on Capitol Hill. Indeed, the *Washington Star* commented as early as May 1954: "House Republican leaders predicted freely, but privately, that Congress will adjourn without acting on bills proposing statehood for either or both of the territories."[84]

Hawaii's Republicans were severely embarrassed by these futile developments in Washington. They were also alarmed that GOP indecision might rebound against the party in local elections. As the communist issue receded during 1954, island Democrats, especially Burns, worked increasingly to wrest power from the old order. The statehood issue, long considered an electoral advantage to Farrington's party, was fast becoming a liability. Without decisive action by the Eisenhower administration, local Republicans could not hope to stem the growing Democratic tide in the islands. King and Farrington thus attempted a series of initiatives aimed at breaking the deadlock in Congress. In April the governor convened a special session of the territorial legislature. It allocated a further forty-five thousand dollars to send a fifty-four member delegation to Washington. The Rules Committee as well as Republicans who had not signed Saylor's discharge petition were the main targets of the visitors (whom disillusioned locals viewed as junketeers rather than lobbyists). The hasty decision to send a very large delegation to Washington was roundly criticized as an unnecessary and extravagant duplication of the ongoing activities of the Statehood Commission. It was also viewed as a partisan GOP attempt to compensate for the failings of fellow Republicans on Capitol Hill. For five days during May the Republican-dominated delegation conducted what Farrington's *Star-Bulletin* exaggeratedly described as "a mass attack on the statehood blockade" in Washington. Both Eisenhower and Nixon met members of the delegation. But the assault was firmly rebuffed when Eisenhower admitted he was anxious to admit only Hawaii. The activities of the visitors from Hawaii did not break down GOP hostility to joint action on both territories. The vigorous, but by now routine, lobbying efforts of Tavares, Jabulka, and Farrington also failed dismally.[85]

These abortive initiatives served only to expose the irrelevance of the expensive statehood campaign. The organized public drive for admission was a necessary initial factor encouraging action by the House. Still, publicity and pleading by Hawaii were insignificant when weighed against the persuasive power of entrenched sectional and political interests in the nation's capital.

If Hawaii's Republicans were disturbed by the likely electoral ramifications of the obstructionist behavior adopted by the Eisenhower administration during 1954, Republicans in Alaska were totally demoralized by it. In the eighteen months which elapsed from the elections of 1952 to the primary elections of April 1954, support for the GOP in

Alaska fell sharply from a record high of 55 percent to less than 25 percent. Confronted with firm evidence that Eisenhower would not accept Alaska, but denied a "forthright explanation" of his position, Alaskans quickly reaffirmed their traditional ties with the Democratic party. The consequences of these developments were obvious. A White House aide advised Eisenhower late in 1954: "The rank and file of Alaskans believe they are being denied statehood arbitrarily. . . . Largely because of this state of mind, the Alaskan Republican Party faces an unmerciful beating in the Territorial elections."[86] He might have added that, because of the relationship between the two statehood bills, the fortunes of the GOP in Hawaii would also be damaged by the behavior of the administration during 1954.

Hawaii's campaign for statehood, and the local Republican party, received a critical blow with the sudden death of Delegate Farrington in June 1954. Known affectionately as "Statehood Joe," Farrington had worked tirelessly to galvanize local support and encourage action by Congress. He served as the territory's nonvoting delegate in Washington for twelve years, and helped transform the campaign after the setbacks that came with Pearl Harbor and martial law into an active, organized, and broadly based movement. Through his newspaper, the influential *Honolulu Star-Bulletin*, and with the close assistance of its editor, Riley Allen, Farrington dominated the statehood drive and gave his party popular and effective leadership. In contrast to the very conservative political complexion of most local Republicans, Farrington was a moderate, flexible politician. While he was prepared to exploit the communist issue in the early 1950s, he also had some friends within the ranks of labor. If he received less electoral support from local Japanese than from whites, Chinese, and Hawaiians, this was primarily a reflection of existing economic, ethnic, and political divisions in the island community. It did not result from a conscious attempt to exploit race for selfish political ends. Farrington's popularity transcended the racial, economic, and social cleavages which still characterized Hawaii, and helped to delay the triumph of the fast-growing Democratic party. The margins of victory which he gained from the local electorate gradually declined after World War II, but Farrington's electoral appeal was more enduring and resilient than that of his party generally. "The people of Hawaii have shown over and over again that they have a rare affection for Joe Farrington and place him distinctly above any sectional, economic or racial interest," a local Democrat had written privately in 1951 when he asked Truman to appoint Farrington governor.[87] In 1954 few Hawaiians, including Farrington's political rivals, would have dissented from this assessment.

A few Democrats, notably some of Japanese descent who were long suspicious of the powerful Republican faction that backed Farrington, later charged that he was prepared only to work for eventual statehood, not immediate admission. As indicated in chapter 5, this accusation first surfaced during 1947–1948 while the young Democrats searched desperately for a flaw in Farrington's political armor. Decades later some Democrats, notably Aoki, continued to claim that this assessment was shared by many congressmen and journalists working in Washington and applied equally to his wife, Elizabeth, who succeeded him as delegate to Congress. "Publicly the Farringtons were for statehood. It was their major political issue. But privately they were always against it," Aoki charged. Other die-hard supporters of Burns have made similar claims, assuming always that Farrington was little more than a puppet of the old guard Republicans and kamaaina haoles. "Make no mistake about this business of statehood for Hawaii. The Republicans never did want it," Samuel Crowningburg-Amalu has written in his glowing tribute to Burns.

> The big business interests in the Islands, the same who governed and ruled the Republicans, had never wanted statehood. They feared statehood, knowing full well that their own powers would be diminished with its coming. Their representatives in Washington, the Republican Delegates to Congress, of course mouthed pious declarations for statehood. But in private they deplored the whole idea. Under a territorial status, the Republicans were secure. With statehood, they were threatened.[88]

This claim served the Democrats well in the political arena, but it was as inaccurate as it was partisan. Conveniently, it assumed that in the 1950s the old guard still dominated every facet of the Republican party, and mistakenly lumped all sugar interests, major business interests, and most Republicans into a solidly anti-statehood bloc. Some Democrats apparently believed the Farringtons were willing participants in a conspiracy hatched on Merchant Street to avert statehood. They failed to appreciate that politics after 1945 were far more open, flexible, and unpredictable than at any time since the early 1900s.

As Elizabeth Farrington has correctly pointed out, although her husband had been drafted into politics in 1933 by "kamaaina sugar types" (notably Clarence Cooke, president of the Bank of Hawaii), he had from the early 1940s distanced himself considerably from this once-dominant faction. During the war he supported the challenge to military government, and during 1946–1952 he cultivated friends within the ILWU and the Japanese community. Mrs. Farrington doubtless exaggerated when she claimed his unflagging sympathy with the unions, but as early as the elections of 1946 he accepted ILWU endorsement, a decision which led to accusations from within the GOP that he was "a communist and everything else." "He happened to be a Republican," Mrs. Farrington stated, "but he wasn't a dyed-in-the-wool party man."

It was this very independence, along with shrewd advice from the editor of his *Star-Bulletin*, Allen, which helped keep his political base secure. At the same time it permitted him to work energetically for statehood—both in Washington and Honolulu—irrespective of the wishes of some conservative members of his party. Through his work as delegate and with the influential *Star-Bulletin* backing his every political move, Farrington made opposition to statehood a heresy in the islands. He "used the paper the whole time for statehood," Elizabeth Farrington recalled, and there is considerable justification for her claim: "If it hadn't been for Joe Farrington and that paper we wouldn't have statehood today."

No convincing evidence exists in the private or public record to support the allegation that the Farringtons, presumably with very skilled duplicity, paid only lip service to statehood. Indeed the private correspondence of the Farringtons with party officials, colleagues, and friends, especially Allen, suggests genuine dedication to the statehood cause. Even Joe Farrington's old political foe Burns has conceded that there was no doubt that he "was really sincere in regard to statehood."[89]

This is not to imply, however, that Farrington always had unqualified support on statehood from all factions of the local Republican party. Nor does it necessarily follow that, as Paul Pratte has attempted to argue, Farrington was "as effective as [he] could be in a Congress with shifting political coalitions." Some contemporaries rightly criticized his unwillingness to promote statehood legislation by back room deals, and regretted his reluctance to foster close working relations with prominent leaders from both sides of the House and Senate.[90] Accustomed to a much gentler tradition of essentially one-party political life during the period of uninterrupted Republican control in the islands, Farrington undoubtedly underestimated the need for tough bargaining and active lobbying in Washington.

In many ways Farrington's death symbolized the end of Republican ascendancy in the islands. Although his widow was narrowly elected to replace him as delegate, during 1952–1956 the Republican party was pushed aside by a confident, disciplined Democratic party. Farrington's untimely death perhaps removed a major obstacle to a Democratic victory at the polls; but the shift to the Democrats was inexorable. It grew out of broad demographic and social changes which gave unprecedented strength to Hawaii's AJAs and to a lesser extent other Asian immigrants. The tide of change long feared by many whites could not be halted, and after 1954 it transformed Hawaiian politics.

No one in the islands was more acutely aware of the direction of political change than Farrington's widow and successor as delegate in Washington. In the final months of 1954 Elizabeth Farrington tried desperately to convince Eisenhower that he must take stronger action on

statehood. Fearing an electoral backlash against local Republicans because of Eisenhower's apparent insincerity over Democratic Alaska, she
warned privately that the administration's pledge on both territories
must be "redeemed" and its "promises maintained." Elizabeth Farrington criticized the fact that although the GOP platform pledged statehood for both territories, presidential pronouncements largely applied
to Hawaii alone. Finally, she argued that self-interest dictated that
Eisenhower act decisively. "If the Administration is desirous of having
added strength in both the Senate and the House in the 84th Congress,"
she emphasized, "it is imperative to get the Hawaii bill through now."
This appeal, li⅃ ᴐ those made throughout 1954 by members of the Statehood Commission, fell on deaf ears. Thus, Elizabeth Farrington wrote
the White House confidentially two weeks later that she wished to meet
personally with Eisenhower. "I urgently need this interview for my
November campaign," she stated realistically. However, the ensuing
campaign photograph of Elizabeth Farrington with the president was
small consolation to those island Republicans who feared they might
lose office because the Eisenhower administration had apparently permitted narrow party considerations to compromise its approach to
statehood.[91]

Eighty-fourth Congress, 1955–1956

The results of the territorial elections in November 1954 had a decisive
impact on every aspect of the statehood issue. The Democrats won
power in the islands for the first time. Their margin of victory was surprisingly wide. In the House they controlled twenty-two of the thirty
seats; in the Senate they won nine of the fifteen positions. In the contest
for delegate to Congress, Elizabeth Farrington defeated Burns. "It
didn't occur to me that I wouldn't win," Mrs. Farrington recalled. "We
didn't have any particular strategy. . . . We just went out like we'd
always done." The election results quickly shattered such complacency
however. Elizabeth Farrington's win reflected sympathy and respect for
the work of her late husband rather than solid majority support for the
GOP. Mrs. Farrington also exploited the communist issue to some effect,
arguing as the campaign gained pre-election momentum, "This is no
time to send to Washington anyone about whom there is any suspicion
of toleration or sympathy for un-American elements." Nonetheless, her
margin of victory was by no means comfortable—960 votes out of a
total of more than 142,000. Although Burns didn't demand a recount,
he later implied that the hand-counted votes might have been tampered
with. "Somebody lost a helluva lot of votes," he wryly commented. Irrespective of the accuracy of this charge (and there were many islanders
who still saw the hand of the hegemony in such events), Burns was

obliged to wait another two years for his long-sought triumph. But his party had finally won undisputed control of the islands' legislature.[92] In the euphoria which followed the Democrats' victory there were perhaps few who paused to wonder how the appointed Republican governor might react. The electoral win could only be translated into concrete policies if King consented and did not exercise his veto power. Nonetheless, Burns was justified in observing later that 1954 was a watershed: "the Republican Party was losing its toehold, foothold, handhold, whatever kind of hold you want. . . . necklock or stranglehold." No longer was Hawaii, in effect, a one-party state.[93]

The Democrats won office primarily by appealing to, and working closely with, the non-Caucasian majority in the islands. The foundations for this success had been laid patiently and deliberately by Burns and his followers. In later years some members of the Burns faction overstated their impact on the rising fortunes of their party. The mid-1950s were a triumph for Burns supporters, but immediately after the war ended, island Democrats had won firm control of Honolulu's Board of Supervisors, and the popular liberal Democrat Wilson was elected mayor. At the same time, the Democrats displaced the GOP on Maui and won half the seats in the territory's lower house. These victories foreshadowed and assisted the later success of younger Democrats. Nonetheless, by 1954 even the most optimistic Democrats were surprised that the landslide victory had come so soon. Under the shrewd guidance of their energetic and tough party chairman, the Democrats consciously and very effectively exploited Hawaii's peculiar ethnic and class structures. They gradually widened their electoral base by maintaining the support of labor groups while appealing also to the expanding, largely non-Caucasian middle class. Candidates and party members were recruited from the newly visible and increasingly articulate and educated nonwhite groups, especially the Japanese. Statehood proponents and local observers had adamantly maintained that Hawaii's people did not engage in bloc voting. But November 1954 confirmed what the younger Democrats had always suspected: ethnicity was a central factor in political preference. (Obviously, the Republican party had also long understood this fact. Certainly Hawaii's white community had seldom endorsed, or voted for, candidates who were not Caucasians.) Race might not have been an overt factor in this campaign, but it underlay the broad political realignment reflected in the 1954 returns. The Democratic ticket was self-consciously nonhaole: "Maybe ninety per cent" of its candidates were of "Oriental ancestry or Pacific ancestry," Burns noted.[94]

The Democratic victory did not suggest that the ethnic makeup of the islands had changed dramatically. Rather, it indicated what younger Democrats and labor union organizers had long believed and encouraged—that the Japanese majority and other nonwhite groups were now able and willing to vote for candidates with similar ethnic backgrounds. These groups, especially the Japanese, were also confident that the election of a majority of non-Caucasians to the legislature would not precipitate a bitter white backlash. Those who realistically expected resentment were determined to confront it head-on, and to expose it as undemocratic and racist. If Hawaii was to justify its assertions that it was democratic and tolerant, then clearly its legislature should represent all significant segments of the island community. In the early 1950s Caucasians still comprised less than 30 percent of Hawaii's people. Citizens of Japanese origin were still the largest ethnic group in the community. Prior to the 1954 elections Caucasians had always constituted a majority in each chamber of the territorial legislature. During 1955–1956, however, twenty-two members of the forty-five-member House of Representatives were of Japanese extraction. Moreover, for the first time, representatives of Korean and Filipino ancestry were elected. Hawaii was on the threshold of genuine representative government—representative, that is, of all ethnic and social groups.[95]

Hawaii's decision to elect a predominantly non-Caucasian, Democratic legislature disturbed many mainlanders. It precipitated a vigorous revival of opposition to statehood based explicitly on racial fears, and further complicated the influence of partisan politics on action by Congress. The ethnic as well as the political complexion of Hawaii's prospective members of Congress were matters of vital concern to many members on Capitol Hill. A. L. Miller, a former Republican chairman of the House Committee on Interior and Insular Affairs and a leading statehood advocate during the early 1950s stated that he was no longer as positively in favor of statehood, partly because Hawaii would not send any Caucasians to Congress. Like many Republicans, however, Miller was also disturbed by the sweeping Democratic victory in the islands in November 1954. Other opponents interpreted the election results as proof of the controlling strength of the Japanese vote and racial bloc voting. Southerners like James Davis (Dem., Ga.) and O. C. Fisher (Dem., Tex.) used the returns to validate their argument that Hawaii's Asians were not yet adequately assimilated to permit statehood. Others, like Smathers, interpreted the election results as further evidence of the "rising tide of Asiatic Communism." Presumably this new tide was related to gains won recently by Communists in China and North Korea. Certainly Smathers' wild assertions were designed to link and exploit both racial and ideological insecurities. Pillion was also publicly convinced that the 1954 election was "a complete victory for the I.L.W.U. and the Communist Party." "Statehood should be rejected now and deferred for an appropriate time when communism no longer threatens the well-being of either Hawaii or the United States," he concluded.[96]

The national election returns also had an important bearing on statehood. The Democrats regained control of both the House and Senate.
But their victory was by no means decisive. In the Senate, forty-eight
Democrats confronted forty-seven Republicans and one independent,
Morse. In the House, the Democrats had a fairly small thirty-one-seat
advantage. The Eisenhower administration was now confronted with a
Democratic Congress, but the Democrats' strength was concentrated
largely in the conservative South. These developments did not augur
well for Hawaii.

Eisenhower's explicit position on statehood early in 1955 was not
appreciably different from that to which he had clung during the previous year. In his state of the Union message in January 1955 he observed that although there was no defensible reason for delaying Hawaiian statehood, the admission of Alaska should await resolution of
Alaska's "complex problems."[97] Yet during the next two years the Republican administration was reluctant to promote either territory, as
the voting trend manifest in 1954 indicated that Hawaii would elect
one, possibly two Democrats to the Senate. Most observers correctly
interpreted this as a permanent and essentially irreversible tendency
rather than a temporary setback for the GOP. At the same time, events
in Alaska confirmed it as a Democratic stronghold.

The political implications of these developments were obvious, especially to the conservative faction in Congress. "Based on the 1954 election returns," Pillion informed a House investigating committee in February 1955, "it appears that, in the event of statehood, Alaska would
surely elect 2 Democratic Senators and Hawaii would be likely to elect 2
Democratic Senators." Cognizant of the delicate balance of power in
Congress, and aware that since the New Deal the Republicans had
become the normal minority party, the Eisenhower administration was
unlikely to make a bad situation worse by adding four new liberal Democrats to the Senate. Pillion succinctly assessed the dilemma confronting
the GOP during the Eighty-fourth Congress.

It is most obvious that the passage of the joint Hawaiian-Alaskan statehood
bill by the Congress would place the Republican Party in a difficult position.
The President would be placed in a political dilemma. By approving statehood for both territories, he would risk the probability that these two territories would return 4 Democratic Senators. If he vetoes statehood, he assumes
the political onus of defeating a measure of popular favor.[98]

But if the statehood question was now politically embarrassing for the
GOP, it was equally a problem for the divided Democratic party.

During 1955–1956 Southern Democrats held most key positions in the
Senate and House. Johnson, the Senate majority leader, was personally
opposed to admitting either territory. His quick rise to power was based
on Southern support, and the ambitious young Texan was not anxious to

compromise his political future by alienating Southern friends—especially when they so strongly overshadowed liberal Democrats in the Senate. Moreover, Rayburn, the Speaker of the House, was also a Texan and an opponent of statehood. Equally important, the reactionary Southerner Smith remained chairman of the House Rules Committee. Not only was Smith an implacable opponent of statehood, he was also the unofficial leader of the anti-civil rights faction in the House. As these three men largely determined what legislation Congress would consider, the prospects of favorable action on Hawaii were indeed slight.

The tactics adopted by both national parties on statehood were not altered by the results of November 1954. Democrats attempted to combine the two bills; Republicans would only endorse Hawaii. However GOP opposition to Alaska was now more explicit and detailed. Alaska's vast size, small population, and economic instability were still cited as basic reasons for denying it statehood. Eisenhower and the Pentagon now also asserted that statehood would seriously damage national defense arrangements. As a territory, 90 percent of Alaska's land was reserved for exclusive federal jurisdiction. Cold war tensions apparently convinced some officials in the Department of Defense that control of this vast close neighbor of the Soviet Union should not be relinquished to an elected government. In part this argument was a transparent attempt to justify Republican partisanship. Still, it appealed to a considerable number of military personnel, conservative congressmen, and a collection of fervent anti-communists.[99] Surprisingly, the Pentagon's guarded position was not shared by the State Department. In 1954 it asserted that statehood for Alaska "would support American foreign policy and strengthen the position of the United States in international relations." Certainly it would add consistency to America's espoused anti-colonialism.[100]

If the State Department was anxious that America should no longer be viewed as a colonial or semi-colonial power, Eisenhower apparently was not. He threatened to veto a combined bill unless substantial areas of Alaska were excluded from the jurisdiction of the proposed state government. Reluctantly, statehood proponents agreed to compromise. They accepted an amendment to the Alaska bill which permitted the federal government to retain exclusive control over 40 percent of the proposed state. However, this concession failed to placate either Eisenhower or the Pentagon. In March 1955 the president shocked the more naive supporters of both territories when he informed the House committee: "I am in doubt that any form of legislation can wholly remove my apprehensions about granting statehood immediately."[101] Those observers who appreciated the realities of partisan politics could hardly have found this an unexpected warning.

Nonetheless, the House Insular Affairs Committee approved a combined bill on March 13 by a vote of nineteen to six.[102] The minority recommended that statehood "be deferred pending an appropriate constitutional amendment to provide for representation in the U.S. Senate on a basis proportionate to population." In the interim, it suggested both territories be given the right to elect their own governors.[103] The 1955–1956 Rules Committee began protracted, hotly contested hearings on the combined bill three days later. The majority of the committee was comprised of Democrats who had previously opposed Hawaii and Republicans hostile to both territories. Thus, when that committee finally agreed to report statehood, it did so with a rule calculated to defeat the legislation. On April 26 it granted a rule which was unacceptable to both Republican supporters of Hawaii and Democrats who wanted both territories admitted.[104] It was correctly described as "a monstrosity of a rule."[105] Proponents had requested that an "open rule" be granted which could permit the combined bill to be separated on the House floor. Instead the Rules Committee gave a "closed rule" which prohibited amendments. Although details of the vote were not made public, Colmer later stated that the closed rule was supported by a two-to-one majority of the twelve-member committee. Presumably the eight Democrats voted to combine the bills, while the four Republicans wanted separate bills. It was widely anticipated that a combined bill would not pass the House. "I support the closed rule," Colmer stated unequivocally. "I am unalterably opposed to the bill."[106]

The House refused to devote substantial time or energy to the combined measure. It was considered briefly on May 9–10 and promptly recommitted to the Insular Affairs Committee, ostensibly for further investigation. This motion, sponsored by Hawaii's old foe Pillion, was carried by 218 votes to 170. Both parties were divided over the motion. In contrast to previous House votes on Hawaii only, however, the GOP offered strongest support for recommittal and hence strongest opposition to statehood. The Democrats were very evenly divided—105 to 107 —while the Republicans divided 113 to 63. Significantly, more than 90 percent of all Democrat votes for recommital came from the eleven Southern States. Georgia, Alabama, Mississippi, Arkansas, North Carolina, South Carolina, and Virginia voted solidly for recommittal. Only six representatives from the remaining four Southern states—Texas, Tennessee, Florida, and Louisiana—opposed recommittal.[107] In contrast, Northern and Western Democrats voted overwhelmingly against Pillion's motion.[108] Predictably, most Republicans who opposed recommittal were liberal representatives of Western states, especially California and Washington. Those voting against recommittal sincerely wanted both territories admitted immediately and concurrently. But in 1955, as in the previous session of Congress, opponents of one or both territories combined to avert affirmative action on either territory. The uncompromising actions of the Rules Committee and GOP intransigence on Alaska made defeat of the combined bill a foregone conclusion. The House debate in 1955 was little more than a charade. Eisenhower tried to salvage something from these murky developments by asserting that each territory should be "considered on its merits." But as the *New York Times* commented, during eight years of exhaustive consideration "merit had always played a much less significant part than politics." In 1955 politics had once again prevailed.[109]

Conscious of her increasingly vulnerable electoral position, Mrs. Farrington again appealed to Eisenhower to give public evidence that he unequivocally supported statehood. "It is not easy for me to go home now and explain why statehood failed," she dejectedly told the president. However, Eisenhower's limp reply was small comfort to Elizabeth Farrington and other island Republicans. He conceded his deep disappointment with the inconclusive events of 1955, but offered no alternative program which might extricate statehood from the constraints of short-term political influences.[110]

No further action was taken on statehood in either chamber during 1955 or 1956. However, members of the Senate Judiciary Committee conducted six days of hearings "on the nature and scope of Soviet penetration of the Hawaiian Islands." Some local cynics suggested that Hawaii's pleasant climate and geography, not a genuine concern with internal security, had drawn these senators away from winter in Washington. But Eastland, the chairman of the subcommittee, and other Southern Democrats fully appreciated the relationship of statehood and civil rights. For this Senate faction at least, the investigation in Hawaii was a serious political exercise. Newspapers in Hawaii and on the mainland merely underlined the obvious when they claimed that the hearings were designed "to build up sentiment in the incoming Congress against another statehood bill."[111]

Eastland's initial trip to the islands was prompted by local residents, especially members of Imua, who opposed statehood and wanted to stifle social and political change in Hawaii. He was supplied with voluminous information by this fervently anti-communist group. Eastland stated that the primary purpose of his trip was to determine why Hawaii's Democratic legislature had reduced the biennial appropriation for the Territorial Subversive Activities Commission from a requested forty-seven thousand dollars to twenty thousand dollars. A rabid segregationist, he was quite willing to intervene on behalf of reactionary local whites in an attempt to undermine the credibility and power of the newly emergent Democratic party in the territory. Nor was Imua, which remained sympathetic to the GOP, reluctant to use a Southern Democrat for this end.[112] Statehood advocates protested that Eastland's free trip to their exotic islands was unrelated to the un-American activities probe, and was instead simply an opportunity for him to collect information with which to fight statehood in the next Congress.

Not surprisingly, his Senate group failed to uncover any new evidence of internal subversion. But its report concluded that "conspiratorial forces" controlled the ILWU and exercised an "influence over the Territory's legislature and over politics in general."[113] The fact that they could not specify the nature or scope of this influence did not deter senators from asserting that it existed. McCarthy's pathetic demise had not convinced all conservative senators that the notion of guilt by association and the use of imprecise smear tactics should be abandoned.

If such unsavory practices continued after the mid-1950s, they now seemed less effective than at any time since the infamous Dies Committee was formed in 1938. Despite Eastland's assertions about Soviet influence, opponents of statehood increasingly found that racism was a more effective weapon than anti-communism. If they could not demonstrate that Hawaii was dominated by Communists, they could at least show that most of Hawaii's people were non-Caucasian. With the decline of McCarthyism and the emergence of a violent national struggle over civil rights from the mid-1950s on, race again became an explicit factor in the statehood debate.

Once the combined bill had been recommitted by the House, the Senate refused to take any action on either territory. Johnson and the Democrats' national chairman, Paul Butler, directed their members not to promote any statehood legislation during 1956. Some liberal Democrats implied they would disobey this instruction, provided Eisenhower gave an assurance that he would not veto any combined or separate statehood measures. During 1956, however, the president refused to give such an undertaking.[114] Although both Hawaii and Alaska won large majorities in public opinion polls, statehood was not a crucial domestic issue. Nor did it appear to be a significant issue in the presidential or congressional elections of 1956. Civil rights was, however, the current pivotal question in national politics; and statehood remained an explicit civil rights issue, as well as a vital ingredient in the liberal-conservative struggle for supremacy in Congress, especially the Senate. Northern Democrats were reluctant to promote statehood during an election year as this would add fresh fuel to the sensitive civil rights issue, and expose the bitter regional animosities which now split the party more deeply than at any time since the New Deal. Neither major party had anything to gain by resurrecting the statehood controversy late in an election year.

The modest civil rights program outlined originally by Truman gained substantial liberal support after World War II. Yet it could never overcome the veto power of conservative opponents in Congress. In the absence of effective action by Congress, or support for tough legislation by Eisenhower, the courts remained the only avenue of change on civil rights. Elected officials were much less responsive to the pressure from black organizations like the NAACP, and less embarrassed by the denial of democracy to black Americans, than was the Supreme Court. In 1954 it moved, albeit gradually, to grant blacks legal equality with other citizens. Although it had previously attempted to expand the rights of black Americans and sometimes criticized discrimination, it had not confronted the most obvious and difficult question which flowed from the practice of racial separation and institutionalized segregation. Since Reconstruction and the proliferation of Jim Crow laws in the South, the courts had essentially accepted the myth that laws could be applied equally even though blacks and whites had access to separate facilities and institutions. In a series of celebrated rulings during 1954, however, the Supreme Court accepted that separate facilities were inherently unequal. In the watershed ruling on *Brown v. Board of Education* it ruled unanimously and precisely:

> We come then to the question presented: Does segregation of children in public schools solely on the basis of race, even though the physical facilities and other tangible factors may be equal, deprive the children of the minority group of equal educational opportunities? We believe that it does. . . . We conclude that in the field of public education "separate but equal" has no place. Separate educational facilities are inherently unequal.

Gradually this decision was generalized to other fields. It represented, nonetheless, an attack only on the legal underpinnings of segregation. It could not ensure changes in social practice. In 1955 the Supreme Court ruled that existing segregation must be ended "with all deliberate speed."[115] But the segregated South conveniently interpreted this as a legal sanction for gradualism and ambivalence. Moreover the Eisenhower administration did not use its executive authority to expedite change. Segregation remained essentially intact. Just as the Fifteenth Amendment had failed to ensure equal voting rights for blacks, so initially the 1954 Supreme Court ruling failed to end segregation and discrimination.[116] The most significant short-term consequence of the ruling lay in the bitter, sometimes violent resistance it precipitated among whites from segregated states. This response had an important bearing on Hawaii's statehood prospects.

It is impossible to separate Southern intransigence on statehood from its hostile reaction to the Supreme Court's desegregation decision. On the one hand this gave rise to the so-called Southern Manifesto which asserted the intention and rights of states to reverse the Court's ruling.[117] It was signed by nineteen senators and eighty-one representatives. (Significantly, nineteen Southern senators had also voted against the combined Hawaii-Alaska bill in 1954.) On the other hand, some Southern states responded in extralegal and illegal ways. The Ku Klux Klan resurfaced. Demonstrations and violence erupted against federal attempts to open schools to black students. Most white supremacists, however, were content to join citizens' councils, which emerged as the most effective public form of resistance to desegregation. Southern determination hardened when Eisenhower submitted a draft civil rights program to Congress in 1956. His modest proposal sought the creation of a civil rights commission, a civil rights section in the Justice Department, and new statutes to widen the civil and voting rights of blacks. This proposal was further diluted before it passed the House in 1956. But, like state-hood legislation, it never reached the floor of the Senate before the Eighty-fourth Congress adjourned. Had Southerners failed to defeat this legislation in committee they would have waged a filibuster against it on the floor of the Senate. Legislation on statehood and civil rights suffered a similar fate because in the eyes of most Southerners at least, the two issues were inextricably linked.

Disenchantment at Home

Separate Hawaii bills had passed the House three times during 1947–1954, while a combined statehood bill won Senate approval in 1954. But during 1955–1956 Congress virtually ignored specific legislation on statehood. Ironically, these two years of inactivity coincided with events in Hawaii which gave statehood new urgency—at least for opponents of the old Republican elite.

The Democrats' victory of 1954 meant that for the first time the com-position and complexion of the territory's legislature closely resembled the community at large. Power in Hawaii did not rest in this elected body however. The new Democratic majority gained office on a plat-form which advocated progressive labor legislation, improved public education, land and tax reforms.[118] For many Republicans the loss of office symbolized the triumph of radical non-Caucasian elements, something which they had successfully averted for more than half a cen-tury. But if the Democrats now controlled the elected legislature, they did not appoint the territory's governor. During 1955 King vetoed sev-enty-one bills approved by the territorial legislature. This action cut the heart out of the Democrats' wide-ranging initiatives. "Never during twenty conservative years of Republican legislatures and Democratic Governors," Daniel Tuttle, Jr., observed, "had a Governor so com-pletely demolished a legislative program." The *New York Times* con-ceded that King's action was "unprecedented." Included in the vetoed legislation were bills increasing property taxes, land reform measures, and progressive labor legislation aimed at amending the Workers' Com-pensation Act.[119] Friction between the elected legislature and the Wash-ington-appointed governor intensified dramatically after 1954. But while King's action frustrated local Democrats, some exploited the new

situation. "Actually," Burns recalled: "King was our good whipping
boy. Because once he vetoed all those bills in the '55 legislature, man,
we were in shape."[120]

When in 1957 the Democrats were able to marshall sufficient votes to
override King's veto of their graduated tax bill, the Eisenhower administration accepted that his behavior might alienate more voters and further entrench the political power of the Democrats. King was now seventy years old and had served four years as governor. The Republican
party was anxious that he be succeeded by a person capable of using the
office to bolster their party's flagging fortunes. He was therefore replaced by William Quinn, who was much younger and far more pragmatic. In contrast to King, Quinn was a malihini haole. He had arrived
in Honolulu two years after the war, less than ten years before his sudden elevation to governor. A self-proclaimed "independent Republican
—of a little different stripe to the old guard here," Quinn had been a
candidate for his party, served as a member of the Statehood Commission, and along with many others had journeyed to Washington to give
evidence on statehood. Recalling his surprise at being summoned to
Washington by Interior Secretary Fred A. Seaton and told of Eisenhower's decision, Quinn noted that the White House had "taken someone
who could never be elected governor and imposed him on the people.
. . . the very thing I'd been preaching against." Nonetheless, Quinn
eagerly accepted the offer. In the intervening two years before statehood he used the position to put a more moderate face on the local
Republican party, and in so doing he built a substantial personal following and helped resuscitate his party.[121]

Hawaii's statehood campaigners were understandably frustrated and
disillusioned by events in Washington in the decade after World War II.
Local Democrats in particular were disturbed that without statehood
and an elected local governor their interests could never be confidently
expressed or satisfied. King's elaborate use of the veto compounded this
disquiet, although many conservative Republicans were delighted that
the status quo could still be protected by an appointee. The sentiments
of territorial senator Ben Dillingham, expressed before the legislature a
few years earlier, typified this opinion. "The people of Hawaii should
know that the only thing that stands between ourselves and chaos," he
claimed, "is the position of the governor." By denying the will of an
elected majority King sparked new awareness—among Democrats at
least—that Hawaii remained subject to a form of colonial rule. Given
the impasse in Congress on statehood, some islanders now demanded
that Hawaii be immediately permitted to elect its own governor. Confident that they would win the 1956 elections, island Democrats pressed
this issue. Considerable support for an elected governor was expressed
throughout the territory. Not all advocates of this compromise were

Democrats. The conservative *Honolulu Advertiser*, for example, argued that a vigorous attempt to get an elected governor might revive support for statehood. Certainly it would demonstrate that Hawaii was, at most, a qualified democracy. There were doubtless some who remembered the *Advertiser*'s previously ambivalent position on statehood and found this apparent enthusiasm for broader democracy most surprising. Some suggested, perhaps uncharitably, that the newspaper supported the proposal because it would simply complicate and further delay statehood.[122]

Predictably, most Republicans opposed the proposal for an elected governor, arguing that it was a politically motivated attempt to attack the GOP and to undermine the statehood cause. King questioned the legality of the proposal. He emphasized that the right to elect their chief executive had never been extended to any of the twenty-nine states which had previously been territories. Like many sincere statehood advocates, King also argued that the proposal would imply that Hawaii was retreating from its demand for that full equality in the Union which could only be attained through statehood. The proposal was dismissed by the *Honolulu Star-Bulletin* as a gradualist approach which would undermine the statehood campaign. The paper also attempted to equate support for an elected governor with support for what it characterized as a fruitless Commonwealth status campaign. A majority of the Republican-dominated Statehood Commission also opposed the proposal because, if approved, it might permit Congress to delay rather than expedite statehood.[123] Despite strong initial support from Democrats and extensive deliberation by the legislature, the proposal was never formally approved. It was a symbol of disenchantment both with Congress and residual Republican strength in the islands rather than a genuine alternative to eventual unqualified statehood.

Growing dissatisfaction with the statehood campaign also provoked other initiatives by the Democrats. They were anxious to identify with the statehood cause, but recognized that the formal campaign could never guarantee success in Congress. In previous years the GOP, through the work of the Farringtons, King, Tavares, and the Republican-controlled Statehood Commission and constitutional convention, had successfully exploited the statehood issue. Yet the Democrats' statehood policy reflected more than political considerations. It was, in part, a recognition that the expensive activities of the commission were, by 1955, largely redundant. Hence when the commission requested a further $150,000 to support its activities during 1955–1956, the Democratic legislature balked. The campaign was granted only $85,000, less than half the average amount given previously by Republican-controlled legislatures.[124]

Openly critical of the "Republican-dominated Commission" and of the governor's partisan appointments to it,[125] Democrats decided to promote statehood essentially through the elected legislature. Many Democrats advocated that Hawaii's citizens should be granted tax concessions by the federal government until they were given full citizenship rights under statehood. Although designed primarily to focus national attention on statehood by reviving the issue of "no taxation without representation," this proposal gained considerable support in Hawaii. In May 1955, the Hawaii House of Representatives passed a resolution asking Congress to grant Hawaii's citizens "relief" from the payment of federal taxes. The resolution originally requested exemption from payment of any federal taxes, but this provision was modified because supporters feared Congress might interpret it as an expression of support for Commonwealth status. However, the territorial senate did not pass the resolution, largely because it might have undermined the statehood campaign. Nonetheless the House-passed resolution was inserted into the *Congressional Record.* It served to reaffirm the fact that although Hawaii's citizens paid federal taxes just as did mainland citizens, they were denied equal political rights with these citizens.[126]

Demands for an elected governor and tax exemptions reflected a decline in active local support for statehood, and general disenchantment with congressional indecision. During 1955–1956, as an aggressive young Democrat, Frank Fasi noted, support for statehood was "at its lowest point since the war."[127] Widespread cynicism had replaced early postwar optimism. Burns observed that few local Japanese still felt statehood would be granted: "Come hell or high water we weren't gonna get it." A leading nisei confirmed this opinion: "I never thought that we would ever, . . . ever get statehood."[128] Hawaii might have enjoyed majority support in Congress, but few congressmen were prepared to push the issue. Most accepted that Southern intransigence could not be overcome in the Senate. Moreover, both national political parties were divided over the Hawaii-Alaska question, and saw little political mileage in resurrecting this divisive issue annually in Congress. "There never was a time when Hawaii had more friends in Congress— or ever a time when we had fewer of our friends working for us," Long observed sadly. Many supporters on Capitol Hill were now decidedly pessimistic. Engle commented, for example, that defeat in the Eighty-fourth Congress "may postpone for many years, if not forever, the entrance of these incorporated territories as States to the union."[129]

Legislation to admit Hawaii made erratic but ultimately disappointing progress in the decade after the war. Those who optimistically expected Hawaii's war record to induce prompt action by Congress must have been sadly disillusioned by the mid-1950s. Proponents' hopes were raised periodically when the House acted; but Senate intransigence and hostility quickly punctured these bursts of optimism. By the end of 1956 the Senate had never voted on a separate Hawaii bill. By manipulating committee procedures, by threatening or initiating a filibuster, opponents defeated Hawaii's bid for statehood. This strategy of delay was complicated and protracted. It was organized and executed by conservative champions of states' rights and white supremacy in both chambers. In seeking partisan political advantage from separate or concurrent entry of Hawaii and Alaska, the major political parties compounded the impact of the obstructive tactics on which the conservatives' veto power ultimately rested. Yet even if party politics had not complicated and permeated every facet of the statehood debate after 1947, it is unlikely that Hawaii could have overcome the determined anti-civil rights faction in Congress. Estimates of the relative influence of racial and political factions in delaying admission might well vary. Moreover the impact of each faction fluctuated markedly. Yet as long as the South interpreted statehood as a threat to its ability to defeat liberal civil rights measures, Hawaii would confront insurmountable procedural obstacles in Congress. The fact that these devices were erected by a minority made them no less effective. Statehood was an important aspect of the divisive and bitter struggle over civil rights after World War II. Unless a compromise could be reached on civil rights generally, there was little prospect of a successful compromise on statehood.

Chapter 8
Compromise Politics:
Alaska First

"Hawaii's prospects for success in this session of Congress are excellent," the Statehood Commission again asserted in early 1957.[1] This time, however, such optimism was not without foundation. Election results in the territories and throughout the nation dramatically undercut the influence of partisan politics on statehood for Hawaii. More importantly, the changed complexion of Congress obliged Southern conservatives to compromise on statehood and civil rights or risk outright defeat on these questions. This is not to suggest, however, that resistance simply evaporated.

A New Delegate and New Tactics in Washington

Eisenhower easily defeated Stevenson again in 1956. But for the first time since 1848 the winning presidential candidate failed to carry either the House or Senate for his party. The Democrats won a two-seat majority in the Senate, and controlled the House by a margin of thirty-seven seats. Eisenhower was clearly more popular than either his party or his liberal Democratic rival. In Hawaii and Alaska the GOP salvaged very little other than the ability to appoint each territory's governor. In both territories the Republicans were soundly defeated. In Hawaii the Democrats won eighteen of the thirty House seats and twelve of the fifteen Senate seats. Both territories also elected Democrats as delegates to Congress. In Hawaii, Burns defeated Mrs. Farrington by a wide sixteen-thousand-vote margin. His victory completed the electoral revolution begun two years before. It confirmed what 1954 had dramatically implied: the long era of Republican ascendancy and authority had ended.

The rise of the new Democratic party and the statehood issue were inextricably linked. Statehood was the central issue in the election campaign which brought Burns his long-sought victory in 1956. Despite a Republican administration in Washington after 1952, the polite efforts of the Farringtons had failed to win congressional support. Increasingly, as the confident young Democrats were very well aware, Hawaii's community accepted (to use Burns' direct language) that such "methods were never gonna win the darn thing," and turned to the Democrats for more forceful initiatives. Furthermore, after the 1954 watershed the divisive struggle between the Democratic legislature and Republican governor convinced many that territorial rule must end immediately. Statehood was increasingly perceived as both a symbol of real democracy and the principal vehicle for achieving this overdue end. In Burns' view only statehood would bring about a change in the distribution of wealth and power. "That was the primary thing in the future," he observed. A decade after the war the ideas espoused by the young Democrats associated with Burns had filtered into the public domain, threatening to become the new orthodoxy in local political rhetoric. Statehood was now projected by the Democrats as the principal way of overcoming the authority and privileges of the conservatives which had long dominated island politics and were still regarded as the power behind the scenes. Furthermore, as we have seen in earlier chapters, the expanding middle class of the islands, which increasingly comprised people of Oriental ancestry, also perceived statehood as a symbol of genuine acceptance into the host society. It would provide confirmation that racism and inequality were not central features of Hawaiian (and by implication American) life. "They wanted statehood so bad," Burns observed frankly, "because they were always the ones given as the reasons why we couldn't get it."[2]

In his perceptive study *The Future of American Politics*, Samuel Lubell argued that the 1930s were an electoral watershed throughout the nation during which the Democrats replaced the GOP as the normal majority party. Under Roosevelt the Democrats constructed a broad-based coalition of Catholic, black, and urban voters.[3] A somewhat similar electoral transformation occurred in Hawaii two decades later. Certainly by the mid-1950s the Republicans had been eclipsed by a vigorous Democratic party, which drew its strength from newly organized labor, wage earners in urban Honolulu, and the descendents of the largest and latest immigrant groups to the islands, especially the Japanese and Filipinos. This new coalition had been nurtured by the experience of war rather than the impact of depression. Younger nonwhite islanders were determined to translate the confidence and aspirations fostered by war into a cohesive political program in the following years. Veterans like Inouye and Matsuo Takabuki who were members of the famous 442nd team and had gained university degrees under the GI Bill epitomized this change. Their experience of inequality at home, enlistment and combat in World War II, veterans' education, and political activism in the 1950s and 1960s closely mirrored the experiences of many black civil rights advocates on the mainland. War was a catalyst for both groups. It would be easy to exaggerate the similarities between nisei and black experiences however. Certainly, no segment of Hawaii's diverse nonwhite population confronted discrimination embedded in a legal apparatus like segregation. Unlike the conditions which shaped race relations in the Southern states, Hawaii's complex racial and ethnic relations were unique within America, stemming from patterns of immigration and settlement peculiar to the island community. Although seldom united in formal political associations, Hawaii's nonwhites comprised a substantial majority of the islands' population—a situation which contrasted fundamentally with the mainland where all nonwhite groups comprised a minority of about 15 percent by the 1950s. The fact that Hawaii's racial and ethnic patterns were unique did not, as we have seen, remove them from the national debate over civil rights and statehood. Moreover, while these patterns had no direct parallel on the mainland, local politics (and hence the statehood drive) were always influenced substantially by them.

Hawaii had not yet sent a citizen of Japanese ancestry to serve as delegate in Washington. Indeed both parties had studiously avoided nominating a descendent of any immigrant Asian group to contest elections for delegate to Congress. Nevertheless, as indicated previously, Hawaii had elected substantial numbers to the local legislature by the mid-1950s. For opponents of statehood this simply confirmed that Hawaii would shortly send nonwhite representatives to Washington. For liberal and moderate Democrats, on the other hand, the ethnic background of Hawaii's representatives was much less significant than their likely political color; and the 1956 elections suggested that Hawaii, like Alaska, would normally send Democrats to the nation's Senate.[4] Any lingering belief that the islands might still be a Republican stronghold was removed. Ironically, Republican opposition to Democratic Alaska had unexpectedly delayed the admission of Republican Hawaii until it too had become a Democratic territory. During his second term as president, Eisenhower had to swallow this bitter political pill or side with a reactionary minority in Congress and reject both territories yet again.

Despite the conspicuous inactivity of both national parties on statehood during 1945–1956, each included immediate admission of Hawaii and Alaska in their platforms for the 1956 elections. At the same time Eisenhower retreated slightly and supported Alaska, on condition that "adequate provision for defense requirements" was included in its legislation. Conscious of the political advantage which might flow to their party from the entry of Hawaii and Alaska, moderate Democrats took the offensive early in 1957. Only "Republican lethargy or deliberate opposition" they charged, could defeat the territories in the Eighty-fifth Congress.[5] Conveniently, this partisan view overlooked the obstructive behavior of Southern members of their own party, as well as the previous reluctance of some moderate Democrats to promote Republican Hawaii.

Under Burns' guidance, and with the increasingly visible support of

Hawaii's Japanese, the Democrats quickly outgrew the communist issue and rose to dominate island politics by the mid-1950s. Burns' enormous energy, shrewd vision, and political acumen were rewarded by the triumph of the Democratic party and his election as delegate to Congress. But if Burns now dominated local politics, he had yet to demonstrate that he was other than a novice in Washington. Like the Farringtons before him, Burns eagerly exploited the statehood issue. He was determined to succeed where his predecessors had failed. Still, success ultimately depended on strong support from national leaders of the Democratic party and the collapse of Southern-led resistance to statehood legislation. Realistically, Burns and the Democrats who controlled Hawaii's legislature recognized that the expensive official statehood campaign was predictable, ineffective, and exhaustive. Under its new chairman, Thurston, the commission continued to send literature to congressmen and more than seventeen hundred mainland newspapers. It also dispatched its respectable members to perform now-familiar rituals before a seemingly endless procession of official hearings by congressional committees. Laden with statistics on every facet of the islands' development, and willing to repeat yet again that Hawaii's people were thoroughly Americanized, these citizens could scarcely have believed that their testimony was necessary, let alone influential. Certainly the local legislature was convinced that the campaign was useless and should be wound down. Thus, it allocated only eighty-five thousand dollars to the commission for the years 1957–1958. However, the rift between the Democratic legislature and the Republican-dominated Statehood Commission persisted after 1956. Moreover, Burns as well as most local Democrats were convinced that direct talks with Johnson and Rayburn, not publicity by the commission, was the only realistic way to break the political deadlock on statehood.[6]

Statehood supporters introduced admission acts rather than enabling bills in the new Congress. This important change in strategy meant that Congress was not required to vote separately on a draft constitution. Burns was largely responsible for the maneuver, although it was made possible by the earlier decision to write and approve a "state" constitution.[7] In 1956 Alaska followed suit and adopted its own "state" constitution. Like Hawaii it now supported only admission acts. Proponents from both territories hoped their bills would be classified as privileged legislation, as this would permit them to bypass the Rules Committee which the bigoted Howard Smith and his aged Southern colleagues still controlled.[8]

After 1956, when the Alaskan electorate endorsed their proposed "state" constitution, Alaska attempted to exploit the so-called Alaska-Tennessee Plan. In 1796 Tennessee had been accepted as a state after holding unauthorized elections and sending a "state" delegation to

Washington. Michigan (1835), Iowa (1846), California (1849), Oregon (1858), and Kansas (1859) had also adopted the Tennessee Plan to expedite statehood. In 1957 Alaska sent two elected "senators" and one "representative" to Washington. When the new Congress convened they were introduced to the Senate from the gallery, but they were never seated in either chamber. During 1949–1950 the Hawaii Statehood Commission had toyed with the idea of employing this plan; but it was rejected largely because proponents naively believed that statehood was imminent.[9] In early 1957 Hawaii's supporters were perhaps equally confident; nevertheless events in the following months again deflated this optimism.

Committees of the House and Senate again conducted extensive hearings on Hawaii early in 1957. This time there was no junketeering and all hearings were held in Washington. Proponents noted with pleased surprise that only one person gave negative testimony to either committee. More importantly, no attempt was made to combine the Hawaii and Alaska bills in committee. Yet there was little enthusiasm in Washington for Hawaii's immediate admission. The Senate Committee on Insular Affairs unanimously backed Hawaii, but only two members were present to endorse its report. The House committee refused to report Hawaii, and neither chamber of Congress debated it during 1957.

Conscious of Hawaii's recent departure from the GOP fold, the Eisenhower administration behaved very inconsistently over Hawaii. It briefly attempted to resurrect the communist issue to justify this ambivalence. Deputy Attorney General William P. Rogers suggested, for example, that communism was "a serious threat to the Territory's economy and politics." GOP leaders now refused to acknowledge publicly that statehood "would reduce the danger of communist infiltration in the islands." Such claims were simply a smoke screen for partisan preoccupations. They did little to enhance Republican support in the islands, and flatly contradicted previous GOP policy.[10] Moreover Eisenhower vacillated and was unable to give firm directives to his party on statehood. The Republicans could not successfully exploit the statehood issue. Nor could they distract attention from it. In the absence of any substantial executive-sponsored legislative program, statehood remained an important, if uninspiring, national issue. Increasingly the Democratic leadership took the initiative on this question, and Hawaii's future rested on developments within the Democratic party.

During 1957 Eisenhower accepted a compromise amendment to the Alaska bill which gave presidents the right to withdraw land from state control if it was deemed essential for defense purposes. The Pentagon and the State Department now agreed that Alaska should be given statehood.[11] However, moderate and liberal Democrats, not Republicans, were the leading proponents of both territories after 1956. Indeed before Congress adjourned that year leaders of the Democratic party gave firm public assurances that separate statehood bills would be debated in both chambers during 1958. Yet the question of statehood had been debated exhaustively before. Unless the anti-civil rights faction could be induced to retreat, any additional debate would again prove frustratingly inconclusive.

Civil Rights and Statehood: The End of Massive Resistance?

The familiar pattern of congressional vacillation on statehood was repeated in 1957. Nonetheless, events in this year signalled the beginning of the end of "massive resistance" by white supremacists against all forms of civil rights legislation. This had an immediate impact on the fortunes of Hawaii and Alaska. Reluctantly, in the face of emerging bipartisan support for at least cosmetic legislation on civil rights, Southern representatives compromised. In late 1957 they withdrew their filibuster against Eisenhower's civil rights bill introduced the previous year. For the first time since the end of Reconstruction more than eighty years before, Congress had approved a specific civil rights measure. This defeat of the Southern faction was more apparent than real however. It was more important for what it foreshadowed than for what it achieved. As the quid pro quo for ending their filibuster, the anti-civil rights faction extracted major concessions over key provisions of the bill. When finally approved it was an emasculated version of Eisenhower's very modest original proposal.[12]

In its final form the bill provided for an Executive Commission on Civil Rights, a Civil Rights Division in the Department of Justice, and empowered the federal government to seek court injunctions against those who sought to obstruct or deprive citizens of their voting rights. But it was a toothless initiative. In return for the two-thirds majority which was necessary to close debate in the Senate, supporters accepted amendments which made it virtually impossible for the attorney general to enforce the act, and reduced penalties under the legislation to a laughably small three hundred dollar maximum or not more than forty-five days imprisonment. In practice the legislation did nothing to boost blacks' access to the vote, and totally ignored their other grievances. Some Southerners bemoaned the fact that their peculiar "way of life" had been irreversibly threatened. In contrast, others, like Senator Richard Russell of Georgia, interpreted the amended and weakened bill as a sweet victory for their section. Yet the white supremacists had been defeated on a civil rights measure—albeit an innocuous one—and pressure for tougher action by Congress continued to build.[13]

From the time of Truman's first civil rights proposals shortly after

World War II (indeed from the era of Reconstruction), pro-segregationists had relied more on manipulating parliamentary procedure than on
majority support to avert change. Events of 1957 suggested, however,
that this strategy was no longer sufficient. By the late 1950s a number of
factors coalesced to undermine the effectiveness of the minority veto.
This development had a dramatic influence on the fate of Hawaii and
Alaska.

Eisenhower's belated decision to introduce civil rights legislation was
a political response to factional changes in Congress which themselves
reflected growing resentment over Southern racial practices. Most vocal
citizens and representatives from outside the South now accepted that
the denial of voting rights to many Southern blacks was an embarrassing anomaly in a country based ostensibly on a concept of freedom and
equality. As old guard, anti-New Deal Republicans were gradually replaced by younger, more flexible representatives in Congress, more
moderate views on race found expression in Washington. In addition,
the growth of Republican support in black districts in the 1956 elections
helped shape an informal coalition of moderate Republicans and Northern Democrats willing to vote for gradual and modest changes to racial
legislation and practices. Referring to its bipartisan leaders in the Senate, Russell appropriately named this unofficial coalition the "Know-
land-Douglas Axis."[14] It comprised a substantial majority of representatives in both chambers. Unlike the well-established conservative
coalition which was based on an arrangement between the two factions
for mutual support on a wide range of issues, this moderate alliance was
temporary, informal, and fluctuating. Nevertheless it did get the 1957
bill through Congress. And in 1958–1959 it reemerged, this time to
ensure decisive action on Alaska and Hawaii.

Confronted with large bipartisan majorities willing to push for modest civil rights legislation after 1956, the Southern faction reluctantly
decided to compromise. The Eisenhower bill surprisingly reached the
Senate floor in 1957. In large part this resulted from the new-found
willingness of moderates to exploit procedural tactics. Knowland, the
leader of the GOP in the Senate, skillfully kept the bill away from Eastland's enclave of reactionaries in the powerful Judiciary Committee. He
was ably supported by the wily Democrat leader Lyndon Johnson, who
had sniffed a shift in the political winds and now sided unashamedly
with Senate moderates. Johnson, a Texan, was conveniently placed to
bargain with fellow Southern Democrats. He was also a back room
negotiator and political numbers man par excellence. Certainly he was
instrumental in persuading his conservative Southern colleagues to
abandon their filibuster. He undoubtedly reasserted what many pro-
segregationists now accepted: that a compromise would be more effective in the long-term than blind resistance. Many opponents of civil

rights anticipated that a protracted filibuster might strengthen the determination of other senators to establish an effective cloture rule. Early in 1957 the Senate had rejected a motion to this effect. Most Republicans, many of whom supported Eisenhower's civil rights measure, voted with Southern Democrats to defeat this effort to end the practice of protracted debate. It is highly probable that at least some Southerners agreed privately not to resist Eisenhower's mild bill in return for Republican support over the cloture issue. Some Southerners certainly appreciated that a prolonged filibuster against the Eisenhower measure might alienate those Republicans previously tolerant of the Southern position on cloture.[15] This in turn might precipitate decisive action against the rules permitting filibuster—something which a bipartisan collection of conservatives had averted earlier in the year.[16] Thus in 1957 the filibuster was withdrawn, and the Senate was permitted to amend and vote on the weak civil rights act.

If any observers still doubted that statehood was tightly linked to the civil rights and states' rights issues, the vote of 1957 must surely have dispelled this misconception. In the House the vote was 126 against the civil rights measure—107 Democrats and 19 Republicans. Significantly, 130 members, representing almost identical constituencies, had previously voted against the separate Hawaii bill. In the Senate 18 Democrats provided the only negative votes. All but one of these represented a Southern state. Virtually all House and Senate opponents of the civil rights act were also opposed to the admission of Hawaii or Alaska. Eastland, Russell, Thurmond, and Smith led the debates and tactics against each of these measures. Given the explicit racism which had permeated the debate over Hawaii and the likely impact of statehood on the Senate's composition, the similar voting patterns evidenced on Hawaii, Alaska, and civil rights from 1947 to 1957 were certainly not unrelated coincidences. In urging Johnson to vote against "this dastardly legislation," this "shameful measure" to give Hawaii equality, many Southerners acknowledged privately the link between these issues. "The admission of these islands to statehood, is fraught with danger," one of Johnson's fellow Texans warned. "To extend such rights would delegate to a polyglot population, with ideologies completely alien to the philosophies of our American heritage, an equal voice in the enactment of laws under which we must live here on the mainland." "We know," the warning concluded, "[Hawaii] would always support legislation detrimental and distasteful to the people of Texas and the entire Southland." Among other objections were that Hawaii: "would add two more senators and a representative of the Hubert Humphrey-James Roosevelt kind"; begin "a flood of Oriental immigration"; "put two Orientals in the United States Senate"; compromise efforts to "keep our Country as white as possible"; and accelerate the eclipse of the "white races of this

Country." Certainly, if Texas is accepted as representative of the South, a substantial minority believed strongly that statehood would result in additional anti-South votes in Congress and hasten the triumph of de-segregation and liberal civil rights legislation. "Being mixed racewise," one of Johnson's constituents noted with alarm, "Hawaiians could be expected to vote for complete integration in America."[17]

The compromise strategy adopted by pro-segregationists in 1957 did not reflect support for Eisenhower's original proposals. By withdrawing their filibuster Southerners gained sufficient reciprocal help to dilute the central provisions of the original bill. Howard Shuman has argued convincingly that "the failure of the filibuster may be regarded as a carefully calculated decision to avoid consequences which would have been worse, from the Southern point of view, than those of the bill as it passed the Senate." Fearing a strong reaction from a majority of sena-tors, the Southerners not only ended their filibuster but even criticized Thurmond for speaking for twenty-four hours in an individual attempt to defeat the legislation. Russell acknowledged that a filibuster was not sustained because in the long-term it would have been counterproduc-tive. "There was not a man among us who was not willing to speak against this iniquitous bill until he dropped in his tracks," Russell stated. "We would have done so, but for the conviction, growing out of our knowledge of the Senate and the experience of many years in this body, that a filibuster was certain to make a bad bill infinitely worse."[18] John-son conceded a similar point when answering a constituent's charge that he had betrayed all Texans by compromising on civil rights. The senator replied to this trenchant criticism that:

> Two choices were open to me in this matter. One was to do nothing and let the extremists take over. The other was to present a reasonable proposal that would attract the support of reasonable men and women everywhere. I took the second choice because I believe this is the way we can block those who believe in forced integration and harsh punitive legislation. The "do noth-ing" course would have left the South exposed to the mercies of the extrem-ists.[19]

C. Vann Woodward, Benjamin Muse, and a number of other authors have argued, however, that the compromise strategy and more concilia-tory rhetoric employed by opponents of civil rights did not necessarily reflect the dissipation of Southern hostility to external intervention in state matters. Rather, it indicated a continued determination to resist federal encroachments on the so-called Southern way of life. In Wood-ward's estimation, the South after the Supreme Court decision of 1954 was more profoundly estranged and wholeheartedly defiant than at any time since Reconstruction. During 1954–1956, for example, the eleven former Confederate states adopted approximately one hundred pro-segregation measures. The flexible strategy employed by the anti-civil rights faction during 1957 was more a response to the exigencies of congressional politics than a suggestion that racial attitudes were quickly moderating in the South.[20] Nonetheless, the very fact that the champions of states' rights had been induced to compromise their position on civil rights legislation in Congress had far-reaching implications for Hawaii.

Passage of the 1957 act was, as Shuman pointed out, the first major defeat for the Southern Democrat–conservative Republican coalition in Congress since 1938.[21] A new majority coalition of liberal Democrats and moderate Republicans was willing to pass civil rights legislation, including statehood for the territories. The 1957 vote also indicated that while four senators from Hawaii and Alaska might increase liberal strength in the Senate, these additional senators would probably not exert a decisive influence on civil rights. The margin of victory in 1957 was sufficiently wide to make the impact of four new votes for civil rights relatively unimportant. Certainly the admission of the new states was not a precondition for passage of a civil rights measure. Moreover the events of 1957 suggested that the filibuster would now be used only sparingly or not at all. Although most Southerners still bitterly opposed the addition of new senators who might support the liberal position on cloture, this preoccupation declined after 1957. Most conservatives now accepted, if reluctantly, that their influence could best be maintained through back room compromises and deals rather than the filibuster. The change of strategy was clearly demonstrated in 1958 when conservative senators failed to invoke a filibuster against statehood and decided to accept a compromise initiated by moderate Democrats. The South abandoned the obstructionist tactics which had served the peculiar interests of its whites so well for more than eighty years.

Hawaii Delayed: A Realistic Concession

If sectional opposition to statehood was breaking down, political obstacles nevertheless still remained. In February 1958, Knowland advised Johnson that the Eisenhower administration would not support Alaska unless the Democrats used their majorities to ensure votes on Hawaii in both the House and the Senate immediately after action was taken on Alaska. Despite the election returns of 1954 and 1956 some members of the GOP continued to view Hawaii as a normally Republican area. As late as February 1958 the *New York Times* reported that it remained a "basic tenet of political faith on Capitol Hill that if Hawaii is admitted it means two Republican Senators, and if Alaska it means two Democratic Senators." It is doubtful if many Republicans still harbored this illusion, although most were anxious to salvage some political advantage for their party by identifying it with the final successful push for statehood. However, many Republicans (including Eisenhower) hesitated, believing that both territories were solidly Democratic.[22] Senator Frank Church (Dem., Idaho) attempted to expose the ambivalent position of the GOP when he told the Senate:

> . . . any effort which has heretofore been made to combine the two statehood bills, under any understanding or arrangement, whether that effort involves simultaneous linking of the bills or a successive consideration of the bills, is an effort which is directed towards combining the opponents of both bills in opposition to each, and thus is not an effort which is in reality designed to serve the interests of the case of statehood for either territory.[23]

Ironically, similar arguments had previously been used by Republicans against Democrats who had insisted in 1953–1954 that the bills be combined.

By 1957–1958, however, sincere supporters of both territories were adamant that the statehood bills were seperate issues, as different as Alaska and Hawaii were geographically and economically. Burns and Alaska's long-serving Democratic delegate to Congress, E. L. Bartlett, agreed early in 1957 to introduce and support separate bills only. With the help of a bipartisan group of congressmen, this strategy was adhered to rigidly. "Separate bills in no way reflect any change whatsoever in my belief," James E. Murray (Dem., Ill.) stated on behalf of twenty-three co-sponsors in the Senate, "that both Alaska and Hawaii are equally ready for statehood, and that both should be accorded equal treatment by the Congress and the Administration." As chairman of the Interior and Insular Affairs Committee, Murray gave a public assurance that the Democrats would demand equal treatment for both territories.[24] But in 1958, as in previous years, his party gave priority to solidly Democratic, white Alaska.

In late January 1958, after persistent appeals by Burns and Bartlett, Johnson convened a private conference of influential Democratic senators. Burns also attended. This meeting agreed that only Alaska would be debated before Congress adjourned. Hawaii was dropped from Johnson's agenda. But in return Johnson undertook to ensure that Southern Democrats would not use procedural devices or the filibuster to defeat Alaska in either chamber. Southern Democrats had clearly accepted this compromise before it was put to Burns and liberal Democratic senators.[25] Again, as in 1957 over civil rights, Johnson had helped to engineer a compromise which preserved surface unity within his party by placating Southern and liberal elements. Most importantly for the Democrats, this compromise averted an embarrassing and divisive public wrangle over a Southern-led filibuster. It also kept the cloture issue safely at bay. If the Democrats' deliberations over statehood were private, their compromise decision was very soon public knowledge. It became obvious that Democrat leaders in the House and Senate did not intend to vote on Hawaii in 1958.[26] With mid-term elections scheduled for November, Democrats were aware that two new senators from Alaska might give them a majority in the next Congress.

Yet political expediency was not the sole incentive for a firm Alaska-only strategy. Many Democrats and a surprisingly large number of Republicans accepted that Alaska's admission would inevitably bring prompt action on Hawaii. The compromise also offered some protection for Southern Democrats as it ensured that, at most, only one liberal state would be admitted in 1958. For the South, Johnson's compromise strategy was at worst a certain way of delaying Hawaii, and at best a means of again defeating both territories. For if Johnson could speak with confidence on Democratic policy, he could not influence Republican tactics, and Southern Democrats apparently believed that Alaska would meet strong resistance from GOP members. Southerners acquiesced to Johnson's compromise in part because they anticipated that the anti-civil rights faction could combine with Republicans opposed to the priority given Democratic Alaska and thereby defeat the separate measure. Eastland and his Southern senate colleagues undoubtedly miscalculated early in 1958, as Republican resistance to "Alaska first" dissolved. Moreover the Southern faction could not overlook the events of the previous year. The civil rights compromise in 1957, and the absence of a filibuster against Alaska in 1958, indicated that conservative Southern Democrats were now prepared to modify their position slightly on states' rights issues in the hope of retaining a substantial, if declining, influence within both their own party and Congress. As Dewey Grantham has noted, the dispute over civil rights after the 1954 Supreme Court decision was the first crack in Southern solidarity. With it Southern sectionalism began a slow and halting decline.[27] Without this important, if imprecise change, neither Alaska nor Hawaii could have overcome the Southern veto in the late 1950s.[28]

Burns played a decisive role in initiating and sustaining the compromise strategy. During 1957 he worked closely with fellow Democrats from Alaska on a possible compromise. "I will work hard for Alaskan statehood," he stated publicly in October 1957. "If it becomes necessary to drop Hawaiian statehood in order to get Alaska through, I will do just that." This concession helped to pave the way for more concrete initiatives involving Johnson and other prominent Democrats like House Speaker Rayburn. Both Johnson and Rayburn had previously opposed immediate statehood. However Rayburn agreed to a compromise strategy late in 1957 after he had been assured by Burns that no attempt would be made to promote Hawaii in 1958. Like many other Southerners, Rayburn remained adamant that Hawaii contained "too many

Japs," but he relented on statehood because he thought the Alaska-first scheme would founder on the rock of combined Republican and Southern Democrat resistance. Johnson was more difficult to convince than Rayburn. He refused to endorse the compromise strategy without first gaining a definite assurance from Burns and Democratic proponents generally that Hawaii would be ignored during the Eighty-fifth Congress. This assurance was given at the meeting convened by Johnson in January 1958.[29] Burns also gave a confidential undertaking to Johnson at this meeting. He informed the Democratic Senate leader that he would initiate moves to recommit the Hawaii bill if Republican supporters attempted to have it considered by the House of Representatives in 1958. Thus Burns agreed to oppose passage of the Hawaii bill during the final session of the Eighty-fifth Congress. As the quid pro quo for this concession, Johnson gave an assurance that he would support consideration of the Hawaii bill by both houses of Congress early in 1959. Johnson, who now claimed publicly that he was both a liberal and a conservative, still refused to commit himself unequivocally to Hawaii's cause. Throughout 1958 he intimated privately that Hawaii would again confront protracted debate if brought before the Senate prematurely. During his first two years in Washington Burns became a self-confessed Johnson man and admitted to being on fairly friendly terms with the powerful Texan. But Johnson remained sensitive to the interests of his Southern colleagues and was, at most, ambivalent over the delicate Hawaiian question until early 1958.[30]

Both Burns and Johnson subsequently denied that any written arrangement or deal had been made over the statehood issue. However the above information, coupled with events during 1958–1959, clearly substantiates the view that an explicit agreement was reached between Burns, Rayburn, and Johnson early in 1958. Pro-statehood Democrats agreed to support the separate admission of Alaska in 1958 and the separate admission of Hawaii in 1959. Anti-statehood Democrats agreed not to wage a filibuster to defeat separate bills, provided only Alaska was considered during 1958.

After reassuring his close political friends in Honolulu of Johnson's pledge that Hawaii would be considered immediately after Alaska, Burns canvassed wider support on Capitol Hill. He wrote Senator Church, for example:

> As perhaps you know—from the meeting I had with Senator Johnson last week—I have taken the position in what I hope is enlightened self-interest that nothing should interfere with success in the consideration of Alaska-S.49. To this end I am perfectly willing and have so advised my constituents that—if necessary—I would remove Hawaii from consideration. I do not think this will be necessary since it is understood that action on Alaska will be completed before Hawaii is brought up. I want statehood.[31]

In a similar vein he informed Senator Murray:

> Alaska and Hawaii should be considered separately . . . Hawaii does not
> want to be the means of killing both. She would rather withdraw to "clear
> the track." The sincerity of her desire for statehood would be suspect if she
> followed any other course.[32]

Burns and other Democratic statehood proponents openly acknowledged their adherence to the Alaska-first strategy. But before the House
approved Alaska they did not publicly concede that they would oppose
attempts to admit Hawaii in 1958. Had this been admitted, the prospects of gaining the necessary bipartisan support for Alaska might have
been seriously undermined. Nonetheless, Murray did acknowledge publicly early in 1958 that the chance of favorable action on Hawaii in the
Eighty-fifth Congress was slight. Nor did any Democratic leader give
the Republicans an assurance that legislation to admit Hawaii would be
considered in 1958. Burns and Church stated only that favorable congressional consideration of Hawaii would "inevitably" follow the admission of Alaska; they neglected, however, to specify whether consideration would be initiated during 1958 or later.[33]

Early in 1958 Republican statehood proponents refused to support
Alaska without an explicit assurance from Democrats that Hawaii
would also be considered by both houses of Congress in 1958. Without
such an assurance, Republican Senate Leader Knowland stated, "it is
very likely that it will be moved that the Hawaii statehood bill be made
the second title of the Alaska statehood bill."[34] However, attempts to
oppose the separate admission of Alaska, or unite the Alaska and
Hawaii bills, were not pursued seriously by GOP leaders. Given the
uninspired program outlined by Eisenhower during his second term as
president, it is not surprising that moderate Republicans relented and
permitted action on statehood. Without a decision on this important, if
long-standing issue, the achievements of Eisenhower's party in Congress
would have been chronically insubstantial. The Republicans had vacillated for too long to benefit from the statehood issue. Ironically, it was
the party supported by most Southerners, the Democrats, which finally
arranged and implemented a successful legislative strategy on statehood. Still, both parties had cynically attempted to exploit the issue
since 1945, and neither could hope to be identified electorally as sincere
crusaders for the rights of American citizens in either territory.

On May 28, 1958, the separate Alaska bill passed the House by a
modest margin—210 votes to 166. Both parties were sharply divided
over the issue, but a majority from each party voted affirmatively.
Democrats divided 118 for, 81 against. Republican support was less
decisive, resulting in a split of 92 votes for, 85 against.[35]

This vote was taken after the Rules Committee was discharged of responsibility for reporting the bill. Under Smith the committee had refused to report either statehood measure. However, both territories were now proceeding by admission bills and could thus be brought directly to the floor by the chairman of the House Interior and Insular Affairs Committee. With the support of Rayburn, who overruled all objections to this procedure, Chairman Leo O'Brien (Dem., N. Y.) brought the "privileged" Alaska measure to the House floor on May 16, 1958. Vigorous opposition from Southerners and conservative Republicans failed to negate the strategy. When a motion by Pillion to recommit the Alaska bill was defeated, moderate Democrats knew that their party's compromise strategy would succeed. Most Southern Democrats, and almost half of the House GOP members, opposed the Alaska bill and supported recommittal. But they could not command sufficient votes to defeat Alaska. Eighty percent of Democrats who opposed Alaska represented former Confederate states.[36] Most Republicans who opposed the separate measure represented large Northern states, but they were joined by a scattered collection of members from smaller and Western states. Republican resistance to Democratic Alaska was stronger than that exhibited against Republican Hawaii in 1947, 1950, or 1953.[37] The informal conservative coalition still provided the core of resistance to statehood, but there were also many moderate Republicans who were reluctant to admit Alaska first and thereby increase Democratic strength in Congress.

Immediately after the House approved Alaska, leading Democrats admitted publicly that Hawaii would not be debated by the Senate or House during 1958. When O'Brien intimated that the Hawaii bill might be discharged from his committee, Burns hurriedly pressed him to withdraw any such proposal. Thus O'Brien advised that attempts to bring Hawaii into the Union would have to be delayed until the next year. Shortly after, Murray informed the Senate that 1958 was not the appropriate time to push for statehood for Hawaii, and concluded: "Anyone who believes Hawaii has a chance of Statehood this session is completely unrealistic." However, to encourage Republican support for the Alaska bill in the Senate, Democrats frequently suggested that Hawaii would be considered by both chambers early in 1959, provided Alaska was admitted in 1958.[38]

The Senate debated the Alaska bill intermittently for a week late in June. Despite Republican threats to resist the separate measure, Southern Democrats led the opposition to it. Stennis unsuccessfully moved that the bill be referred to the Armed Services Committee for additional consideration. Eastland raised two points of order, but both were decisively rejected. A motion by Almer Monroney (Dem., Okla.) to substitute Commonwealth status for statehood was defeated by fifty votes to twenty-nine. Thurmond moved that a large section of northern Alaska be excluded from the proposed state and reserved for federal control. This amendment was also rejected by a decisive majority. Although these moves were designed to delay Alaska's admission, they were supported by only a few Republicans. Most Southern Democrats vigorously opposed the bill, but they did not initiate a filibuster against it. On June 30, 1958, the Senate passed the Alaska bill by an overwhelming sixty-four votes to twenty. More Republicans than Democrats voted for Alaska. A bipartisan group of thirty-one Democrats and thirty-three Republicans voted affirmatively. Only thirteen Democrats and seven Republicans opposed the bill. Five Southern states—Arkansas, Georgia, Mississippi, South Carolina, and Virginia—voted solidly against it, providing half of the total opposition votes. Some Southern Democrats, notably Johnson, Smathers, and Ralph Yarborough (Tex.) abstained from voting.[39] In the light of Johnson's later efforts to be identified as a leading proponent of civil rights, his refusal to vote for Alaska appears extremely inconsistent. Political ambitions clearly weighed heavier with Johnson than democratic principles. He was reluctant to alienate his Southern supporters within the Democratic party by voting for Alaska. At the same time however, he encouraged Southerners to seek accommodation with the moderate mainstream of their party. Johnson, and the Democratic party generally, later reaped the political harvest of this skillful juggling act.

The compromise Alaska-first tactic confronted Eisenhower's party with a complex political dilemma. By 1958 it had been outmaneuvered on statehood. Pro-statehood Republicans were understandably reluctant to collaborate with Southern Democrats in order to defeat the separate Alaska bill. This action would have undermined bipartisan support for Hawaii and exposed the GOP to the charge that it, much more than the Democratic party, wished to defeat both territories. Most Republicans were also very reluctant to be associated with any maneuver which might jeopardize statehood, as this issue now constituted a central portion of Eisenhower's very modest legislative program. Nor could the GOP encourage attempts to combine the Hawaii and Alaska bills without displaying considerable hypocrisy. Before 1957 it had consistently denounced similar efforts by Democrats as a cynical political exercise designed to defeat both territories. Democrats like Murray were, by 1958, eager to point this out. Also, as the *New York Times* remarked, the Republican party was reluctant to continue its "unremitting hostility" to Alaska because this may have alienated local voters and further consolidated Democratic strength in this region.[40] Defeat of the Alaska-first strategy might also have adverse repercussions for Republican candidates in the 1958 elections in Hawaii. Hence, mainstream Republicans could no longer afford to vacillate over statehood. Finally, many GOP members genuinely believed that they could gain the support of liberal Democrats and admit Hawaii late in 1958, immediately after Alaska had paved the way through Congress.[41]

Burns, along with other Democrats, was confident Alaska's admission would foreshadow favorable action on Hawaii. But predictably, majority leaders in Congress refused to schedule a debate on Hawaii during 1958. Johnson stated that the Senate would only debate the issue after the House had acted. Few congressmen were surprised, however, when the House Insular Affairs Committee refused to report Hawaii to the floor until the last day of the final session of the Eighty-fifty Congress.[42] The Democrats had closed ranks behind Johnson's strategy. To ensure that the compromise was not breached, Southern conservatives indicated that they might have to initiate a "prolonged debate" in the Senate if the Hawaii bill was discussed.[43] House Majority Leader John McCormack (Mass.) predicted that Hawaii would definitely be debated in 1959. Burns advised his constituents that attempts to promote consideration of Hawaii late in 1958 might endanger its strong chances in 1959. Similarly, Church emphasized the excellence of Hawaii's prospects, provided no attempt was made to initiate consideration before 1959.[44]

Admission early in the new Congress was now a foregone conclusion. As had so often been the case since 1945, Hawaii's fate was determined before it reached the floor of either chamber. Reports from Washington vindicated the public confidence of Burns, Johnson, and others when they estimated that Hawaii could confidently anticipate at least seventy favorable Senate votes in 1959. Shortly before the national elections were held, Johnson denied that he had ever made "commitments, trades or deals concerning Hawaii." However, he also stated:

> I believe the Senate Interior Committee will easily in the next session report the Hawaii bill. I believe the Senate Democratic Policy Committee will schedule it for debate, and early in the session there will be plenty of time to debate it. Due to the wise counsel of Delegate Burns and others who have put their country ahead of politics, Hawaii has the best chance for admission at the next session it has ever had.

Johnson was confident that "a number of former opponents" would support the Hawaii bill, or at least "not oppose it so vigorously" as before. Democrats were convinced that Southern statehood opponents would not filibuster to defeat the Hawaii bill in 1959. In the light of these developments, Johnson's definition of "commitments, trades and deals" must have been a very formal one indeed. Few congressmen or reporters accepted as either genuine or accurate his public claim that such an arrangement did not exist. As Ernest Gruening later noted, Johnson "cleared the way so that [statehood] legislation wouldn't be impeded."[45]

The compromise Johnson strategy was vehemently criticized. The

New York Times led the assault, charging that Hawaii's legitimate rights had again been defeated by "subterfuge and obstruction." "There is absolutely no honorable excuse for the manipulation that is preventing the issue from coming to a vote," the newspaper observed shortly after Alaska was approved. The *Washington Post* was equally disturbed.[46] In Congress Republicans attacked the strategy as a partisan, "politically advantageous" maneuver designed to increase Democratic party numbers in the Senate. While signing the Alaska bill into law on July 7, 1958, Eisenhower stated that he was "extremely disturbed over reports that no action is contemplated by the current Congress on pending legislation to admit Hawaii."[47]

If Eisenhower and GOP congressmen were powerless to break the Democrats' strategy, similar endeavors by islanders from both parties were destined to fail also. Nonetheless on July 6, 1958, an official delegation of eight members arrived in Washington to lobby for statehood. It was appointed by the Statehood Commission and led by its Republican-appointed chairman, Lorrin P. Thurston. (More than sixty years earlier Thurston's father had journeyed to Washington seeking annexation and protection of the small white elite in the islands. As late as 1948 Lorrin P. Thurston had refused to endorse statehood, fearing it seems that it would promote the interests of Hawaii's non-Caucasian majority. Now a decade later he led the islands' official campaign for equality. Few local observers failed to see the irony in these developments, especially those of Japanese ancestry who remembered the attitudes expressed by the *Advertiser* during martial law and the late 1940s.) In addition to this official delegation, local Democrats Oren Long and Vincent Esposito, and Republicans Mrs. Farrington, King, and the newly appointed governor, Quinn, also journeyed to Washington. Despite three weeks of active lobbying on Capitol Hill, the Democrats' strategy remained unchanged. Quinn's heated encounter with Johnson typified the response of the Democratic leadership to these lobbying efforts. "I'm setting the agenda" for the Senate, Johnson angrily told Quinn. "I'll determine when things will be called-up and when they won't." Hawaii's lobbyists were left in absolutely no doubt that the Democrats would not shift from their agreed strategy in 1958. Rayburn told Mrs. Farrington unequivocally: "Hawaii will have to wait until next year."[48]

Understandably, local Democrats from the Burns camp were not enthusiastic supporters of these lobbying activities, as they were directed against a strategy which Burns not only supported but helped to engineer. Island Republicans exploited this situation enthusiastically in the months preceding the 1958 elections. Quinn accused Burns of complicity in a "dark compromise" designed to ensure the defeat of Hawaii and condemned his refusal to "strike while the iron is hot." The Statehood

Commission, which remained firmly controlled by appointed Republicans, refused to sanction the compromise Alaska-first tactic. Mrs. Farrington went so far as to charge that her old adversary had permanently jeopardized statehood. "No man on the face of the globe has set statehood back as far as Jack Burns," she claimed in August 1958. Republicans also criticized Burns and Democratic members of the territorial legislature for refusing to support the Statehood Commission actively or forcefully.[49] Many Democrats, including Burns, viewed the commission as moribund, expensive, and a de facto wing of the Republican party. Some partisans of Burns, including Wright in his study of Hawaii's "second revolution," have claimed that "a number of members of the Statehood Commission . . . had advocated every move likely to jeopardize statehood." Admitting that not all commission members acted out of a desire to undermine admission, this view nevertheless maintained that the strategy the commission promoted in 1958 "—tying Hawaii to the Alaska Bill, and when this failed, trying to rush passage of the Hawaii Bill at the close of the session—were actions most likely to kill the Hawaii Bill."[50] Certainly Burns did his utmost to dissuade the commission from pursuing such tactics, fearing that they might upset his fragile agreement with Johnson. Nevertheless, in the absence of concrete evidence to the contrary it must be assumed that all commission members genuinely believed their tactics were in the best interests of statehood. Denied full knowledge of the Burns-Johnson strategy, and anxious to be identified with the final successful stage of the long statehood struggle, they were understandably determined to exploit the changed circumstances of 1958.

The territorial electorate was apparently unmoved by the virulent criticism levelled against Burns and his supporters. In the elections of November 4, 1958, the Democrats' strategy on statehood was formally tested. It was the central issue in the election campaign. Burns won a handsome victory over his Republican opponent, Farrant Turner. The Democratic party again won control of both houses of the recently reapportioned legislature. It enjoyed majorities of almost two to one in the House (thirty-three seats to eighteen) and Senate (sixteen seats to nine). While statehood was not the only issue contested in these elections, the returns nonetheless constituted an expression of strong support for Burns' decision to sanction Alaska first in order to break the perennial political impasse on Capitol Hill. Most islanders apparently accepted that Hawaii would be admitted immediately after the new Congress convened.

Chapter 9

Fiftieth State

Statehood 1959: Still a Divisive Issue

Viewed objectively, Hawaii was better equipped for statehood than Alaska. Numerous congressional committees acknowledged this. Yet during the 1950s Alaska consistently enjoyed stronger mainland support than Hawaii. Six national Gallup polls, conducted during 1950–1958, all revealed greater opposition to the immediate admission of Hawaii than Alaska. The proportion of mainlanders willing to accept either territory as a state also declined significantly during this decade. For Alaska it dropped from 81 percent to 73 percent of those polled. For Hawaii it fell from 76 percent to only 63 percent. As both territories were non-contiguous, important strategically, incorporated for long periods, and supported small populations, the only significant variable which might have influenced the differences in mainland opinion was the composition of Hawaii's population. The issue of communist influence appears to be the only other variable which might have induced greater resistance to Hawaii. Yet the decline in mainland support for the islands coincided with the gradual retreat of internal security as a rousing national issue. It appears that public disenchantment with Hawaii increased as the nature of its mixed population became more widely known. Ironically, this was a direct but obviously unwanted consequence of the vigorous publicity campaign conducted by supporters. It is hazardous to draw inferences from opinion polls, but the consistency of these returns for 1950–1958 suggests that racial factors remained the primary influence on mainland attitudes toward Hawaii's bid for admission.[1]

Other evidence supports this interpretation. As we have seen throughout this study, Southerners provided the backbone of all opposition to Hawaii. The Congressional correspondent of the *New York Times*, William S. White, concluded that hostility to Hawaii reflected "the quite plain fact that some Senators are afraid of the color of some of the people of Hawaii." Nor was this concern restricted to a few congressmen. As late as 1957 the *Tulsa Tribune* asked rhetorically: "Do we want to put a couple of Japs in the Senate of the United States?" It concluded that the admission of the "polyglot people" of Hawaii would

inject foreign concepts and traditions into Congress.[2] A booklet by
Drew Smith on *The Menace of Hawaiian Statehood*, published in New
Orleans in 1957, protested that Hawaii's admission would aggravate
racial tensions by allowing unchecked immigration of Asians. "The car-
dinal and crucial fact to be borne in mind," Smith claimed, "is that this
nation is an extension of European civilization and has received none of
her generative impulses from Asia. It is the blood of Europe that went
into the settling of America and the greatness that has been attained will
be perpetuated only so long as that unity of blood remains substantially
unimpaired." The subtitles of this booklet expressed succinctly the reactionary arguments that had almost invariably surfaced whenever statehood was debated after 1898. They included: "A Menacing Precedent,"
"The Caucasions are Rapidly Disappearing in Hawaii," "America an
Extension of European Civilization," "The Japanese Control Hawaii,"
and "Immigration Threat." According to George Lehleitner, a Louisiana businessman who worked energetically for Hawaii in an attempt to
break down Southern intransigence, Smith's crude assertions provided
invaluable ammunition for opponents of Hawaii.[3] Smith, along with
many opponents of the islands, was incapable of recognizing the contribution of African or Asian immigrants to America's traditions and development. His notions were an unashamed rehash of simple nineteenth-century social Darwinism. There were still some, however, who
found such opinions comforting. Clearly, as Murray noted with dismay,
racism was a crucial factor in the protracted statehood dispute. The
Democrats' decision to give priority to Alaska over Hawaii in 1958 was
influenced by more than partisan self-interest; it reflected also a belief
that predominantly white Alaska would confront less hostility in Congress than multiracial Hawaii.[4]

After 1957 most Southerners felt it politic to adopt conciliatory rhetoric when opposing civil rights or related bills in Congress. Nonetheless,
in 1959 Thurmond and other intractable opponents continued to criticize Hawaii's admission on racial grounds. He conceded that "the Japanese are as truly moral as any other race of civilized human beings," and
accepted that societies could coexist, despite differences in "heritages"
and "outlooks." However, Thurmond argued, Rudyard Kipling had
been correct when he wrote "the immortal words 'East is East and West
is West, and never the twain shall meet.' " As Asians and Hawaiians
constituted more than 70 percent of Hawaii's population, and as these
groups had a heritage and culture "fundamentally different" from that
of the West, the senator concluded, statehood should not be granted.
Some House opponents were equally convinced that Hawaii's racial
composition made statehood impossible. Howard Smith argued simply
that Hawaii would be a "foreign state." "With a population so radically
different from the rest of the United States," another Southerner assert-

ed, "[Hawaii] cannot possibly qualify as one of the United States."⁵ Supporters of segregation and white supremacy remained reluctant to grant full and equal citizenship rights to any Americans who were nonwhite.

Perennial disputes over the balance of party strength in the Senate, as we have seen, complicated and delayed congressional action on Hawaii after 1946. Attempts by both major political parties to exploit statehood for partisan ends inflated the strength and effectiveness of opposition to Hawaii for more than a decade. Yet behind virtually every facet of resistance lay states' rights issues. Throughout 1945–1959 the core of resistance to Hawaii was provided by those states anxious to remain immune from interference by the central government and those congressmen who felt the more populous states were disadvantaged by the constitutional provisions for equal representation of all states in the Senate. These issues had been raised but not completely resolved when the original thirteen states accepted the federal Constitution. They had resurfaced with tragic consequences in the bitter sectional strife which precipitated the Civil War. No territory has entered the Union without confronting resistance based on the belief that the power of existing states would be eroded by any additions to the Senate. The threatened erosion of states' rights, foreshadowed in Truman's civil rights program and confirmed by the Supreme Court's decision of 1954, solidified Southern opposition to the entry of multiracial Hawaii or liberal Alaska. The anti-civil rights faction opposed statehood because in the longterm it might contribute to an expanded role for the federal government in racial questions. Howard Smith, an unbending foe of Hawaii and a leading apologist of segregation, claimed that "the centralization of power in the Federal Government is an evil that will eventually destroy the carefully preserved concept of free, sovereign and independent states."⁶ Sectional jealousy and attempts to preserve the peculiar pattern of race relations in the South underpinned such views. The states' rights argument was a direct, if slightly muted, echo of the rationale for secession advanced by the South before the Civil War. Obviously, the Southern states could not now defend their rights by withdrawing from the Union. But as we have seen throughout this book, they believed they could help prevent any erosion of their power by stopping new states from joining the Union.

Pillion acknowledged the vital relationship between states' rights and proposed statehood legislation when he told the House:

The past 25 years can be noted for the vast and alarming growth and concentration of power in the National Government. A parallel concentration continues to take place in the executive branch of our government. These increasing concentrations of power coincide with a reduction of powers of the States, the loss of sovereign rights and liberties of the people, and deprivations of the legislative powers and responsibilities of Congress.

> Statehood for these Territories would accentuate the inequalities of national
> representation. It would tend to strengthen the national concept and weaken
> States rights. It would increase the pace of nationalization of local govern-
> ment services and concentrate power in the Federal Government and in the
> executive branch.[7]

This argument was, a White House aide remarked, an opinion "as old as the Republic itself." It had repeatedly been raised and rejected as the Union expanded from thirteen to forty-eight states. States rights' argu- ments were not confined to Southerners determined to protect their par- ticular way of life. Many congressmen who were not Dixiecrats were influenced by the calculation that on the average, one senator repre- sented approximately 17 million citizens, while Hawaii would qualify for one senator per 223,000 citizens.[8] Southern conservatives skillfully exploited bipartisan and cross-sectional anxieties about the long-term consequences of equal representation of states in the Senate. Willis Rob- ertson (Dem., Va.) denied that Southern opposition to Hawaii in the Senate was motivated by either racism or resistance to the possibility of two new Republican senators. He told the Senate:

> Our objection is far more fundamental. It is the same objection voiced . . .
> more than 100 years ago by Daniel Webster with respect to Utah and New
> Mexico, when he said: "I have the strongest objection to a premature cre-
> ation of States. . . . The bringing in of small states with a representation in
> the Senate equal to the representation of the largest states in the Union, and
> with a very small number of people, deranges and disturbs the proper bal-
> ance between the Senate and the House of Representatives."[9]

The threat to the so-called Southern way of life posed by the snowball- ing drive for desegregation and effective civil rights legislation could be resisted, perhaps defeated, if white Southerners retained their relative strength in the Senate. The long-term success of Southern resistance hinged upon the continued effectiveness of the filibuster. In the past, "prolonged debate" had delayed or negated federal encroachments on what Howard Smith called "the rights of the sovereign States and the individual liberties of our people."[10] (Clearly Smith's definition of peo- ple excluded fellow Mississippians who were black.) As Paul H. Douglas (Dem., Ill.) pointed out, many Southerners still feared the addition of four senators who would favor civil rights legislation, or an effective cloture rule.[11] Gruening observed that the issue was essentially the same as before the Civil War. Southerners, he suggested, were still "trying to prevent states that might upset their balance of power from joining the Union."[12] Yet as events surrounding the civil rights and Alaska bills of 1957–1958 implied, outright obstruction of moderate legislation did not automatically serve the long-term interests of the conservative cham- pions of states' rights.

Within the islands, debates over the nature and extent of Americanization and assimilation were the more palatable public aspects of a
deeper controversy over racial questions and statehood. Overt objections to possible Japanese control of the local legislature and representatives in Washington were seldom voiced during the late 1950s. Nevertheless this concern remained a basic determinant of local antipathy to
possible changes in the structure and nature of island government. The
growth of a strong Democratic party, a confident middle class, and
assertive anti-Republican political leaders were widely accepted as related indices of the new status and strength of nisei in postwar Hawaii.
These trends exacerbated the fears of those insecure residents who could
not accommodate to the emergence of genuinely representative government in their community. This concern still dominated the material
supplied by statehood opponents to congressional investigating teams.
The findings of three extensive private surveys conducted during 1956–
1959 also suggest the continued existence of a relationship between anti-
Japanese feelings and opposition to statehood.

In 1956 the Honolulu Chamber of Commerce commissioned a confidential survey to determine whether it should actively promote statehood. Although only slightly more than half of its three thousand members replied, 64 percent answered affirmatively. "Significantly," the
Star-Bulletin noted, "Caucasian members, members in the higher income brackets . . . did not vote as strongly for active promotion as did
the Chamber members who are non-Caucasian, in modest income
brackets." Opposition to an active campaign did not necessarily imply
hostility to statehood per se. Nonetheless a large minority (36 percent of
respondents) would not support such a campaign. Almost half of all
members of the Chamber were apparently uninterested in statehood or
happy with the status quo. It is difficult to generalize confidently from
these figures. While they suggest disproportionately strong resistance to
statehood from Caucasians, this might have resulted from economic as
well as racial considerations. Certainly some high-income members,
especially those with interests in real property, believed that territorial
government should be maintained in order to avert radical changes in
the islands' tax structure.[13]

The results of a public opinion poll of Oahu residents in 1958 correlate closely with the findings of the survey by the Chamber of Commerce. The poll revealed that 27 percent of citizens of Hawaiian or
part-Hawaiian ancestry and 23 percent of all Caucasians opposed statehood. Only one major ethnic group, the Japanese, indicated majority
support for immediate statehood. Fuchs observed that a breakdown of
opinions expressed by members of major ethnic groups indicated that
"62 per cent of the citizens of Japanese ancestry, 44 per cent of the Chinese, 39 per cent of the Filipinos, 33 per cent of the haoles, and only 30

per cent of Hawaiians and part-Hawaiians" favored immediate statehood. Almost one-quarter of all persons interviewed were uncommitted
on the statehood question.[14]

An intensive survey conducted in the fourteenth representative district on Oahu in 1959 also revealed considerable opposition to statehood. A little over one-third of all Caucasians interviewed expressed
opposition to statehood, or were uncommitted on the issue. Nearly as
many Hawaiians and part-Hawaiians concurred. In this same survey,
60 percent of all Hawaiians and part-Hawaiians expressed opposition to
the Japanese racial group because it exercised undue influence in the
territory. Residents of the fourteenth district were also asked if any
"racial group or groups in the Islands had too much power." Of those
who answered positively, "nearly nine out of ten Hawaiians and Chinese, eight out of ten Filipinos and haoles, and nearly seven out of ten
respondents of Portuguese extraction specified the Japanese."[15] Clearly,
racial hostility against the Japanese majority in the territory remained
substantial. This resentment was expressed by some residents as opposition to statehood. Removal of the appointed governor was expected to
compound growing Japanese political strength. A belief that "the Japs
are taking over" was expressed often by members of all minor ethnic
groups, although not all residents who feared growing Japanese influence translated this alarm into resistance to statehood.[16] Also, as previously indicated, opposition derived from a combination of racial,
political, and economic factors. However, the evidence of these Oahu
surveys cannot be accepted uncritically.

A variety of evidence suggests that by 1959 local support for immediate admission was more general than the surveys implied. Fuchs conceded that the results inflated the numerical strength of opponents of
statehood. The 1959 survey indicated that respondents who remained
neutral on statehood, or who, though opposed, would accept it if it
came, would be likely to vote in favor of statehood in a clear "Yes or No"
referendum.[17] In the 1958 territorial elections for delegate to Congress,
the anti-statehood candidate, Edward A. Brennan, received less than 1
percent of the total votes cast. More than 88 percent of all registered
voters cast ballots in this election. Thus, approximately 87 percent of all
voters were prepared to support pro-statehood Democratic or Republican candidates for delegate. The most conclusive evidence of the limited
support for continued territorial rule or the Commonwealth alternative
was expressed by Hawaii's electorate in 1959. Shortly after Congress
passed the statehood bill in March, a plebiscite was held to ratify the
decision. By an overwhelming majority, 132,938 votes to 7,854, Hawaii's people accepted the statehood bill. This was the most accurate
gauge of statehood opinion, and it suggested that less than 6 percent of
Hawaii's adult citizens felt strongly enough to register outright opposi-

tion. Almost 90 percent of all eligible voters cast ballots in the plebiscite. This was the heaviest election turnout in Hawaii's history.[18] Tuttle commented that both the size of the turnout and the affirmative vote surpassed even the most optimistic expectations.[19] Even if it is conceded that many of those opposed to statehood did not register their opinions at the ballot box, the anti-statehood faction could not have comprised more than about 15 percent of Hawaii's citizens by 1959. The reliability of the opinion surveys conducted from 1956–1959 is thus suspect. Local opposition was not as strong as these surveys suggested.

If the surveys exaggerated the numerical strength of opposition to statehood, they nonetheless demonstrated that resistance was relatively strongest among citizens of Caucasian, Hawaiian, or part-Hawaiian ancestry. Paradoxically, however, the leading advocates of statehood were also representatives of these groups: Farrington was a Republican of Caucasian ancestry; King a Republican with part-Hawaiian ancestry; and Burns a Democrat of Caucasian extraction. Although the Japanese ethnic group provided the most unqualified support for statehood, no nisei played a vital role in the public campaign for admission. On the statehood issue, as within politics generally, Hawaii's Japanese trod warily, conscious always that assertiveness might precipitate a negative reaction from other racial groups in the islands, and perhaps bind these groups into a cohesive anti-Japanese majority. The considerable degree of political unity which developed among haoles, some part-Hawaiians, and some Chinese under the banner of the Republican party, and the fact that only a handful of Japanese belonged to this party, was an informal but important political manifestation of a unity based largely on shared feelings about the Japanese.

Local statehood opponents and Commonwealth advocates comprised a small minority in Hawaii after 1945. Yet during the protracted campaign for admission they exerted an influence disproportionate to their small numbers. They retarded the statehood drive by opposing the official campaign, supplying material to congressional opponents, and promoting Commonwealth status as an alternative to immediate statehood. Led by a curious collection of locals, most notably Walter Dillingham, Stainback, Campbell, Stokes, and Hill, the anti-statehood faction undermined the unity of the affirmative campaign, and precipitated prolonged and often bitter divisions over statehood and issues allegedly related to it, especially the threat to internal security and American values posed by Hawaii's Japanese community. In the late 1950s a small but wealthy minority continued to cling tenaciously to the status quo. Hostility to statehood still correlated closely with opposition to trade unions, an elected governor, and new tax laws, as well as with fear of Hawaii's Japanese.

Some "influential businessmen" and "a minority of large employers,"

Leverett A. Chapin, associate editor of the *Denver Post*, observed in 1958, believed "an elected State government would be less favorable to business than a Territorial government headed by a governor appointed by the President of the United States and armed with authority to veto acts of the legislature." The prospect of a liberal Democratic state government, unrestrained by an appointed governor, alarmed some sections of business. After 1954 the Democrats attempted to remove the taxation anomalies which favored large landowners. But this initial assault on land and tax privileges in the islands was effectively blunted by Governor King, who wielded his veto power ruthlessly. King's behavior reflected his belief that the Democrat-controlled legislature was full of "New Deal ideas" and "wanted to soak the rich."[20] As late as the eve of statehood the Republican party sought special dispensations for large landholders in proposed tax reform measures. Party chairman Ed Bryan stated unashamedly that these concessions would enable "the big landowner to help himself." Few Democrats were surprised when their tax assessment bill was vetoed by Quinn in 1959. The wealthy backers of Imua were adamant that the New Dealism of Hawaii's Democratic party could best be resisted with an appointed governor.[21] In sharp contrast, local Democrats argued that unqualified democracy under statehood was essential if "the feudal system of land ownership which discourages economic development" and the "tax system designed to favor the wealthy" were to be altered.[22]

In 1959 the communist issue and Commonwealth argument remained the rallying points of public opposition to statehood, both locally and on Capitol Hill. In the final debates, for example, old foes Pillion and Eastland revived the charge that Communists had captured and retained political and economic control of the islands. By subtly infiltrating the ILWU, the local Democratic party and even the local Republican party, the reactionary stalwarts again charged, communism had penetrated the very fabric of political life in the vulnerable territory. McCarthyism died a very slow death in some quarters on Capitol Hill. With a vigor which belied both his age and the general unpopularity of his cause, Eastland asserted that Congress was preparing to act on the statehood bill "in an atmosphere of almost hysterical excitement." A decision to elevate the "Communist controlled" territory to statehood, he concluded in now-familiar language, would constitute a "serious threat to the internal security of the United States." Pillion was also convinced (if his words in any way reflected his actual opinions) that statehood would permit "four Soviet agents to take seats in the U.S. Congress."[23] Given the activities of Imua, some islanders apparently believed such wild accusations. The allegations were totally without substance and had a negligible impact on the final phase of the statehood debate. Nevertheless, during the late 1940s and early 1950s,

against a background of cold war insecurity and the McCarthy witch-
hunts, they provided a convenient overt rationale for opposition to
statehood based on racial and sectional factors. Even though genuine
concern with internal subversion did not initiate hostility to statehood
nor substantially intensify existing opposition, public charges of communist influence were employed more often and promoted more exhaustively than any other single argument used against Hawaii after
the war.

"This Communist question is used as an argument against Statehood
as perennially as spring grass," Church observed wryly at a Senate hearing in 1957. Yet even at this late stage administration spokesmen close to
Eisenhower refused to firmly endorse immediate admission, ostensibly
because of Hawaii's vulnerability to subversion. Deputy Attorney General Rogers warned senators that before they approved Hawaii, "Consideration must be given to the extent of influence and control Communists, Communist sympathizers and their associates may be able to
exert, particularly through the I.L.W.U. in the Islands." Such charges
were as irrelevant to the statehood issue in the late 1950s as they had
been a decade earlier; but they were still viewed sympathetically by
many conservative Republicans, and some members of Eisenhower's
staff. They were also supported indirectly by the *Star-Bulletin*, which
claimed as late as 1957 that a communist conspiracy existed in Hawaii.[24] Many who had profited from the old order in the islands were
seemingly unable to differentiate between New Deal liberals, elected
trade union leaders, and Communists during the 1950s. These blurred
distinctions simplified the rhetoric of local politics in a decade of unprecedented change, and provided a climate which the anti-statehood
faction hoped to exploit.

Most efforts to undermine the statehood drive throughout the 1950s
were financed or coordinated by Imua—an organization dedicated to
defending unrestrained capitalism, paternalism between haoles and
Hawaiians, and white political and economic supremacy. Its members
were the most vigorous and well organized opponents of the forces
which threatened to transform island life after the war. Imua's explicit
function was to highlight the extent of subversion within the islands. In
1958, for example, with Walter Dillingham as chairman of its fund-rais-
ing committee, Imua spent ninety-two thousand dollars in an attempt
to expose such activities.[25] Its budget for this year exceeded that of the
Statehood Commission. Although it was not officially an anti-statehood
organization, Thurston, Quinn, and Burns emphasized independently
and correctly that the activities of this three-thousand-member association had a direct, largely negative bearing on the statehood campaign.[26]
It was both an anti-communist and anti-Japanese organization, and its
publicity and very existence accentuated tensions between labor and

employer groups, as well as across ethnic lines. It was the last resort of kamaaina haoles unwilling to accommodate to Hawaii's more flexible political and racial climate. Samuel P. King has observed that beneath Imua's avowed anti-communism was an undercurrent of apprehension about statehood, and this apprehension was racial in origin. Indeed, King concluded, "The communism part was secondary." Leaders of the organization maintained publicly Imua's neutrality on the statehood question. In 1958 however, Imua's leading spokesman, Lyle G. Phillips, told the American Conference of National Associations to Combat Communism that the primary function of Hawaii's Statehood Commission was to "cover-up the Communist Menace." Hawaii did not deserve statehood, he claimed, "until the present threat of subversive control over territorial life ends." (By the same curious logic it might have been argued that democracy be suspended throughout the nation until the threat of communism had evaporated.) Phillips supported his position by contending that a considerable segment of Hawaii's labor force was under Communist control, that Communists were in a position to tip the balance of power, and that they exerted increasingly an influence on Hawaii's government and economy. Later in 1958 the directors of Imua endorsed this view.[27] All of this simply confirmed what most island residents had long suspected about Imua's attitude to statehood.

Yet the sound and fury over communism throughout the 1950s failed to convince many observers that this was a central, genuine concern of local opponents of statehood. Chapin commented, for example, that there was "a growing conviction that the constant to-do about 'Communism' is nurtured by persons who for political, economic, tax or land-ownership reasons, would like to keep Hawaii as a Territory." He might have added that the issue was also a camouflage for racism. Chapin's politely understated conclusion was nonetheless accurate: "part of the emphasis on the 'Communist' menace," he wrote in the *Denver Post*, "may be a subtle device for defeating the granting of statehood."[28]

Despite the much-publicized and persistent efforts of Imua, the communist issue did not have a significant impact on Hawaii's statehood bid after 1956. The general disrepute of McCarthyism reduced the appeal of this argument, although Imua clung doggedly to it. In addition, a range of specific developments in Hawaii confirmed that internal subversion was not a political or economic threat. In June 1957 an appeal by the seven labor leaders convicted under the Smith Act was finally upheld. The number of man-days lost through strike activity declined gradually in the period 1951–1957. The percentage of island workers enrolled in the ILWU also declined in these years, as the economic significance of agriculture was eroded by the growth of tourism and service industries. By 1958 only 10 percent of Hawaii's 210,000 workers belonged to the ILWU. Legislative initiatives promoted by the union, notably repeal of the Dock Seizure Law of 1950, were usually defeated. Moreover, as Thurston pointed out, economic prosperity and increased investment in Hawaii by mainland enterprises were firm evidence that left-wing labor was a spent force in the islands.[29] Hawaii's Anti-Subversive Activities Commission reported confidently in 1959 that "the opponents of statehood have not been able to cite a single instance of Communist domination or control in the Territory."[30] The harsh union-management conflicts which erupted during 1945–1950 gradually subsided during the 1950s as a result of the growth of a larger middle class, general economic prosperity for the major ethnic groups, and a progressive local Democratic party. The central conflicts over equal access to education and employment, taxation, landownership, and employment conditions had largely been transferred from the industrial to the political arena. This neutralized some of the earlier bitterness, although at the time of statehood these issues were still unresolved. They were deadlocked in the conflict between the Democratic legislature and the Republican-appointed governor.

The economic argument against statehood was usually translated into support for Commonwealth status. Proponents of the Commonwealth option, many of whom were wealthy members of Imua, argued throughout the 1950s that Hawaii could be disincorporated and granted a political status similar to that accorded Puerto Rico. This might exempt Hawaii's residents from paying federal taxes. Stainback (forever out of step with local Democrats) and Brennan led this campaign in the late 1950s, but it did not command significant numerical support.[31] Earlier, however, many businessmen and landholders had supported it. In 1957 the Honolulu Chamber of Commerce investigated the legal aspects of the Commonwealth proposal. A special six-member committee comprising Tavares, Anthony, A. G. Smith, W. C. Tsukiyama, W. B. Stephenson, and Walter Chuck appraised the proposal but reported against it. In the 1958 election for delegate to Congress, the Commonwealth candidate, Brennan, received less than 1 percent of all votes cast. Not surprisingly, the 1958 House committee investigating statehood detected little enthusiasm for Commonwealth among Hawaii's citizens. It conceded, however, that "a rather articulate minority," led largely by the irrepressible Stainback, continued to support it as an alternative to immediate statehood.[32] By the late 1950s few islanders accepted the argument that Commonwealth status would end federal taxes. Most people now recognized the fiscal arrangements between Puerto Rico and Washington as a unique situation made possible by a Supreme Court ruling "that Puerto Rico was a non-incorporated territory," and that in legislating for it "Congress was not bound by the constitutional clauses requiring uniformity of taxation" within the nation.[33] Most Hawaiians were by now also at least dimly aware that Commonwealth status had not brought prosperity or full citizenship rights to the bulk of Puerto Rico's very disadvantaged people.

Only a small minority of islanders viewed statehood as an economic liability. On the contrary, economic self-interest had initiated and helped sustain Hawaii's organized campaign for admission after the depression. In the late 1950s self-interest remained a tangible and urgent stimulant to demands for immediate political equality with the states. Before the war the powerful sugar companies had pressed for statehood in order to end discrimination by Congress against offshore producers. The influence of sugar interests on the islands' economy and politics was diluted after the war as a result of the rapid diversification of Hawaii's economic base. Even so the sugar and pineapple corporations remained by far the largest single category of private enterprise in the territory. The annual value of plantation production by the late 1950s was approximately $250 million. Nevertheless federal expenditure on the armed forces and related activities was now the principal source of capital. In 1957, for example, defense expenditure totalled approximately $300 million. Manufacturing and tourism were the most rapidly expanding activities. Investments by mainland corporations took off in the early 1950s, leading to the establishment of a range of wholesale and retail organizations along with finance and investment institutions which were linked directly with these operations throughout the nation. In the decade after the war the value of mainland commerce with Hawaii exceeded that for all but five countries—the United Kingdom, Canada, Japan, France, and Germany. The islands were an integral factor in the nation's economy. After 1945 new, more competitive retail firms emerged, and the availability of goods and patterns of consumption came increasingly to mirror those of the mainland. The old monopoly of the Big Five had not disintegrated, but it was under challenge, especially in the commercial and retail fields. By the early 1950s approximately one thousand corporations did business in the islands. Two of the three leading pineapple companies, the California Packing Corporation and Libby, McNeill and Libby, were mainland based and competed nationally. The Big Five still dominated sugar and related activities, but genuine competition was developing in most business fields. More than thirty thousand individuals or corporations had business licenses in the territory; in excess of thirty thousand stockholders held interests in the largest 831 corporations; and mainland retailers like Sears Roebuck and Kress competed with locally owned enterprises. In general, however, the ownership of the means of production, distribution, and exchange remained more concentrated in the territory than in any existing state.[34]

Hawaii's unique island geography, settlement patterns, and territorial status provided a precarious base for economic growth. Despite diversification, its economy depended largely on export earnings from agriculture and defense appropriations. When in 1949 federal expenditure in the territory fell by about one-quarter, the unemployment level rose to almost one-fifth of the total local work force. At the same time welfare fund and unemployment compensation expenditures consumed about 20 percent of the total territorial budget.[35] The Korean War temporarily relieved this serious local depression, but most business and labor interests were by the late 1950s deeply aware that continued economic growth and stability demanded further diversification of industry, increased levels of capital investment, an equitable sugar quota, and consistently high levels of expenditure on defense. They anticipated that statehood would help provide conditions essential for such crucial developments. Evidence to this effect was submitted to the last congressional investigating team by the Honolulu Chamber of Commerce, Hawaiian Electric Company, Mutual Telephone Company, the Sugar Planters' Association, and the Pineapple Growers Association.[36] Governor Quinn observed that Hawaii had a "mature, expanding, and healthy economy," but he also testified that statehood would dramatically accelerate local economic expansion. The *Star-Bulletin* commented that the majority of Honolulu's business community viewed statehood as an economic stimulus. Statehood Commission Chairman Thurston did not exaggerate when he estimated that, "Over 80% of our sugar and pineapple executives, all our public utilities, all our transportation companies, the majority of banks and small businessmen" wanted immediate statehood.[37] Conscious of the fact that Hawaii consistently paid more in federal taxes than it received in federal appropriations, most business interests believed statehood might help to reverse this situation.

The sugar industry remained concerned with its vulnerability to neglect or discrimination by Congress. Memories of the Jones-Costigan Act had dimmed but had not been extinguished. They were kept alive by incidents after the war which obliged Hawaii to protest further unfair treatment by Congress. Under the 1946 sugar price support program, for example, the islands were lumped with Puerto Rico and the Virgin Islands as offshore producers. This disadvantaged Hawaii in relation to mainland producers, ignored its special incorporated status, and worse still, did not even accord it parity with Cuba. Although Hawaii was eventually given equal treatment with Cuba,[38] like the Jones-Costigan furor, this incident underlined the islands' susceptibility to arbitrary actions by Washington. In 1959 economist Robert M. Kamins remarked that sugar producers wanted equal representation with the various states in Congress as this would help preserve Hawaii's existing market quota and permit its elected representatives to pressure for an enlarged quota.[39] Executives of four of the five major sugar corporations were convinced that Hawaiian sugar would "never secure equitable treatment until it has the political power that accompanies statehood."[40] The amount of sugar which could be refined in Hawaii was still determined by Congress. Sugar interests could not "bargain for bigger sugar quotas and proper treatment of the industry," the *Honolulu Advertiser* stated, "without voting representation in Congress."[41] Moreover, producers of other agricultural commodities believed statehood would ensure equitable "coverage for their crops under the farm support program."[42] Henry A. White, president of the influential Hawaiian Pineapple Company, had earlier stated: "Hawaii is too important economically to be represented in Congress only by non-voting delegates."[43]

Throughout the the postwar years, as in 1935, most of the major sugar interests were apparently convinced that statehood was an economic necessity. If some sugar families and corporation executives remained ambivalent over likely political consequences of statehood, such doubts were rarely expressed publicly. Chauncey B. Wightman, secretary of the powerful Sugar Planters' Association, informed the House subcommittee in 1946: "it is important that Hawaii's sugar industry has adequate support and protection from discrimination that it has suffered in the past." During the war, a sugar shortage in the United States led to the removal of quota restrictions on Hawaii's sugar. Indeed, during this period island producers were encouraged to grow as much sugar as possible. However, producers in Hawaii expected quota restrictions to be reimposed after the war, and as a result anticipated a partial loss of their existing 12 to 14 percent share of the national market. Thus, as in 1935, they actively supported statehood because they believed equal representation in Congress was essential if Hawaii was to preserve its share of the national market. Wightman succinctly expressed the concern of Hawaii's sugar interests:

> Sugar production and marketing is controlled by Congress. . . . As a Territory our representation in Congress is solely through our one Delegate. When we add up all the States on the mainland where sugar cane and sugar beets are grown and processed and where refineries for Cuban sugar are located, we find the total is 26. Those 26 States interested in sugar are represented in Congress by 52 Senators and more than 250 Members of the House of Representatives; a clear majority of both Houses. Certainly Hawaii deserves more than one delegate, not only to represent the sugar industry but to represent all of Hawaii's interests.[44]

What was good for sugar interests in the islands was also beneficial to business generally. The decision of the Honolulu Chamber of Commerce to endorse statehood after the war was similarly based on a belief that equal representation in Congress would protect all business interests. This view, coupled with the fact that by 1946 Hawaii paid more in federal taxes than fourteen of the states, prompted a majority of businessmen to protest that continued territorial status was "inequitable for half a million people and unsound for their business."[45] Constant vigilance and loud appeals for equity were still necessary after the war, although in general discrimination or neglect by Congress was not severe. Nonetheless, during the 1930s and 1940s the islands had experienced unfair treatment by Congress under the sugar price support scheme.[46] Representatives with the power to vote on Capitol Hill were considered essential if Hawaii was to protect its business interests and press for additional federal government assistance to offset any losses in revenue which might result from reduced national defense expenditure in the Pacific region. Statehood would thus help support the pillars of the local economy, especially agriculture and the military. In addition, most businesses and political leaders anticipated that national business confidence in Hawaii would be greatly increased by the granting of statehood. They expected that mainland capital investment in island businesses would be rapidly accentuated, and industry and commerce further diversified. Thurston predicted that "a period of unprecedented economic expansion for Hawaii" would be initiated by statehood.[47]

Political factors also exerted strong influence on the statehood campaign. Demands for equal political rights, unqualified citizenship, and even "no taxation without representation"[48] reflected the genuine demands of an increasing majority of Hawaii's residents for full political rights as United States citizens. Indeed by 1945 more than 85 percent of Hawaii's 502,000 people were United States citizens.[49] Under territorial government, these citizens were denied full citizenship rights but subject to federal laws and taxes. Increasingly after 1945 local support for statehood was motivated by a desire to gain political representation in national decision making along with self-government for the territory. Under the Organic Act, Congress could veto or modify any legislation passed by the territory's legislature. In fact, during the war the president was able to dispense with the requirements of the Organic Act and impose military government. Local citizens were powerless to stop this radical initiative, and failed even to moderate the worst abuses which emerged during more than three years of tight military control. Furthermore, despite passage of the Hawaii Bill of Rights in 1923, some congressional legislation concerning labor relations, industrial and agricultural development, transportation, finance, as well as public health, education, and welfare appropriations continued to discriminate against Hawaii in comparison with the states.[50] Special petitions in Congress by the various delegates from Hawaii usually rectified all major discrimination. But Governor Stainback had expressed the concern of many islanders when he pointed out that as a territory Hawaii was forced to gain equal treatment from Congress and some executive departments of the federal government by special appeals, rather than through normal political representation. Because it was a territory, Elizabeth Farrington recalled, Hawaii was compelled to attempt to attach itself to federal aid programs by legislative amendment. Such appropriations did not accrue automatically as they did to the states.[51]

With two crucial exceptions—the impositions of the Jones-Costigan Act and military rule—Hawaii did not suffer acutely from inequitable legislation. Indeed, on a per capita basis federal appropriations to Hawaii exceeded in value those granted a majority of states. In 1940, before wartime defense needs temporarily inflated federal government expenditure in Hawaii, per-capita federal grants and expenditures to the territory totalled $36.53, and exceeded those made to thirty states. In the fiscal year 1944 Hawaii's internal revenue payments exceeded those of fourteen states, but direct federal government payments, relief, and other aid exceeded those made to twelve states.[52] As most states experienced similar minor discrepancies between federal tax payments and aid received, local proponents could not reasonably protest that Washington discriminated uniquely against Hawaii, nor could they use this complaint as a lever for admission. Proponents did not deny that Hawaii usually received equitable financial treatment from federal agencies, rather they stressed that without statehood discrimination was possible and could not be effectively resisted. Only representation and voting power in Congress, proponents argued, would irrevocably remove the prospect of future discrimination.[53]

The belief that statehood would transfer land to local rather than federal control was another powerful economic stimulant to the campaign for immediate admission. Section 5, part (d), of the admission bill required all federal agencies with jurisdiction over land in the islands to advise within five years of statehood whether continued federal control of this land was necessary. The president was given discretionary power to return all or portions of such lands to local control.[54] As previously indicated, land was very scarce, ownership sharply concentrated, and competition for commercial, industrial, and housing land acute. After the Democrats came to power in 1954 the issue of land distribution, tax, and use was a central political preoccupation. Thus the prospect of a return of substantial federal land to local control for industrial, housing, or public use intensified support for immediate statehood.[55] This prospect appealed especially to the new, essentially nonhaole middle class, which did not enjoy substantial direct ownership of real property.

The islands never experienced severe discrimination by Congress once military government was ruled unconstitutional. Nevertheless, the Organic Act and various decisions by Congress continued to impose disadvantages which states of the Union did not experience. "Discrimination in Federal legislation is not as frequent as it used to be," Quinn told a Senate committee in 1957, "but we still have to be jealously watchful and petition for inclusion in Federal legislation which affects all states equally."[56] Hawaii was initially excluded from the federal Highways Act of 1956 and had to petition Congress for inclusion in this program.[57] Because it was excluded from the federal defense highway scheme, the territory was forced to collect an additional $2 million annually in local taxation. Federal public welfare aid to Hawaii was not apportioned on an equal basis with aid to the states. The 1958 welfare assistance program, for example, excluded Hawaii from federal benefits valued at approximately $240,000 annually.[58] The estimated additional cost of state government for Hawaii was $400,000 per annum. However, statehood proponents were confident that this cost would be comfortably compensated for by the increase in federal appropriations which voting representatives in the House and Senate could secure for the islands.[59]

Numerous other material and administrative advantages were expected to follow from statehood. Under the Organic Act, territorial government was inflexible and sometimes inefficient. The *Honolulu Advertiser* made the point that statehood was crucial to the efficient functioning of local government. It commented, in effect, that the territorial legislature often concerned itself with requests to Washington over matters which, as a state, would have been handled locally or, if appropriate, would have been presented to Congress by its representatives or senators. During 1955, for example, the territorial legislature issued thirty-nine joint resolutions requesting permission from Congress to legislate on a variety of local matters. In addition, Congress often delayed the appointment of government officers in Hawaii. This sometimes led to a suspension of normal administrative processes in the territory. Even the appointment of governors was occasionally delayed, especially before the war. Washington was sometimes slow to replace judges of territorial courts, and on at least one occasion during the 1950s this problem severely curtailed the work of Hawaii's supreme court.[60] Although it had become a ritual, Hawaii was even obliged to petition each year for permission to convene its elected legislature. Trivial matters were also subject to Washington's approval. "Why should we have to go through the process of petition by legislative resolution if we want to use the lands at Ponohawaii South, for church purposes?" the *Advertiser* asked rhetorically. It protested, like many witnesses before the various investigating teams dispatched from Washington, that the Organic Act was inflexible and outmoded. "We are so tightly bound at the moment," the *Advertiser* complained, "that the Legislature had to petition Congress on behalf of the Kauai supervisors to give free school bus transportation to youngsters living more than 10 miles away from their school."[61] Hawaii's appointed governors often found it necessary to lobby self-consciously in Washington to ensure equal treatment for the islands on a range of minor matters. Presidential approval was necessary before the governor could permit funds to be raised locally through a bond issue. This lack of administrative autonomy disturbed representatives of both major political parties in the islands and all appointed governors after 1945.[62] Martial law had made this an acutely sensitive, persistent issue. After the war most politicians viewed the continued denial of unqualified democracy for island citizens with a mixture of concern and cynicism.

This disenchantment was most pronounced among progressive local Democrats who deeply resented the appointments made by the Truman administration to positions in the executive and judicial branches of the territory's government. Stainback and to a much lesser extent his successor, Long, were viewed by most local Democrats as conservative, uninspired leaders who had been foisted on island Democrats by administration officials in Washington with little interest in or awareness of local conditions. As early as November 1948 the Democratic Central Committee in Honolulu had requested that Truman remove the conservative Tennessee-born governor from office. Three years later the secretary of Hawaii's Democratic party, David A. Benz, made similar appeals to Washington. Stainback "works closely with the large business interests who are definitely Republican," Benz claimed. Local progressives were particularly alarmed with the appointments made by Stainback, charging that less than 20 percent went to recognized Democrats.[63] Even after Long was appointed to replace Stainback, many local Democrats complained that their party would never be revitalized while it suffered "seriously from neglect and indifference as shown by former Governor Stainback and present Governor Long."[64] Interestingly, the Republican party when it held sway in island politics was seldom alarmed by the activities of these ostensibly Democratic governors. Moreover, when the Republicans lost control of the elected legislature after 1954 their interests were well served by governors and officials appointed by a sympathetic Eisenhower administration in Washington. As we have seen, King and Quinn used their positions to resist Democrat-sponsored change and to rejuvenate the GOP. This merely compounded Democrat hostility to territorial government generally, and appointed governors in particular.

Appeals for statehood which focused on the anomaly of taxation without representation remained a central factor throughout the long campaign for equality. During 1898–1959 Hawaii contributed more than $2 billion in taxes to the federal government. In the fiscal year ending June 30, 1958, the territory paid $166 million in federal taxes. It thus paid more taxes than ten of the existing states. On a per capita basis, residents of Hawaii paid higher taxes than residents of twenty existing states. Yet, as statehood proponents emphasized, the United States government picked up only a small portion of the cost of territorial government, and paid nothing at all for local government in Hawaii. Denied voting representation in Congress, Hawaii could influence neither the raising nor the spending of federal tax money. Moreover the appointed governor could, through use of the veto, control the expenditure of territorial revenue by the local legislature and nullify important domestic legislation. Hawaii's citizens were subjected to all of the obligations of mainland citizens, but denied complete citizenship rights. Most citizens of Hawaii accepted that, "Taxation without Representation is proper and legal only during the period of pupilage of a Territory destined to become a State."[65] However, by the 1950s an overwhelming majority of citizens believed that Hawaii was thoroughly qualified for statehood and had unquestionably completed its period of pupilage. This view was shared by a substantial majority of congressmen throughout the 1950s. But it was not until 1959 that this sentiment was permitted to prevail on Capitol Hill.

Congress Finally Acts

"Everything that can be said . . . on the subject of Hawaii statehood, for or against, has been said," Alaska's new senator, Bartlett, commented most appropriately early in 1959.[66] Few people believed that further debate would influence a single vote in Congress. Ritualistically, however, both sides resurrected their familiar arguments and marshalled speakers to attack or defend Hawaii. Opponents dutifully repeated statements which had for fifteen years provided an effective rationalization for racial and states' rights objections to Hawaii's appeals for statehood. Now, however, this group could not rely on procedural tactics to veto or avert action by Congress. Without this weapon, their arguments were futile.

The favorable political conditions which brought Alaska statehood in 1958 were not disrupted by the national election results of that year. Indeed the composition of the new Congress further enhanced the prospects of early action on Hawaii as foreshadowed in the Johnson-Burns compromise strategy. The Democrats won massive majorities in both chambers of the new Congress. In the House their majority was increased to 128; in the Senate it rose to 30. Hawaii, and Burns, benefitted from the fact that Johnson retained his position as Senate majority leader. Moreover Democratic gains were made primarily in non-Southern constituencies.[67] Thus conservative strength within the majority party was weaker in 1959 than in 1958. Southern intransigents could not dictate party policy on statehood or civil rights, although in both chambers they were virtually the only opponents of Hawaii's ambitions.

Republican strength was cut dramatically by the election results of
1958, but those GOP members who retained office did not desert Democratic Hawaii. Thus in the Eighty-sixth Congress Hawaii enjoyed
strong bipartisan support similar to that which had previously brought
Alaska statehood. Also, in 1959 as in 1958, opponents were not prepared to use a filibuster against statehood legislation. The South was
now increasingly split over racial issues and congressional tactics. Even
its most inflexible representatives appreciated that they could not afford
to alienate moderate opinion in Congress and thereby risk a backlash in
the form of tougher legislation on civil rights. Against this background
prompt affirmative action on Hawaii seemed certain.

Congress acted with almost embarrassing haste in the early months of
1959. Hearings were conducted by the House Committee on Interior
and Insular Affairs for three days in January. A week earlier a report
was issued by a special subcommittee based on hearings held in Hawaii
in late 1958. It concluded that the territory was "entitled to statehood
by every fair test and precedent," and dismissed allegations made by
friends of Imua that the islands were strongly influenced by Communists and un-American elements. On February 4 the full House committee approved the Hawaii Bill (H.R. 4221) by an overwhelming twenty-
five votes to four. Fourteen Democrats—none of whom represented
Southern constituencies—and eleven Republicans supported the bill in
committee. A motion by Dwight Rogers to delay debate indefinitely
was rejected. However, the committee did accept an amendment which
reduced Hawaii's proposed representation in Congress. Although the
islands were entitled to two representatives under the existing appor-
tionment scheme, opponents contended that it should be granted one
representative because eighty-nine existing representative districts had
larger constituencies than those proposed for Hawaii. Proponents accepted the amendment partly to counteract the potential opposition of
some Southerners to the statehood bill, and partly because they expected future reapportionments would grant Hawaii two representatives.[68]

The final House Interior and Insular Affairs Committee report was
issued on February 11, 1959. Eighteen reports were published during
1935–1959. Only one of these opposed statehood. The 1959 report reiterated that Hawaii met the traditional requirements for entry, and
concluded that "the grant of statehood will be in the best interests of the
people of the entire Nation as well as the half million Americans who
now reside in the Territory that has been an incorporated part of the
United States for fifty-eight years." Significantly, this favorable report
was issued earlier in the congressional session than any previous report.
House leaders agreed to commence floor consideration of the Hawaii
bill at the first possible moment.[69]

The Senate also initiated early, decisive action. On February 25 a subcommittee conducted brief hearings in Washington. The following day it reported a bill identical to that approved by the full House committee. On March 3 the full Senate Committee on Interior and Insular Affairs unanimously approved this bill.[70] Johnson assured statehood proponents in March that: "as soon as the bill is ready, we will schedule it for immediate consideration by the Senate."[71] This decisive preliminary action was unprecedented.

Opposition by obstructionists on the House Rules Committee was easily overcome in 1959. Four of its members, including the inveterate reactionary Chairman Smith remained hostile to Hawaii. But as Rogers conceded, they could not permanently block "the granting of a rule."[72] Like Alaska, Hawaii was now promoted with an admission act and classified by the House Interior Committee as privileged legislation. Thus the Rules Committee could be bypassed. However, strong opposition was expressed by Smith, Pillion, Rogers, and Colmer during prolonged Rules Committee hearings in late February and early March. Proponents had anticipated this development, and specified in the 1959 House Interior Committee report that the privileged Hawaii bill be taken directly to the floor if the Rules Committee failed to release it for debate within a "reasonable period."[73] This threat induced conservatives to withdraw their opposition, and permitted a normal vote by the Rules Committee.

On March 10, 1959, Johnson honored the agreement which he had concluded with Burns and other statehood sympathizers in January 1958. In what the *New York Times* called "a surprise move" he scheduled a debate on Hawaii for the following day. At the same time the House Rules Committee agreed by seven votes to four to report the Hawaii bill and also scheduled a debate for March 11. The final phase of the compromise strategy was now being implemented. Specific pressure from Democratic leaders in both chambers, especially Johnson and Rayburn, now resulted in decisive action. In accordance with assurances given late in 1958 by Johnson and Burns, Hawaii was to be considered early in the Eighty-sixth Congress.[74]

Debate on the Hawaii statehood bill commenced in the Senate on March 11, 1959. "From the outset," the *New York Times* observed, "approval of statehood for Hawaii was a settled matter." A motion by Thurmond to recommit the bill to committee with instructions to further investigate the possibility of granting the territory Commonwealth status was rejected by a voice vote. In sharp contrast to previous years, Senate opponents did not attempt to prolong the debate. After less than one day of consideration, the Senate voted. The Hawaii statehood bill was approved by an overwhelming seventy-six votes to fifteen.[75]

On the same day the House of Representatives adopted a rule permitting immediate debate on Hawaii, by an overwhelming 338 votes to 69.

On March 12, 1959, unanimous consent was granted to substitute the Senate approved bill (S. 50) for the House Bill (H.R. 4221). The House rejected a motion by Pillion to recommit the bill for further consideration. An amendment moved by W. R. Poage (Dem., Tex.) to permit the future inclusion of all Pacific possessions of the United States into the state of Hawaii was also rejected. Following six hours of debate, the House passed the Hawaii statehood bill by an impressive majority of 323 votes to 89.[76] Thus, "after one of the fastest actions by Congress in years," the *New York Times* commented, "only the mechanics of admitting a new state remain before Hawaii joins the Union." The irony of such rapid (if very belated) action by Congress did not escape observers in Hawaii or on Capitol Hill. It was the final, crucial aspect of the Burns-Johnson strategy initiated early in 1958.

The fact that congressional old guards of each party had thwarted Hawaii for so many years was conveniently ignored as Democrats and Republicans alike anxiously sought to be identified with the victory of 1959. Republican leaders in both Honolulu and Washington were convinced that Burns and his friends would portray statehood as a strictly partisan triumph. In anticipation of the final vote, Quinn was rushed to Washington, where he attempted, with reasonable success, to salvage for his party some kudos for passage of the bill. Republican spokesmen were quick to point out that Democrats had always provided the core of opposition and statehood had been won finally under a Republican administration. In contrast, Democrats were confident that they would win credit for breaking the impasse which had perenially defeated Hawaii. Predictably, island Democrats were quick to thank Johnson for his valuable assistance to Hawaii's delegate. Prominent Republicans were much less grateful: "Johnson was against us the whole time until the end," Elizabeth Farrington claimed, "then he came up as the hero—he and Jack Burns."[77] Predictably, Johnson praised the efforts of fellow Democrats and stated: "if any man is entitled to full credit for Hawaiian statehood, Burns is that person." In the short-term, Johnson's assessment was justified. But Burns' achievements rested, ultimately, on foundations laid down for over a quarter of a century by his Republican predecessors in Washington, notably Sam King and Statehood Joe Farrington. Without the painstaking and long-frustrated efforts of a large number of Republicans and Democrats alike, the statehood campaign would not have borne fruit in 1959.[78]

The Southern wing of the Democratic party was virtually the only opponent of the final statehood bill. However, because the Democrats held large majorities in both chambers of the Eighty-sixth Congress, its members also provided more affirmative votes in both the House and Senate than did Republicans. In the House, 203 Democrats and 120 Republicans voted affirmatively; 65 Democrats and 24 Republicans voted negatively. Virtually all negative Democratic votes were cast by

Southerners. Most negative Republican votes were cast by representatives of large Northern states. Twenty-eight states voted unanimously for statehood.[79]

In the Senate, 46 Democrats and 30 Republicans voted for Hawaii in 1959. Fourteen Democrats and only 1 Republican voted against it. As in the House, most Southerners remained hostile. All but 1 Senate opponent of the 1959 bill represented a former Confederate state. Alabama, Arkansas, Georgia, Mississippi, South Carolina, and Virginia all voted solidly against the bill. Smathers (Fla.) and Allen J. Ellender (Dem., La.), also voted negatively. All but 1 of the 14 Southern senators who voted against Hawaii also voted with the 18 opponents of the 1959 civil rights bill. Eleven of these 14 senators voted against the Alaska bill in 1958. Senate resistance to a separate Hawaii bill had dissipated dramatically during the 1950s. In 1948 51 senators in effect voted against Hawaii's separate admission by supporting recommittal of a Hawaii bill. Although the Senate did not vote on a separate Hawaii bill until 1959, by 1954 a majority of senators supported concurrent admission of Hawaii and Alaska. Thus, by 1954, when Hawaii was temporarily divorced from partisan politics, it enjoyed majority support in the Senate. By 1959 this support had grown further, and now constituted an overwhelming majority of senators. But the proportion of Southern senators opposed to Hawaii remained fairly constant after the war. This contrasted markedly with the gradual but decisive breakdown of resistance among congressmen from other states.[80]

It must be emphasized, however, that in the House after 1946, and in the Senate after 1954 at the latest, separate admission of Hawaii enjoyed majority support. Despite its relationship to the Alaska statehood issue, Hawaii passed the House in 1947, 1950, and 1953. Although the Senate recommitted a separate Hawaii bill in 1948, it never voted to reject such a bill outright. Moreover, the proposal to grant Hawaii Commonwealth status was never supported by more than a third of the Senate.[81] In 1954 a substantial majority of senators endorsed the joint Hawaii-Alaska bill. Yet until the late 1950s very few senators were willing to actively promote a separate bill. Generally, they were irresolute rather than enthusiastic or strongly committed.

It should also be acknowledged that while the South always provided the nucleus of resistance to Hawaii, a substantial minority of Southern representatives dissented firmly from this position. In the House, for example, most of Louisiana's large delegation had always endorsed Hawaii's aspirations. Representatives from Florida and Tennessee also provided many affirmative votes throughout 1947–1959. In the Senate, Kefauver (Tenn.), Holland (Fla.), and Long (La.) actively promoted Hawaii's admission in 1954 and 1959. Moreover, Southerners Johnson and Rayburn gave decisive support to the compromise strategy adopted by the Democratic party in 1958. Without this somewhat overdue assis-

tance a compromise strategy could not have been implemented. Ultimately, Burns later claimed, "Southerners got the damn thing [state-
hood] through."[82] The irony of this fact could not have escaped Hawaii's
people, whose statehood ambitions were perennially frustrated by
Southern-led resistance after 1945.

Last Steps to Equal Status

Eisenhower signed the Hawaii statehood bill on March 18, 1959. As
amended in committee earlier that year, however, it did not immediately grant statehood. Three important provisions of the legislation had
to be ratified by Hawaii's citizens before the president could issue a
proclamation of admission. In addition, the islands were expected to
elect their new state delegation to Congress before Eisenhower took this
irreversible action.

The referendum on the provisions of the statehood bill was scheduled
for June 26, 1959. Three related proposals were thus placed before
Hawaii's electors. The first asked whether Hawaii should be admitted
immediately into the Union, while the second and third asked electors
to ratify the boundary and land provisions of the Act of Congress approved on March 18. Unless each of these clauses was accepted by a majority of its citizens the bill would not become law. This cumbersome
procedure was necessitated by changes made in the controversial land
control and boundary sections of the statehood legislation after Hawaii
had ratified its proposed state constitution in 1950. Voters had to cast a
"Yes" or "No" reply to each proposal. The referendum was, as the
Honolulu Advertiser emphasized, "the deciding factor in Hawaii's admission to the Union as the 50th State."[83]

Public enthusiasm for statehood quickly resurfaced after the decisive
events in Congress during March. Proponents were confident that a
direct vote on statehood would result in ratification by a majority of "at
least three-to-one" and possibly "five-to-one." Nonetheless, nothing was
taken for granted. A vigorous campaign was launched to ensure that the
statehood bill finally became law. The campaign slogan was as simple
as it was effective: "Vote Yes! Yes! Yes!" It was promoted enthusiastically
by the legislature, the Statehood Commission, all major newspapers,
Governor Quinn, and Delegate Burns.[84] Now that admission was definitely imminent, local politicians jostled unceremoniously to be identified as leaders of the successful struggle. Throughout the postwar years
identification with the statehood drive had been an automatic reflex for
virtually all aspiring politicians. Doc Hill was the only political survivor
who had opposed statehood, although as an appointed official Stainback had also been able to ignore electoral pressure and work against
statehood.

Surprisingly perhaps local opponents did not rally against the referendum proposals. Advocates of Commonwealth status were rarely vocal during 1959. Nor did those who had once been identified as against statehood voice their opposition in the pre-plebiscite campaign. Having suffered a humiliating defeat in the 1958 elections, advocates of Commonwealth status like Campbell and Stainback accepted reluctantly that a campaign against a "Yes" vote would be futile and perhaps expensive.[85] Ratification was a foregone conclusion and those who had waged a protracted battle against statehood were now obliged to concede this fact. While this conservative local faction had worked energetically to torpedo statehood, it had not influenced decisively the perennial setbacks encountered by statehood proponents after 1945. Ultimately these reversals resulted from the blatant use of veto tactics by an intolerant minority in Congress.

In the plebiscite on the statehood bill, held on June 27, 1959, the numerical weakness of local statehood opponents was unambiguously revealed. Only 7,854 local citizens rejected the admission act. In sharp contrast, 132,938 accepted it without qualification. A majority of more than seventeen to one voted "Yes" to each of the three sections of the plebiscite. In keeping with Hawaii's established record of high voter turnout, 99 percent of those registered to vote did so. It might be argued that most of those who stayed away from the polls were expressing passive dissent or general alienation from the American political system and by implication expressing hostility to statehood as well. Even if these nonvoters are combined with those who voted negatively in the 1959 plebiscite, however, not more than 17 percent of Hawaii's total electorate were opposed to immediate admission.

Obviously, this is an inflated estimate, as failure to vote did not necessarily imply opposition to statehood.[86] In only one of the islands' 240 voting precincts did a majority vote against the provisions of the plebiscite. The unique exception was the small, privately owned, isolated island of Niihau. It voted seventy to eighteen against statehood. All eighteen representative districts in the territory provided affirmative majorities of at least eleven to one. The smallest (but still very substantial) margin came from the seventeenth district of Oahu, which included an area, from Kahala to Koko Head, where some of Hawaii's most prosperous residents lived. On a per capita basis, this was perhaps the wealthiest district in the islands.[87] The highest income sections of the haole community—the same group which sustained Imua—continued to offer the strongest resistance to statehood. Those who had profited most under territorial rule were the most reluctant to encourage its dissolution. But as indicated previously, even among this group an overwhelming majority now viewed statehood as compatible with their interests.

Commenting on the results of the plebiscite the *Star-Bulletin* noted appropriately: "The extent of the victory surprised even those who worked hardest for it."[88] With elections for Hawaii's first state representatives and governor imminent, there was no shortage of aspiring local politicians anxious to be identified with this hard-won and very popular victory. Both major parties claimed responsibility for the triumph. In the euphoria which accompanied admission and Hawaii's first genuinely democratic elections, most politicians conveniently ignored the cynical way in which their national parties had for so many years behaved, permitting action to be delayed in the hope of exploiting statehood for short-term political gain.

That Hawaii had been denied equality and autonomy as a state until after much of Asia, the Indian subcontinent, and Africa had been decolonized was also generally overlooked. For a nation long preoccupied with its unique role as an anti-imperialist champion of democracy at home and abroad, the delay over Hawaii should have occasioned considerable uneasiness and embarrassment. In the years of intense cold war strain and constant accusations by each side against the imperialist ambitions of the other, the semi-colonial status of Hawaii was an irritating anomaly for officials in Washington. Understandably the State Department welcomed the granting of equality to Alaska and Hawaii as an action which would enhance American foreign policy and strengthen the nation's position generally, and particularly in the United Nations. Privately, the department conceded that "the extent to which we manifest our support for the aspirations of dependent peoples for self-government" was one of "the more important tests applied to American policy and actions by the nations of Asia, the Near East, Africa and Latin America." Not only would the ending of territorial rule in Alaska and Hawaii "rebound to our credit among these nations," it concluded in predictable cold war terms, but such "action would also be in stark contrast to the policies of the Soviet Union which practices a systematic denial of political liberty in the areas where it exercises control."[89]

Statehood proponents had occasionally attempted to capitalize on such international issues. A territory "is a creature of the National Government, which can change its form of government at will, and legislate for it without any regard for its wishes," the official campaign claimed in the late 1940s and early 1950s. Proponents occasionally asserted that statehood "would be a plus factor in our cold war against communism"; that it would "greatly increase the prestige and dignity" of the United States "in the worldwide struggle of ideologies which now threatens our way of life." Seldom, however, were the phrases colonial or semi-colonial status applied explicitly to Hawaii. Usually proponents were content to argue in polite terms that statehood would increase U.S. prestige the world over. At most only oblique references were made to the anomalous position of the territory in an ostensibly anti-colonial nation.

"Statehood is in the national interest," the Statehood Commission stated during the Korean War. It would "give effect in dynamic fashion to the principles of self-government which this country is making tremendous sacrifices to establish among the people of the world."[90] Given the procrastination and delay which confronted the statehood drive at every turn after 1945, many congressmen and senators were apparently unconvinced of the need to integrate "in dynamic fashion" the rhetoric of anti-colonialism with the practice of internal self-government for all Americans. Some who sincerely supported Hawaii emphasized the "national advantage" of removing it from a semi-colonial status. Engle argued, for example, that statehood had international significance in that it would demonstrate firmly that the United States was committed to complete political equality for all citizens, regardless of their ethnicity. Black civil rights proponents bolstered their demands for an end to segregation with similar assertions in the 1950s. Liberal commentators occasionally highlighted the connections between colonialism, racism, civil rights, and self-government for Hawaii's people. "If statehood should be denied," the *Denver Post* commented in 1959, "this country will be guilty of colonial exploitation, and Hawaii must eventually, for its own best interests, demand an independent status."[91] The Philippines had won independence in 1946 and Puerto Rico was granted increased home rule in 1952. Although some Filipinos and many Puerto Ricans were disturbed by the nature and levels of American influence in their islands after these formal political changes, both areas were now essentially self-governing. Unless Hawaii was also granted statehood, or genuine political autonomy and self-government, it would remain a nagging contradiction of Washington's espoused support for decolonization. During the cold war contest for the hearts and minds of all underdeveloped emerging states, this was a persuasive national consideration.

On July 28, 1959, Hawaii's people took the first decisive step toward the exercise of real self-government since the coup of 1893. After the most vigorous and expensive political campaign in their history, islanders elected their first state delegations to Washington, a state legislature, and a state governor. The results seemed to validate the persistent claims of statehood advocates that Hawaii was not dominated by any one political party or ethnic group. If 1954–1956 marked the end of GOP ascendency, 1959 indicated firmly that the Democrats would not enjoy a long period of unchallenged supremacy. For the first time since annexation control of the islands' legislature was divided—Republicans surprisingly regained control of the Senate, while the faction-torn Democratic party won only a precarious majority in the House. Representatives from all substantial ethnic groups won office. Slightly more than half of all elected offices in the new state were won by Americans of Asian ancestry, including Filipinos. Members of the three major ethnic groups, affiliated with both major political parties, were elected to serve in Congress. Representation in the Senate was split between a wealthy Republican of Chinese extraction, Hiram L. Fong, and a former appointed haole governor, the moderate and essentially independent Democrat Long. The one position in the House of Representatives went to Burns' talented and popular protégé, Inouye. It was with the understanding that Long would not seek reelection that Inouye agreed to serve a brief apprenticeship in the House before replacing Long as a Democratic candidate for the Senate.[92]

Despite Inouye's easy victory, the overall results of 1959 shocked the Democrats. Led energetically by Quinn, moderate and independent Republicans reversed the electoral trends of the 1950s. The first state election was the closest in the islands' history. Political cleavages were less predictable and far more fluid than in most mainland states. An opinion poll conducted in 1958 revealed that almost half of Hawaii's electors perceived themselves as independents. In general, at the time of statehood the Republicans who polled most strongly were those who were least associated with the conservative older wing of their party. Included in this group were Honolulu Mayor Neil Blaisdell, Quinn, Fong, and a number of unlikely converts to the moderate fold, including Frank Judd and Hebden Porteus. Independent Democrats also fared well, notably Gill and Esposito, who criticized Burns' authoritarian control of the party and dissociated themselves from a traditional pillar of the party, the ILWU. Both parties now contained energetic younger members who represented a wide cross section of Hawaii's ethnic communities, although nisei were far more likely to be Democrats than Republicans. Both parties now made strong attempts to cultivate support from the fast-growing part-Hawaiian population. The revival of the Republican party's fortunes at the time of statehood rested partly on its willingness to recognize and exploit the fact that in Hawaii ethnicity and politics could never be divorced—a lesson which Burns had long understood. Apart from Fong and Quinn, the Republicans nominated a person of Japanese ancestry, Wilfred Tsukiyama, as a candidate for the Senate; a Hawaiian-Chinese, James Kealoha, as lieutenant governor; and a person of Portuguese ancestry, Charles Silva, for the House of Representatives. "This was a formidable team from the ethnic standpoint," Fong observed. "Ethnically, we couldn't have done better, except that probably we could have gotten a person of Filipino ancestry."[93]

The results of the state's first elections were as unexpected as they were encouraging for those who had argued throughout the statehood campaign that Hawaii's citizens were not likely to vote in rigid blocs along ethnic lines. Their claims that Hawaii would eagerly embrace full democracy were also vindicated. A record 93 percent of all eligible voters cast ballots in the first state elections.

However, this huge turnout was small consolation for the most effective local proponent of statehood, Burns. Uncharacteristically perhaps, he accepted the advice of his party that he should run for governor, and not contest the U.S. Senate, where he was assured of a seat. Democrats were anxious to ensure that their party win the governorship and hence the appointment of the hundreds of officials required under the terms of the state constitution. The first state governor would exercise unique powers of appointment. And in the light of their experiences under appointed governors (including nominally Democratic ones like Stainback) local Democrats were determined to replace the incumbent appointee, Quinn, with a committed Democrat. The Republican party, representing the still-powerful interests of the Chamber of Commerce and the plantation owners, worked desperately against Burns, as Aoki recalled, "because they wanted to protect everything they had." To limit change at home, the power of the Democrats had to be curtailed. It was widely believed that a Democratic majority under a progressive Democratic governor would mount an assault on the pillars of oligarchic power—including the sharply concentrated land and property ownership which was supported by perhaps the most regressive and inequitable taxation arrangements in the Union. Though the Democrats attached great importance to the first state elections, the ease of their political victories after 1954 had generated complacency within the party. "They didn't do the militant work amongst the rank and file of which they were so capable," Quinn later acknowledged. Confident that his success in Washington would assure him victory over Quinn, Burns returned to the islands relatively late in the campaign—too late to overhaul the substantial electoral support which his popular liberal Republican opponent had nurtured as governor after his unexpected appointment by Eisenhower. The power so eagerly sought by Burns and his party faithfuls in 1959 remained surprisingly in Republican hands. But Burns was a political fighter and he soon triumphed over his Republican opponents and liberal critics within his own party. He dominated island politics in the 1960s and early 1970s much as he had dominated his own party in the 1950s. He had to wait until 1962, however, before he could muster electoral support equal to his ambitions.[94]

The high voter turnout, revival of the Republican party, and the varied ethnic composition of the state's first elected representatives appeared to negate the fears of Japanese control which had always sustained opposition to statehood. The election results were, as it turned out, an aberration: they provided only a brief respite for both the Republican party and those who equated statehood with the political triumph of Hawaii's Japanese and their resilient haole leader Burns. In the next state election, in 1962, the political trends of the 1950s resurfaced and the Burns faction returned to dominate the first two decades of state government. Burns defeated Quinn in the race for the governorship; Inouye easily defeated Ben Dillingham in the contest for the junior Senate seat; and Spark Matsunaga, a veteran of the 100th Battalion, replaced Inouye in the House of Representatives. A second House seat allocated to Hawaii was won by Tom Gill who, despite differences with the Burns group, ran on a Democratic unity ticket. Throughout the 1960s and early 1970s the Burns group, based overwhelmingly on the support of Hawaii's Japanese, became the "new establishment" in local political life. Only Hawaii's senior senator, the self-confessed maverick Republican Fong, was able to swim successfully against this tide. Fong's personal stature, not his party affiliations, accounted for his unique political achievements. Thus, the decline of the Republican party, signalled so starkly by the electoral returns of 1954 and 1956, continued after statehood.

In island politics generally whites still exerted a disproportionately strong influence. But as was indicated by election returns throughout the 1960s (along with the mutterings of some insecure haoles), this power was quickly being eclipsed by other ethnic groups, especially the Japanese. For those native Hawaiians who had previously received some comfort from haole paternalism, the spectre of a state government dominated by voters of Asian descent was an unsettling prospect. Some locals suggested uncharitably that the growth of Japanese political power vindicated the long-standing (if seldom public) charge that statehood would mean the end of haole dominance in the islands. In conventional, formal political terms this fear was not without substance, although the eclipse of haole authority in the arena of electoral politics was slow and uneven. In economic and social terms this charge was widely exaggerated. Statehood quickly brought the numerous ethnic and class groups into more open political conflict. The distribution of wealth and opportunity changed relatively slowly, however, remaining biased in favor of kamaaina haoles and Chinese. With statehood Hawaii was becoming more equal, but it was far from an egalitarian society, even in the narrow sense of affording equal opportunity to members of a particular generation. Ethnic and class divisions were persistent, although far more flexible than at any time since annexation.[95]

After ratifying the statehood bill and electing its state representatives, Hawaii had finally completed the steps preliminary to statehood. Eisenhower formally proclaimed "the admission of the State of Hawaii into the Union on an equal footing with the other States" on August 21, 1959. Yet even this largely ceremonial act was marred by heated partisan controversy, as Burns was not invited to witness the president sign the documents formally admitting Hawaii. This might have been an honest mistake on the part of White House staff—although Elizabeth Farrington was convinced the president "purposely" and "deliberately" did not invite Burns because the Republicans and the Farringtons were responsible for Hawaii's victory. Island Democrats angrily claimed that Eisenhower's refusal to include Burns in the statehood ceremony was a deliberate slight against the person they (with predictable partisanship) regarded as the "father of statehood." Inouye and Rayburn, both close friends of Burns, were among those who attended. "We were angered when we were advised that you were not invited—not by any unintentional oversight but by design," Inouye later wrote Burns, and "Speaker Rayburn made his distress known to the President." According to Murai, Rayburn took one of the pens used to sign the documents and told Eisenhower: " 'I'm going to give this pen to Jack Burns, the father of the Statehood bill.' " Many local Republicans undoubtedly came to regret this unfortunate incident, for if island Democrats were distressed by this episode, in later years they nonetheless eagerly exploited it for electoral purposes.[96]

The new state was to be governed under the terms of the constitution which its citizens had drafted and ratified almost a decade earlier. All territorial laws and procedures not explicitly altered by the admission bill remained in force, although some were subsequently changed by the state's legislature. Statehood gave Hawaii self-government within the framework of the United States Constitution and Union. Under Article 4, Section 2, of the federal Constitution, all citizens of new states were entitled "to all the privileges and immunities of citizens of the several states." Hawaii's citizens were thus granted complete and irrevocable voting representation in the United States Senate and House of Representatives, the right to participate in the selection of the nation's president and vice president, and the right to vote on proposed amendments to the United States Constitution. They were also granted authority to determine "the extent of powers to be exercised by their own legislature," and the right to have "local justice administered by judges selected under local authority rather than by Federal appointees."[97] The qualified rights which came with territorial citizenship were replaced by full and equal citizenship rights.

As this book has previously indicated, the provisions of Hawaii's constitution granted the local legislature much broader law-making powers than did the Organic Act. No longer was legislation passed by the local legislature subject to possible veto by Congress or a governor appointed by Congress. Article 10 of the United States Constitution stipulated: "The powers not delegated to the United States by the Constitution, nor prohibited by it to the States, are reserved to the States respectively, or to the people." Thus, as a state, Hawaii gained the right to legislate on all matters not specifically reserved for federal jurisdiction. Moreover, it was for the first time assured its fair share of federal grants, appropriations, and production quotas. Voting representation in Congress afforded equitable protection of Hawaii's political and economic interests for the first time since incorporation into the Union in 1900. An expanding desire to achieve this equality with existing states, along with unqualified citizenship rights, had helped sustain the formal statehood campaign for more than a quarter of a century. Initially confined largely to disgruntled sugar growers, this demand grew rapidly as a result of war, military government, and broad socioeconomic changes in the immediate postwar years.

In the final analysis the acceptance of Hawaii as a state derived from legal precedents which were reinforced by internal demographic, economic, social, and political developments during sixty years of political tutelage. These changes were in turn highlighted and promoted by an exhaustive and expensive campaign rooted firmly in the assumption that statehood was not only desirable but inevitable under the terms of the United States Constitution.

As an incorporated territory, an inchoate state, Hawaii could not legally be denied statehood permanently. After 1900 United States policy relating to territorial possessions consistently recognized that Hawaii and, after 1912, Alaska were entitled to eventual statehood. No determined attempt was made to grant either territory independence or increased home rule. In contrast, after 1901, American policy in the Philippines sought to create conditions which would permit the territory to acquire independence. Increased self-government was granted the Philippines in 1916 and 1934, and in 1946 independence was granted. The other major unincorporated territory belonging to the United States, Puerto Rico, was granted increased local autonomy as a Commonwealth within the American federal system in 1952. Congressional policy toward Hawaii was premised on judicial opinions which classified Hawaii as an incorporated territory entitled to equal partnership in the Union as a state. Similarly, Hawaii's campaign for statehood was confidently predicated on a belief that statehood might be delayed but could not be denied by Congress. This assumption was confirmed by the various reports of congressional investigating committees. The 1959 House committee report, like those of previous years, emphasized the legality of Hawaii's appeals for admission:

> The citizens of Hawaii are in precisely the same legal and political status today as were the residents of the Northwest Territory when they were admitted to full citizenship. . . . they are residents of an incorporated Territory, one to which the Constitution was extended by the 55th Congress more than half a century ago, thus incorporating it into the Union.

Although Congress could not be compelled to admit any territory, no incorporated area which met the traditional requirements for statehood had ever been permanently denied equality as a state. When confronted with an inactive Congress in the early 1950s, however, some disillusioned islanders felt that their territory might never gain full statehood. The unique political status granted Puerto Rico strengthened this belief, and encouraged a small proportion of statehood supporters to flirt with the Commonwealth alternative. Only one territory, New Mexico, remained tied to its incorporated territorial status for longer than Hawaii —one year longer in fact, a total of sixty years. Usually, however, this was a brief transitionary status. The thirty states which passed through periods as incorporated territories remained subject to this system of government on average for less than twenty-one years.[98]

By 1959 an overwhelming majority of congressmen and island citizens accepted that the territory was not only legally entitled to statehood, but fully capable of supporting it. Before World War II a joint House-Senate committee had concluded that Hawaii had satisfied all the requirements set for territories up until then. With the important exception of Butler's report of 1949, no subsequent House or Senate report contradicted this finding. By 1959 Hawaii undisputably had the requisite population and resources for the operation of a state government and could contribute its share in support of the federal government. Its population had increased to 620,000—more than three times the population of Alaska in 1958, and larger than the populations of all but one territory at the time of admission. Approximately 85 percent of Hawaii's people were United States' citizens. More than 98 percent of all secondary school children were citizens. Its population was larger than that of five existing states—Vermont, Wyoming, Nevada, Delaware, and Alaska. Economically also Hawaii was qualified for immediate statehood. During 1945–1959 the islands' economy underwent unprecedented diversification and growth. Individual per capita income increased from $1,328 in 1945 to $2,274 in 1959. Despite its relatively small population, in the fiscal year 1957–1958 Hawaii paid more in federal taxes than ten states. The 1959 House investigating committee correctly concluded that Hawaii's population was "sufficiently large," and its "resources sufficiently developed, beyond question, to support statehood."[99]

After the Pacific War the bulk of Hawaii's people consistently supported immediate statehood. In 1950 they ratified a proposed state constitution by an overwhelming margin, despite the reservations of some labor groups. The landslide approval given the statehood plebiscite in 1959, along with the impressive voter turnouts for this poll and the first state elections, substantiated beyond doubt proponents' claims that Hawaii's people earnestly wanted statehood. Neither outright local resistance nor support for an alternative status ever gained wide support. Moreover during the 1950s internal opposition to statehood was relatively stronger in Alaska than in Hawaii.[100]

The protracted campaign for statehood was made possible by an underlying consensus on the issue which dated from 1945 at the latest. Arguments which emphasized that the islands were both thoroughly qualified for admission and legally entitled to it always formed the nucleus of the long official drive for equality. These views were accepted by more than 90 percent of prominent national newspapers,[101] reiterated monotonously by the various investigating committees of the House and Senate, and repeated tirelessly by local proponents in testimony to these committees. In addition, they provided the backbone of arguments advanced by statehood supporters in the numerous, often lengthy debates in Congress during 1947–1959.[102] The Statehood Commission was largely responsible for coordinating and promoting these publicity activities. For more than a decade it spent, on average, more than one hundred thousand dollars annually to support its activities in Honolulu and Washington. It distributed information to approximately 1,700 mainland newspapers, published and distributed various booklets and letters, provided extensive testimony to all House and Senate investigating committees, sent delegates to lobby on Capitol Hill, and in effect wrote many of the speeches used by supporters in Congress. It distributed more than twenty-five thousand publications, pamphlets or letters annually. With the active support of King, Farrington, Tavares, Long, Thurston, and Quinn, the campaign effectively demonstrated "that Hawaii wanted, deserved, and was fully qualified for statehood."[103]

The campaign was a vital, if undramatic precondition for acceptance by Congress, but publicity alone could not overcome the entrenched racial, states' rights, and political interests which perennially frustrated Hawaii's legitimate aspirations. The impact of the formal campaign was often indirect or essentially covert, but it was nonetheless substantial. In the decade after 1948, for example, support within the Senate increased almost fourfold, although popular approval as expressed in opinion polls declined marginally. Support from members of the House also rose substantially during these years. Without this significant, if gradual expansion of support, especially in the Senate, the political and sectional impasse over Hawaii would not have been broken in 1958–1959. Many islanders were justifiably disillusioned with the nature and effectiveness of the formal campaign by the late 1950s. But in the long-term this systematic propaganda and lobbying exercise played a crucial role in Hawaii's successful bid for statehood.

In the sixty years which elapsed after annexation, Washington had little incentive to break, or indeed alter, its formal relationship with Hawaii. American interests in such vital areas as immigration and defense were well served by its direct control over the islands after 1898. While Japan's assault on Pearl Harbor precipitated America's entry into war against the Axis states in Europe as well as Asia, Roosevelt had previously committed his country unambiguously to the Allied cause. Indeed, some historians have argued that this provoked Japan into preemptive action in December 1941. Events in Asia and Europe throughout 1940–1941 made it virtually impossible for the United States to remain permanently aloof from the war. Certainly its special association with Hawaii was not primarily responsible for its participation in the conflict, although this relationship did precipitate the actual declaration of war. Washington's firm control over the islands also boosted the nation's ability to plan for and wage war in the Pacific. It was not obliged to negotiate with a sovereign people. Nor was it restrained by constitutional protections which would have applied to Hawaii's people had they lived in an American state. Martial law demonstrated that, in a crisis at least, territoriality permitted Washington to exercise unchecked authority over every aspect of island life—even if such activities were later deemed unconstitutional. If it had been an independent country, a colony of another nation, or an equal American state, Washington would presumably have acted differently in Hawaii during the war with Japan.

Material as well as strategic and military advantages accrued to the United States as a result of its special association with Hawaii. As indicated previously, the islands were an important, stable, and profitable area for the investment of mainland capital. They were also a more important purchaser of American exports than all but five countries. From the 1870s on many American nationals profited greatly from their agricultural and commercial ventures in the islands. Territoriality had formally protected the interests of this group, ensured stability, delayed full-fledged democracy, helped prolong haole authority, and integrated the islands irrevocably into the national economy. After annexation the material interests of Hawaii's American citizens usually coincided with the national economic interest, and were in part dependent upon sympathetic action by Washington.

The triumph of Americanization in ideological, political, and economic terms by the early 1950s confirmed the integration of the islands into the national community. Hawaii's interests were now essentially inseparable from those of the nation generally. Despite the persistence of ethnic and socioeconomic stratification in Hawaii, its peoples overwhelmingly accepted that they shared values and interests common not only to the island community but to the nation at large. Most mainlanders, congressmen, national newspapers, corporate and business interests agreed that the islands could not now be cut adrift without seriously damaging the national interest. It was no mere coincidence that arguments employed by expansionists in the 1890s to justify annexation were sometimes repeated verbatim to promote statehood as late as 1959. The

day before Congress finally approved Hawaii's admission, for example,
Senator Thomas Kuchel quoted a statement made by Charles Henry to
the House on June 6, 1898:

> We want these islands because of their value from a naval and military point
> of view; we want them on account of the commercial advantages they will
> bring to our country; we want them in order that no foreign power may use
> them as a base of operations against us in time of war; we want them because
> they are more contiguous to our territory than to that of any other nation.[104]

If considerations of national advantage prompted annexation, they also
remained a persuasive influence on demands for statehood. National
interests were not restricted to economic or strategic benefits however.
Equally important, as most statehood advocates argued after the war,
were ideological issues. Most accepted that a continued semi-colonial
status, whether it be as a territory or a commonwealth, was inconsistent
with the nation's political traditions.[105] This same argument, applied
domestically, helped foster unprecedented support for an attack on segregation and institutional racism after the Supreme Court's historic ruling in 1954.

In the 1890s the advantages of annexation were regarded as self-evident. But in the 1950s it was more difficult to define or assess the actual
rewards which an intimate association with Hawaii brought to the
nation. The last House committee to investigate statehood conceded this
point. It was impossible "to prove in precise terms the exact extent to
which the residents of the older States would be benefitted" if Hawaii
was given statehood, it concluded in 1959.[106] But in the light of America's professed enthusiasm for self-government, democracy, and anti-
imperialism, it could not (without considerable hypocrisy) retain the
islands as a territory. Some Americans were adamant that Hawaii
should be granted national independence, as both territorial status and
statehood flatly contradicted policies pursued by the United States in
giving the Philippines independence and encouraging the decolonization of Asia, Africa, and the Caribbean. By retaining Hawaii and making it a state, the American Parents' Association asked rhetorically,
"Aren't we supplying a perfect example of so-called capitalist imperialism which can be exploited by the Communists?"[107] Few endorsed this
view, least of all the overwhelming majority of islanders who so eagerly
sought immediate statehood. Yet when viewed against the rising tide of
decolonization abroad and demands for racial equality at home, many
Americans undoubtedly accepted that Hawaii's unequal and dependent
territorial status was an embarrassing anomaly. If national interest had
once dictated that the islands be annexed and incorporated, it now suggested that territorial rule was inappropriate. Thus statehood was pro-

claimed, in banner headlines, as a "Message for [the] Free World." Official American opinion welcoming Hawaii as an equal in the Union was expressed in predictable cold war rhetoric and ignored the long years of territorial rule. In words typical of statements by the White House and State Department, the director of the U.S. Information Agency, George Allen, wrote about the effects of statehood:

> America will gain strength, respect and reassurance at a time when forces of intolerance threaten the free peoples of the world. . . . As the only State in the Union with a striking Asian heritage, the example of Hawaii can have a profound effect on the so-called uncommitted nations of Asia. . . .
> Statehood for Hawaii should prove a convincing answer to overseas critics who have made a great issue of our race problems. It proves to others that, far from crushing minorities, we are glad to have them.[108]

Hawaii's status was no longer a political anomaly; it had been transformed into an ideological asset in the struggle for the so-called uncommitted peoples of the world. In this context statehood was interpreted as genuine victory for America's political, "moral and spiritual values." Hawaii would prove, Allen concluded, that "democracy and freedom are not only desirable but workable as well."

After sixty years as an inchoate American state and three generations of pervasive Americanization, virtually no one seriously contemplated giving Hawaii self-government as an independent, sovereign nation. Given the proliferation of small decolonized nations in the Pacific during the 1960s and 1970s this might have been considered a possible alternative to continued territorial rule. But Hawaii was too thoroughly integrated into America's economic, political, and ideological structures and patterns to even contemplate this alternative. Nor did many Hawaiians interpret a status similar to that accorded Puerto Rico as a reasonable alternative to statehood. Shared American experiences and common interests dictated after the 1930s that the statehood pledge given during 1898–1900 should be honored. Annexation had occurred fundamentally because the interests and aspirations of Hawaii's small but powerful American community overlapped with and complemented Washington's expanding aims in the Pacific and Asia. In 1959 virtually all of Hawaii's people, irrespective of race or traditions, believed their interests could best be served by integrated political equality with the existing American states.

In the 1890s Hawaii's people and the nation's political representatives were deeply divided over annexation. By the late 1950s, however, local and national conflicts over Hawaii's future had subsided, and Congress moved finally to honor the promises implied in 1898 when the United

States seized formal control of the islands. By granting Hawaii's people equality within the Union, statehood resolved a nagging and embarrassing inconsistency in American politics. It demonstrated a belated commitment to democratic principles which Hawaii's semi-colonial territorial status had long contradicted and compromised.

Conclusion:
"We All Haoles?"

When the United States flag was raised over the Hawaiian islands in the 1890s it was welcomed enthusiastically by a small but determined minority of white settlers. Revolution against the old Hawaiian order and annexation foreclosed the islands to possible control by another nation. Hawaii was a prize easily won during America's outward imperialist thrust at the turn of the century. But very few Hawaiians initially sanctioned this forced transformation of their vulnerable community into an American possession. The islands were subsequently ruled as a semi-colonial appendage of the United States. Hawaii's people were denied full-fledged political democracy at home, and not afforded equality with citizens on the mainland. These explicit administrative and political arrangements did not challenge but rather reinforced the authority of the powerful white elite which dominated the islands after the coup of 1893. Hawaii's native peoples resigned themselves reluctantly to these imposed changes—changes which symbolized the eclipse and eventual subordination of their traditional way of life to imported norms and patterns. Native Hawaiians had been conspicuously absent from the ceremony which marked the transfer of sovereignty over their islands to Washington and signalled the triumph of American values and institutions over those indigenous to the islands. Yet when statehood was eventually granted, only a minority of Hawaiians and part-Hawaiians resisted, perceiving it as the final irreversible step toward foreign domination of their society.

Along with most members of the islands' various ethnic groups, descendents of Hawaii's original inhabitants generally welcomed statehood. Ironically, those who now resisted were more concerned with the influence of residents with Asian ancestry than with the more pervasive pressures of Americanization. But in the years after 1959 the long-dormant undercurrent of Hawaiian nationalism resurfaced in a self-conscious movement called the Hawaiian renaissance. This development symbolized Hawaiian resistance to foreign influences of all kinds, especially haole culture. It was an attempt to reawaken cultural pride and political awareness among a generally disadvantaged native population. But it was not restricted to empty, symbolic gestures. It gave rise to demands for land rights and compensation for past injustices, formation

of a state-run Office of Hawaiian Affairs, approval by Congress of a
Native Hawaiians Study Commission, and moves to win special recognition as an indigenous people.[1]

The strength of anti-imperialist sentiment in Congress during the
1890s indicated that many Americans believed the forced incorporation
of Hawaii's people into the American political system was neither necessary nor appropriate. But if opposition to expansion and colonialism
was strong, it did not prevail. Later, after almost three generations of
white control and territorial administration, few Americans doubted
that Hawaii's future should lie within the American system. Sharp disagreement existed over the political rights and constitutional status appropriate for Hawaii, but even the most bitter opponents of statehood
rarely contemplated giving it formal independence outside the political
ambit of the United States. Nor would such a decision have turned back
the tide of Americanization which transformed the island community
ineluctably after the late nineteenth century, and which accelerated
sharply as a result of war against Japan. Like annexation, statehood
was essentially an explicit reflection of underlying developments which
drew Hawaii increasingly toward the United States. These forces, in
turn, gave rise to the convenient fiction that Hawaii's people had
always wanted to be absorbed into the American body politic.

During World War II and the cold war internal pressures for ideological consensus and national unity were intense. At the same time, decolonization began to transform the international order, and criticism of
colonialism in any form became a dominant international sentiment.
Embarrassed by the unresolved dependent status of Hawaii, Americans
were officially encouraged to believe that their country had been invited to annex the islands and would quickly grant them statehood. As late
as 1957, for example, Eisenhower's Interior secretary, Fred A. Seaton,
expressed this view in a press release. "Through the nineteenth century,
as ties of friendship and trade grew stronger, the desire of Hawaiians to
be Americans became more vocal," he asserted. "Ever since the Hawaiian people . . . have pursued this goal with diligence."[2] This argument
was compatible with America's espoused anti-colonialism and consistent with its cold war rhetoric. It conveniently averted criticism of
America as a colonial power by claiming that Hawaii's people had
encouraged annexation. But this view overlooked the strength of local
resistance to the events of 1893 and 1898, and ignored internal divisions
over statehood as well as hostility to territorial rule throughout 1900–
1959.

Phrases like "We All Haoles" or "Now We Are All Haoles" were
widely used to symbolize the acceptance of Hawaii's diverse peoples as
Americans under statehood. Rather like Lind's phrase "One People Out
of Many," these words implied that all Hawaiians were assimilated,

indistinguishable Americans.[3] After World War II the word haole was usually applied to white American settlers in the islands. Hence statehood was popularly perceived as the final stage in the Americanization and assimilation of Hawaii's people. But haole had traditionally meant foreigner or stranger. In the general euphoria which greeted statehood few pondered the irony of phrases like "We All Haoles." Certainly, Hawaii's various ethnic groups had internalized the dominant values of American society. Most island citizens were genuinely acculturized, and had anxiously sought to demonstrate their loyalty and fundamental Americanism during the years of war against Japan, the cold war, and McCarthyism. For Hawaii's native peoples, this process had exacerbated the erosion and distortion of their traditional values and customs. As the descendents of imported Asian laborers began to play an active, open role in local political and economic affairs, the relative influence of Hawaiians or part-Hawaiians declined further. In a sense, native Hawaiians had become haoles, or strangers, in their own land, submerged beneath the powerful white minority and a newly assertive Asian majority.

In another sense, however, it is highly misleading to claim that Hawaii's peoples were "all haoles," because the term had definite economic and social connotations; it implied that Hawaii was a broadly egalitarian society. Indeed, the slogan "We All Haoles" certainly exaggerates the degree of structural assimilation experienced by the nonwhite majority. The overwhelming support for immediate statehood was an index of widely shared political aspirations and democratic values resulting from pervasive Americanization over almost a century. It did not, however, reflect broad structural unity, the dissolution of ethnic diversity, or uniform patterns of acculturation across the numerous ethnic and class cleavages which still fragmented Hawaii's uniquely complex society.

In a way the statehood question exposed the limits of assimilation in Hawaii. It sharpened the deep-rooted contest for political authority in the islands—a contest which derived from demands by the bulk of its nonwhite people for access to political office and economic opportunities traditionally reserved for the haole elite. Not until immediately after World War II, when substantial numbers of local-born citizens of Asian extraction were sufficiently confident to confront the old order, however, did this conflict become the central concern of local politics and a vital aspect of the struggle for statehood. Most islanders who were uneasy about statehood feared that it would hasten unwelcome changes. This concern was proportionately strongest among haoles and Hawaiians, and weakest among the emerging Japanese group. Some whites, especially those with substantial property and wealth, were determined to resist any developments which might threaten their advantaged position in the islands. Yet even before statehood the power and privileges of the old order were under serious challenge—especially after the electoral watershed of 1954. In addition, some Hawaiians and part-Hawaiians clung to territorial rule rather than foster further Americanization under statehood. Others were reluctant to formally sanction the loss of their land and culture by accepting a new status as an American state—particularly if this state might be controlled by its most recent settlers, those of Asian descent.

For Hawaii's numerous Asian minorities, especially the large group of Japanese, statehood was much more than a belated symbol of social acceptance by American society at large. "Now we are able to make our own decisions," one of Hawaii's nisei leaders observed. "We have a chance now to correct the system." Others of Japanese extraction welcomed statehood as a kind of victory over the apprehension of many Caucasians that the Asian population of Hawaii was too large to permit such a step. "It symbolized," Murai observed in words used frequently by local Japanese after the war, that "we were no longer a second class citizen as far as the United States is concerned. We're first class citizens on [an] equal footing with other states in the Union." Fong, Hawaii's most distinguished leader of Chinese descent, also viewed statehood in this light. It ended Hawaii's status as America's "step-child," he stated, and brought genuine equality.[4] Statehood was a tangible, necessary step toward democracy at home and self-government free from the arbitrary authority of officials appointed by Washington. Significantly, although both the haole and Hawaiian minorities remained divided over immediate statehood until 1959, citizens of Japanese, Chinese, and Filipino ancestry overwhelmingly supported the drive for statehood. In general, those who felt most stifled and disadvantaged under the old territorial administration were the most anxious to embrace statehood. Virtually all island citizens who were descended from Asian immigrants welcomed it as a crucial step toward wider access to genuine political equality and improved economic and social opportunities.

It became clear after 1945 that the loyalty, acculturation, and assimilation of Hawaii's multiracial community were not the stumbling blocks to statehood. Multiracialism itself was the issue. There was a powerful minority, both in the islands and throughout the nation, who held fervently that race was the fundamental criterion of Americanism. Being essentially nonwhite, Hawaii's people would thus never be suitable candidates for unqualified American citizenship. Racism, manifest in a variety of ways, was therefore the central obstacle to statehood. Locally, it sustained virtually every effort to defeat, delay, or divert statehood. Nationally, it merged Hawaii's aspiration for political equality into the most divisive conflict in domestic politics after the New Deal—protracted dispute over civil rights for nonwhite Americans. And it was the relationship between statehood and this divisive national conflict which determined Hawaii's fate until 1959.

The central battles over Hawaii took place in Congress, where statehood was perceived as a threat to the political and sectional status quo. In particular, the powerful conservative faction interpreted it as a direct challenge to the racial practices, sectional influence, congressional authority, and traditional states' rights of the segregated South. Statehood for the islands had important implications for a range of related domestic issues which preoccupied Congress during the bitter postwar struggle to grant all Americans equality under the Constitution, irrespective of race. In general, the opponents of civil rights for black Americans refused also to accept the liberal, multiracial Hawaiian society as an equal with the existing states. Hawaii thus confronted a complex series of obstructionist strategies which were unashamedly designed to deny its citizens voting representation in Congress and democracy at home. These tactics were rationalized by charges that Hawaii's predominantly Asian population was by definition un-American, uniquely susceptible to subversion from within by enemy aliens during conflict with Japan and by communist sympathizers during confrontation with the Soviet Union. These wild assertions complicated debate and action on Hawaii. But they were never substantiated, and were in large part convenient substitute arguments for opposition which derived from sectional and states' rights considerations. However, such assertions did reflect and exploit the racial, political, and ideological insecurities of a substantial minority of Americans during the 1940s and 1950s.

The decision to accept a noncontiguous possession as a state was an unprecedented development in United States history. Although this step had been anticipated shortly after annexation when the islands were formally designated an incorporated territory, statehood irrevocably extended the boundaries of the nation beyond their traditional continental limits. It also incorporated into the Union a state with a population predominantly of Asian extraction. "By voting the admission of Hawaii, America's frontier has moved into the Asian world," an American official concluded.[5] Certainly, the nation's frontier now formally extended into the Pacific, as Mahan and other imperialists had anticipated a century earlier. But the idea that the islands were a part of Asia constituted a sadly insensitive view of Hawaii's native peoples and their history. It was a view dictated by ideological pressures and a desire to use Hawaii's admission to statehood as a weapon in the cold war. The unique ethnic composition of Hawaii's community, not its particular geography, was for sixty years the underlying barrier to its attempts to emulate all other incorporated territories and gain statehood.

Despite America's vocal support for freedom, democracy, and decolonization abroad during the cold war, Congress was frustratingly indecisive in its attempts to establish these conditions at home. During the 1940s and 1950s it was slow to guarantee full civil rights for black Americans. At the same time it refused to end Hawaii's dependent status and qualified rights until 1959. By contrast, other noncontiguous and essentially nonwhite possessions acquired by the United States at the turn of the century, as well as many European colonies in Asia and Africa, were formally decolonized before Hawaii was finally elevated to statehood.

Appendixes

APPENDIX 1

Delegates to the Constitutional Convention, Honolulu, 1950.

First Representative District
Nelson Doi
Teruo Ihara
Frank Luiz
Richard Lyman, Jr.
Tom Okino
Thomas Sakakihara
James Yamamato
Takao Yamauchi

Second Representative District
Peter Kawahara
Earl Nielsen
Sakuichi Sakai
Charles Silva

Third Representative District
Marguerite Ashford
J. Pia Cockett
Kazuo Kage
Harold Kido
Harold Rice
W. O. Smith
Richard St. Sure
Cable Wirtz
Arthur Woolaway

Fourth Representative District
J. Garner Anthony
Samuel Apoliona, Jr.
A. H. Castro
Ann Corbett
Flora Hayes
William Heen
Elizabeth Kellerman
Katsumi Kometani
John Lai

Nils Larsen
Herbert Lee
W. H. Loper
John Phillips
Hebden Porteus
Harold Roberts
C. Nils Tavares
Henry White
B. O. Wist

Fifth Representative District
Trude Akua
Edward Bryan
George Dowson
Hiram Fong
Yasutaka Fukushima
James Gilliland
E. B. Holroyde
Frank Kam
Masao Kanemaru
Charles Kauhane
Samuel King
Chuck Mau
Steere Noda
Frederick Ohrt
Herbert Richards
Clarence Shimamura
Arthur Trask
James Trask

Sixth Representative District
Matsuki Arashiro
Randolph Crossley
H. S. Kawakami
Jack Mizuha
Charles Rice
Toshio Serizawa

APPENDIX 2

Summary of Debates in Congress on Hawaii*

CHAMBER	DATES	APPROXIMATE DURATION	RESOLUTION	SPEAKERS FOR	AGAINST
House	June 30, 1947	4 hours	Statehood Bill	27	6
Senate	May 17, 18, 20, 1948	3 days	Knowland Resolution	4	2
House	Mar. 3, 6, 1950	4 hours	Statehood Bill	32	4
House	Mar. 9, 10, 1953	4 hours	Statehood Bill	32	29
Senate	Jan. 27, Feb. 26; Mar. 4, 9–12, 15–19, 29–31; Apr. 1, 1955	16 days	Statehood and Related Bills		
House	May 9, 10, 1955	2 days	Alaskan Statehood	27	13
Senate	Mar. 11, 1959	1 day	Statehood Bill	28	5
House	Mar. 11, 12, 1959	6 hours	Statehood Bill	70	10
Total Speakers				247	80

* Adapted from Donald Dedman, "The Functions of Discourse in the Hawaiian Statehood Debates," *Speech Monographs* 33, no. 1 (1966):37.

Abbreviations

AH	Archives of Hawaii, Honolulu
CN	*Congress and the Nation*
CQA	*Congressional Quarterly Almanac*
CR	*Congressional Record*
EP	Dwight D. Eisenhower Papers, Eisenhower Library, Abiline, Kansas
FP	Joseph R. Farrington Papers, Archives of Hawaii, Honolulu
HA	*Honolulu Advertiser*
HH	House of Representatives Hearings
HH-SH	Joint Congressional Hearings
HR	House of Representatives Reports
HR-SR	Joint Congressional Reports
HSB	*Honolulu Star-Bulletin*
HSC	Hawaii Statehood Commission
HSCP	Hawaii Statehood Commission Papers, Archives of Hawaii, Honolulu
HSPA	Hawaii Sugar Planters' Association
JABOHP	John A. Burns Oral History Project, Hamilton Library, University of Hawaii, Honolulu
JP	Lyndon Baines Johnson Papers, Lyndon Baines Johnson Library, Austin, Texas
NYT	*New York Times*
SH	Senate Hearings
SR	Senate Reports
TL	Harry S. Truman Library, Independence, Missouri
TP	Harry S. Truman Papers, Harry S. Truman Library

Notes

Introduction

1. Secretary of State James G. Blaine to James H. Comley (U.S. minister in Hawaii), Dec. 1, 1881, Senate Executive Docs., 53d Cong., 2d sess., no. 13 (serial 3160), pp. 8–9.

2. Scholarship in this field is discussed in the Notes throughout Chap. 1.

3. My special indebtedness to these scholars is acknowledged throughout this book in both the text and the notes. Lawrence Fuchs and Gavan Daws have also written short but penetrating accounts of the statehood issue, especially its relation to local politics. A number of other books and articles give short, largely noninterpretive accounts. In addition, Charles Hunter, late professor of history at the University of Hawaii, published a paper in 1958 which discussed some aspects of "Congress and Statehood for Hawaii." Donald Dedmon has written extensively about the long congressional debate on Hawaii in terms of a case study on modern political communications (see Bibliography for the works by these authors).

4. John Masefield, "The Everlasting Mercy," in his *Poems* (London, 1923), p. 61.

5. This observation is clearly influenced by Carl Becker's aphorism about the nature of the American Revolution.

6. Dedmon, "Analysis of the Argument," p. 445.

7. William R. Brock, *Conflict and Transformation: The United States, 1844–1877* (Harmondsworth, 1973), p. 24.

8. John Mathews, *The American Constitutional System* (New York, 1940), p. 53.

9. Daniel J. Boorstin, *The Americans*, vol. 2, *The National Experience* (New York, 1965), p. 423.

Chapter 1. Toward Annexation

1. Plesur, *America's Outward Thrust*, p. 205.

2. Lind, *Hawaii's People*, pp. 6–9.

3. Fuchs, *Hawaii Pono*, pp. 22–23

4. For the debate over Hawaii's population, see Robert C. Schmitt, "How Many Hawaiians?"; also his "New Estimates of the Pre-censal Population of Hawaii," *Journal of Polynesian Society* 88(1971):237–43; Howells, *Pacific Islanders*, pp. 16, 18. A number of excellent studies have been written on Hawaii before annexation and its relations with the United States. Perhaps the most rewarding are: Julius Pratt, *Expansionists of 1898*, and "The Hawaiian Revolution: A Reinterpretation," *Pacific Historical Review* (Sept. 1932); Russ, *Hawaiian Republic*; Stevens, *American Expansion in Hawaii*; Merze Tate, *United States and the Hawaiian Kingdom*, and *Hawaii: Reciprocity or Annexa-*

tion (East Lansing, Mich., 1968); Kuykendall, *Hawaiian Kingdom;* Daws, *Shoal of Time;* and Bradley, *American Frontier in Hawaii.* Malo to Kaahumanu II, Aug. 18, 1837, U.K. Foreign Office Records, quoted in Daws, *Shoal of Time,* p. 106.

5. Burrows, *Hawaiian Americans,* pp. 41–43. For figures on the decline of the native population, see Lind *Hawaii's People,* pp. 16–19.

6. Pendleton, "Reversal of Roles," pp. 26–32; Aller, *Labor Relations in the Hawaiian Sugar Industry.*

7. Fuchs, *Hawaii Pono,* pp. 86–105; *Planter's Monthly,* May 1883, p. 25; Lind, *Hawaii's People,* p. 27; Nordyke, *Peopling of Hawaii,* pp. 29–35; and generally, Glick, *Sojourners and Settlers.*

8. Lind, *Hawaii's People;* Nordyke, *Peopling of Hawaii.*

9. Fuchs, *Hawaii Pono,* pp. 17–43, 68–149; Lind, *Hawaii's People,* pp. 15–38; Nordyke, *Peopling of Hawaii,* pp. 22–55.

10. Fuchs, *Hawaii Pono,* p. 37.

11. The view that American expansion occurred in two phases, linked by a common expansionist ideology, is perhaps best expressed by Richard W. Van Alstyne, *The Rising American Empire* (Oxford, 1960). An interesting, more complex attempt to link American expansion to four stages of economic growth is Eblen's *First and Second United States Empires.*

12. Cf. President Harrison's view, "The Constitution follows the flag," with Secretary of State Elihu Root's response, "Yes . . . the Constitution follows the flag, but doesn't quite catch up with it" (quoted in Beisner, *From Old Diplomacy to New,* p. 216).

13. Incorporation is discussed at length in the first section of Chap. 2.

14. Fillmore, quoted in James D. Richardson, ed., *A Compilation of the Messages and Papers of the Presidents,* vol. 6, Dec. 2, 1851 (New York, 1897–1916), p. 2656.

15. Kuykendall, "Destined to be American," p. 33; Hyams, "Tough Job," *HA,* p. 2. See also Brookes, *Rivalry in the Pacific Islands,* p. 91.

16. Commodore Matthew C. Perry, quoted in S. E. Morison and H. S. Commager, *The Growth of the American Republic,* vol. 1 (New York, 1962), p. 406.

17. SR5, p. 9; *HA,* June 23, 1959; Hunter, "Forty-ninth State?", p. 10.

18. Daws, *Shoal of Time,* pp. 147–53; Barber, *Hawaii: Restless Rampart,* p. 98.

19. Donald M. Dozer, "Anti-Expansionism during the Johnson Administration," *Pacific Historical Review* 12(1943):253–75; Patterson, "United States and Hawaii Reciprocity," pp. 14–26; Thomas J. Osborne, "Trade or War? America's Annexation of Hawaii Reconsidered," *Pacific Historical Review* 50(Aug. 1981): 285–307.

20. Tate, *United States and the Hawaiian Kingdom,* pp. 34–43; *HA,* June 23, 1959.

21. See generally Plesur, *America's Outward Thrust;* and Beisner, *From Old Diplomacy to New.*

22. Lodge, quoted in Beisner, *From Old Diplomacy to New,* p. 13.

23. Platt, quoted in Peter N. Carroll and David W. Noble, *The Free and the Unfree: A New History of the United States* (Harmondsworth, 1977), p. 307.

24. Alfred T. Mahan, "Hawaii and Our Future Sea Power," pp. 1–11.

25. Williams, *The Roots of the Modern American Empire* (New York, 1969); La Feber, *The New Empire*; McCormick, *China Market*. Cf. Paul A. Varg, "The Myth of the China Market, 1890–1914," *American Historical Review* 73(Feb. 1968):742–58; Beisner, *From Old Diplomacy to New*, esp. pp. 17–27; and M. Young, "American Expansion," pp. 176–201.

26. See note 25 above.

27. Blaine to James H. Comley (U.S. minister in Hawaii), Dec. 1, 1881, Senate Executive Docs., 53d Cong., 2d sess., no. 13 (serial 3160), pp. 8, 9.

28. McKinley, quoted in SR5, p. 9.

29. Senator George F. Hoar, Hanna, and Depew, all quoted in Carl N. Degler, *Out of Our Past: The Forces that Shaped Modern America*, 3d ed. (New York, 1970), pp. 430–31.

30. M. Young, "American Expansion," pp. 185–86.

31. See generally Healy, *U.S. Expansionism*.

32. John W. Burgess, *Political Science and Comparative Constitutional Law* (Boston, 1890), pp. 37–45.

33. Quoted in Degler, *Out of Our Past*, p. 427.

34. Osborne, *Empire Can Wait*, esp. p. 136. This is an excellent "post-revisionist" study of the anti-imperialists, which argues convincingly that the coup against the Hawaiian monarchy in 1893 initiated America's "Great Debate" over empire. See also Pratt, *Expansionists of 1898*, p. 225; C. Campbell, *Transformation of American Foreign Relations*, pp. 235–37.

35. Longfield Gorman, "The Administration and Hawaii," *North American Review* 165(1897):379; Broussard, *CR*, June 14, 1898, 31, pt. 7, p. 5938; Cooley, "Grave Obstacles to Hawaiian Annexation," p. 406.

36. John M. Morton to William Hunter, Nov. 25, 1879, Consular Dispatches, Honolulu, no. 18, quoted in Plesur, *America's Outward Thrust*, pp. 204–11. See also Tate, *United States and the Hawaiian Kingdom*, pp. 38–43; Dozer, "Anti-Expansionism during the Johnson Administration"; Daws, *Shoal of Time*, pp. 197–206; Kuykendall, *Hawaiian Kingdom*, vol. 3, pp. 24–39.

37. Plesur, *America's Outward Thrust*, pp. 205–6.

38. Tate, *United States and the Hawaiian Kingdom*, pp. 38–43; Plesur, *America's Outward Thrust*, pp. 204–11.

39. For newspaper opinions, see New York *Herald*, July 25, 1887, and Sept. 12, 1887; *New York Daily Tribune*, June 24, 1879; *Sacramento Daily Record-Union*, Jan. 24, 1887; and *San Francisco Merchant*, Feb. 10, 1882. Also, Merze Tate, "British Opposition to the Cession of Pearl Harbor," *Pacific Historical Review* 29(Nov. 1960):381–94; and Plesur, *America's Outward Thrust*, pp. 209–10.

40. Volwiler, *Correspondence Between Harrison and Blaine*, pp. 204–6.

41. These events are discussed at length in a number of studies. See, for example, Pratt, *Expansionists of 1898*; Daws, *Shoal of Time*; and Kuykendall and Day, *Hawaii: A History*.

42. Hopkins to Thurston, Dec. 29, 1892, in Lorrin A. Thurston, *Memoirs of the Hawaiian Revolution*, ed. Andrew Farrell (Honolulu, 1936), pp. 242–43.

43. For detailed accounts of the revolution see Tate, *United States and the Hawaiian Kingdom*, pp. 155–93; Stevens, *American Expansion in Hawaii*, pp.

215–29; Russ, *Hawaiian Republic*, generally; and Daws, *Shoal of Time*, pp. 251–92.

44. Stevens to Foster, Jan. 19, 1893, U.S. Dept. of State, *Foreign Relations 1894*, app. 2, p. 398.

45. Hunter, "Statehood Issue Almost Blocked Annexation," *HA*, p. 4, and "Forty-ninth State?", pp. 10–12.

46. See note 45 above. For population figures, see Lind, *Hawaii's People*, p. 28.

47. Stevens to Foster, Feb. 8, 1893, and Stevens to Capt. Wiltse, Feb. 1, 1893, U.S. Dept. of State, *Foreign Relations 1894*, app. 2, pp. 404–5.

48. Devine, "John W. Foster," esp. pp. 47–48.

49. Ibid.; Johnson, quoted in *CR*, June 15, 1898, 31, pt. 7, pp. 5967–98.

50. Devine, "John W. Foster"; Daws, *Shoal of Time*, pp. 270–80.

51. Lind, *Hawaii's People*, pp. 26–31; Nordyke, *Peopling of Hawaii*, pp. 22–58; Fuchs, *Hawaii Pono*, pp. 112–35.

52. Bailey, "Japan's Protest," esp. pp. 46, 51–55; Russ, *Hawaiian Republic*, pp. 131, 139, 155–56.

53. Smith to Hawaiian minister of Foreign Affairs Henry E. Cooper, Mar. 26, 1897, quoted in Pratt, *Expansionists of 1898*, p. 216; Hunter, "Statehood Issue Almost Blocked Annexation," *HA*, p. 4.

54. Russ, *Hawaiian Republic*, pp. 173–74; Bailey, "Japan's Protest," p. 59.

55. Capt. Albert S. Baker to Secretary of the Navy John D. Long, Aug. 30, and Sept. 15, 1897, quoted in C. Campbell, *Transformation of American Foreign Relations*, pp. 233–34; Roosevelt, quoted by Hunter, "Statehood Issue Almost Blocked Annexation," *HA*, p. 4.

56. *Honolulu Star*, n.d., quoted in Fuchs, *Hawaii Pono*, p. 36.

57. Hunter, "Statehood Issue Almost Blocked Annexation," *HA*, p. 4.

58. Champ Clark (Dem., Mo.), *CR*, June 14, 1898, 31, pt. 7, p. 6019. Also, Hunter, "Statehood Issue Almost Blocked Annexation," *HA*, p. 4; and Daws, *Shoal of Time*, pp. 285–92.

59. New York *Sun*, n.d., quoted in Beisner, *From Old Diplomacy to New*, p. 116. Cf. Osborne, *Empire Can Wait*, in which the impact of the war with Spain and Hawaii's military importance are viewed as subordinate factors in the decision to annex Hawaii. Osborne argues that Hawaii was a springboard to all of Asia, not only the Philippines. This fact gained new importance in the spring of 1898 as the European powers moved to carve China into spheres of exclusive national influence. America's acquisition of Hawaii was now urgent, he argues, if it was to restrain these powers or win a share of the China market itself (see esp. pp. 135–36 for a succinct statement of this view).

60. See the first section of Chap. 2 of this book.

61. See, for example, C. Campbell, *Transformation of American Foreign Policy*, pp. 291–94.

62. William Henry Seward to Z. S. Spalding, July 5, 1868, *Papers Relating to the Foreign Relations of the United States, 1892*, app. 2, p. 144, quoted in Plesur, *America's Outward Thrust*, p. 5.

63. This assertion is heavily influenced by the work of La Feber, *The New Empire*; Plesur, *America's Outward Thrust*; and M. Young, "American Expansion."

64. William B. Tansill (Legislative Reference Service) to Senator Clinton Anderson, Apr. 1, 1954, container 536, Anderson Papers; Westal W. Willoughby, *The Constitutional Law of the United States*, 1910, vol. 1 (New York, 1927 ed.), p. 429.

65. Daws, *Shoal of Time*, p. 291.

66. Dinell et al., *Hawaiian Homes Program*, pp. 1–3; Lind, *Hawaii's People*, p. 28. "Hawaiians" made up 19.3 percent of the population, "part-Hawaiians" comprised 5.1 percent in 1900.

67. H. M. Sewall (U.S. minister to Hawaii) to W. R. Day, Aug. 6, 1898, quoted in Russ, *Hawaiian Republic*, pp. 364–65.

68. See John Fitzgerald (Mass.) and Richard Bland (Mo.), *CR*, June 13, 1898, and June 15, 1898, 31, pt. 7, pp. 5967–98.

69. House Committee on Foreign Relations, *Report*, H.R. 1355 (minority opinion), 55th Cong., 2d sess., vol. 2, p. 1898.

70. See the following reports on this ceremony: "Hawaii," *Nation* 68(Aug. 25, 1898):139; Beardslee, "Pilekias," p. 475. In 1900 Hawaiians and part-Hawaiians comprised 24.4 percent of the population. In contrast, Japanese constituted 39.7 percent, Chinese 16.7 percent, and "Caucasians" 17.3 percent (see Lind, *Hawaii's People*, p. 28).

Chapter 2. Incorporated But Not Equal

1. As Hunter has pointed out: "Those who had overthrown the monarchy and anxiously sought annexation also cautioned against statehood because 'it would be unsafe to give all the powers of the state to the present electorate.'" See Charles H. Hunter, *HA*, Feb. 8, 1953, "Statehood Issue Almost Blocked Annexation," *HA*, and "Forty-ninth State?", p. 10.

2. Lind, *Hawaii's People*, pp. 10, 93; Fuchs, *Hawaii Pono*, esp. pp. 36–67.

3. "Joint Resolution No. 55 [55th Cong.] to Provide for Annexing the Hawaiian Islands to the United States," HR8, app. D, pp. 60–61; Dill, *Statehood for Hawaii*, p. 25; Houston, "Implied Statehood Promise Given," *HA*; Ralph S. Kuykendall, "The Evolution of Hawaii's Government," SH1, p. 139. In 1910, Section 5 of the Organic Act was amended because several executive departments of the federal government differed in their rulings as to "whether general appropriations applying to the States as a whole were applicable to Hawaii." As amended, Section 5 read: "That the Constitution, and except as otherwise provided, all the laws of the U.S., including the laws carrying general appropriations, which are not locally applicable, shall have the same force and effect within the territory as elsewhere in the U.S." (Hawaii Equal Rights Commission, *Hawaii: Integral Part*, p. 6).

4. Dill, *Statehood for Hawaii*, p. 26. Dill concluded: "So many similar statements can be found in the opinions of the Supreme Court and inferior courts, that the principle announced 'in this decision' is now part of the constitutional law of the United States." See also Kinevan, "Alaska and Hawaii," p. 278; Frank P. Huddle, "Admission of New States," in *Editorial Research Reports*, vol. 1 (Mar. 20, 1946), pp. 185–98, HSCP.

5. Swisher, *American Constitutional Development*, pp. 476–81; HR8, p. 3 (this report cites U.S. court decisions: 182 U.S. 305; 190 U.S. 197; 389 U.S.

537). See also SR5, p. 10; and Barber, *Hawaii: Restless Rampart*, p. 99. Cf. Hunter's argument that: "Both houses of Congress . . . refused to pass measures that would have denied future statehood to the Islands. Other than this (and the precedent that a territorial status had heretofore resulted in eventual statehood) there was no indication during the process of annexation nor in the creation of a form of government for the Territory of Hawaii that statehood was intended, promised or implied" ("Forty-ninth State?", pp. 10–11).

6. Westal W. Willoughby, *The Constitutional Law of the United States*, 1910, vol. 1 (New York, 1927 ed.), p. 407; *CN* 1:1499, 1503–07. Kuykendall, "Evolution of Hawaii's Government," SH1, pp. 139–41; Dill, *Statehood for Hawaii*, p. 25; Houston, "Implied Statehood Promise Given," *HA*.

7. Fuchs, *Hawaii Pono*, p. 152. See also Robert M. C. Littler, *The Governance of Hawaii* (Stanford, 1929), p. 14; Baker, "Human Nature in Hawaii," p. 453.

8. Burns, JABOHP, tape 3, pp. 6–8, tape 8, pp. 8–9, tape 7, p. 11 (references to JABOHP tapes and page nos. hereafter abbreviated: 3.6–8; 8.8–9; etc.); Daws, *Shoal of Time*, p. 312.

9. According to Representative Hanna (Hawaii House of Representatives), all 726 directorships in these eighty-nine corporations were held by Caucasians in 1936 (HH3, pp. 801–11).

10. Lind, "Hawaiian Backgrounds," p. 7.

11. Edward P. Dole, quoted in U.S. Congress, *Report of Subcommittee on Pacific Islands and Puerto Rico on General Conditions in Hawaii*, vol. 1 (Washington, 1903), p. 10.

12. Wright, *Disenchanted Isles*, pp. 21–37 (Thurston is quoted on pp. 28, 61).

13. Royal M. Mead, House Committee on Immigration and Naturalization, *Labor Problems in Hawaii*, Hearings, 67th Cong., 1st sess., 1921, p. 391.

14. *Evening Bulletin*, Mar. 6, 1901, p. 4; SR5, p. 10; *Friend*, June 1911, quoted in Hyams, "Tough Job," *HA*.

15. *Evening Bulletin*, Mar. 7, 1903, p. 1; *NYT*, Mar. 13, 1959, p. 13; *Pacific Commercial Advertiser*, Feb. 27, 1919, p. 5; Hyams, "Tough Job," *HA*.

16. *HSB*, Jan. 19, 1920, p. 6. The *Pacific Commercial Advertiser*, which became the *Honolulu Advertiser* in 1919, remained opposed to statehood until after World War II.

17. Wright, *Disenchanted Isles*, pp. 21–37; Daws, *Shoal of Time*, pp. 293–338; and Fuchs, *Hawaii Pono*, pp. 153–259.

18. See note 17 above.

19. Fuchs, *Hawaii Pono*, p. 162.

20. Allan A. Spitz, "Land Aspects of the Hawaiian Homes Program" (Honolulu, 1964); Dinell et al., *Hawaiian Homes Program*, pp. 1–10.

21. Lind, *Hawaii's People*, pp. 4–38, Nordyke, *Peopling of Hawaii*, pp. 22–83.

22. See note 21 above, esp. Lind, Table, p. 28.

23. Dept. of Planning and Research, State of Hawaii, *Historical Statistics*, p. 8. See also Lind, *Hawaii's People*, pp. 7–8, 28; Daws, *Shoal of Time*, p. 316; Adams, "Statehood for Hawaii," p. 5.

24. Daws, *Shoal of Time*, p. 316; Palmer, *Human Side of Hawaii*, p. xiii; Cooke to Victor Houston, Apr. 1933, Houston Papers, quoted in Fuchs, *Hawaii Pono*, p. 408.

25. *HSB*, Jan. 19, 1920, p. 6; Neal, "Hawaii's Land and Labor Problems," pp. 389–97; Stoddard, *Rising Tide of Color*, pp. 279–80; Fuchs, *Hawaii Pono*, pp. 171–81.

26. Burns, JABOHP, 1.11; 2.19; 3.7–8; 7.11–12; 8.8–9; Dept. of Planning and Research, State of Hawaii, *Historical Statistics*, p. 25; HH3, p. 548. See also Fuchs, *Hawaii Pono*, pp. 174–181.

27. Daniel Inouye and Lawrence Elliott, *Journey to Washington* (Englewood Cliffs, N.J., 1967), p. 209.

28. Meller, "Legislative Party Profile," p. 111.

29. Aoki, JABOHP, 12.45–46; Burns, JABOHP, 1.11; 2.19; 3.7–8; 7.11–12; and 8.8–9.

30. Fong, interview with Chou, tape 2, p. 176–82; Fong, interview with author; Quinn, interview with author; Chou, "Education of a Senator," pp. 306–28.

31. Gill, quoted in Wright, *Disenchanted Isles*, p. 237.

32. Murai, JABOHP, 2.4–7, 14, 40–44; Aoki, JABOHP, 12.45–46; Kido, JABOHP, 1.9, 18, 22ff.; Hirai, JABOHP, 1.41; Mau, JABOHP, tapes 31, 32, generally; Quinn, interview with author.

33. For example, after working in Honolulu's business community for several years, Fred H. Merrill observed: "Before the war and during the early part of the war, the Bank of Hawaii wouldn't make a loan to an Oriental. They didn't want an Oriental customer" (Chou, "Education of a Senator," p. 392).

34. Hirai, JABOHP, 1.41.

35. *HA*, quoted in Wright, *Disenchanted Isles*, pp. 52–53.

36. These events are discussed at length by Wright, *Disenchanted Isles*, pp. 45–63; Fuchs, *Hawaii Pono*, pp. 206, 225.

37. Chou, "Education of a Senator," pp. 306–28; Fong, interview with Chou, 21.176–82; Fong, interview with author.

38. *HSB*, Mar. 10, 1924, p. 1; Hyams, "Tough Job," *HA*, p. 2; *HA*, Apr. 17, 1923, p. 1; Houston, HH1, p. 94.

39. Daws, *Shoal of Time*, pp. 303, 321, 346; *HA*, July 10, 1927, p. 1; Fuchs, *Hawaii Pono*, p. 178. Thurston had supported annexation as a means of preventing the establishment of an "alien" stronghold in Hawaii. L. A. Thurston, *Handbook*, p. 3.

40. Hunter, "Forty-ninth State?", p. 11; Barber, *Hawaii: Restless Rampart*, pp. 103–5; *HA*, Dec. 2, 1930, p. 1, June 23, 1959.

41. Daws, *Shoal of Time*, p. 333; C. Nils Tavares, "Some Incidents, Humorous and Otherwise, of the Statehood Struggle" (Paper delivered Jan. 5, 1970), pp. 5–8, Tavares Private Papers. The vote in the House of Representatives was twenty-three in favor, none against; in the Senate, thirteen in favor, two against.

42. Barber, *Hawaii: Restless Rampart*, p. 105. For an excellent, detailed reconstruction of this case, see Daws, *Shoal of Time*, pp. 317–26, *New York American*, quoted in ibid., p. 329.

43. *Hawaii Hochi*, Apr. 10, 1932; Crowningburg-Amalu, *Jack Burns*, p. 29.

44. *Hawaii Hochi*, Apr. 30, 1932.

45. Judge Edward M. Watson, HH1, p. 273. See also Hunter, "Forty-ninth State?", p. 12 (Hunter emphasized that Roosevelt was "annoyed among other things by the inability of the Island Democrats to unite on a local candidate for Governor"); A. G. M. Robertson, HH1, p. 35; U.S. Senator Frank Church, SH8, p. 21; Barber, *Hawaii: Restless Rampart*, p. 109.

46. Barber, *Hawaii: Restless Rampart*, p. 108; Hyams, "Tough Job," *HA*, p. 2; Daws, *Shoal of Time*, p. 330.

47. *HSB*, Apr. 20, 1934, p. 4; Daws, *Shoal of Time*, p. 331; Adams, "Statehood for Hawaii," p. 4; Cooke, *Jones-Costigan Act*, pp. 3, 6–7.

48. Cooke, *Jones-Costigan Act*, pp. 10–11; *HSB*, Sept. 5, 1934, p. 6; Barber, *Hawaii: Restless Rampart*, p. 110.

49. Robertson, HH1, p. 35. In 1938 Hawaii regained an equitable portion of the national sugar market.

50. John Waterhouse, in *HSB*, Apr. 20, 1934, p. 1.

51. Richard A. Cooke, in ibid.

52. *HSB*, Sept. 5, 1934, p. 6.

53. Tavares, "Incidents in the Statehood Struggle," p. 8.

54. Wright, *Disenchanted Isles*, p. 183.

55. Barber, *Hawaii: Restless Rampart*, p. 112; Hunter, "Forty-ninth State?", p. 12; HR-SR1, pp. 94–95.

56. HSC, "Abstract of Congressional Investigations of Statehood for Hawaii" (Honolulu, n.d., Mimeo.), pp. 3–4.

57. Houston and Hawaii Equal Rights Commission, HH1, pp. 93, 7–11. See also *NYT*, June 1, 1935, p. 9; *NYT*, Oct. 20, 1935, p. 29.

58. HH1, pp. 11–12, 329; *NYT*, June 1, 1935, p. 9; HSC, "Abstract of Congressional Investigations," pp. 4–5.

59. Chairman Eugene B. Crowe, in *NYT*, Oct. 20, 1935, p. 29.

60. *HSB*, Aug. 6, 1937, p. 1; HR-SR1, pp. 94–95. Seven members, none of whom were senators, went to Hawaii to conduct the hearings.

61. Barber, *Hawaii: Restless Rampart*, pp. 113–14. For details of the activities of the commission, see generally Hawaii Equal Rights Commission Papers.

62. HH-SH1, pp. 9, 94–95. See also *HSB*, Oct. 15, 1937, p. 1.

63. *HSB*, Sept. 12, 1934, p. 6; *HSB*, Oct. 4, 1937, p. 1; Stokes, HH-SH1, pp. 246–72; *NYT*, Feb. 19, 1938, p. 14; HH2, p. 164.

64. *HA*, Oct. 18, 1937, p. 1; *HSB*, Oct. 18, 1937, p. 2. On the island of Hawaii, for example, seven of the ten people who gave evidence opposed statehood. However, these findings were contradicted by the returns from the 1940 plebiscite on statehood (see note 95 below).

65. HR-SR1, p. 95.

66. HR-SR1, pp. 93–94.

67. HR-SR1, pp. 94–95; Roesch, "Hawaiian Statehood Plebiscite," pp. 1–11.

68. Indeed, his attempt to defend Hawaii's mixed, predominantly Asian population from the charge that it was un-American and potentially disloyal resulted in him being known in Congress (not entirely unaffectionately) as "Sanpan Sam" (E. Farrington, interview with McDowell).

69. King to Vitousek, May 5, 1938, King Papers.

70. Roesch, "Hawaiian Statehood Plebiscite," pp. 9–10. My discussion of this episode is influenced substantially by Roesch's thorough study.

71. *HSB*, Apr. 1, May 17, 1939, and Feb. 24, 1940. The question was written in Hawaiian as well as English. This might have convinced some that the islands were not yet thoroughly American, but proponents wanted to avoid the possibility of alienating Hawaiian or part-Hawaiian voters. See John Snell to King, May 13, 1939, King Papers.

72. *HSB*, Apr. 1, 1939, p. 1; *HSB*, Apr. 25, 1940, p. 4; Barber, *Hawaii: Restless Rampart*, p. 119.

73. Roesch, "Hawaiian Statehood Plebiscite," generally; *HA*, June 23, 1959.

74. Mrs. Farrington recalled, for example, that during receptions for visiting congressional investigators members of the HSPA would argue the merits of statehood while "their wives would be on the other side of the room whispering against it" (E. Farrington, interview with McDowell).

75. Waterhouse to Wallace M. Alexander, n.d., King Papers.

76. *HSB*, July 18, 1940, p. 8.

77. Fong, interview with author. Also, Fong, interview with Chou. James P. Winne to King, Oct. 13, 1939, King Papers. Winne, an employee of the HSPA, not only performed the duties of a liaison officer between industry and the Republican party but regularly served as national committeeman for the latter.

78. *HSB*, Apr. 22, 1940.

79. *HSB*, Sept. 23, 1940.

80. The *Nippu Jiji*, Sept. 24, 1940, for example, quoted other statements by Gunji encouraging Hawaii's Japanese to be loyal Americans and suggested that Gunji had simply meant to state that Hawaii's Japanese were prepared to tolerate the bitterness and discrimination which accompanied the growing rift between Tokyo and Washington.

81. *HA*, Apr. 25, 1940; *Nippu Jiji*, July 23, 1940.

82. See, for example, *HSB*, Oct. 1, 1940; *HA*, Oct. 14, 1940.

83. *Hawaii Hochi*, Mar. 21, 1940; *Nippu Jiji*, Jan. 20, 1940. In a letter to King, John Snell acknowledged that pressure against the use of this program was being mounted by "a well-known veterans" group, presumably the American Legion. Snell to King, June 7, 1939, King Papers; *HSB*, Aug. 9, 1940; *HA*, Aug. 10, 1940.

84. *HA*, Oct. 4, 22–24, 1940.

85. King was the leading exponent of this view. See, for example, King to Cogswell, Sept. 30, 1940, King Papers; King to Ezra Crane, editor, *Maui News*, July 13, 1940, King Papers.

86. See Albert Wray, "The Menace of Dual Citizenship," *Paradise of the Pacific* (May 1940), p. 9; editorial, *Islander* (Oct. 1940); and Roesch, "Hawaiian Statehood Plebiscite," pp. 121, 125.

87. See note 86 above; *HSB*, July 19, Aug. 12, 29, Sept. 25, Nov. 1, 1940; *Hawaii Hochi*, July 29, 1940; and *HA*, Sept. 23, Nov. 5, 1940.

88. *HA*, Oct. 8, 11, 15, 17, 31, Nov. 4, 1940; *Nippu Jiji*, Sept. 21, Oct. 23, 1940; *Hawaii Hochi*, Oct. 1, 24, 1940.

89. In 1940 these papers had a combined circulation of more than 26,000, serving a "Japanese" population of 157,000 (see Roesch, "Hawaiian Statehood Plebiscite," p. 122).

90. Ibid., esp. pp. 90–92.

91. Stokes, HH-SH1, pp. 246–72; *HA*, Apr. 17, 1940, p. 6.

92. Vitousek to King, Oct. 10, 1940, King to Cogswell, Aug. 4, 1940, King to William George, Nov. 18, 1940, King Papers; and Equal Rights Commission, Minutes, Oct. 9, 1940, Trask Papers, AH. See Roesch, "Hawaiian Statehood Plebiscite," esp. pp. 144–71.

93. U.S. Bureau of Education, *A Survey of Education in Hawaii*, Bulletin 16 (1920), p. 20.

94. *HSB*, Oct. 31, 1940; King to Crane, July 13, 1940, King to George, Nov. 18, 1940, King Papers.

95. The total number of registered voters in 1940 was 87,312. In the plebiscite, 46,174 voted "Yes," while 22,428 voted "No"—a total of 68,602. Lind, *Hawaii's People*, p. 97. Cf. Secretary of Hawaii, *Official Tabulation: Statehood Plebiscite, Nov. 5, 1940* (Honolulu, 1940).

96. The belief that the sugar interests could deliver the outer islands to the GOP before the war was shared by many islanders from both major parties. Fong, Quinn, interviews with author. Also Roesch, "Hawaiian Statehood Plebiscite," p. 171.

97. Roesch's detailed investigation of the plebiscite supports this interpretation. See his "Hawaiian Statehood Plebiscite," esp. pp. 145, 170–71.

98. Snell to Jean Pohold, Dec. 30, 1940, Poindexter Papers, AH, quoted in ibid., p. 168; *NYT*, Aug. 7, 1940, p. 1; *New Republic*, Jan. 24, 1940, p. 101.

99. *HA*, Apr. 26, 1940; Roesch, "Hawaiian Statehood Plebiscite," p. 165.

100. Cogswell to John Moir, Nov. 25, 1940, quoted in Roesch, "Hawaiian Statehood Plebiscite," p. 164; King to George, Nov. 18, 1940, King Papers.

101. In 1946, 60 percent favored Hawaii statehood, 19 percent opposed. See *Christian Science Monitor*, Jan. 14, 1946, sec. 2, p. 9; HSC, *Statehood for Hawaii*, pp. 12–13.

102. See generally R. A. Esthus, "President Roosevelt's Commitment to Britain to Intervene in a Pacific War," *Mississippi Valley Historical Review* 50(June 1963):28–38; and Roger Bell, *Unequal Allies: Australian-American Relations and the Pacific War* (Melbourne, 1977), pp. 17–34.

103. See *NYT*, Sept. 15, 1940, sec. 4, p. 5.

104. Zalburg, *A Spark is Struck*, p. 197.

105. *NYT*, Sept. 15, 1940, sec. 4, p. 5, Nov. 19, 1940, p. 22.

Chapter 3. The Tests of War

1. Senate Joint Committee, *Investigation of the Pearl Harbor Attack. Report.* 79th Cong., 2d sess., 1946, p. 65. Numerous books have been published on the Pearl Harbor attack. The most recent and most thorough is Gordon W. Prange, Donald M. Goldstein, and Katherine V. Dillon, *At Dawn We Slept: The Untold Story of Pearl Harbor* (New York, 1981). A minute reconstruction of events, this book details the failure of military authorities on Oahu to respond appropriately to the many signals of attack given unwittingly by the Japanese during the days before the actual assault. A less convincing, "revisionist" view is John Toland, *Infamy: Pearl Harbor and Its Aftermath* (New York, 1981).

2. Anthony to Stainback, Dec. 1, 1942, in Zalburg, *A Spark is Struck*, p. 65.

3. Stainback, as governor of the territory from 1942 to 1950, was a notable exception to this generalization—he opposed military rule, but from 1947 on also opposed statehood (see Chaps. 5 and 7).

4. Anthony, *Hawaii Under Army Rule*, p. 203.

5. Matthew Meehan (international secretary, ILWU), quoted in Zalburg, *A Spark is Struck*, p. 99.

6. Burns, JABOHP, 4.1–18; and Aoki, JABOHP, 12.33; 13.3–4; Peyton Ford to Truman, Aug. 29, 1949, H. G. Morrison (acting attorney general) to W. D. Hassett (secretary to the president), Aug. 29, 1949, TP Office File; Anthony, *Hawaii Under Army Rule*, esp. pp. 41–45; and Johannessen, *Hawaiian Labor Movement*, pp. 194–95; Fuchs, *Hawaii Pono*, pp. 299–301, 354–55; Zalburg, *A Spark is Struck*, pp. 64–65, 92, 96, 99.

7. Symes, "What About Hawaii?", pp. 533–34; Waldron, "New Star in the Union?", p. 36.

8. Burns, JABOHP, tapes 3, 4, Murai, JABOHP, 1.18. See generally Anthony, *Hawaii Under Military Rule*.

9. Burns, JABOHP, 4.2–3; 2.7; 6.2–3, and Aoki, JABOHP, tape 13, esp. pp. 45–47.

10. See note 9 above. Also Kido, JABOHP, 1.1–3; Murai, JABOHP, 1.12–15, 26–30.

11. De Witt quoted in Rostow, "Our Worst Wartime Mistake," p. 195. See also Allen, *Hawaii's War Years*, pp. 364, 395–401.

12. Aoki, JABOHP, 12.33; 13.2–4; Burns, JABOHP, 3.1–2; 5.6–10, 17. Also B. Smith, *Americans from Japan*, pp. 181–85.

13. Burns, JABOHP, 2.6–7; 4.1–18; Yoshida, HH-SI1, p. 315.

14. Murai, JABOHP, 1.24–26; 2.2–5; Hirai, JABOHP, 1.12; Burns, JABOHP, 4.8, 12–15; see General Mark W. Clark, quoted in HSC, *Statehood for Hawaii*, p. 56 (see also pp. 54–57); Fuchs, *Hawaii Pono*, pp. 304–7; Mullins, *Hawaiian Journey*, p. 105; *HA*, June 23, 1959, p. 9.

15. *HA*, Oct. 2, 1942, p. 8.

16. Murai, JABOHP, 1.24–26; 2.1–18; Hirai, JABOHP, 1.12; HSC, *Statehood for Hawaii*, pp. 54–57.

17. *HSB*, Feb. 26, 1945, p. 4; King, HH3, p. 35.

18. Kido, JABOHP, 1.11; Oshiro, JABOHP, 2.11–12; Murai, JABOHP, 1.26; 2.37; Daniel Inouye and Lawrence Elliott, *Journey to Washington* (Englewood Cliffs, N.J., 1969), pp. xix–xx.

19. See generally Fuchs, *Hawaii Pono*, pp. 299–301; Wright, *Disenchanted Isles*, pp. 101–3; Zalburg, *A Spark is Struck*, pp. 64–69.

20. Benjamin Thoron (director of Territorial Affairs, U.S. Interior and Insular Affairs Dept.), quoted in Anthony, *Hawaii Under Army Rule*, pp. 29–30.

21. Burns, JABOHP, 4.4; 5.6–10, 17; Anthony, *Hawaii Under Army Rule*, pp. 101–3; and Allen, *Hawaii's War Years*, esp. pp. 131–50, 166–84, 391–402; Zalburg, *A Spark is Struck*, pp. 64–69.

22. See note 21 above. See also Wright, *Disenchanted Isles*, pp. 101–3; Fuchs, *Hawaii Pono*, pp. 299–301.

23. Ralph S. Kuykendall, "The Evolution of Government," SH1, p. 139;

HSB, Dec. 8, 1945, p. 1; McLane, "Territory of Hawaii," p. 65; Daws, *Shoal of Time*, p. 357.

24. Tavares, in *HSB*, Dec. 8, 1945, p. 1.

25. Burns, JABOHP, 5.11–12. Cf. Fong, interview with author.

26. *HSB*, July 5, 1945, p. 6.

27. *NYT*, Dec. 23, 1945, p. 6; J. Farrington, *CR*, Jan. 29, 1946, 92, pt. 9, p. A315; HSC, *Statehood for Hawaii*.

28. Appendix, "Report of the Subcommittee on Territories," HH3, pp. 546–50C. Subcommittee members were: Larcade, James J. Delaney (N.Y.), George P. Miller (Calif.), Homer D. Angell (Oreg.), Dean P. Taylor (N.Y.), and Farrington.

29. HSC, *Hawaii and Statehood* (1951), p. 54.

30. Fred A. Seaton, secretary of Interior, Press Release, Apr. 2, 1957, TP Office File.

31. Editorial, *Christian Science Monitor*, Jan. 14, 1946, inserted by J. Farrington in *CR*, Feb. 8, 1946, 92, pt. 9, p. A608.

32. HH5, p. 73; SR5, p. 39.

33. Shaplen, "A Reporter at Large," pt. 1, p. 75.

34. Emerson, "America's Policy Towards Pacific Dependencies," p. 2; *HSB*, July 23, 1945, p. 3; and McLane, "Territory of Hawaii," p. 57.

35. This issue is discussed at length in the following chapters.

Chapter 4. Postwar Hawaii

1. HR8, p. 12; *CR*, Mar. 11, 1959, 105, pt. 3, p. 3844.

2. Lind, *Hawaii's People*, pp. 106–15. See generally Adams, *Peoples of Hawaii*, and Adams, *Interracial Marriage in Hawaii*.

3. Lind, *Hawaii's People*, p. 115.

4. HSC, *Hawaii and Statehood* (1951), pp. 54–55.

5. See generally Gordon, "Assimilation in America," pp. 263, 265–66, 269–71, 273–85. These ideas are developed more fully in Gordon, *Assimilation in American Life*.

6. See note 5 above; Parenti, "Ethnic Politics," esp. pp. 717–22, 724–26.

7. Gunnar Myrdal, *An American Dilemma*, vol. 1 (New York, 1964), esp. pp. 24, 78, 101; Robert K. Merton, "Discrimination and the American Creed," in *The Study of Society*, ed. Peter I. Rose, 2d ed. (New York, 1970), pp. 449–57.

8. Richard J. Meister, ed., *Race and Ethnicity in Modern America* (Lexington, 1974), p. 2. This idea of a "pleasing uniformity" was first expressed by J. Hector St. John de Crèvecoeur in 1782, in his essay, "What is an American?", but it persisted into the twentieth century when it was expressed formally in Americanization campaigns and informally in the tacit acceptance of assimilation into Anglo-American norms as legitimate and necessary for minority groups.

9. This evidence was directly reflected in all majority reports on statehood after 1945. See, for example, Report of the Subcommittee on Territories, HH3, pp. 6–31.

10. See, for example, Dworkin and Dworkin, *Minority Report*, pp. 1–130; G. E. Lenski, *Power and Privilege: A Theory of Social Stratification* (New

York, 1966), esp. pp. 73–83, 395–402; G. Bowker and J. Carrier, eds., *Race and Ethnic Relations: A Reader* (New York, 1976), chap. 1; Parenti, "Ethnic Politics"; Gordon, "Assimilation in America"; Will Herberg, *Protestant-Catholic-Jew* (New York, 1955); Kurt B. Mayer, "Social Stratification in Two Equalitarian Societies: Australia and the United States," in *Class, Status and Power*, ed., Reinhard Bendix and Seymour Martin Lipsett (London, 1970), pp. 149–61; Seymour Martin Lipsett, "Value Patterns, Class, and the Democratic Policy: The United States and Great Britain," in ibid., pp. 161–71; Joe R. Feagin and Clairece B. Feagin, *Discrimination American Style* (Englewood Cliffs, N.J., 1978), pp. 1–41; Robert H. Wiebe, *The Segmented Society: An Introduction to the Meaning of America* (New York, 1975), esp. pp. 90–125.

11. Lind, *Hawaii's People*, pp. 106–10; Andrew W. Lind, "Hawaii in the Race Relations Continuum of the Pacific," *Social Process* 25(1961–1962):12.

12. Lind, HH3, p. 559. For details of intermarriage, see Chan and Yamamura, "Interracial Marriage and Divorce in Hawaii," pp. 77–84.

13. Lind, *Hawaii's People*, pp. 103–15.

14. Lind, *Hawaii's People*, p. 115. See Cordon, SH2, pp. 360–61; B. F. Kneubuhl, SH2, p. 232.

15. Lind, *Hawaii's People*, pp. 107, 111.

16. Appendix, "Report of the Subcommittee on Territories," HH3, p. 548. After 1945 there was a gradual increase in the number of nisei members in the legislature.

17. *Christian Science Monitor*, Jan. 14, 1946, sec. 2, p. 9, HSCP. For details of race relations in Hawaii, see HH3, pp. 234–35, 255–56, 262–63, 487–88, 509–11, 534–36, 597–99, 600–604.

18. Lind, HH3, p. 559.

19. Cheng, "Assimilation in Hawaii," pp. 24–25.

20. Wiebe, *Segmented Society*, pp. x–xi, 90–91, 111–12.

21. Nordyke, *Peopling of Hawaii*, pp. 32–35, 62; Appendix, "Report of the Subcommittee on Territories," HH3, pp. 550–50a. For the notion of America as an affluent consensus society by the 1950s, see David Potter, *People of Plenty* (Chicago, 1954).

22. In 1958, for example, almost 90 percent of eligible voters participated in local elections. In contrast mainland voter turnout rarely rose above 60 percent.

23. HR1.

24. Gruening, quoted in Edward R. Burke to Hugh Butler, Jan. 24, 1948 (copies to J. Farrington and Truman), copy in TP Office File; Aoki, JABOHP, 12.33; 13.2–4; 14.1–4.

25. See, for example, Haas and Resurrection, *Politics and Prejudice*, pp. 32–51.

26. Lind, "Hawaii's Race Relations," p. 60.

27. SR5, p. 8; See Lind, *Hawaii's People*, pp. 28, 85–106.

28. HSC, *Hawaii . . . and Statehood* (Honolulu, [1949]), pp. 48–49.

29. Midkiff, "Economic Determinants of Education," pp. 85–86, 199; Oshiro, JABOHP, 1.8–11; Kido, JABOHP, 1.5–8.

30. Hawaii Committee on Education in Post-war Reconstruction, *Post-War Needs*, pp. iii–3, 45.

31. Gruening, quoted in Burke to Butler, Jan. 24, 1948, TP Office File; Bur-

rows, *Hawaiian Americans*, pp. 167–68; B. Smith, *Americans from Japan*, p. 147. For details of the Americanization movement and the implicit demands of Americanization, see, for example, Hill, "Americanization Movement," pp. 609–35; Higham, *Strangers in the Land*, esp. pp. 234–63.

32. Lind, *Hawaii's People*, pp. 81, 91–92, 107.

33. See B. Smith, *Americans from Japan*, esp. p. 166; Burrows, *Hawaiian Americans*, p. 85; Norbeck, *Pineapple Town*, esp. p. 118; Matsuoka, "Race Preference in Hawaii," pp. 635–41.

34. This reaction is discussed in detail in Chaps. 5 and 6 of this book. Aoki, JABOHP, 12.36–37, 46–47; 13.11, 37; Mau, JABOHP, 31.1–8, 17–18; 32.49; Fuchs, *Hawaii Pono*, pp. 178–79, 181.

35. See note 34 above. See also Kuykendall and Day, *Hawaii: A History*, esp. p. 283.

36. In 1956, for example, more than 130,000 tourists visited Hawaii, adding $66 million to Hawaii's annual income. For evidence that tourism was expected to become the major industry by the 1960s, see Seaton, Press Release, Apr. 2, 1957, EP; and generally Inagaki, "Economic Planning and Development in Hawaii."

37. Lind, *Hawaii's People*, pp. 73, 78–80, 95–100; Ball and Yamamura, "Ethnic Discrimination," pp. 687–94.

38. Norbeck, *Pineapple Town*, p. 118; Evelyn Yama and Margaret Freeman, "Race Relations within a Business Firm in Honolulu," *Social Process* 18(1953): 1–12; Mau, JABOHP, 31.1–9, 17–18; 32.46.

39. Ball and Yamamura, "Ethnic Discrimination," pp. 687–94; Oshiro, JABOHP, 1.479; Hirai, JABOHP, 1.7, 12, 41; Kido, JABOHP, 1.17–19; Murai, JABOHP, 1.3–11; Richardson, JABOHP, pp. 4–5, 15; and Wright, *Disenchanted Isles*, p. 223.

40. Stainback to Chapman, Oct. 18, 1950, Chapman Papers; Fuchs, *Hawaii Pono*, pp. 442–49; Kinloch and Borders, "Racial Stereotypes and Social Distance," pp. 368–77; M. Smith, "Measuring Ethnocentrism in Hilo," pp. 220–37; and Frederick Samuels, "Color Sensitivity Among Honolulu's Haoles and Japanese," *Race* (Oct. 1969):203–12.

41. Robin M. Williams, Jr., "Prejudice and Society," in *The American Negro Reference Book*, ed. J. P. Davis (Englewood Cliffs, N.J., 1966), pp. 727–30; Mau, JABOHP, 31.17–19; Aoki, JABOHP, 13.16; pt. 2, tape 1, pp. 1, 8–15, 38.

42. Daws, *Shoal of Time*, p. 30; Fuchs, *Hawaii Pono*, p. 258; Victor Houston, *Rehabilitation of Native Hawaiians* . . . (Washington, 1921), p. 3, Anderson Papers.

43. Aoki, JABOHP, 13.26–28; 14.20–22; "Report of the Subcommittee on Territories," HH3, pp. 11, 26; *HA*, Feb. 25, 1945. For a detailed summary of the concentration of landownership and the taxation advantages enjoyed by large landowners, see Hulten, "Report of the Mayor"; and Public Administration Service of Chicago, "Report to Governor William H. Quinn on Territorial Tax Assessment Procedures" (Chicago, 1958).

44. Li, "Chinese Americans," pp. 297–324; Lind, *Hawaii's People*, pp. 92–103; Fuchs, *Hawaii Pono*, pp. 430–49. See also Hormann, "A Note on Hawaii's Minorities"; Burns, JABOHP, 3.10–14. N. Young, "Changes in Values," pp. 228, 239–41.

45. See note 44 above. Also, Kinloch and Borders, "Racial Stereotypes and Social Distance," pp. 368–69.

46. Ima, "Japanese Americans," pp. 268, 279–83; Burns, JABOHP, 3.10–14; Haas and Resurrection, *Politics and Prejudice*, pp. 1–9. See generally also Ogawa, *Jan Ken Po*, and *Kodomo no tame ni*.

47. Frank E. Midkiff to J. Farrington, Dec. 14, 1950, TP Office File; Stainback to Krug, Sept. 15, 1947, Chapman Papers; Norbeck, *Pineapple Town*, p. 123; Fuchs, *Hawaii Pono*, pp. 440–43; Haas and Resurrection, *Politics and Prejudice*, pp. 45–46.

48. Lind, "Hawaii in the Race Relations Continuum," p. 13.

49. Burns, JABOHP, 3.10–14; E. Farrington, interview with Chou, p. 39.

50. Aoki, JABOHP, 12.36, 46–47; pt. 2, tape 1, p. 1; pt. 2, pp. 8–9; Burns, JABOHP, 3.10–14; Mau, JABOHP, 31.1–8; 32.39.

51. Alice Campbell, "Frank Comments by a Feminist Legislator," *Paradise of the Pacific* 56, no. 7(July 1944):12, 30; A. Campbell, in *HSB*, May 29, 1947, p. 2; A. Campbell, HH3, p. 482; Appendix, "Report of the Subcommittee on Territories," HH3, p. 547.

52. See note 51 above; Nordyke, *Peopling of Hawaii*, appendices, table 3. In March 1959, the month in which Hawaii's statehood bill finally passed both houses of Congress, Mrs. Campbell celebrated her seventy-fifth birthday by proclaiming: "Some people call me the 'untamed woman.' Others call me more complimentary things. Some say 'princess,' 'queen.' But to me the greatest, most beautiful thing I could ever be called is a Hawaiian." The *Advertiser* described Mrs. Campbell's estate at Ewa as a place which "will be forever Hawaii . . . Old Hawaii with its cherished traditions and passing customs" (*HA*, Mar. 23, 1959).

53. Matsuoka, "Race Preferences in Hawaii," pp. 635–41; B. Smith, *Americans from Japan*, p. 166; Norbeck *Pineapple Town*, p. 118; Yamamura and Sakumoto, "Residential Segregation in Honolulu"; Burrows, *Hawaiian Americans*, p. 85; Burns, JABOHP, 3.10–14.

54. Yama and Freeman, "Race Relations within a Business," pp. 19–25; Kinloch and Borders, "Racial Stereotypes and Social Distance," pp. 368–77; Hormann, "Significance of the Palikiko Case," pp. 1–12.

55. Fuchs, *Hawaii Pono*, p. 42; Hirai, JABOHP, p. 12, Murai, JABOHP, 2.3.

56. HSC, *Hawaii and Statehood* (1951), p. 48.

57. Louis Cain, HH2, pp. 23–25.

Chapter 5. Issues Confused

1. *HSB*, July 27, 1945, HSPA Scrapbook, 1945. Members of the Equal Rights Committee were: Stainback (chairman), Robertson, Marguerite K. Ashford, Riley H. Allen, and Arthur K. Trask.

2. *HA*, May 11, 1946, p. 1; *HSB*, May 11, 1946, pp. 1–7.

3. See note 2 above. Also *HA*, Feb. 28, 1946, p. 1; *HA*, Mar. 1, 1946, p. 1; *HA*, Mar. 6, 1946, p. 2; Krug to Truman, July 3, 1946, TP Office File. Stainback was born in Somerville, Tennessee, in 1883. He received a B.A. degree from Princeton University in 1907 and the J.D. degree in 1912 from the University of Chicago. He then went to Hawaii, where he engaged in private practice

until 1914. He was then appointed attorney general of the territory, a position he held until November 1917, when he entered the United States Army. Following army service he again entered general law practice in Hawaii and later served as United States attorney for the territory of Hawaii from March 14, 1935, until November 13, 1940, when he was sworn in as United States district judge for the territory. He held this position until he was appointed governor in 1942. For evidence of local support for Stainback's reappointment, see the correspondence of Longley (acting chairman, Territorial Central Committee, Democratic party) to Hassett, Feb. 5, 1946, TP Office File. By 1948, however, the attitude of the Democratic party in Hawaii had changed dramatically (see Mitsuyuki Kido [acting secretary of the Territorial Central Committee, Democratic party] to Oscar Chapman [secretary of the Interior], Nov. 26, 1948, Chapman Papers.) Despite persistent appeals for Stainback's dismissal, Truman asserted late in 1948 that he had "no intention of doing this" (see handwritten comments by Truman on C. W. Bonham to General Harry H. Vaughan [White House aide], Nov. 17, 1948, TP Office File).

4. Executive Secretary, Citizens' Statehood Committee, Report, Nov. 25, 1946, FP.

5. Richard J. Welch (Rep., Calif.), CR, June 30, 1947, 93, pt. 6, pp. 7916–17. See also Clair Engle (Dem., Calif.), ibid., p. 7929. Fifty-nine newspapers with a daily circulation of approximately 9 million were included in this survey. Editorials from forty-five of the forty-eight states favored statehood. During 1947–1948 the HSC surveyed the editorial opinions of 282 newspapers with a combined circulation of more than 25 million. Approximately 94 percent of these newspapers supported statehood. Included in these newspapers were: *Washington Post, Los Angeles Times, San Francisco Chronicle, Miami Herald, Atlanta Constitution, Chicago Tribune, Kansas City Star, Newark News,* and *New York Times.* See SH2, p. 488.

6. *HSB,* Feb. 25, 1947, p. 1; HSC, "Report, 1947–48," p. 3, (Honolulu, Mimeo., SL); *HA,* Feb. 28, 1946, p. 1, Mar. 1, 1946, p. 1, Mar. 6, 1946, p. 2. J. Farrington to Allen, editor, *HSB,* Feb. 26, 1948, folder titled "Riley Allen," FP; *HSB,* May 16, 1947, HSPA Scrapbook, 1947; HSC, "Report 1947–48," p. 3.

7. HSC, "Report, 1947–48," pp. 1, 3–4; *HSB,* May 16, 1947, HSPA Scrapbook, 1947. Membership of the HSC underwent many changes in the following years, although Sam King was undoubtedly its most important and long-serving member. From 1949–1959 its members were: 1949–1951—Robert C. Hogan (chairman), Katsuro Miho, Arthur D. Woolaway, Bush, Rice, Metzger, and Thurston; 1951–1953—King (chairman), Mrs. Gerald Corbett, Ernest B. De Silva, Trask, Miho, Woolaway, Rice, and Thurston; 1953–1955—C. Nils Tavares (chairman), Wayne E. Ellis, Flora K. Hayes, Miho, Metzger, Woolaway, Trask, and Thurston; 1955–1957—Lorrin P. Thurston (chairman), Dr. Philip M. Corboy, John M. Fox, Harriet Magoon, William F. Quinn, Wayne Ellis, J. Pia Cockett, Miho, and De Silva; 1957–1959—Lorrin P. Thurston (chairman), William H. Heen, Wallace S. Fujiyama, K. C. Leebrick, O. P. Soares, Mrs. Magoon, Dr. Corboy, Ellis, and De Silva.

8. HSC, "Report, 1947–48," pp. iii–iv.

9. The roles of Farrington and Burns are discussed in the following chapters. For evidence of the lobbying activities of the commission in Washington,

see, for example: Frank McNaughton to Bob Girvin, Jan. 28, 1948, Frank McNaughton Papers, TL; Memo (no author given) for Truman, Apr. 14, 1948, TP Office File; Lau Ah Chew (chairman, Hawaii Central Committee, Democratic party) to Truman and reply by Matthew Connelly (secretary to the president), May 14, 1948, TP Office File; or Jack M. Fox (member of Statehood Commission) to James Hagerty (secretary to the president), Mar. 26, 1957, EP Office File.

10. See HSC publications and pamphlets in the Bibliography of this book; HSC, "Report, 1947–48," pp. 3–6. See generally HSCP, various folders titled "Requests from Congressmen," "Congress-Speeches."

11. Farrington, *CR*, July 2, 1946, 92, pt. 11, p. A3877.

12. *HSB*, Feb. 15, 1946, p. 4; Homer R. Jones, *CR*, June 16, 1946, 92, pt. 11, p. A2906; HSC, "Report, 1947–48," p. 4.

13. HSC, *Statehood for Hawaii*, p. 13; Engle, *CR*, June 30, 1947, 93, pt. 6, p. 7929.

14. HR1, p. 11; HH5.

15. Krug, HH5, HH5, p. 41.

16. *NYT*, Mar. 8, 1947, p. 11; Ernest W. Green (vice president, HSPA), HH5, p. 185; Wightman, HH5, pp. 192–93; *HA*, Mar. 7, 1947, p. 11.

17. HR1, pp. 11, 21; Allen, *CR*, June 30, 1947, 93, pt. 6, p. 7912.

18. Larcade p. 7918, Welch p. 7916–17, Engle p. 7928, Brown p. 7928, McDonough p. 7929–30, Farrington p. 7917–18, Mansfield p. 7921, all in *CR*, June 30, 1947, 93, pt. 6; *HSB*, July 1, 1947, pp. 1, 6; *CN* 1:46a–47a.

19. *NYT*, July 1, 1947, p. 1; *HSB*, July 3, 1947, p. 6.

20. *CN* 1:46a–47a.

21. Dept. of Planning and Research, State of Hawaii, *Historical Statistics*, p. 25; *HSB*, June 27, 1946, p. 4; *Portland Press Herald*, July 3, 1947, quoted by Hugh Butler in *CR*, July 25, 1947, 93, pt. 8, p. 10178.

22. Frank P. Huddle, "Admission of the New States," in *Editorial Research Reports*, vol. 1 (Mar. 20, 1946), pp. 197–98, HSCP. See also *CN* 1:1498–1500; Gruening, *Battle for Alaska Statehood*, p. 2.

23. *HSB*, June 7, 1946, HSPA Scrapbook, 1946; Appendix K, "National Party Planks on Statehood, 1900–1950," SR5, pp. 62–64. Until the mid-1950s defense reasons were usually cited publicly by GOP leaders to explain the party's reluctance to accept Alaska. But within the Eisenhower administration political factors were equally persuasive. A memo by a White House aide for Eisenhower stated, for example: "A great deal of time and attention has been devoted by . . . administration leaders to the question of statehood for Alaska. It has been discussed frequently at the regular White House meetings of the legislative leaders, and it has been the subject of White House Staff Meetings and conferences with the Interior Department." The memo conceded that "important military considerations" were involved in the Alaska issue, but it also highlighted voting trends in the territory. In 1950 the GOP received 55 percent of the total vote, Democrats 45 percent. In 1954, however, the GOP won less than 25 percent of the vote, the Democrats 75 percent to 80 percent (Apr. 8, 1954, EP Office File).

24. *Christian Science Monitor*, July 2, 1947, inserted by Knowland in *CR*, July 14, 1947, 93, pt. 12, p. A3494.

25. *HA*, July 2, 1947, p. 2; *HSB*, July 3, 1947, HSPA Scrapbook, 1947.

26. See, for example, John A. Hamilton (executive vice president of the Chamber of Commerce of Honolulu), pp. 4–6, Joseph A. Kaholokula (member, Territorial House of Representatives, business agent of the ILWU, CIO), pp. 346–47, Samuel Wilder King, pp. 257, 334, Wilford Richardson (Hawaiian Civic Association), pp. 41–42, Gregg M. Sinclair (president, University of Hawaii), pp. 166, 293, E. J. Burns (Central Committee, Republican party), p. 283, Charles M. Hite (Central Committee, Democratic party), p. 283, all in SH2. See generally Contents, ibid., pp. iii, viii.

27. *NYT*, Apr. 16, 1948, p. 2; *HSB*, Mar. 19, 1948, p. 1; *NYT*, Mar. 20, 1948, p. 7.

28. *NYT*, Apr. 18, 1948, sec. 4, p. 8.

29. McNaughton to Don Bermington (White House aide), May 10, 1948, Frank McNaughton Papers, TL; *NYT*, May 9, 1948, p. 48; *HSB*, May 8, 1948, p. 1.

30. McNaughton to Bermington, May 10, 1948, McNaughton Papers.

31. SH2, p. 11.

32. Krock, in *NYT*, May 11, 1948, p. 24.

33. *Washington Evening Star*, May 14, 1948, quoted by Knowland in *CR*, May 17, 1948, 94, pt. 5, p. 5902; *NYT*, May 21, 1948, p. 16; *CN* 1:45a.

34. *CN* 1:50a. All but two Senate supporters of statehood in 1948 backed the imposition of cloture in 1949. In contrast, most of those who opposed statehood (i.e., the Knowland resolution) in 1948 opposed the imposition of cloture in 1949.

35. *CN* 1:45a, 50a. The vote for cloture was much stronger than that for the Knowland resolution, partly because there were more Northern Democrats in the new Senate.

36. *HSB*, May 20, 1948, p. 1.

37. *Washington Sunday Star*, May 23, 1948, quoted by Larcade in *CR*, May 24, 1948, 94, pt. 5, p. 6352; *HSB*, May 20, 1948, p. 1.

38. *Jackson Clarion Ledger*, July 3, 1947, quoted by Butler in *CR*, July 21, 1947, 93, pt. 8, p. 9468.

39. *Houston Post*, July 4, 1947, quoted by Butler in ibid.

40. *HSB*, Feb. 15, 1946, p. 4; Farrington, *CR*, July 2, 1946, 92, pt. 11, p. A3877.

41. Larcade, *CR*, June 30, 1947, 93, pt. 6, p. 7921; Eastland, quoted in *Omaha World-Herald*, Dec. 24, 1953; Paul, "The Power of Seniority," p. 145, 174. The view that "racial prejudice" was the "major obstacle" to statehood was shared by many statehood advocates (see, for example, E. Farrington, interview with McDowell, and interview with Chou, pp. 22–23).

42. Preston, *CR*, June 30, 1947, 93, pt. 6, p. 7936.

43. Hale, ibid., p. 7934.

44. See, for example, California Joint Immigration Committee to Representative Hale, Mar. 21, 1947, folder titled "Statehood-Racial," FP. Arthur M. Churchill (Portland, Oreg.), typewritten paper, 29pp., titled "Dangerous Factors in Proposed Hawaii Statehood," folder titled "Statehood Opposition," FP.

45. *Portland Press Herald*, July 3, 1947, and *Portland Evening Express*, July 5, 1947, quoted by Butler in *CR*, July 25, 1947, 93, pt. 8, p. 10178.

46. *Topeka Daily Capital*, July 3, 1947, *Jackson Clarion Ledger*, July 3, 1947, and *Houston Post*, July 4, 1947, quoted by Butler in *CR*, July 21, 1947, 93, pt. 8, pp. 9467–78.

47. Coudert, *CR*, June 30, 1947, 93, pt. 6, p. 7935; *CN* 1:46a–47a.

48. *NYT*, Jan. 8, 1948, p. 4; *NYT*, Feb. 3, 1948, p. 22.

49. See note 48 above.

50. Truman diary, Feb. 2, 1948, and letter to Ernest W. Roberts, Aug. 8, 1948, in Robert H. Ferrell, ed., *Off the Record: The Private Papers of Harry S. Truman* (New York, 1980), pp. 122, 146–47.

51. Key, *Southern Politics*, p. 369. Representatives from districts with substantial Negro or urban populations in particular tended to diverge from traditional Southern voting behavior.

52. *NYT*, May 11, 1948, p. 24.

53. *CN* 1:1500, 1597, 1615–17.

54. Truman diary, Nov. 30, 1950, and letter to Mary Jane Truman, Nov. 14, 1950, in Ferrell, *Off the Record*, pp. 118, 201.

55. Berman, "Civil Rights and Civil Liberties," p. 194.

56. Key, *Southern Politics*, p. 359.

57. Oscar T. Barck, Jr., *A History of the United States Since 1945* (New York, 1965), p. 82.

58. Shoemaker, cited by Jack Hall in HH3, p. 132.

59. Hall, HH3, pp. 131–32. Interesting, detailed, but very partial accounts of the early union recruitment and the relationships between new unionism and the emerging Democratic party under Burns can be found in JABOHP, esp. Burns, tapes 5, 7, 8, and Aoki, tape 12.

60. ILWU, *I.L.W.U. Story*, pp. 30, 32–33; Johannessen, *Hawaiian Labor Movement*, p. 23; Fong, interview with author. Another prominent postwar Republican, William Quinn, recalled, however, that the Republican party showed few signs of change until the mid-1950s, when it was obliged to confront the prospect of Democratic victories in both the legislature and the contest for delegate to Congress (Quinn, interview with author).

61. Hall, HH3, p. 133.

62. Johannessen, *Hawaiian Labor Movement*, p. 107.

63. Ibid., p. 119.

64. ILWU, *I.L.W.U. Story*, p. 34.

65. Rademaker, "Exercise of Union Power," pp. 228–31.

66. O'Brien, *The Plot to Sovietize Hawaii*, pp. 14–15; Hall, HH3, p. 133.

67. Dept. of Planning and Research, State of Hawaii, *Historical Statistics*, p. 25; Rademaker, "Exercise of Union Power," p. 230.

68. Tuttle, "Contending Forces," p. 43.

69. Kido, JABOHP, 1.23; Murai, JABOHP, 2.35.

70. Kido, JABOHP, 1.23; Murai, JABOHP, 2.35.

71. Burns, JABOHP, 7.3–4; 8.1–5. E. Farrington, interview with Chou, pp. 41–42.

72. Mau, JABOHP, 31.19–26; 32.1–2, 31–32. See also note 74 below.

73. Quinn, interview with author; Fong, interview with author; Fong, interview with Chou, p. 598. Cf. E. Farrington, interview with Chou, p. 78, where Farrington denies that her party "left-out" the "Oriental boys." They chose

Burns because the Democrats were in power in Washington, and thus Burns had the power patronage—something which AJAs were keen to benefit from.

74. Aoki, JABOHP, 12.8, 24; 13.16, 32, 35–36; 14.14, 21–23, 29; Burns, JABOHP, 7.3–14; 8.1–5; Mau, JABOHP, 31.19–26; 32.1–2, 31–33.

75. Mau, JABOHP, 31.24; 32.31–33, 50–55; Aoki, JABOHP, 12.16.

76. A. W. Van Valkenburg, HH3, p. 264.

77. Stokes, HH3, pp. 245–46.

78. Hormann, "Sociological Observations on Statehood," p. 4.

79. Alice Campbell. Her family was the second largest landowner in the territory.

80. Hormann, "Sociological Observations on Statehood," pp. 4–5.

81. Faye (president, Chamber of Commerce of Honolulu), HH3, p. 415. The Chamber of Commerce comprised 804 Caucasians and part-Hawaiians, 302 Japanese, 141 Chinese, 34 Koreans, and 26 Filipinos.

82. *Hilo Tribune-Herald*, Jan. 15, 1946, HSPA Scrapbook, 1946.

83. *HA*, Jan. 23, 1946, HSPA Scrapbook, 1946; Hill, SH2, p. 70, Hill to Butler, Feb. 2, 1948, SH2, pp. 469–70; Quinn, interview with author.

84. Appendix, "Report of the Subcommittee on Territories," HH3, p. 550b.

85. A. Campbell, HH3, p. 481; *HA*, Mar. 3, 1945, p. 1; Chou, "Education of a Senator," p. 26.

86. A. Campbell and Stokes, HH3, pp. 481, 486–88.

87. Bolte, HH3, pp. 47–48; Appendix, "Report of the Subcommittee on Territories," p. 548; *NYT*, Jan. 6, 1945, sec. 4, p. 7; HH3, pp. 436, 451, 461; Lind, *Hawaii's People*, pp. 91–92; Cheng, "Assimilation in Hawaii," p. 240.

88. Hall, HH3, p. 133; Appendix, "Report of the Subcommittee on Territories," HH3, p. 550c.

89. J. A. Krug (secretary of Interior), HH4, p. 3.

90. King, HH4, pp. 35–36.

91. A. Campbell, pp. 483–84, and Stokes, p. 246, HH3. The Larcade subcommittee concluded: "there is a concentration of landholdings in the hands of a few persons, companies or estates" (Mar. 11, 1946, TP Office File, pp. 11, 26).

92. The formal statehood campaign conceded that the Big Five issue was an obstacle to statehood. See, for example, HSC, *Hawaii and Statehood* (1951), pp. 61–64.

93. *HA*, Dec. 4, 1945, HSPA Scrapbook, 1945.

94. A. Campbell, HH3, pp. 483–84.

95. Kido, JABOHP, 2.9; Fong, interview with Chou, 2.177–82.

96. Mau, JABOHP, 31.17–18; Aoki, JABOHP, 14.1–4; Burns, JABOHP, 5.5–6, 9–10, 19; and HSC, *Hawaii and Statehood* (1951), p. 64.

97. Appendix, "Report of the Subcommittee on Territories," HH3, pp. 550–50a.

98. Fuchs, *Hawaii Pono*, p. 311; *HA*, Apr. 10, 1947, p. 1, May 28, 1947, p. 1.

99. *NYT*, July 1, 1947, p. 1; Adolph J. Sabath, *CR*, June 30, 1947, 93, pt. 6, p. 7913.

100. See, for example, Alice Campbell to editor, *HA*, published in *HA*, Oct. 22, 1947, HSPA Scrapbook, 1947; Roy Clippinger (Rep., Ill.) and Earl Wilson (Rep., Ind.), in *HA*, Oct. 25, 1947, HSPA Scrapbook, 1947.

101. *HSB*, Mar. 13, 1948, p. 8, Sept. 16, 1947, p. 1; *Hilo Tribune-Herald*, Feb. 11, 1948, HSPA Scrapbook, 1947; *HA*, July 1, 1947, p. 1; *NYT*, Sept. 18, 1947, p. 27.

102. *NYT*, Nov. 12, 1947, p. 34, Nov. 23, 1947, p. 16; *HSB*, Nov. 1, 1947, p. 6.

103. *HSB*, Nov. 1, 1947, p. 6. E. Farrington, interview with Chou, pp. 25–26, and interview with McDowell. Farrington was president and general manager of the *HSB* from 1939 until his death in 1954 and retained considerable control over the editorial opinions expressed in the *HSB* while he was delegate to Congress. See generally, correspondence between Farrington and Allen, editor, *HSB*, 1943–1954, various folders titled "Riley Allen," FP. See also A. Campbell to Truman, Nov. 19, 1948, TP Office File; Joe Keenan to Connelly, Nov. 5, 1948, ibid.

104. Louis Hartz, *The Liberal Tradition in America* (New York, 1955), p. 211; Griffith, *Politics of Fear*, pp. 30–33.

105. McCarran, quoted in John P. Roche, *The Quest for the Dream: The Development of Civil Rights and Human Relations in Modern America* (Chicago, 1968), p. 221.

106. *HA*, Dec. 7, 1947, p. 1. Also *HSB*, Dec. 13, 1947, p. 1; HSC, "Report, 1947–48," p. 5; *Hilo Tribune-Herald*, Oct. 9, 1947, HSPA Scrapbook, 1947.

107. SR1, p. 10.

108. *Houston Post*, July 4, 1947, quoted by Butler in *CR*, July 21, 1947, 93, pt. 8, p. 9468.

109. Hill, SH2, p. 70; Hill to Butler, Feb. 2, 1948, published in SH2, pp. 469–70.

110. Hill, statement of Sept. 11, 1944, quoted in Honolulu *Record*, Dec. 7, 1950.

111. Dillingham, SH2, pp. 290, 402; E. Farrington, interview with McDowell; King interview with McDowell; Fuchs, *Hawaii Pono*, p. 372.

112. Powell, SH2, pp. 419–20, A. Campbell, SH2, pp. 410–13. Campbell claimed there was danger of an "Oriental Alliance" of sections of the local community with the international Communist party; Stokes, SH2, p. 92. *HSB*, Apr. 14, 1959: Daws, *Shoal of Time*, p. 383.

113. SR1, p. 5.

114. O'Brien, *The Plot to Sovietize Hawaii*, p. 65.

115. Fuchs, *Hawaii Pono*, p. 310; Earl A. Nielson (acting chairman, Democratic Central Committee, Hawaii) to Truman, Feb. 29, 1951, TP Office File.

116. *HSB*, Mar. 13, 1948, p. 8; Stainback, quoted in O'Brien, *The Plot to Sovietize Hawaii*, pp. 62–63. See also Stainback to Krug, Sept. 15, 1947, TP Office File; Stainback to Chapman, May 14, 1948, Chapman Papers.

117. Mitsuyuki Kido (acting secretary, Territorial Central Committee, Democratic party) to Truman, Nov. 13, 1948, TP Office File; Stainback to Chapman, May 14, 1948, Chapman Papers.

118. Burns, JABOHP, 7.1–19; Aoki, JABOHP, pt. 2, tape 1, p. 8; Mau, JABOHP, 32.42, 49.

119. Stainback to Krug, Sept. 15, 1947, TP Office File; Stainback to Chapman, May 14, 1948, Chapman Papers.

120. HR3, pp. 1, 10–11, 23; House Un-American Activities, *Report*, Mar. 29, 1944, quoted in HR3, p. 2; *HA*, Jan. 19, 1948, quoted by Butler in *CR*, May 20, 1948, 94, pt. 5, p. 6168; Lasky, "Red Wedge in Hawaii," *Plain Talk*, May 1948, quoted by Butler in *CR*, May 17, 1948, 94, pt. 5, pp. 5930–32. See also O'Brien, *The Plot to Sovietize Hawaii*, esp. p. 304; HR3, pp. 6–7. Although Bridges was found guilty of perjury and sentenced to five years in jail after a trial lasting eighty-one days in 1949, his conviction was overturned on technical grounds by the Supreme Court in 1954. The following year the Eisenhower administration abandoned efforts to prosecute. See David Caute, *The Great Fear: The Anti-Communist Purge Under Truman and Eisenhower* (New York, 1978), pp. 237–38.

121. Allen to Farrington, Mar. 3, 1948, folder titled "Riley Allen," FP. See also *HA*, June 14, 1948, HSPA Scrapbook, 1948; *HSB*, Sept. 2, 1948, HSPA Scrapbook, 1948; *NYT*, Nov. 14, 1948, p. 47; *HSB*, Aug. 28, 1948, p. 1; Stainback to Chapman, May 14, 1948, Chapman Papers; Fuchs, *Hawaii Pono*, pp. 313–14.

122. Wilson, SH2; Wilson to Osborn A. Pearson (assistant postmaster general), Apr. 30, 1952, Chapman Papers.

123. Hawaiian Civil Liberties, Press Release, Aug. 6, 1948, in HR3, p. 11.

124. *NYT*, Nov. 4, 1948, p. 2; *HSB*, Sept. 2, 1948, HSPA Scrapbook, 1948.

125. Stainback to Chapman, May 14, 1948, quoted in Fuchs, *Hawaii Pono*, pp. 312–13. These letters suggested that Stainback was anxious to justify his ambivalence over statehood to national leaders of the Democratic party.

126. *HA*, Jan. 19, 1948, quoted by Butler in *CR*, May 20, 1948, 94, pt. 5, p. 6168.

127. Dept. of Planning and Research, State of Hawaii, *Historical Statistics*, p. 25; Office of the Secretary of Hawaii, *Hawaii: Election Results, Official Tabulation, 1946–1959*, folder of unnumbered folios.

128. See, for example, *HA*, June 14, 1948, HSPA Scrapbook, 1948; *HSB*, Sept. 2, 1948, HSPA Scrapbook, 1948; *NYT*, Nov. 14, 1948, p. 47; *HSB*, Aug. 28, 1948, p. 1.

129. Farrington, *CR*, Dec. 31, 1948, 94, pt. 12, p. A5377.

130. See generally HSPA Scrapbooks, 1949–1952.

131. See, for example, O'Brien, *The Plot to Sovietize Hawaii*, pp. 52–53; Butler, *CR*, Aug. 30, 1949, 95, pt. 9, p. 12465.

132. *HSB*, Jan. 5, 1949, p. 1; Kefauver, although a Southern Democrat, was a supporter of statehood in the House in 1947. *NYT*, Jan. 4, 1949, p. 4; *HSB*, Jan. 3, 1949, p. 1; McLane, "Report of the Washington Office," May–Aug. 1949, p. 1; *HSB*, Jan. 18, 1949, p. 1.

133. Aoki, JABOHP, 12.36–42; Mau, JABOHP, 32.41–44.

134. Mau, JABOHP, 32.41–44.

135. The Hawaii Statehood Commission maintained an office in Washington, 1947–1959, but was never listed officially as a lobby group. See *CN* 1:1585–90; *HSB*, Jan. 24, 1949, p. 8; *HA*, Jan. 23, 1949, p. 1; HSC, "Report, 1949–50," p. 11. See also note 13 of this chapter, and Burns to Donald Dawson (White House aide), Mar. 6, 1949, TP Office File; McNaughton to Phinizy Adams, Mar. 11, 1949, McNaughton Papers; Burns, JABOHP, 8.22; 9.25; Aoki, JABOHP, 12.36–37; Mau, JABOHP, 32.41–44.

136. HSC, "Report, 1949–50," pp. 2, 4, 7. Statehood Commission Chairman Longley died during 1949. Commission members during 1949–1950 were: King (chairman), Metzger, Thurston, Rice, and new members Katsuro Miho, Arthur D. Woolaway, Robert G. Hogan, and Bush; *HSB*, Feb. 28, 1949, p. 1; *HSB*, Mar. 1, 1949, p. 1.

137. HSC, "Report, 1949–50," p. 1; *NYT*, Mar. 6, 1949, sec. 4, p. 10.

138. *HSB*, May 16, 1949, p. 1; *HSB*, May 17, 1949, p. 1; *HSB*, May 20, 1949, p. 1.

139. McLane, "Report of the Washington Office," May–Aug. 1949, pp. 3–4.

140. *Washington Post*, May 27, 1949, HSCP; *HA*, Mar. 9, 1949, p. 1.

141. *NYT*, July 23, 1949, p. 3; McLane, "Report of the Washington Office," May–Aug. 1949, pp. 5–6.

142. McLane, "Report of the Washington Office," May–Aug. 1949, p. 4; *Washington Post*, May 27, 1949, HSCP; *Los Angeles Daily Examiner*, July 27, 1949, HSCP.

143. See note 142 above; *Washington Post*, May 27, 1949, HSCP. *HA*, Mar. 9, 1947, p. 1; *CN* 1:1500.

144. Butler, *CR*, June 23, 1949, 95, pt. 6, p. 8175.

145. HR2, pp. 52, 57.

146. Butler, *CR*, June 23, 1949, 95, pt. 6, p. 8171. This committee allegedly comprised: Kimoto, Hall, Freeman, McElrath, Mrs. Robert McElrath, Eileen Fujimoto, Charles Fujimoto, Koichi Imori, Vossbrink, and Hyun. Butler alleged that Communist party members controlled every committee during the convention, ibid., pp. 8172–75.

147. Butler to Esther Van Orsdel, July 15, 1947; Butler to A. Pickard, Aug. 22, 1947; and Butler to Ben Kuroki (owner of the *York* [Nebr.]), June 10, 1951; Butler, "Report from Washington, No. 9," Sept. 7, 1951. All in Butler MS, quoted in Paul, "The Power of Seniority," pp. 141, 143, 146. Butler, *CR*, Aug. 30, 1949, p. 12465; *HSB*, June 25, 1949, HSPA Scrapbook, 1949.

148. Ichiro Izuka, *The Truth about Communism in Hawaii*, quoted by Butler in *CR*, May 20, 1948, 94, pt. 5, pp. 6169–74.

149. Butler, *CR*, June 23, 1949, 95, pt. 6, p. 8175.

150. Johannessen, *Hawaiian Labor Movement*, pp. 131–32. See also ILWU, *I.L.W.U. Story*, pp. 35–38.

151. Shoemaker, "Economic Transformation Since the War," p. 10.

152. *NYT*, June 10, 1949, p. 14; Johannessen, *Hawaiian Labor Movement*, pp. 128–29. Through his contacts in Washington, Burns influenced the settlement. Burns, JABOHP, 8.20–24; 9.2–4.

153. Claude A. Jagger (president of Hawaii Economic Foundation) to Steelman (assistant to Truman), July 25, 1949, TP Office File; Jagger to C. G. Ross (secretary to Truman), May 12, 1949, TP Office File; F. Simplich, Jr., Memo for A. G. Budge (president, Castle and Cooke), Aug. 19, 1952, TP Office File.

154. *HA*, Sept. 9, 1949, HSPA Scrapbook, 1949.

155. McNaughton to Birmington, June 23, 27, 1949, McNaughton Papers; Butler, *CR*, June 27, 1949, 95, pt. 6, pp. 8405–06.

156. *NYT*, June 26, 1949, p. 38; King to Krug, June 30, 1949, container 74, Krug Papers.

157. HSC, *Hawaii and Statehood* (1951), p. 94; Cordon, *CR*, Mar. 31, 1950, 96, pt. 4, p. 4464.

158. Farrington, *CR*, Oct. 19, 1949, 95, pt. 16, p. A6475; Cordon, *CR*, Mar. 31, 1950, 96, pt. 4, p. 4464; Jagger to Ross, May 12, 1949, TP Office File; Stainback to Chapman, Aug. 11, 1949, Chapman Papers.

159. Hiram L. Fong, SH3, pp. 188–89, Chou, "Education of a Senator," p. 593; Farrington, *CR*, July 25, 1950, 96, pt. 16, p. A5379.

160. Farrington, *CR*, Oct. 19, 1949, 95, pt. 16, p. A6475.

161. Edward R. Burke (legal counsel to the HSC) to Butler, July 5, 1949, quoted by Mansfield in *CR*, July 19, 1949, 95, pt. 14, pp. A4663–64.

162. In the Hawaiian language *imua* means "go forward." *HSB*, June 5, 1949, pp. 1, 4; *HSB*, June 28, 1949, p. 6; *HA*, June 28, 1948, p. 2; Fuchs, *Hawaii Pono*, p. 367, 372; Burns, JABOHP, 9.2–4.

163. *HSB*, Jan. 12, 1950, p. 1; *HSB*, Jan. 20, 1950, p. 1.

164. For details of the procedure by which a bill can be discharged from a House committee, see *CN* 1:169a. Before a discharge resolution can be moved it must have the support of 218 House members. *HSB*, Jan. 23, 1950, p. 1; Peterson, *CR*, Jan. 23, 1950, 96, pt. 1, pp. 783–84.

165. *NYT*, Jan. 24, 1950, p. 23. See also statement by Representative McCormack in *HSB*, Mar. 10, 1950, p. 6.

166. *CN* 1:54a–55a; *NYT*, Mar. 4, 1950, pp. 1, 4; Gruening, *Battle for Alaska Statehood*, p. 43; *HSB*, Apr. 4, 1950, p. 2; *NYT*, Mar. 7, 1950, p. 1.

167. Cox, Hale, and Angell, *CR*, Mar. 6, 1950, 96, pt. 3, pp. 2871–72.

168. Sixty members did not vote. See *CN* 1:46a–47a.

169. *CR*, Mar. 7, 1950, 96, pt. 3, p. 2947. One independent also voted negatively. See also Cheng, "Assimilation in Hawaii," p. 16; *Hawaii Statehood News*, Mar. 10, 1950, HSCP.

170. HSC, "Report, 1949–50," pp. 2, 6–8; *HSB*, Apr. 6, 1950, p. 1.

171. See, for example, Stainback to Chapman, Oct. 11, 1950, Chapman Papers. Cf. Stainback to Chapman, Aug. 11, 1949, Chapman Papers.

172. *HSB*, Apr. 4, 1950, p. 1; ILWU, *I.L.W.U. Story*, p. 70.

173. *NYT*, Apr. 20, 1950, p. 4. See also Appendix I, "The Annual Report of the Committee on Un-American Activities of the United States House of Representatives for the Year 1950," SR5, pp. 42–45. Izuka, Paul Crouch, and Kageyama were among those who admitted former Communist party affiliations.

174. Carr, *House Committee on Un-American Activities*, p. 173. See *NYT*, Apr. 9, 1950, p. 40, for a list of committee members. *U.S. News and World Report*, Mar. 30, 1950, p. 35; HH7, pp. 1940, 1945, 1958, 1961, 1970, 1977, 1987, 2013, 2014, 2019, 2020, 2021, 2040, 2042, 2043–2047, 2054–58; Mau, JABOHP, 31.24; 32.50–53.

175. *NYT*, Apr. 16, 1950, sec. 4, p. 2.

176. Representative Harold Velde (Rep., Ill., and member of the 1950 House Committee on Un-American Activities), SH3, p. 262. Velde's testimony cited a statement by Hoover.

177. Carr, *House Committee on Un-American Activities*, p. 173.

178. Walter, quoted in ibid., p. 171.

179. Nixon, *HSB*, Feb. 20, 1950, HSPA Scrapbook, 1950.

180. See generally SH3. See also *HSB*, May 2, 1950, p. 1; Carr, *House Committee on Un-American Activities*, p. 173.

181. *NYT*, June 29, 1950, p. 8; *CN* 1:1500; SR3, pp. 1–47.

182. SR3, pp. 47, 55–58.

183. *HA*, May 20, 1950, p. 1; *NYT*, July 6, 1950, p. 47, May 8, 1950, p. 20.

184. Charles R. Adrian and Charles Press, *The American Political Process* (New York, 1965), p. 437.

185. *HSB*, July 14, 1950, p. 1.

186. *NYT*, Nov. 26, 1950, sec. 4, p. 1; *CN* 1:10.

187. In the 1950 elections in Hawaii, the Republicans retained control of the legislature. See Dept. of Planning and Research, State of Hawaii, *Historical Statistics*, p. 25.

188. *NYT*, Nov. 29, 1950, p. 36; *HSB*, Nov. 28, 1958, p. 1; Gruening, *Battle for Alaska Statehood*, pp. 55–56.

189. Gruening, *Battle for Alaska Statehood*, pp. 55–56; see statement by Stennis in *NYT*, Nov. 29, 1950, p. 37; *NYT*, Dec. 5, 1950, p. 16; *HSB*, Dec. 4, 1950, p. 1.

190. *CN* 1:1500.

191. Truman to Ernest W. Roberts, Aug. 18, 1948, and Truman diary, Nov. 30, 1950, in Ferrell, *Off the Record*, pp. 146–47, 201–2.

192. *CN* 1:1599.

193. *CN* 1:1426. The compromise rule "required the votes of two-thirds of the entire Senate membership to invoke cloture (instead of two-thirds of those present and voting) but allowed cloture to operate on any pending business or motion, with the exception of debate on motions to change Senate rules themselves, on which cloture would not operate as before."

194. Anderson to H. D. Halfhill, Mar. 23, 1953, container 541, Anderson Papers.

195. HSC, *Hawaii and Statehood* (1951), p. 72.

Chapter 6. A Constitution in Search of a State

1. McLane, "Report of the Washington Office," May–Aug. 1949, p. 7.

2. McLane, Exhibit 53, "Hawaii Plans Its First State Convention," SH2, p. 435; "Constitutional Convention," p. 4. These fifteen states were: Arkansas, June 5, 1836; California, Sept. 9, 1850; Florida, Mar. 3, 1845; Idaho, July 3, 1890; Iowa, Dec. 28, 1846; Kansas, Jan. 29, 1861; Kentucky, June 1, 1792; Maine, Mar. 15, 1820; Michigan, Jan. 26, 1837; Oregon, Feb. 14, 1859; Tennessee, June 1, 1796; Vermont, Mar. 4, 1791; Texas, Dec. 29, 1845; West Virginia, June 20, 1863; Wyoming, July 10, 1890. See also HSC, *Hawaii and Statehood* (1951), p. 68.

3. McLane, "Report of the Washington Office," May–Aug. 1949, p. 7.

4. *HSB*, July 22, 1949, p. 2.

5. McLane, Exhibit 53, "Hawaii Plans First State Convention," SH2, pp. 436–37.

6. *HSB*, Mar. 22, 1950, p. 1; *NYT*, Nov. 15, 1949, p. 20; *NYT*, Feb. 11, 1950, p. 13.

7. "Constitutional Convention," p. 4. Approximately one-third of all delegates had not been nominated previously for political office. See also Harold S. Roberts, "Hawaii Molds State Constitution," *Christian Science Monitor.*

8. Roberts, "Hawaii Molds State Constitution," *Christian Science Monitor.*

9. Lind, *Hawaii's People,* p. 28. In 1950 there were approximately sixty-one thousand Filipino residents in Hawaii.

10. Roberts, "Hawaii Molds State Constitution," *Christian Science Monitor.*

11. Ibid. Nineteen of the delegates were lawyers. The remainder, Roberts observed, "represented a broad cross-section of the community, 'including two former attorneys general, two pineapple company presidents, members of the territorial legislature, five women, a labor union representative and a university student.' " Cf. Chou, "Education of a Senator," p. 581.

12. "Constitutional Convention," p. 4.

13. *NYT,* Apr. 7, 1950, p. 4.

14. *HSB,* Apr. 4, 1950, p. 6; *HSB,* Apr. 15, 1950, p. 1; *HSB,* Apr. 16, 1950, p. 1; *NYT,* Apr. 15, 1950, p. 1.

15. *HSB,* Apr. 10, 1950, p. 1; *NYT,* Apr. 11, 1950, p. 1; *HSB,* Apr. 12, 1950, p. 3a.

16. *HSB,* Apr. 11, 1950, p. 1. See also Appendix I, "The Annual Report of the Committee on Un-American Activities of the United States House of Representatives for the Year 1950," SR5, pp. 43–44.

17. Appendix I, "Report on Un-American Activities," SR5, p. 44; *HA,* Apr. 21, 1950, p. 1; *HSB,* Apr. 12, 1950, p. 39.

18. Harold S. Roberts, "Preface," in Conrad and Kamins, *Proceedings of the Constitutional Convention,* 1:vii. Silva was replaced as delegate by Matsuki Arashiro. Kageyama was replaced by John R. Phillips. For a complete list of convention delegates, see Appendix 1 of this book; Appendix I, "Report on Un-American Activities," SR5, p. 43.

19. *HSB,* Apr. 4, 1950, p. 6; Roberts, "Preface," pp. v–xi.

20. *HSB,* July 22, 1950, p. 1.

21. *HSB,* Oct. 11, 1950, p. 1. Ben Dillingham was the son of Walter F. Dillingham.

22. *HSB,* Sept. 29, 1950, p. 1; Chou, "Education of a Senator," p. 601.

23. *HSB,* Oct. 11, 1950, p. 1.

24. HSC, "Report, 1949–50," pp. 6–8.

25. *HSB,* Sept. 30, 1950, p. 1.

26. *HSB,* May 27, 1950, p. 3; *HA,* June 10, 1950, p. 10; Fong, interview with author; Conrad and Kamins, *Proceedings of the Constitutional Convention,* 2:320–30.

27. *HSB,* Oct. 17, 1950, p. 5.

28. Appendix J, "The Constitution of the State of Hawaii," SR5, p. 56; HSC, *Statehood for Hawaii,* p. 61.

29. *HSB,* Nov. 8, 1950, p. 1; *NYT,* Nov. 9, 1950, p. 39; *HSB,* Sept. 30, 1950, p. 1.

30. Appendix J, "Constitution of the State of Hawaii," SR5, pp. 45, 46, 54.

31. Ibid., p. 55; Roberts, "Hawaii Molds State Constitution," *Christian Science Monitor.*

32. Appendix J, "Constitution of the State of Hawaii," SR5, pp. 50–51; James

M. Burns and John W. Peltason, *Government by the People: The Dynamics of American National, State and Local Government* (Englewood Cliffs, N.J., 1966), p. 743.

33. Appendix J, "Constitution of the State of Hawaii," SR5, pp. 51–52.

34. S. Gale Lowrie, "Constitution for Hawaii," *American Political Science Review* 45(Sept. 1951):771.

35. Appendix J, "Constitution of the State of Hawaii," SR5, pp. 46, 49–51.

36. Lowrie, "Constitution for Hawaii," p. 771.

37. Ibid., p. 772; Appendix J, "Constitution of the State of Hawaii," SR5, p. 48.

38. Appendix J, "Constitution of the State of Hawaii," SR5, p. 48.

39. Ibid., p. 46; Roberts, "Hawaii Molds State Constitution," *Christian Science Monitor.*

40. Bebout, quoted in Roberts, "Preface," p. x.

41. Richard S. Childs (chairman of the Council of the National Municipal League), quoted in ibid.

42. Lowrie, "Constitution for Hawaii," p. 774.

43. *HSB*, Sept. 28, 1950, p. 8.

44. Bebout, quoted in Roberts, "Preface," p. x; Burns and Peltason, *Government by the People*, p. 743; Lowrie, "Constitution for Hawaii," p. 774.

45. Butler, *CR*, June 23, 1949, 95, pt. 6, p. 8175.

46. SR5, p. 14.

47. Fong, SH3, pp. 190–92; Appendix I, "Report on Un-American Activities," SR5, pp. 42–45.

48. McLane, "Report of the Washington Office," May–Aug. 1949, p. 7.

49. Norman Meller, *With An Understanding Heart* (New York, 1971), p. 84, quoted in Chou, "Education of a Senator," p. 599.

50. Fong, quoted in Chou, "Education of a Senator," p. 596.

Chapter 7. Politics of Nonaction

1. Woodrow Wilson, *Congressional Government* (New York, 1956 ed.), p. 83.

2. Ira Katznelson and Mark Kesselman, *The Politics of Power: A Critical Introduction to American Government* (New York, 1975), p. 308. See also Brenner, "Committee Conflict," pp. 98–100.

3. Fred I. Greenstein, *The American Party System and the American People* (Englewood Cliffs, N.J., 1963), pp. 87–88. See also Katznelson and Kesselman, *Politics of Power*, pp. 304–13.

4. HSC, "Report, 1949–50," pp. 1–5. McLane became administrative assistant to the governor of Hawaii.

5. Burns, JABOHP, 7.4–5, 20–25; 8.22; 9.2; Mau, JABOHP, 31.18–30; Richardson, JABOHP, 1.4–5, 14; Kido, JABOHP, 2.10–16; and Aoki, JABOHP, 14.4, and pt. 2, tape 1, pp. 1–9; Chapman to Truman, Mar. 6, 1951, TP Office File. Born in 1889 in Altoona, Kansas, Long studied at the University of Michigan and Columbia before he and his family settled in Hawaii. From 1919 to 1946 he was a prominent figure in the educational and civil life of the islands, spending twelve years as superintendent of public instruction. In 1946 he was

appointed secretary of Hawaii, a position which he held until his elevation to governor. Burns claimed Long was the "number one choice," but Mau's far more detailed and convincing recollection indicates that he was a compromise candidate. See also *NYT*, Apr. 21, 1951, p. 15; *NYT*, May 2, 1950, p. 52; *NYT*, Mar. 27, 1951, p. 32; *HSB*, Mar. 31, 1950, p. 1; *HA*, Apr. 1, 1950, p. 1.

6. Kido, JABOHP, 2.10–16.

7. SR5, pp. 1, 69; *HA*, Apr. 4, 1951, p. 3; *NYT*, Feb. 21, 1951, p. 25; *HA*, Feb. 21, 1951, p. 2; *NYT*, Apr. 4, 1951, p. 18; *HA*, Apr. 4, 1951, p. 3. See also *CR*, May 21, 1951, 97, pt. 4, p. 5487.

8. SR5, pp. 67–69; *U.S. News and World Report*, Mar. 20, 1951, p. 35. The minority report concluded: "We feel strongly that Hawaii should not be granted statehood until we are sure we are not adding a red star to the 48 white ones of the American flag."

9. SR5, pp. 15–16; *NYT*, Apr. 4, 1951, p. 18; *HA*, Apr. 4, 1951, p. 3; *CR*, May 21, 1951, 97, pt. 4, p. 5487; HSC, *Hawaii and Statehood* (1951), p. 60.

10. O'Mahoney, *CR*, July 23, 1951, 97, pt. 7, p. 8652; McFarland, *CR*, Oct. 20, 1951, 97, pt. 10, p. 13681; *NYT*, Jan. 27, 1952, sec. 4, p. 9; *HA*, Apr. 4, 1951, p. 3.

11. *NYT*, Jan. 27, 1952, sec. 4, p. 9, and Feb. 7, 1952, p. 28; *HSB*, Jan. 24, 1952, p. 1, Jan. 19, 1952, p. 1, and Feb. 5, 1952, p. 1; and HSC, "Report, 1951–52," p. 5.

12. Gruening, *Battle for Alaska Statehood*, p. 57; *NYT*, Feb. 7, 1952, p. 28, and Feb. 28, 1952, pp. 1, 17.

13. *Congressional Quarterly Almanac: 82d Congress, 2d session, 1952* 8(Washington, 1953):295, 230 (hereafter cited as *CQA*).

14. *CN* 1:1503, 1506.

15. *HSB*, Mar. 10, 1953, p. 1; *NYT*, May 23, 1953, p. 25; Smathers, SH5, p. 460.

16. See, for example, William Crozier, Jr., to Smathers, June 29, 1953, SH5, pp. 475–77; SH5, pp. 587–600, 426, 472–73, 450–53.

17. *HA*, Mar. 24, 1954, p. 9. Hughes was Campbell's attorney.

18. Stainback, *Commonwealth for Hawaii*, pp. 2–5. See also Stainback, *Desirability of Commonwealth; HA*, Mar. 24, 1954, p. 9; *CN* 1:1506.

19. *Hilo Tribune-Herald*, July 23, 1953, HSPA Scrapbook, 1953; *HSB*, Mar. 30, 1954, HSPA Scrapbook, 1954. See also J. Garner Anthony to editor, *HSB*, published Mar. 30, 1954.

20. See *HA*, July 15, 1954, HSPA Scrapbook, 1954. *HA*, July 21, 1954, HSPA Scrapbook, 1954; Hughes to Butler, May 1, 1953, quoted in SH5, p. 428.

21. *HA*, Dec. 11, and July 21, 1954, HSPA Scrapbook, 1954; *NYT*, July 27, 1954, p. 1.

22. See, for example, the extensive information on Commonwealth status inserted in SH5, pp. 587–600, 426, 472–73, 450–53.

23. *CN* 1:46a; *NYT*, Feb. 28, 1952, pp. 1, 17. The twelve states which voted solidly against recommital were: California, Oregon, Montana, Connecticut, Minnesota, Rhode Island, New York, New Mexico, Wyoming, Vermont, West Virginia, and Washington. Only three Southern Democrats—Spessard L. Holland (Fla.), John J. Sparkman (Ala.), and Estes Kefauver (Tenn.) opposed recommittal. They were joined by senators from two border states, Oklahoma

and Kentucky. Old guard Republicans who supported recommittal included Taft, Bridges, Malone, Millikin, Butler, and Jenner.

24. *Newsweek*, Mar. 10, 1952, p. 28; *Time*, Mar. 10, 1952, p. 10.

25. *NYT*, Mar. 4, 1952, p. 1, Feb. 28, 1952, pp. 1, 17; *HSB*, Mar. 3, 1952, p. 1. Voting against recommital of Alaskan statehood (i.e., for statehood) were twenty-four Democrats and twenty Republicans. Voting for consideration of Hawaii were only six Democrats and twenty-six Republicans.

26. Farrington attended the Republican National Convention and Long attended the Democratic National Convention. They influenced the pro-statehood planks adopted by their respective parties. See *HA*, July 22, 1952, p. 2; *HSB*, July 10, 1952, p. 8; *NYT*, Jan. 7, 1953, p. 82.

27. Included in these were Albert Gore (Dem., Tenn.), Frank Barrett (Rep., Wyo.), Charles Potter (Rep., Mich.), and Mike Mansfield (Dem., Mont.). Although O'Mahoney, a leading Senate proponent, was defeated, two opponents of Hawaii, McKellar and Tom Connally (Dem., Tex.) were also defeated. Connally was a vehement critic of Hawaii. He reportedly stated in the Senate that "two Japs from Hawaii did not equal one Texan." As reported in the *Congressional Record*, however, his comments read: "I think I am a better American than a great many people who live in Hawaii. . . . The majority of the people there are not of American ancestry or descent" (see Connally, *CR*, Mar. 3, 1952, 98, pt. 2, p. 1719). *Denver Post*, n.d., quoted in Gruening, *Battle for Alaska Statehood*, p. 59; *CN* 1:13.

28. *HSB*, July 8, 1952; E. Farrington to Justus F. Paul, Nov. 18, 1965, and Butler to J. L. McMaster, Mar. 16, 1953, Butler MS, quoted in Paul, "The Power of Seniority," pp. 144, 146–47.

29. Quinn, interview with author; E. Farrington, interview with McDowell; E. Farrington, JABOHP, p. 18.

30. HSC, "Report, 1951–52," pp. 8–11. See also Ernest Gruening, "Statehood for Alaska," in Latham, *Statehood for Hawaii and Alaska*, p. 19.

31. *HA*, Jan. 15, 1953, p. 1; *Washington Post*, Feb. 23, 1953, HSCP; Gruening, "Statehood for Alaska," p. 19.

32. *NYT*, Feb. 3, 1953, p. 12; *Louisville Courier-Journal*, n.d., inserted by E. L. Bartlett in *CR*, Mar. 2, 1953, 99, pt. 9, p. A1080; Mack, *CR*, Mar. 10, 1953, 99, pt. 2, p. 1824; *HSB*, Feb. 20, 1953, p. 1.

33. *NYT*, Jan. 7, 1953, p. 82; *NYT*, Feb. 8, 1953, p. 58; HR4, p. 57; Gruening, *Battle for Alaska Statehood*, p. 59.

34. HSC, "Report, 1953–54," pp. 18–19; HSC, "Report, 1951–52," p. 14 (includes information on commission activities early in 1953); *HSB*, Feb. 23, 1953, p. 1; C. Nils Tavares, "Some Incidents, Humorous and Otherwise, of the Statehood Struggle" (Paper delivered Jan. 5, 1970), p. 11, Tavares Private Papers; SH4.

35. Fuchs, *Hawaii Pono*, p. 379.

36. HR4, p. 4; Tavares, "Incidents of the Statehood Struggle," pp. 13–14. On the island of Oahu alone, there were at least seventy-five areas over which the federal government would have exercised exclusive jurisdiction. See also J. Lee Rankin (assistant U.S. attorney general) to Cordon, Jan. 13, 1954, and Anderson to King, June 15, 1953, container 541, Anderson Papers.

37. Tavares, "Incidents of the Statehood Struggle," pp. 18–21. A complete

transcript of the confidential Senate committee discussion of the proposed state boundaries of Hawaii is contained in: Senate Committee on Interior and Insular Affairs (C.I.I.A.), "Stenographic Transcript of Hearings Before the C.I.I.A.," pts. 1, 2, 4, 5, 6, Mar. 12, 13, 16, 17, and May 12, 1953 (Mimeographed copy). See also Senate C.I.I.A., "Executive Session—Confidential Stenographic Transcript of Hearings," vol. 1, "Submerged Lands—Outer Continental Shelf and Statehood for Alaska and Hawaii" (Mimeographed copy). SH5, p. 10; Roger W. Jones (assistant director for legislative reference, White House) to Bernard M. Stanley, Apr. 27, 1953, EP. The final boundaries of the proposed state conformed with the wishes of the Pentagon, not the Interior Department. Burns' later claim that he was responsible for excluding Palmyra Island and thus quickening the passage of the statehood bill seems inaccurate in light of Tavares' role and the evidence above. (Cf. Burns, JABOHP, 10.19–22.)

38. *CQA, 83d Cong., 1st sess., 1953* 9(Washington, 1953):302; Pillion, *CR*, Mar. 16, 1953, 99, pt. 9, p. A1297.

39. *NYT*, Mar. 4, 1953, p. 16; *CQA, 83d Cong., 1st sess., 1953* 9:302.

40. *HSB*, Mar. 3, 1953, p. 1; *NYT*, Mar. 4, 1953, p. 16; HR4, p. 16.

41. *HSB*, Mar. 5, 1953, p. 1; Smith, quoted in *CQA, 83d Cong., 1st sess., 1953* 9:302.

42. See, for example, Walter Rodgers (Dem., Tex.), Pillion, Davis, Coudert, and Donovan, *CR*, Mar. 9, 1953, 99, pt. 2, pp. 764–68, 1772–77, 1799.

43. Smith, ibid., p. 1761. Miller refuted this statement, claiming that a majority of the population of Florida was Negro when it was admitted as a state. See *NYT*, Mar. 10, 1953, p. 19.

44. McCormack, p. 1780, Engle, p. 1822, Thomas Lane (Dem., Mass.), p. 1821, all in *CR*, Mar. 9, 1953, 99, pt. 2.

45. *NYT*, Mar. 11, 1953, p. 18; *HSB*, Mar. 10, 1953, p. 1; Saylor, quoted in *Newsweek*, Mar. 23, 1953, pp. 29–30.

46. *CR*, Mar. 10, 1953, 99, pt. 2, pp. 1813–14, 1817–22; see also *CQA, 83d Cong., 1st sess., 1953* 9:303.

47. *CR*, Mar. 10, 1953, 99, pt. 2, pp. 1828–29.

48. In 1947, seventy-seven Democrats opposed the Hawaii bill. In 1950, eighty-eight Democrats were opposed. However, in 1953, one hundred Democrats voted negatively. One independent representative also opposed Hawaii in 1953.

49. As in previous years some Southern Democrats supported Hawaii. Six of Louisiana's seven representatives voted for Hawaii in 1953. Moreover, Virginia, which had previously voted solidly against Hawaii's admission, provided two affirmative votes in 1953. See *CR*, Mar. 10, 1953, 99, pt. 2, pp. 1828–29.

50. *NYT*, May 13, 1953, p. 22; *CQA, 83d Cong., 2d sess., 1953* 9:303. Democrat committee members who had previously indicated support for Hawaii were Anderson, Murray, and Henry M. Jackson. However, four committee Democrats—Smathers, Russell Long (La.), Price Daniel (Tex.), and Earle Clements (Kt.)—were expected to oppose both territories.

51. This was confirmed by the fact that the Hawaii bill was sponsored by eight Republicans and six Democrats. In contrast, the Alaska bill was sponsored by nine Democrats and the Independent, Morse. *NYT*, May 15, 1953, p. 6.

52. *NYT*, June 26, 1953, p. 18.

53. SH5, pp. 504–52, 445–77, 221–51, 471, 262, 426–27, 117.

54. McNamara, "Hawaii's Smith Act Case," pp. iv–vi, 1–3, 116–19, 135–41, 169–70. Metzger, who was a member of the Statehood Commission, stated: "I have known Jack Hall, between twelve and fifteen years. He is fearlessly honest, an excellent law abiding citizen. . . . I have never heard his loyalty questioned." Many others agreed. See, for example, Burns, JABOHP, 9.12. The "Hawaii seven" were freed early in 1958 by an appeals court in San Francisco after a U.S. Supreme Court ruling of 1957 stated that mere membership in the Communist party and "preaching abstractly" were insufficient grounds for a conviction under the Smith Act.

55. See, for example, questions by Smathers and Malone during the presentation of testimony by statehood proponents during the 1953 Senate hearings, SH5, pp. 159–81. Burns, JABOHP, 9.12; Aoki, JABOHP, 13.11.

56. Coke to Smathers, n.d., quoted in SH5, p. 471.

57. See, for example, *HA*, July 7, 1953, quoted by Smathers in *CR*, July 16, 1953, 99, pt. 3, pp. 8941–42. See also Eastland's reference to the exposure of communism in Hawaii by the *HSB*, the newspaper "owned by the esteemed Delegate from Hawaii, Mr. Farrington," in *CR*, Apr. 13, 1953, 99, pt. 3, pp. 2987–88.

58. *HA*, Apr. 17, 1953, sec. 2, p. 1; *HSB*, Dec. 28, 1953, HSPA Scrapbook, 1953; *HSB*, Nov. 12, 1953, HSPA Scrapbook, 1953.

59. Apart from members of the Dillingham family, Imua's backers allegedly included George Burgess of the Hawaiian Pineapple Company, Ed Schneider of the Bank of Hawaii, H. C. Eichelberger of American Factors, and Thomas G. Singlehurst of the Bishop Trust Company. Zalburg, *A Spark is Struck*, p. 392; *HSB*, Sept. 19, 1958; Fuchs, *Hawaii Pono*, pp. 371–73. See also *NYT*, Jan. 27, 1952, sec. 4, p. 9; *HSB*, Jan. 19, 1952, p. 1.

60. Smathers, *CR*, July 16, 1953, 99, pt. 3, pp. 8941–42; Eastland, *CR*, Apr. 13, 1953, 99, pt. 3, pp. 2987–88.

61. *San Francisco Examiner*, July 2, 1953, HSCP.

62. Anderson, *CR*, Jan. 11, 1954, 100, pt. 1, p. 102.

63. *NYT*, Jan. 8, 1954, p. 10.

64. See Anderson, quoting a statement by Eastland, *CR*, Jan. 18, 1954, 100, pt. 1, p. 350.

65. *HSB*, Jan. 13, 1954, p. 1; *NYT*, Jan. 14, 1954, p. 13. Smathers requested an investigation of communism in Hawaii by Senator McCarthy's Government Operations Committee, but this was refused.

66. *NYT*, Jan. 20, 1954, pp. 1, 15, *HSB*, Jan. 19, 1954, p. 1.

67. *NYT*, Jan. 26, 1954, p. 16; *HA*, Jan. 22, 1954, p. 1; *NYT*, Feb. 14, 1954, sec. 4, p. 7. Gruening, "Statehood for Alaska," p. 77.

68. *NYT*, Jan. 28, 1954, p. 8; *HA*, Feb. 8, 1954, p. 1; *NYT*, Feb. 5, 1954, p. 10.

69. *CR*, Mar. 4, 1954, 100, pt. 2, p. 2633ff.

70. Quoted in Griffith, *Politics of Fear*, p. 205.

71. *HSB*, Mar. 4, 1954, HSPA Scrapbook, 1954. See, for example, Jackson, quoted in *HSB*, Mar. 11, 1954, p. 1; *HA*, Mar. 6, 1954, p. 1.

72. Anderson, *CR*, Feb. 26, 1954, 100, pt. 2, p. 2377; *NYT*, Mar. 12, 1954, pp. 1, 13; *CR*, Mar. 11, 1954, 100, pt. 3, p. 3091; *HSB*, Mar. 12, 1954, p. 1; Farrington's newspaper suggested that a "considerable number of Republican Senators who voted against combining the bills" were not opposed to the admission of Alaska. See also Memo for Eisenhower, Aug. 8, 1954, EP.

73. Holland, *CR*, Mar. 11, 1954, 100, pt. 3, p. 3076.

74. *HSB*, Mar. 12, 1954, p. 1.

75. *NYT*, Mar. 14, 1954, sec. 4, p. 2; *NYT*, Mar. 17, 1954, p. 1; Eastland, *CR*, Mar. 16, 1954, 100, pt. 3, p. 3330.

76. Monroney, *CR*, Apr. 1, 1954, 100, pt. 4, p. 4321. Smathers pointed out that there were only four senators present on March 17, 1954. See Smathers, *CR*, Mar. 17, 1954, 100, pt. 3, p. 3380; *CR*, Mar. 16–18, 1954, 100, pt. 3, pp. 3325–30, 3382–3405, 3396–4405; *HSB*, Mar. 19, 1954, HSPA Scrapbook, 1954.

77. *CR*, Apr. 1, 1954, 100, pt. 4, pp. 4332, 4339; *CR*, Mar. 18, 1954, 100, pt. 3, pp. 3499, 3508.

78. *CR*, Apr. 1, 1954, 100, pt. 4, p. 4343. Details of the vote are also given in *CN* 1:63a. The three Southern Democrat supporters were Long, Kefauver, and Holland. GOP opponents included Homer Ferguson (Mich.), chairman of the Republican Party Policy Committee, Prescott Bush (Conn.), Malone (Nev.), John Butler (Md.), Andrew Schoeppel (Kans.), and Herman Welker (Idaho).

79. Fulbright, *CR*, Mar. 9, 1954, 100, pt. 3, p. 3954; *NYT*, Mar. 28, 1954, p. 56. *Time* observed shortly after the vote that "Martin made no secret of Republican plans to let the bill die quietly" (Apr. 12, 1954, p. 15).

80. *CQA, 83d Cong., 2d sess., 1954* 10(Washington, 1954):397; *NYT*, Apr. 6, 1954, p. 1; E. Farrington, JABOHP, p. 26.

81. *NYT*, Apr. 6, 1954, p. 1; *HA*, Apr. 4, 1954, p. 1; *NYT*, Apr. 8, 1954, p. 20.

82. Miller, *CR*, Apr. 12, 1954, 100, pt. 4, p. 5002; *HSB*, Mar. 12, 1954, p. 1; *NYT*, Apr. 13, 1954, p. 28; *NYT*, July 27, 1954, p. 1; *HSB*, Apr. 14, 1954, p. 1. Only five members of the Rules Committee wanted to convene a joint House-Senate conference.

83. *NYT*, May 14, 1954, p. 33, May 15, 1954, p. 11, May 17, 1954, p. 1.

84. *Washington Post*, May 20, 1954, HSCP.

85. HSC, "Report, 1953–54," p. 8. The delegation comprised "the Governor and aide, 3 commission members, 6 island businessmen, 6 veterans, 2 University of Hawaii students, 1 Public Relations Official, 25 Representatives and 8 Senators." *HSB*, Apr. 27, 1954, p. 1, May 15, 1954, HSPA Scrapbook, 1954; *HA*, May 10, 1954, HSPA Scrapbook, 1954.

86. Memo for Eisenhower, Aug. 8, 1954, EP.

87. Eric Beecroft to Oscar Chapman, Feb. 6, 1951, Dotty Papers.

88. Aoki, quoted in Pratte, "Ke alaka'i," pp. 256–57. See also ibid., pp. 255, 282. Crowningburg-Amalu, *Jack Burns*, p. 403; Aoki, JABOHP, 12.36–42.

89. E. Farrington, JABOHP, pp. 1–5, 11–16, 22–26; E. Farrington, interview with McDowell; Burns, JABOHP, 3.5, and 10.20–21. Pratte, "Ke alaka'i," pp. 256–57, 282, endorses this view.

90. Pratte, "Ke alaka'i," pp. 256–57, 282.

91. E. Farrington to Eisenhower, Aug. 8, 1954, and to Thomas Stevens (secretary to the president), Aug. 21, 1954, EP; Mrs. Farrington to James C. Hagerty, Sept. 20, 1954, and Memo for Eisenhower, Aug. 8, 1954, EP. Follow-

ing her late husband's example, Mrs. Farrington generally heeded the astute political advice offered by Riley Allen, who as editor of the *Bulletin* was a powerful force in island life, especially in the decade after the war (see Zalburg, *A Spark is Struck*, pp. 380–81, 605).

92. Burns, JABOHP, 10.7; E. Farrington, in *HSB*, July 29, 1954, HSPA Scrapbook, 1954.

93. Burns, JABOHP, 10.6–13; 5.11; 7.17; Aoki, JABOHP, 13.35–36; 14.21–23; Mau, JABOHP, 32.56–58; Dept. of Planning and Research, State of Hawaii, *Historical Statistics*, p. 25; Fuchs, *Hawaii Pono*, pp. 182–83, 329; Daws, *Shoal of Time*, pp. 364–65; Office of the Secretary of Hawaii, *Hawaii: Election Results, Official Tabulation, 1946–1959*, folder of unnumbered folios, SL; Pillion, HH9, p. 301. There was also a pronounced swing to the Democrats in Alaska in 1954. Democrats won twelve of the sixteen seats in Alaska's senate, and all but three of the twenty-four seats in the lower house. This had a direct bearing on Hawaii's statehood bid in the following years.

94. Burns, JABOHP, 3.13; 5.11; 7.17; Mau, JABOHP, 32.56–58; Fong, interview with author.

95. Dept. of Planning and Research, State of Hawaii, *Historical Statistics*, p. 8; Kamins, "The Month the Clock Stopped," pp. 18, 28; Fuchs, *Hawaii Pono*, pp. 308–22.

96. *HSB*, Dec. 16, 1954, p. 1; *HSB*, Dec. 18, 1954, HSPA Scrapbook, 1954. Stennis, *CR*, Mar. 8, 1954, 100, pt. 3, p. 3482; Pillion, HH9, p. 307. See also similar statements by opponents of statehood, *CR*, May 10, 1955, 101, pt. 5, pp. 5915–19, 5934.

97. *HSB*, Jan. 6, 1955, p. 1. See also Thurston B. Morton (assistant secretary of Interior) to Murray (chairman, Committee on Internal Affairs), Feb. 28, 1955, EP.

98. Pillion, HH9, pp. 300–301. See also Fuchs, *Hawaii Pono*, pp. 308–22, 328.

99. *HSB*, May 8, 1955, HSPA Scrapbook, 1955; C. E. Wilson (secretary, Dept. of Defense) to Murray, Feb. 15, 1955, quoted in SH6, p. 22; *NYT*, Feb. 23, 1955, p. 26; Gruening, in *NYT*, Feb. 23, 1955, p. 26; Gruening, *Battle for Alaska Statehood*, p. 52; *CQA, 84th Cong., 1st sess., 1955* 11(Washington, 1955), p. 373. See also *NYT*, Feb. 17, 1955, p. 17.

100. Morton to Murray, Feb. 4, 1955, quoted in SH6, pp. 22, 21. See also *NYT*, Feb. 23, 1955, p. 26.

101. *HSB*, Feb. 16, 1955, HSPA Scrapbook, 1955; Eisenhower to Miller, Mar. 31, 1955, quoted in *CQA, 84th Cong., 1st sess., 1955* 11:373.

102. *NYT*, Feb. 17, 1955, p. 17.

103. HR5, p. 125.

104. *HA*, Apr. 27, 1955, p. 1. For details of how Rules Committee members voted in 1953, see *CN* 1:64a–65a. For information on the undemocratic structure and operation of the Rules Committee, see Otten, "How Twelve Men Control Congress," p. 34.

105. Miller, *CR*, May 9, 1955, 101, pt. 5, p. 5880.

106. *CQA, 84th Cong., 1st sess., 1955* 11:374; Colmer, *CR*, May 9, 1955, 101, pt. 5, p. 5878.

107. *CR*, May 10, 1955, 101, pt. 5, pp. 5975–76; *CN* 1:70a–71a.

108. *CN* 1:70a–71a. For example, all eleven Democratic representatives from Illinois, and all but two of the nineteen Democratic representatives from New York opposed recommittal.

109. *NYT,* May 12, 1955, p. 28.

110. *CQA, 84th Cong., 1st sess., 1955* 11:374. See also *Time,* May 23, 1955, p. 15: Mrs. Farrington to Eisenhower, Sept. 15, 1955, and Eisenhower to Mrs. Farrington, Oct. 1, 1955, EP. See also Mrs. Farrington to General Wilton B. Persons (White House aide), Sept. 15, 1955, EP.

111. SR7, pp. 33–35, *NYT,* Nov. 16, 1956, p. 26.

112. *NYT,* Nov. 4, 1956, p. 2. Eastland stated that the investigation's primary purpose was to determine why the Hawaii legislature had reduced the biennial appropriation for the Territorial Subversive Activities Commission from a requested forty-seven thousand dollars to twenty thousand dollars. Eastland's investigation was prompted in part by the extensive material (supplied to congressional statehood opponents by Imua) which purportedly detailed the growing strength of communism in Hawaii. See, for example, *HA,* Mar. 24, 1955, and *HSB,* Apr. 20, 1955, both in HSPA Scrapbook, 1955.

113. SR7, p. 37.

114. *NYT,* May 11, 1955, p. 1; *HSB,* Dec. 26, 1955, p. 1; *HSB,* Jan. 6, 1956, p. 1.

115. For details of these decisions and materials relating to them, see Doc. Nos. 617, 628, in Henry Steel Commager, ed., *Documents of American History,* 7th ed. (New York, 1963), pp. 619–22, 641–43.

116. *CN* 1:1597, 1620–21.

117. "Southern Declaration on Integration," Mar. 12, 1956, quoted in Commager, *Documents of American History,* p. 641. For a detailed discussion of the white South's reaction to pressure for desegregation after 1954, see Wilhoit, *Politics of Massive Resistance.*

118. Kamins, "The Month the Clock Stopped," p. 19.

119. Tuttle, "Politics in Paradise," pp. 32, 42; *NYT,* May 13, 1956, p. 46.

120. Burns, JABOHP, 10.17–18.

121. Quinn, interview with author; Fong, interview with author.

122. Meller, "Centralization in Hawaii," p. 54; *HSB,* May 9, 1956, HSPA Scrapbook, 1956; Zalburg, *A Spark is Struck,* p. 381.

123. *NYT,* May 13, 1956, p. 46; *HSB,* May 9, 1956, HSPA Scrapbook, 1956. See also *NYT,* Nov. 11, 1956, p. 53.

124. *HA,* Feb. 19, 1955, HSPA Scrapbook, 1955; HSC, "Report, 1955–56," pp. 11–12.

125. *HSB,* Sept. 25, 1956, HSPA Scrapbook, 1956. Hawaii Democrat Robert G. Dodge, for example, charged that King had appointed a majority of Republicans to the commission and destroyed the bipartisanship of the statehood campaign.

126. *HSB,* May 24, 1955, p. 1; *CR,* May 31, 1955, 101, pt. 6, p. 6168.

127. Fasi to editor, *HA,* Nov. 9, 1955, HSPA Scrapbook, 1955. See also *Time,* May 23, 1955, p. 15.

128. Burns, JABOHP, 7.17; Aoki, JABOHP, 13.16.

129. Long, quoted in *HSB,* Apr. 5, 1956, HSPA Scrapbook, 1956. Engle, quoted in *Time,* May 23, 1955, p. 15.

Chapter 8. Compromise Politics

1. HSC, "Report, 1955–56," pp. 2, 11–12 (includes material relating to early 1957).

2. Burns, JABOHP, 3.3–6; Aoki, JABOHP, 12.36–42, and 13.16–17, 37–38.

3. Lubell, *Future of American Politics.*

4. *CN* 1:22; Dept. of Planning and Research, State of Hawaii, *Historical Statistics,* p. 25; *HSB,* Nov. 24, 1956, HSPA Scrapbook, 1956. The composition of the Hawaii legislature was: House of Representatives, Democrats eighteen and Republicans twelve; Senate, Democrats twelve and Republicans three. The Alaskan delegate, E. L. Bartlett, was reelected to his seventh term. Office of the Secretary of Hawaii, *Hawaii: Election Results, Official Tabulation, 1946–1959,* folder of unnumbered folios; *HSB,* Nov. 8, 1956, p. 1; *HA,* Nov. 8, 1956, p. 1.

5. HSC, "Report, 1955–56," p. 10; *NYT,* Aug. 22, 1956, p. 16; Anderson, quoted in *HSB,* Jan. 21, 1957, p. 1.

6. HSC, "Report, 1957–58," pp. 1–2, 11; see also SH7, pp. 34, 48–49, 104–9. Burns, interview with author; Aoki, JABOHP, 12.36–42; Mau, JABOHP, 32.41–44; Burns, JABOHP, 3.4–6.

7. Burns, interview with author; *CQA, 85th Cong., 1st sess., 1957* 13(Washington, 1958):646–47. See also Aspinal, *CR,* July 10, 1958, 104, pt. 10, p. 13449.

8. Burns, SH7, p. 7. See also Murray, *CR,* Jan. 7, 1957, 103, pt. 1, p. 258; Gruening, *Battle for Alaska Statehood,* pp. 71–72; Aoki, JABOHP, 12.36–42.

9. *CQA, 85th Cong., 1st sess., 1957* 13:646–47; Aspinal, *CR,* July 10, 1958, 104, pt. 10, p. 13449; HSC, "Report, 1949–50," p. 11; Burns, interview with author. The various Hawaii Statehood Commission reports issued after 1950 did not refer to the possible adoption of a "Tennessee Plan." Burns rejected the idea, viewing it as appropriate for Alaska should it proceed first, but unnecessary for Hawaii.

10. Rogers to Jackson, Mar. 28, 1957, inserted in SH7, pp. 1–2. See also *HSB,* Apr. 2, 1957, p. 1; *NYT,* Apr. 2, 1957, p. 7; Nixon, quoted in *HSB,* Feb. 20, 1950, HSPA Scrapbook, 1950; Carr, *House Committee on Un-American Activities,* p. 171.

11. *CQA, 85th Cong., 1st sess., 1957* 13:648; *NYT,* Mar. 26, 1957, p. 20. See also Vice Admiral G. L. Russell, deputy chief of Naval Operations, representing the Dept. of Defense, SH7, p. 53; *Washington Post,* Feb. 7, 1958, quoted by Murray in *CR,* Feb. 10, 1958, 104, pt. 2, p. 1905. This provision was made in Section 10 of the Alaska Statehood Bill. However, since the admission of Alaska in 1958, the U.S. government has never withdrawn any land from state jurisdiction. Gruening (*Battle for Alaska Statehood,* pp. 94–95) suggests that Interior Secretary Seaton, a sincere statehood advocate, was largely responsible for gaining Eisenhower's acceptance of immediate statehood for Alaska in 1957–1958. Later in this chapter, however, I have indicated that Republican acceptance of the Alaska bill resulted from the influence of a combination of factors more important than Seaton's influence on Eisenhower.

12. *NYT,* July 26, 1957, p. 36; *CQA, 85th Cong., 1st sess., 1957* 13:645; *CR,* Aug. 30, 1957, 103, pt. 12, p. 16693. Wilhoit (*Politics of Massive Resistance,*

pp. 41–51, 201–30) dates the breakdown of "massive resistance" from the early 1960s, but my study suggests that cracks appeared in its facade on Capitol Hill during 1957.

13. Dan Lacy, *The White Use of Blacks in America* (New York, 1972), p. 195.

14. D. Berman, *A Bill Becomes Law*, pp. 3, 136. Berman writes that Eisenhower "chose equivocation and inaction rather than resolute leadership on civil rights."

15. Shuman, "Senate Rules and Civil Rights," p. 969. It should not be inferred that Southern senators were in unanimous agreement over the related issues of cloture, civil rights, and the filibuster in 1957. Nevertheless, a solid majority of congressmen from Southern states shared fundamentally similar views on these issues.

16. *CN* 1:1621.

17. *CN* 1:74a, 76a–77a, for details of the House vote on the 1957 Civil Rights Bill. In 1947, 133 representatives opposed statehood for Hawaii; in 1950, 111 representatives opposed the Hawaii bill; and in 1953, 138 representatives voted negatively. These opinions were expressed in letters to Johnson by: J. M. Cunningham, Jan. 6, 1959; F. O. Oberwetter, Jan. 29, 1959; R. Orr, Mar. 19, 1959; A. E. Burges, Jan. 11, 1959; F. M. Gossett, Mar. 9, 1959; W. M. Michels, Jan. 28, 1959; A. R. Durham, Mar. 5, 1959. A poll conducted in one congressional electoral district in Texas during 1958 revealed that 67 percent favored statehood, 17 percent opposed it, and 16 percent were uncertain. Given the negative voting behavior of most Southern representatives, the strength of Southern hostility to statehood was perhaps assumed to be stronger throughout the South than this poll indicated. Johnson's late change on Hawaii might have been influenced by such information. See L. Westbrook to Johnson, May 20, 1957, JP, Senate Papers, 1957–1958.

18. Shuman, "Senate Rules and Civil Rights," pp. 974–75.

19. Johnson to A. R. Durham, Mar. 18, 1959, and Durham to Johnson, Mar. 5, 1959, file of George Reedy, JP, Senate Papers, 1958–1960.

20. Grantham, "Politics of Sectionalism," pp. 48–49; Woodward, quoted in ibid., p. 48.

21. Shuman, "Senate Rules and Civil Rights," pp. 957, 961; D. Berman, *A Bill Becomes Law*, pp. 136–37.

22. *NYT*, Feb. 7, 1958, p. 12; *NYT*, Feb. 10, 1958, p. 22; *Washington Post*, Feb. 7, 1958, quoted by Murray in *CR*, Feb. 10, 1958, 104, pt. 2, p. 1905; *NYT*, Feb. 23, 1958, sec. 4, p. 7.

23. Church, *CR*, Mar. 3, 1958, 104, pt. 3, p. 3200.

24. Murray, *CR*, Jan. 7, 1957, 103, pt. 1, p. 258, and *CR*, Mar. 3, 1958, 104, pt. 3, p. 3200; Murray, statement made Jan. 7, 1957, quoted by Morton in *CR*, Aug. 8, 1958, 104, pt. 13, p. 16665.

25. *HSB*, Jan. 28, 1958, p. 1; Burns to Church, Feb. 5, 1958, quoted by Church in *CR*, May 5, 1958, 104, pt. 6, p. 7988; Burns, interview with author. Burns, 3.5; 9.26; 10.20–21; Aoki, 12.36–42; all in JABOHP. Those attending this conference were Burns, Johnson, Paul H. Douglas (Ill.), Joseph Clark (Pa.), Theodore Green (R.I.), Church, Anderson, Murray, Mansfield, and representatives of Henry Jackson (Wash.), Warren Magnuson (Wash.), and Holland.

26. *CQA, 85th Cong., 2d sess., 1958* 14(Washington, 1959):285.

27. Church, quoted in *HSB*, Jan. 28, 1958, p. 1 (see also O'Brien, Burns, *CR*, July 14, 1958, 104, pt. 10, pp. 13738–39); Grantham, *Politics of Sectionalism*, pp. 54–55.

28. As this study has demonstrated, the Southern faction was always the principal stumbling block to action by Congress. Burns appreciated this fact, although as a Democrat he was often embarrassed by it. Yet Theon Wright in his most sympathetic portrait of Burns has asserted—on the basis of conspicuously little evidence—that Burns "must have been aware . . . that the real opposition to Hawaii's statehood did not come from the South—as was popularly supposed in Hawaii—nor from Washington. It came from Hawaii itself, from the *Kamaaina haoles*." If local opposition did largely derive from this group, such opposition did not at any stage in the struggles after 1945 influence decisively the fate of any legislation before Congress. At most it provided support for congressmen already committed to defeating Hawaii. Burns' actions as delegate in Washington suggest conclusively that he, along with most of his supporters, fully appreciated that local opposition to statehood was now relatively insignificant, and that the only battle still to be won was with the anti–civil rights faction of his own party. The argument advanced by Wright simply echoes the partisan assertions of Democrats made in the 1950s. Anxious to use the local haole elite as a convenient political whipping boy, these Democrats consistently exaggerated its power and influence. Failure to appreciate the relationships between statehood and the Southern position on civil rights has obscured from most observers, including Wright, the real obstacles to admission. Wright accepts the views of Southerners understandably anxious to deny that issues of race had any bearing on the statehood question. Thus he implies that the people of Hawaii "were wrong in suspecting that Southern members of Congress would block statehood due to racial hostility or the communist menace," and that they assumed incorrectly "that Southern Senators and Representatives would oppose statehood for Hawaii because they did not want dark-skinned Hawaiians or saffron-hued Asians sitting by them in the halls of Congress." Yet it was not Southern antagonism to Hawaii's nonwhites per se (or simple racism) which motivated the core of Southern opposition to statehood. Rather, as this book has demonstrated, it was the relationship of Hawaii and Alaska statehood to other civil rights legislation in Congress which was decisive. Wright's study simply ignores the central aspects and implications of this relationship, and thus it fails to analyze the real barriers to statehood for Hawaii. (See Wright, *Disenchanted Isles*, esp. pp. 203–4, 210.)

29. Burns, quoted by Murray in *CR*, June 23, 1958, 104, pt. 9, p. 11945; *HSB*, Oct. 16, 1957, p. 1; Burns, JABOHP, 3.5; 9.26; 10.20–21. Gruening, interview with Franke, tape 1, p. 13.

30. Burns to Church, Feb. 5, 1958, quoted by Church in *CR*, May 5, 1958, 104, pt. 6, p. 7988. See also Burns to Murray, Feb. 18, 1958, quoted by Murray in *CR*, Mar. 3, 1958, 104, pt. 6, p. 3200; Burns, interview with author, May 7, 1970; Johnson to E. M. Thacker (friend and rancher from Oahu), July 21, 1958, JP, Senate Papers, 1958; and *Lubbock-Avalanche-Journal* (Tex.), Jan. 4, 1959, JP, Senate Papers, 1958.

31. Murai, JABOHP, pp. 35–36; Burns to Church, Feb. 5, 1958, quoted by Church in *CR*, May 5, 1958, 104, pt. 6, p. 7988.

32. Burns to Murray, Feb. 18, 1958, quoted by Murray in *CR*, Mar. 3, 1958, 104, pt. 4, p. 3200.

33. *HSB*, Feb. 12, 1958, HSPA Scrapbook, 1958; *HSB*, Jan. 28, 1958, p. 1. See also *CR*, May 5, 1958, 104, pt. 6, p. 7986.

34. Knowland, *CR*, May 5, 1958, 104, pt. 6, p. 7986.

35. *CN* 1:78a–79a.

36. Hunter, "Congress and Statehood for Hawaii," p. 374; *HA*, June 8, 1958, p. 1; Gruening, *Battle for Alaska Statehood*, p. 104; *HSB*, May 19, 1958, p. 1; *HA*, June 8, 1958, p. 1; *CN* 1:78a–79a.

37. Eighty-five Republicans opposed the Alaska bill in 1958. In contrast, only thirty-seven Republicans opposed the Hawaii bill in 1953.

38. *HA*, May 29, 1958, HSPA Scrapbook, 1958; Murray, *CR*, June 23, 1958, 104, pt. 9, p. 11945; Gruening, quoted in *HSB*, June 6, 1958, HSPA Scrapbook, 1958.

39. Gruening, *Battle for Alaska Statehood*, p. 104; *CR*, June 30, 1958, 104, pt. 9, p. 12650; *CN* 1:75a. For evidence of Johnson's equivocal position in 1958, see Johnson to E. M. Thacker, July 15, 1958, and July 21, 1958, file of George Reedy, JP, Senate Papers, 1958–1960.

40. Murray, *CR*, June 23, 1958, 104, pt. 9, pp. 11944–45; *NYT*, June 8, 1958, sec. 4, p. 9.

41. Timothy Sheehan (Rep., Ill.), *CR*, July 16, 1958, 104, pt. 10, p. 13734; Morton, *CR*, Aug. 18, 1958, 104, pt. 13, pp. 16664–65; Gruening, *Battle for Alaska Statehood*, p. 104; Church, *CR*, May 5, 1958, 104, pt. 6, p. 7986.

42. *NYT*, July 9, 1958, p. 12; see also, Jacob K. Javits (Rep., N.Y.), *CR*, July 10, 1958, 104, pt. 10, p. 13318; Hunter, "Congress and Statehood for Hawaii," p. 375. For details of committee delays, see *NYT*, July 9, 1958, p. 12; *NYT*, Aug. 7, 1958, p. 20.

43. *NYT*, July 25, 1958, p. 18.

44. See *CR*, July 10, 1958, 104, pt. 10, p. 13377; *HA*, July 2, 1958, HSPA Scrapbook, 1958. See also Burns, *CR*, July 14, 1958, 104, pt. 10, p. 13739, Watkins, ibid., pp. 13668–69.

45. *HA*, July 2, 1958, HSPA Scrapbook, 1958; *HA*, July 9, 1958, p. 1; Johnson, quoted in *NYT*, Nov. 2, 1958, p. 56. Gruening, interview with Franke, tape 1, p. 14.

46. *NYT*, July 25, 1958, p. 18; *Washington Post*, July 3, 1958, HSCP.

47. Sheehan, *CR*, July 14, 1958, 104, pt. 10, p. 13734; *HA*, July 8, 1958, p. 1.

48. Quinn, interview with author; E. Farrington, interview with McDowell. Quinn, something of a political novice in 1958, was shocked by the intense rebuke he received from Johnson, and was angered by Burns' refusal to support the lobbying efforts of the Hawaii delegation in 1958. HSC, "Report, 1957–58," p. 5. See also *HA*, July 3, 1958, p. 1; *HA*, July 7, 1958, p. 1; *CQA, 85th Cong., 2d sess., 1958* 14:285; Thacker to Johnson, July 10, 1958, file of George Reedy, JP, Senate Papers, 1958–1960.

49. Quinn, quoted in *HSB*, July 29, 1958, p. 1; HSC, "Report, 1957–58," pp. 1–5; Mrs. Farrington, quoted in *HSB*, Aug. 18, 1958, p. 1. See also *HA*, July 24, 1958, p. 1; *HA*, July 27, 1958, p. 1. Quinn, interview with author.

50. Wright, *Disenchanted Isles*, p. 213.

Chapter 9. Fiftieth State

1. Church, *CR*, Mar. 3, 1958, 104, pt. 3, p. 3199. Polls conducted by the American Institute of Public Opinion during 1950–1958 on Hawaiian and Alaskan statehood indicated:

	FAVOR (%)	OPPOSE (%)	NO OPINION (%)
Alaska			
1950	81	8	11
1953	78	10	12
1955	82	9	9
1956	74	10	16
1957	71	8	21
1958	73	6	21
Hawaii			
1950	76	10	14
1953	72	14	14
1955	78	12	10
1956	71	11	18
1957	64	14	22
1958	65	12	23

2. White, quoted in *HSB*, May 1, 1957, HSPA Scrapbook, 1957; *Tulsa Tribune*, Mar. 30, 1957, inserted in SH7, p. 99.

3. Drew L. Smith, *The Menace of Hawaiian Statehood* (New Orleans, 1957), pp. 1–11. See Lehleitner to King, Nov. 14, 1957, "George H. Lehleitner—Correspondence," HSCP. Certainly Smith's pamphlet was widely used in the late 1950s. (See, for example, L. MacDonald to Johnson, Mar. 11, 1959, file of George Reedy, JP, Senate Papers, 1958–1960.)

4. Murray, SH7, p. 99. See also Mike Masaoka (Washington representative of the Japanese American Citizens League), Testimony, SH7, p. 42. Masaoka correctly observed: " . . . the covert fear of admitting into the Union a State whose residents are dominantly of Asian extraction has been one of the primary obstacles blocking Congressional approval of statehood for Hawaii."

5. Thurmond, *CR*, Mar. 11, 1959, 105, pt. 3, pp. 3881, 3878; Smith, quoted in *HSB*, Feb. 26, 1959, p. 1; Davis, *CR*, Mar. 12, 1959, 105, pt. 3, p. 4015.

6. Smith, Keynote Address at the 1960 convention of the Democratic party of Virginia, quoted in Peter H. Odegard, ed., *American Government: Readings and Documents* (New York, 1964), p. 471.

7. Pillion, *CR*, Mar. 10, 1955, 101, pt. 2, p. 2688.

8. Pillion, *CR*, Mar. 9, 1959, 105, pt. 3, p. 3703. Gerald D. Morgan (administrative assistant to the president) to Pillion, Dec. 15, 1953, EP Office File.

9. Robertson, *CR*, Mar. 10, 1953, 99, pt. 2, pp. 2052–53.

10. Smith, quoted in Odegard, *American Government*, p. 473.

11. Paul H. Douglas, in *Time*, Mar. 10, 1952, p. 10; *CN* 1:1415–16, 50a, 62a, 74a.

12. Gruening, quoted in *HSB*, Dec. 8, 1955, HSPA Scrapbook, 1955.

13. *HSB*, Jan. 27, 1958, HSPA Scrapbook, 1958.

14. Fuchs, *Hawaii Pono*, pp. 412–13; ibid., p. 482. Fuchs cites "Political

Opinion and Party Preference," the Hawaii Poll of Public Opinion, research
division of Robert S. Craig Associates, Honolulu, 1958–1959: "The sample of
this survey of voter opinion on the island of Oahu was developed by the area
probability method. The number of interviews conducted in each representative district was in proportion to the number of voters in that district with a
total of 1,321 respondents interviewed in the winter of 1958–1959."

15. Fuchs, *Hawaii Pono*, pp. 413, 482. Fuchs cites "Survey of Political,
Social, Economic, Ethnic Opinions and Attitudes in the 14th Representative
District of Oahu," conducted by the Social Science Research Council in 1959:
"An intensive and detailed survey of 457 voters comprising a sample drawn by
an accepted random method of selecting every Nth name from voter lists was
conducted in the Spring of 1959. The 14th district was chosen because of its cos-
mopolitan and socioeconomic characteristics."

16. See Fuchs, *Hawaii Pono*, p. 413.

17. Ibid., pp. 413; 482. As these surveys were all conducted on the island of
Oahu only, they cannot be interpreted as reliable evidence of opinions in the
territory generally. Moreover, the large percentage of negative replies to the
questions on statehood possibly resulted in part from the particular wording of
the questions asked.

18. Office of the Secretary of Hawaii, *Hawaii: Election Results, Official
Tabulation, 1946–1959*, folder of unnumbered folios; HR8, p. 15; *HSB*, June
28, 1959, p. 1.

19. Tuttle, "Hawaii's Two Party System," p. 5.

20. Chapin (associate editor, *Denver Post*), "Forty-Ninth State," *Denver
Post*, Jan. 14, 1958, inserted in SH8, p. 24; Fuchs, *Hawaii Pono*, p. 424–32;
King, quoted in an article by Chapin on Hawaiian statehood, published in
HSB, Jan. 22, 1958, HSPA Scrapbook, 1958.

21. Bryan, quoted in Fuchs, *Hawaii Pono*, pp. 429–30; Dillingham, in Chapin article, in *HSB*, Jan. 22, 1958.

22. See generally Chapin, "Forty-Ninth State," *Denver Post*, Jan. 14, 1958,
in SH8, pp. 24–25.

23. Pillion, *CR*, Mar. 9, 1959, 105, pt. 3, p. 3704; Eastland, *CR*, Mar. 11,
1959, 105, pt. 3, pp. 3869–75.

24. *HSB*, Aug. 28, 1957, HSPA Scrapbook, 1957; Rogers to Senator Henry M.
Jackson (chairman, Senate Subcommittee on Territories), Mar. 28, 1957, EP
(Church quoted in press clipping attached to memo).

25. Chapin, "Forty-Ninth State," *Denver Post*, Jan. 14, 1958, in SH8, pp.
27–28.

26. Lorrin P. Thurston, *Communism Does Not and Never Will Control
Hawaii*, published in SH7, pp. 23–29; Quinn, quoted in *HA*, Dec. 10, 1957,
p. 1, and *HSB*, Sept. 23, 1958, p. 1; Burns, quoted in *HSB*, Sept. 18, 1958, p. 6.

27. King, interview with McDowell; John T. Jenkins (executive vice president, Hawaii Residents Association) to Pillion, Mar. 25, 1955, "Imua" folder,
HSCP; Lyle G. Phillips, "The Communist Grip in Hawaii," pp. 8–9, "Imua"
folder, HSCP.

28. Chapin, "Forty-Ninth State," *Denver Post*, Jan. 17, 1958, in SH8, p. 28.

29. Hawaii Employers Council, "Research Report: Strikes and Work Stoppages, United States and Hawaii" (Aug. 1957), inserted in SH7, p. 105; "State-

ment in Refutation of the Statement of Congressman Pillion in Opposition to Statehood" (Honolulu, n.d., Mimeo, HSPA Scrapbook, 1958); L. P. Thurston, "Communism Does Not Control Hawaii," in SH7, pp. 23–24.

30. Stewart French (chief counsel, Hawaii Subversive Activities Commission), Testimony, SH8, p. 79.

31. Roberts, "The Commonwealth Proposal," *HA*, Aug. 31, 1958; *HSB*, July 17, 1957, p. 4.

32. *HSB*, Jan. 28, 1957, HSPA Scrapbook, 1957; HR7, p. 58.

33. Roberts, "The Commonwealth Proposal," *HA*, Aug. 31, 1958 and Sept. 2, 1958, HSPA Scrapbook, 1958.

34. Kamins, "What Statehood Means to Hawaii," p. 61; Roger Ernst (assistant secretary of Interior) to Senator Byrd, Mar. 10, 1959, inserted by Kuchel in *CR*, Mar. 11, 1959, 105, pt. 3, p. 3852; Mark, "Emerging Patterns," pp. 16–17.

35. Jagger to Ross, May 12, 1949, TP Office File; Simplich to Budge, Aug. 19, 1952, TP Office File.

36. This view was widely held. See, for example, evidence presented on behalf of the Honolulu Chamber of Commerce, Hawaiian Electric Co., Mutual Telephone Co., the HSPA, and the Hawaii Pineapple Growers Assoc., HH11, pp. 86–90.

37. Quinn, Testimony, HH11, p. 34; *HSB*, Feb. 3, 1958, HSPA Scrapbook, 1958; Thurston, quoted in Ross and Kiester, "Hawaii Wants Statehood Now," p. 9.

38. John R. Steelman (director, War Mobilization and Reconversion, director, Economic Stabilization), Policy Statement, and Press Release, Nov. 6, 1946, TP Office File.

39. Kamins, "What Statehood Means to Hawaii," p. 61.

40. Herman Pheeger (attorney for HSPA) to Budge, n.d., cited in *HA*, Mar. 23, 1958, HSPA Scrapbook, 1958.

41. *HA*, Mar. 23, 1958, HSPA Scrapbook, 1958. See also statement by J. Walter Cameron (vice president and general manager, Alexander and Baldwin), ibid.

42. Kamins, "What Statehood Means to Hawaii," p. 61; Ross and Kiester, "Hawaii Wants Statehood Now," p. 9; Jackson, Testimony, SH7, pp. 87–88.

43. White, quoted in editorial, *New York Herald Tribune*, June 9, 1947, HSCP.

44. Wightman, HH3, p. 564; Steelman, Nov. 6, 1946, TP Office File.

45. H. P. Faye (president, Chamber of Commerce of Honolulu), HH3, pp. 415–16, 6–8; editorial, *New York Herald Tribune*, June 9, 1947, HSCP.

46. Steelman, Memo, Nov. 6, 1946, TP Office File.

47. L. P. Thurston, quoted in *HA*, Mar. 11, 1958, HSPA Scrapbook, 1958. This view was widespread, see, for example, Quinn, Testimony, SH7, pp. 48–49.

48. Stainback, HH3, p. 18; Senator Knowland, *CR*, May 20, 1948, 94, pt. 5, p. 6161.

49. Appendix, "Report of the Subcommittee on Territories," HH3, pp. 547–48.

50. Stainback, HH3, pp. 18–19, King, HH3, pp. 42–43; *HSB*, Dec. 22, 1945, p. 1.

51. Stainback, HH3, pp. 18–19, E. Farrington, interview with Chou, p. 50. See also numerous appeals by Stainback and other territorial officials, in TP Office File.

52. Exhibit 4H, presented by the Equal Rights Commission, "Federal Grants and Expenditures to States and Territory of Hawaii, on per capita basis, by rank of states, 1940," HH3, pp. 662–63, and Exhibit 4G, presented by the Equal Rights Commission, "Expenditures made by the Federal Government as direct payments to the States and Territories . . . fiscal year 1944," HH3, p. 662.

53. *HSB*, Dec. 22, 1944, p. 1.

54. HH8, p. 19.

55. Fuchs, *Hawaii Pono*, pp. 426–27. See also Meller, "Hawaii: The Fiftieth State," p. 491. Kamins, "What Statehood Means to Hawaii," p. 62.

56. Quinn, Testimony, SH7, p. 49.

57. *HSB*, Oct. 16, 1957, p. 1.

58. Roy E. Brown (director, Tax Foundation of Hawaii), cited in *HA*, Feb. 1, 1959, HSPA Scrapbook, 1959.

59. *HSB*, Sept. 30, 1955, HSPA Scrapbook, 1955.

60. Quinn, Testimony, SH7, pp. 48–49.

61. *HA*, Aug. 31, 1955, HSPA Scrapbook, 1955.

62. Stainback to Krug, Nov. 13, 1947, Chapman Papers. Local politicians and party members were also often acutely disturbed by the nature of appointments made by both the Truman and Eisenhower administrations. See, for example, Stainback to Krug, Sept. 15, 1947, TP Office File.

63. Bonham to Major General Vaughan, Nov. 17, 1948, TP Office File; Benz, quoted in Vaughan to Truman, Feb. 3, 1951, TP Office File.

64. Wilson to Pearson, Apr. 30, 1952, TP Office File. Wilson's view was supported by "young" Democrats and promoted in Washington by Vincent O. Esposito.

65. Meller, "Centralization in Hawaii," p. 55; *HSB*, May 24, 1955, p. 1; HSC, *Statehood for Hawaii*, p. 34; *HA*, July 8, 1955, HSPA Scrapbook, 1955.

66. Bartlett, Testimony, SH8, p. 50.

67. *CN* 1:29, 31a.

68. *NYT*, Jan. 31, 1959, p. 8; *CQA, 86th Cong., 1st sess., 1959* 15(Washington, 1960):174; *NYT*, Feb. 5, 1959, p. 40; *HSB*, Feb. 5, 1959, p. 1; *HSB*, Jan. 15, 1959, p. 1; *HSB*, Feb. 5, 1959, p. 1. The vote on this motion was twenty-one to six.

69. HR8, pp. 12–13; *HSB*, Feb. 4, 1959, p. 1; *NYT*, Jan. 30, 1959, p. 10.

70. *NYT*, Feb. 26, 1959, p. 16. See also *CQA, 86th Cong., 1st sess., 1959* 15:174; *NYT*, Feb. 27, 1959, p. 14; *HSB*, Mar. 3, 1959, p. 1.

71. Johnson, *CR*, Mar. 11, 1959, 105, pt. 3, p. 3845.

72. *HA*, Jan. 29, 1959, HSPA Scrapbook, 1959; *HSB*, Mar. 10, 1959, p. 1.

73. Hunter, "Congress and Statehood for Hawaii," p. 374; *HSB*, Feb. 26, 1959, p. 1; *NYT*, Mar. 4, 1959, p. 1; *NYT*, Mar. 6, 1959, p. 17. Pillion was again the most determined House opponent. See, for example, a copy of his statement to the Rules Committee, *CR*, Mar. 9, 1959, p. A1910; HR8, p. 7.

74. *NYT*, Mar. 11, 1959, p. 1. Four Southern Democrats—Smith, Colmer, Rogers, and Davis—opposed the rule. Burns, interview with author. Burns also emphasized the role played by Rayburn in promoting this decision. Burns, JABOHP, 9.25; 10.20.

75. *NYT*, Mar. 12, 1959, pp. 1, 4; Thurmond, *CR*, Mar. 11, 1959, 105, pt. 3, pp. 3882, 3890.

76. *CR*, Mar. 11, 1959, 105, pt. 3, p. 3905; *CQA, 86th Cong., 1st sess., 1959* 15:174; Poage, *CR*, Mar. 12, 1959, 105, pt. 3, p. 4034; *CN* 1:82a–83a.

77. *NYT*, Mar. 13, 1959, p. 1; Johnson to E. A. Cahill, Sept. 2, 1959, and Cahill to Johnson, Aug. 24, 1959, "LBJ," JP subject file; and W. S. Richardson to Johnson, Mar. 15, 1959, JP, Senate Papers. E. Farrington, interviews with McDowell.

78. Included in this large group were the members of the Equal Rights Commission, the HSC, various delegations of islanders to Washington, and hundreds of supporters who gave testimony to numerous investigating committees or worked for the official campaign after its inception in 1935. Apart from King, the Farringtons, and Burns, the most prominent advocates of statehood were: Governors Long and Quinn, Tavares, Allen, Lehleitner, and Jabulka. Despite the passage of years the public squabble over the relative roles of Farrington and Burns continues. Recently Elizabeth Farrington charged, for example, that "all the work had been done before Jack Burns went to Congress . . . he just happened to be in Congress when it passed" (interview with McDowell).

79. *CN* 1:64a–65a, 80a, 82a–83a. The solidly Democratic Southern states of Arkansas and Mississippi voted unanimously against the bill. The twenty-nine representatives from Alabama, Georgia, and Virginia provided only three favorable votes. A large majority of representatives from North Carolina and Texas also opposed admission. The eleven Southern states provided sixty-seven opposition votes. Four of these votes were cast by Republican representatives of Southern constituencies. Only two Democrats who did not represent former Confederate states opposed the legislation. The large Northern states—Illinois, Michigan, New York, Ohio, and Pennsylvania—provided seventeen opposition votes. All but one of these were cast by Republicans.

80. *CN* 1:45a, 63a, 64a–65a, 74a, 75a, 80a, 82a–83a. Thirty-two senators who voted for recommittal in 1948 were replaced during 1948–1959 by senators who endorsed statehood. Moreover, thirteen senators retained office during 1948–1959 who had supported recommittal in 1948, but endorsed statehood in 1959. Four senators who opposed recommittal retained their seats and supported statehood in 1959. Fourteen senators who opposed recommittal were replaced by statehood supporters after 1948. In contrast, only two senators, Hill and Sparkman of Alabama, changed from supporters of statehood in 1948 to opponents of statehood in 1959. All 1948 opponents who retained office and had altered their positions on statehood by 1959 represented non-Southern constituencies. Nine Southern senators retained office during 1948–1959 and consistently opposed statehood. Five Southern opponents in 1948 were replaced by statehood opponents prior to 1959. Only three Southern senators who opposed statehood in 1948 were replaced by statehood supporters prior to 1959.

81. In 1954, for example, only twenty-four senators voted to grant Hawaii Commonwealth status.

82. Burns, JABOHP, 3.5.

83. *HA*, May 28, 1959, HSPA Scrapbook, 1959; *NYT*, Mar. 19, 1959, p. 1; HR8, pp. 4, 20. The boundaries of the new state were not identical to those of the territory. As previously noted, during 1953–1954 compromise boundary

provisions were incorporated into the statehood legislation. Thus, Palmyra
Island—a small privately owned island 960 miles south of Honolulu—was
excluded from the new state. Compromise land provisions also negotiated during 1953–1954 were made effective when statehood was granted. The state government was given title to all lands formally held by the territory. However, an
important section of the statehood bill provided that Hawaii might receive
grants of federally controlled land in the five years immediately after admission
to statehood. Provision was made for the United States president or Congress to
stipulate during this period that certain areas of land which had been under
federal control prior to 1959 be retained under such control. After five years
any land not claimed by the federal government reverted to the permanent control of the state. The Hawaiian electorate ratified these boundary and land provisions during the 1959 statehood referendum.

84. *HSB*, Feb. 5, 1959, HSPA Scrapbook, 1959; *HA*, June 24, 1959, HSPA
Scrapbook, 1959.

85. *HSB*, June 29, 1959, p. 7. See, for example, statements by Mrs. Campbell, Hogan, and Stainback, quoted in *HSB*, Mar. 20, 1959, HSPA Scrapbook,
1959.

86. *HSB*, June 29, 1959, p. 1; *NYT*, June 29, 1959, p. 22.

87. *HSB*, June 29, 1959, p. 7. The votes on the three propositions were "relatively equal"; *HSB*, June 30, 1959, p. 1.

88. *HSB*, June 29, 1959, p. 7.

89. Doc. No. 7, EP, Assistant Secretary of State Morton to Senator Murray,
Feb. 4, 1955, EP Office File.

90. HSC, *Statehood for Hawaii*, pp. 36, 71; W. J. Pickett to Johnson, Feb. 7,
1959; J. L. Lewis to Johnson, Feb. 24, 1959; and P. W. Chun, Jr., to Johnson,
Mar. 30, 1959; all in file of George Reedy, JP, Senate Papers, 1958–1960.

91. Engle, *CR*, Mar. 9, 1959, 105, pt. 3, p. 3685; *Denver Post*, Feb. 24, 1959,
inserted by Allott in *CR*, Mar. 11, 1959, 105, pt. 3, pp. 3858–59; Kuchel, *CR*,
Mar. 11, 1959, 105, pt. 3, p. 3846.

92. Burns, JABOHP, 5.6–8; 7.12; 10.6, 11–13; Hirai, JABOHP, p. 35. In
many respects Inouye symbolized the emergence of postwar Japanese influence
in the Democratic party and island politics generally. A veteran of the celebrated 442nd Regiment, who had lost an arm in combat, Inouye had been educated under the GI Bill and entered politics after the war along with a number
of confident and talented younger nisei and sansei who were determined to
challenge the old Republican haole order. He was rewarded in 1959 with a
large majority in his bid to enter Congress.

93. Quinn, interview with author; Fong, interview with author; Fong, interview with Chou, p. 4; Aoki, JABOHP, 13.21–38; Burns, JABOHP, 10.1–3. For
partisan views of why Burns was defeated in 1959, see JABOHP, Dan Inouye,
tape 27 (quest. 9); William Richardson, tape 34 (quest. 6); Matsuo Takabuki,
tape 35 (quest. 5).

94. See note 93 above; also Fuchs, *Hawaii Pono*, pp. 346–53.

95. See note 94 above.

96. E. Farrington, interview with Chou, p. 28; Inouye to Burns, Mar. 30,
1963, quoted in Crowningburg-Amalu, *Jack Burns*, p. 63; Murai, JABOHP,
2.35.

97. *NYT*, Aug. 22, 1959, pp. 1, 6; HR8, pp. 22, 13. This provision was included in Section 15 of the statehood bill.

98. HR8, p. 12; HSC, *Hawaii and Statehood* (1951), pp. 12–18; George E. Taylor, *The Philippines and the United States: Problems of Partnership* (New York, 1964), pp. 61–62, 65; Emerson, "Puerto Rico and American Policy," pp. 10–11. This article includes a general comparison of the political status of all United States territories and possessions prior to the admission of Hawaii and Alaska to statehood. For a more specific analysis of the political status of these areas, see *CN* 1:1497–1514; Swisher, *American Constitutional Development*, p. 480. See also the first section of Chap. 2 of this book.

99. HR-SR1, pp. 94–95; HR8, p. 12; HSC, *Statehood for Hawaii*, pp. 1, 33, 34.

100. *CN* 1:1500–1501. Alaska ratified the proposed state constitution by a two-to-one majority in 1956. Hawaii's constitution was ratified by a five-to-one majority. The ratification vote of the Hawaii statehood bill was also much stronger than the corresponding vote on the Alaska bill.

101. See, for example, extracts from 103 mainland newspapers, inserted by Allott in *CR*, Mar. 11, 1959, 105, pt. 3, pp. 3858–65.

102. See generally Dedmon, "An Analysis of the Argument." For details of the duration and dates of all congressional debates on Hawaii statehood, see App. 2 to this book.

103. Jabulka, quoted in *HSB*, Apr. 23, 1959; Dedmon, "Discourse in the Statehood Debate," p. 30.

104. Kuchel, *CR*, Mar. 11, 1959, 105, pt. 3, p. 4850.

105. See, for example, Seaton, Press Release, Apr. 2, 1957, EP Office File.

106. HR8, esp. pp. 1–12.

107. American Parents' Association to Robert Taft, Mar. 1, 1953, copy in container 536, Anderson Papers.

108. Allen, article titled "The Hawaii Story—Message for Free World," *HA*, June 23, 1959, pt. 1, p. 15.

Conclusion

1. See, for example, articles by Gerry Burris, *HA*, Dec. 10 and 12, 1982; Mullins, *Hawaiian Journey*, pp. 116–23; and Shaplen, "A Reporter at Large," pts. 1, 2.

2. Seaton, May 2, 1957, EP.

3. See, for example, *Newsweek*, Mar. 23, 1959, pp. 38–39; Lind, *Hawaii's People*, pp. 106–15; and Daws, *Shoal of Time*, pp. 339–96 (Chap. titled "Now We Are All Haoles").

4. Oshiro, JABOHP, 2.14–15; Murai, JABOHP, 2.27, 37; Fong, interview with author.

5. Allen, in *HA*, June 23, 1959, p. 15.

Select Bibliography

Manuscript and Oral History Sources

Although much of Hawaii's statehood history is relatively recent, this fact has not substantially restricted access to manuscript sources. Ultimately, statehood was a less sensitive domestic issue in postwar politics than either civil rights or McCarthyism, and this has helped to expedite the release of manuscript sources relating to it. But statehood was also a protracted, divisive, and very public issue, both locally and on Capitol Hill. For example, more than seven thousand pages of testimony (two million words) were taken on it for over a quarter of a century. Hence the small amount of manuscript material not yet available, most notably the private papers of John A. Burns, can reasonably be compensated for by use of more accessible materials, including newspapers, congressional debates and hearings, and interviews with participants. Recently, the Eisenhower, Truman, and Johnson libraries have released a valuable range of materials relating both to statehood and the administration of Hawaii as a territory. These documents have proved important sources for this study. In large part, however, this book is based on sources located in the Hawaiian and Pacific Collection (housed until 1977 in the Gregg M. Sinclair Library, University of Hawaii, and now located in the university's Hamilton Library) and on the materials housed in the Archives of Hawaii, Kekauluohi Building, Iolani Palace grounds, Honolulu. The Hawaiian and Pacific Collection includes approximately fifteen thousand references, all of which are conveniently catalogued according to subject. The Archives of Hawaii houses an extensive collection of manuscript sources on virtually every facet of Hawaii's history as a territory. Although many of these materials have not been catalogued, I was generously given unrestricted access to them. The intimate accounts of twentieth-century Hawaii available in the ambitious John A. Burns Oral History Project have also been of inestimable value in the preparation of this book. Apart from the extensive central interviews with Burns, those conducted with Daniel Aoki, Chuck Mau, Robert Oshiro, Mitsuyuki Kido, Ernest Murai, Seichi Hirai, William Richardson, and Elizabeth Farrington were most helpful. Future historians of Hawaii will doubtless be as indebted as I am to Stuart Gerry Brown, Daniel Boylan, and Paul Hooper for undertaking this major oral history project. Also helpful were Michaelyn Chou's lengthy interviews with Hiram Fong and Elizabeth Farrington, which form part of the oral history series "The Modern Congress in American History." (Unless otherwise indicated, all sources listed below are located in the Hawaiian and Pacific Collection, Hamilton Library. Abbreviations used are those in the list of Abbreviations which precedes the Notes.)

Allen, Riley. Correspondence with the Farringtons, 1943–1956. AH.

Anderson, Clinton P. Papers, 1938–1972. Library of Congress. Especially containers 483–84, 518, 535–37, 541.

Aoki, Daniel. Interviews, JABOHP, tapes 12, 13, 14, and pt. 2, tape 1, Mar. 24, 1975–May 31, 1977. Aoki was confidential assistant to Burns 1968–1974 and these frank interviews, while very informative, also indicate a strong, uncritical respect for Burns and his achievements.

Burns, John A. Interviews, JABOHP, tapes 1–11, Jan. 1–Feb. 12, 1975. An invaluable source for all students of Hawaii after the late 1930s. While extremely informative and direct, like all oral histories Burns' recollections are sometimes inaccurate or very selective. Burns conceded this problem throughout the interviews when he noted, for example, "Memory is a funny thing" (tape 9, p. 1), and "My chronological clock doesn't work too good" (tape 8, p. 5). Nonetheless, because of the thoughtful and thorough structure of this project, the interviews with Burns are revealing and exhaustive. They are especially helpful on the impact of war, formative years of the Democratic party, factionalism within the party, ethnicity and politics, labor history, anti-communism, and statehood.

———. Interview with author, May 7, 1970.

Chaplin, George. Interview, JABOHP, June 5, 1978.

Chapman, Oscar L. Papers. TL. Especially correspondence with Stainback, Long, Truman, Hawaii Democratic party Central Committee, Wilson, Krug.

Dotty, Dale E. Papers. TL. Especially correspondence with Chapman, Truman.

Eisenhower, Dwight D. Papers. Dwight D. Eisenhower Library, Abilene, Kansas. Various files relating to Hawaii, Alaska, statehood, Republican party in Hawaii, and administration of the territory. Especially correspondence with the Farringtons, Seaton, King, Quinn, and various aides.

Farrington, Elizabeth. Various Papers, especially 1954–1956. HSCP.

———. Interview, JABOHP, May 26, 1976. Slightly disappointing on the statehood issue, but contains some interesting recollections on the Republican party and the roles the Farringtons played in island politics.

———. Interviews with Michaelyn Chou, 1978. Titled "Memories of Elizabeth P. Farrington," Oral History Interviews, "The Modern Congress in American History" series. Mimeo. Transcripts in Hawaiian and Pacific Collection and Library of Congress.

———. Interview with Patience McDowell, Dec. 2, 1982. In possession of interviewer.

Farrington, Joseph R., Hawaii Delegate to Congress, 1943–1954. Papers. Thirty-nine boxes, uncatalogued. AH. Especially useful were newspaper clippings and editorial opinions in folders titled "Newspapers—Editorial Comment (Statehood)," "Magazines—Editorial Comment (Statehood)," "Statehood Editorials," and "Statehood Clippings." Also helpful was the correspondence between Delegate Farrington and Riley Allen (editor, *Honolulu Star-Bulletin*), 1946–1954, contained in various folders titled "Riley Allen."

Fong, Hiram. Interviews with Michaelyn Chou, 1978–1979. Titled "Memories of Hiram L. Fong," Oral History Interviews, "The Modern Congress in American History" series. Mimeo. Transcripts in Hawaiian and Pacific Collection and Library of Congress.

————. Interview with author, Dec. 9, 1982.

Gruening, Ernest. Interview with B. Frantz, Apr. 23, 1974. Transcript in Lyndon Baines Johnson Library.

Hawaii Equal Rights Commission. Papers. Uncatalogued. AH.

Hawaii Statehood Commission, 1947–1959. Papers. Twenty-five boxes, uncatalogued. AH. This voluminous collection of documents includes uncatalogued materials relevant to virtually all aspects of the history of statehood. These materials were used extensively, but not exhaustively. Most valuable were the collections of editorial opinions from over two hundred newspapers and magazines; biennial reports and financial statements of the commission; and numerous books, pamphlets, and news sheets issued by the commission. The various collections of pamphlets, statistics, news clippings, and private correspondence grouped in folders under specific topics relevant to the statehood issue were also helpful. Extensive use was made of materials relating to the International Longshoremen's and Warehousemen's Union; Labor and Communism in Hawaii; the Hawaii Residents' Association (Imua); the Hawaiian Sugar Planters' Association; Commonwealth Status for Hawaii; the Constitutional Convention, 1950; and Congressional Hearings and Reports, both on Statehood and Un-American Activities in Hawaii. Also useful was the voluminous private correspondence of various individual opponents and supporters of statehood.

Hawaii Statehood Commission. Reports, 1947–1959. Seven reports. Each report includes details of the commission's activities during the biennium.

Hirai, Seichi (Shadow). Interview, JABOHP, June 1, 1978.

Johnson, Lyndon Baines. Papers. Lyndon Baines Johnson Library, Austin, Texas. Especially Senate Papers 1957, 1958, 1959, Subject File "Hawaiian Statehood" (containers 288, 1026, 1165); Office File of George Reedy, 1958–1960 (container 427); and LBJ Subject File.

Kido, Mitsuyuki. Interviews, JABOHP, tape 1, July 17, 1975, and tape 2, July 31, 1975.

King, Samuel Wilder. Papers. AH.

King, Samuel P. Interview with Patience McDowell, Dec. 11, 1982. In possession of interviewer.

Krug, Julius. Papers, 1936–1950. Library of Congress.

Mau, Chuck. Interviews, JABOHP, tapes 31, 32, Sept. 21, 1975. A most interesting and very detailed series of recollections by one who worked closely with Burns after the war but split with his faction of the Democratic party over the communist issue during 1950–1952. Excellent on the specific issue of statehood and what it represented to Hawaii's Chinese and Japanese peoples.

McLane, George H. "Report of the Washington Office, Hawaii Statehood Commission." HSCP.

McNaughton, Frank. Papers. TL.

Murai, Ernest. Interviews, JABOHP. Tape 1, July 1, 1975, and tape 2, July 8, 1975, are excellent—concise, detailed, and informative.

Oshiro, Robert. Interviews, JABOHP. Tape 1, Jan. 22, 1977, tape 2, Feb. 8, 1977, and tape 3, Feb. 10, 1977, were most helpful.

Quinn, William. Interview with author, Dec. 10, 1982.

———. Interview with Patience McDowell, Dec. 1982. In possession of interviewer.

Reinecke, John. Interview with author, Feb. 11, 1970.

Richardson, William. Interviews, JABOHP. Tape 1, Feb. 2, 1976, especially useful.

Taft, Robert. Papers, 1889–1953. Library of Congress. Especially container 287.

Tavares, C. Nils. Interview with author, Mar. 10, 1970.

Truman, Harry S. Papers. TL. Especially Office File, various correspondence of Stainback, Long, Chapman, Krug, Ickes, McCarran, Butler, and local Democrats (e.g., Metzger, Wilson, Mau).

Congressional Documents and U.S. Government Publications

Hearings: House of Representatives (HH)

HH1. U.S. Congress. House. Committee on Territories. *To Enable the People of Hawaii to Form a Constitution and State Government. Hearings*, on H.R. 3045. 74th Cong., 1st sess., May 31, 1935.

HH2. U.S. Congress. House. Committee on Territories. *Statehood for Hawaii. Hearings*, before a subcommittee of the Committee on Territories, on H.R. 3034. 74th Cong., 1st sess., Oct. 7–18, 1935.

HH3. U.S. Congress. House. Committee on Territories. *Statehood for Hawaii. Hearings*, before a subcommittee of the Committee on Territories, on H.R. 236. 79th Cong., 2d sess., Jan. 7–18, 1946.

HH4. U.S. Congress. House. Committee on Territories. *Enabling the People of Hawaii to Form a Constitution and State Government and to be Admitted into the Union on an Equal Footing with the Original States. Hearings*, on H.R. 3643. 79th Cong., 1st sess., June 4, 1946.

HH5. U.S. Congress. House. Committee on Public Lands. *Statehood for Hawaii. Hearings*, on H.R. 49, H.R. 50, H.R. 51, H.R. 52, H.R. 53, H.R. 54, H.R. 55, H.R. 56, H.R. 579, H.R. 1125, H.R. 1758. 79th Cong., 2d sess., Mar. 7–19, 1947.

HH6. U.S. Congress. House. Committee on Public Lands. *Statehood for Hawaii. Hearings*, before a subcommittee on Territorial and Insular Possessions of the Committee on Public Lands, on H.R. 49 and related bills. 81st Cong., 1st sess., Mar. 3, 8, 1949.

HH7. U.S. Congress. House. Committee on Un-American Activities. *Communist Activities in the Territory of Hawaii. Hearings.* 81st Cong., 2d sess., pt. 3, Apr. 17–19, 1950, and 82d Cong., 1st sess., pt. 4, July 6, 1951.

HH8. U.S. Congress. House. Committee on Interior and Insular Affairs. *Statehood for Hawaii. Hearings*, before a subcommittee on Territorial and

Insular Possessions of the Committee on Territorial and Insular Affairs, on H.R. 21, H.R. 49, H.R. 205, H.R. 1745, H.R. 2981. 83d Cong., 1st sess., Feb. 23–27, 1953

HH9. U.S. Congress. House. Committee on Interior and Insular Affairs. *Hawaii-Alaska Statehood. Hearings,* on H.R. 2535, H.R. 2536. 84th Cong., 1st sess., Jan. 25–31, and Feb. 2–16, 1955.

HH10. U.S. Congress. House. Committee on Interior and Insular Affairs. *Statehood for Hawaii. Hearings,* before a subcommittee on Territorial and Insular Affairs of the Committee on Interior and Insular Affairs, on H.R. 49, H.R. 339, H.R. 1246, H.R. 1243. 85th Cong., 1st sess., Apr. 8–16, 1957.

HH11. U.S. Congress. House. Committee on Interior and Insular Affairs. *Statehood for Hawaii. Hearings,* on H.R. 50, H.R. 88. 86th Cong., 1st sess., Jan. 26–28, and Feb. 4, 1959.

Reports: House of Representatives (HR)

HR1. U.S. Congress. House. Committee on Public Lands. *Enabling the People of Hawaii to Form a Constitution and State Government and to be Admitted into the Union on an Equal Footing with the Original States. Report* No. 194, to accompany H.R. 49. 80th Cong., 1st sess., Mar. 27, 1947.

HR2. U.S. Congress. House. Committee on Public Lands. *Enabling the People of Hawaii to Form a Constitution and State Government and to be Admitted into the Union on an Equal Footing with the Original States. Report* No. 254, to accompany H.R. 49. 81st Cong., 1st sess., Mar. 10, 1949.

HR3. U.S. Congress. House. Committee on Un-American Activities. *Hawaii Civil Liberties Committee: A Communist Front. Report* No. 2986. 81st Cong., 2d sess., June 23, 1950.

HR4. U.S. Congress. House. Committee on Interior and Insular Affairs. *Enabling the People of Hawaii to Form a Constitution and State Government and to be Admitted into the Union on an Equal Footing with the Original States. Report* No. 109, to accompany H.R. 3575. 83d Cong., 1st sess., Mar. 3, 1953.

HR5. U.S. Congress. House. Committee on Interior and Insular Affairs. *Enabling the People of Hawaii and Alaska Each to Form a Constitution and State Government and to be Admitted into the Union on an Equal Footing with the Original States. Report* No. 88, to accompany H.R. 2535. 84th Cong., 1st sess., Mar. 3, 1955.

HR6. U.S. Congress. House. Committee on Interior and Insular Affairs. *Hawaii Statehood. Report* No. 2700, to accompany H.R. 48. 85th Cong., 2d sess., Aug. 23, 1958.

HR7. U.S. Congress. House. Committee on Interior and Insular Affairs. *Hawaii Statehood. Report* No. 39, pursuant to H.R. 94. 85th Cong., 2d sess., Dec. 8, 1958.

HR8. U.S. Congress. House. Committee on Interior and Insular Affairs. *Hawaii Statehood. Report* No. 32, to accompany H.R. 5221. 86th Cong., 1st sess., Feb. 11, 1959.

Hearings: Joint, House-Senate (HH-SH)

HH-SH1. U.S. Congress. Joint Committee on Hawaii. *Statehood for Hawaii. Hearings*, on S. Con. Res. 18. 75th Cong., 2d sess., Oct. 8–22, 1937.

HH-SH2. U.S. Congress. Committee on Interior and Insular Affairs. *Statehood for Hawaii. Hearings*, on S. 49, S. 51, H.R. 3575. 83d Cong., 2d sess., Jan. 13–19, 1954.

Reports: Joint, House-Senate (HR-SR)

HR-SR1. U.S. Congress. Joint Committee on Hawaii. *Statehood for Hawaii. Report*, from the Chairman of the Joint Committee Transmitting Pursuant to S. Con. Res. 18. 75th Cong., 3d sess., Jan. 5, 1938.

Hearings: Senate (SH)

SH1. U.S. Congress. Senate. Committee on Territories and Insular Affairs. *Administration in Hawaii. Hearings.* 72d Cong., 2d sess., Jan. 16, 1933.

SH2. U.S. Congress. Senate. Committee on Public Lands. *Statehood for Hawaii. Hearings*, before a subcommittee on Territories and Insular Affairs, on H.R. 49, S. 114. 80th Cong., 2d sess., Jan. 5–20, and Apr. 14, 1948.

SH3. U.S. Congress. Senate. Committee on Interior and Insular Affairs. *Hawaii Statehood. Hearings*, on H.R. 49, S. 156, S. 1782. 81st Cong., 2d sess., May 1–5, 1950.

SH4. U.S. Congress. Senate. Committee on Interior and Insular Affairs. *Statehood for Hawaii. Hearings*, before a subcommittee on Territorial and Insular Possessions, on S. 49, S. 51. 83d Cong., 1st sess., Mar. 6, 1953.

SH5. U.S. Congress. Senate. Committee on Interior and Insular Affairs. *Statehood for Hawaii. Hearings*, on H.R. 49, S. 51, H.R. 3575. 83d Cong., 2d sess., June 29–30, July 1–11, 1953, and Jan. 7–8, 1954.

SH6. U.S. Congress. Senate. Committee on Interior and Insular Affairs. *Alaska-Hawaii Statehood, Elective Governor, and Commonwealth Status. Hearings*, on S. 49, S. 399, S. 401. 81st Cong., 4th sess., Feb. 21–28, 1955.

SH7. U.S. Congress. Senate. Committee on Interior and Insular Affairs. *Statehood for Hawaii. Hearings*, on S. 50, S. 36. 85th Cong., 1st sess., Apr. 1–2, 1957.

SH8. U.S. Congress. Senate. Committee on Interior and Insular Affairs. *Statehood for Hawaii. Hearings*, before a subcommittee on Territorial and Insular Affairs, on S. 50. 86th Cong., 1st sess., Feb. 25, 1959.

Reports: Senate (SR)

SR1. U.S. Congress. Senate. Committee on Interior and Insular Affairs. *Statehood for Hawaii. Report*, on H.R. 49, S. 114. 80th Cong., 2d sess., Feb. 12, 1948.

SR2. U.S. Congress. Senate. Committee on Interior and Insular Affairs. *Statehood for Hawaii: Communist Penetration of the Hawaiian Islands. Report*, to accompany H.R. 49. 81st Cong., 1st sess., June 21, 1949.

SR3. U.S. Congress. Senate. Committee on Interior and Insular Affairs. *State-*

hood for Hawaii. Report No. 1928, to accompany H.R. 49. 81st Cong.,
2d sess., June 29, 1950.

SR4. U.S. Congress. Senate. Committee on Interior and Insular Affairs. *Statehood for Hawaii. Report* No. 1928 (supplementary), to accompany H.R.
45. 81st Cong., 2d sess., Aug. 28, 1950.

SR5. U.S. Congress. Senate. Committee on Interior and Insular Affairs. *Statehood for Hawaii. Report* No. 314, to accompany S.49. 82d Cong., 1st
sess., May 8, 1951.

SR6. U.S. Congress. Senate. Committee on Interior and Insular Affairs.
Hawaii Statehood. Report No. 886, to accompany S. 49. 83d Cong., 2d
sess., Jan. 27, 1954.

SR7. U.S. Congress. Senate. Committee on the Judiciary. *Report of the Subcommittee to Investigate the Administration of the Internal Security Act
and Other Internal Security Laws* (sec. 3). *Report* (no no.). 84th Cong.,
2d sess., Dec. 31, 1956.

SR8. U.S. Congress. Senate. Committee on Interior and Insular Affairs. *Providing for the Admission of the State of Hawaii into the Union. Report*
No. 1164, to accompany S. 50. 85th Cong., 1st sess., Aug. 29, 1957.

SR9. U.S. Congress. Senate. Committee on Interior and Insular Affairs. *Statehood for Hawaii. Report* No. 80, to accompany S. 50. 86th Cong., 1st
sess., Mar. 5, 1959.

U.S. Congress, *Congressional Record.* Bound vols., 1897–1900, 1935–1959.
Washington.

U.S. Congress, Senate Committee on Foreign Relations. *Papers Relating to the
Annexation of the Hawaiian Islands.* Washington, 1893.

U.S. Department of State, *Foreign Relations of the U.S., 1894.* Washington,
1895.

Hawaii Government Publications

Hawaii Attorney General's Office. "Incorporated Territories of Hawaii and
Alaska and the Proposed Commonwealth Status." Honolulu, 1954.
Mimeo.

Hawaii Attorney General's Office. *Explanation of the Three Propositions to be
Submitted to the Voters on June 27, 1959, Pursuant to Public Law 86-3.*
86th Congress. Honolulu, 1959.

Hawaii Attorney General's Office. "Report to the Members of the Thirtieth Territorial Legislature on the Factors and Problems which the Territory
Faces in Becoming a State." Honolulu, 1959. Mimeo.

Hawaii Commission on Subversive Activities. *Report on Subversive Activities to
the Legislature of the Territory of Hawaii.* Honolulu, 1951.

Hawaii (Territory) Committee on Education in Post-War Reconstruction. *Post-
War Needs of Education in Hawaii.* Honolulu, 1945.

Hawaii (Territory) Department of Public Instruction. *Moral and Ethical Values
in the Public Schools of Hawaii,* by F. Deal Crooker. Honolulu, 1949.

Hawaii (Territory) Governor's Advisory Committee on Education. *Survey of
Schools and Industry in Hawaii.* Honolulu, 1931.

Hawaii (Territory) Hawaiian Homes Commission. *Report to the Legislature of*

Hawaii. Various, 15 vols., 1924–1956. Copies held in Library of Congress.

Hawaii Joint Legislature Interim Committee. *The Constitution of the State of Hawaii.* Honolulu, 1959.

Hawaii Public Archives Department of Accounting and General Services. *Official Publications of the Territory of Hawaii, 1909–1959.* Honolulu, 1962.

Unpublished Materials and Theses

Ahn, Elizabeth S. "Government Intervention in the 1949 Hawaii Longshoremen's Strike." Master's thesis, University of Hawaii, 1950.

Aller, Curtis C. "The Evolution of Hawaiian Labor Relations: From Benevolent Paternalism to Mature Collective Bargaining." Master's thesis, Harvard University, 1958.

Chou, Michaelyn P. "The Education of a Senator, Hiram L. Fong, from 1906 to 1954." Ph.D. diss., University of Hawaii, 1980.

Dedmon, Donald M. "An Analysis of the Argument in the Debate on the Admission of Hawaii to the Union." Ph.D. diss., University of Iowa, 1961.

Galloway, Eilene, ed. "Statehood for Hawaii and Alaska." U.S. Library of Congress, Legislative Reference Service, Washington, 1950. Mimeo.

Hawaii Citizens' Statehood Committee. "Statehood for Hawaii." Honolulu, 1946. Mimeo.

Hawaii Statehood Commission. "Statehood Precedents: How Certain of the States were Brought into the Union." Honolulu, 1953. Mimeo. AH.

Hawaii University, Ethnic Studies Program. "Chinese in Hawaii." Honolulu, n.d. Mimeo.

Hulten, John J. "Report of the Mayor and the Board of Supervisors of the City and County of Honolulu." Honolulu, 1958.

Inagaki, John Y. "Economic Planning and Development in Hawaii, 1937–57." Master's thesis, University of Hawaii, 1957.

Kim, Bernice B. H. "The Koreans in Hawaii." Master's thesis, University of Hawaii, 1937.

Legislative Reference Bureau, University of Hawaii. "A Statehood Factbook." Honolulu, 1954. Mimeo.

McNamara, Robert M. "Hawaii's Smith Act Case." Master's thesis, University of Hawaii, 1960.

Meller, Norman. "Hawaii: A Study of Centralization." Ph.D. diss., University of Chicago, 1955. Available Library of Congress.

Midkiff, Frank E. "The Economic Determinants of Education in Hawaii." Ph.D. diss., Yale University, 1935. Available Library of Congress.

Odo, Franklin S. "Communism and Labor in Hawaii." Bachelor's thesis, Princeton University, 1962.

Phillips, Paul C. "Hawaii's Democrats: A Study of Factionalism." Ph.D. diss., University of Hawaii, 1979.

Pratte, Paul A. "Ke Alaka'i: The Role of the *Honolulu Star-Bulletin* in the Hawaiian Statehood Movement." Ph.D. diss., University of Hawaii, 1976.

Roesch, Richard L. "The Hawaiian Statehood Plebiscite of 1940." Master's thesis, University of Hawaii, 1952.

Spitz, Allan A., "The Hawaiian Homes Program: A Study in Ideological Transplantation." Ph.D. diss., Michigan State University, 1964.

Stueber, Ralph K. "Hawaii: A Case Study in Development Education, 1778–1960." Ph.D. diss., University of Wisconsin, 1964.

Books, Articles in Books, and Pamphlets

Adams, Romanzo C. *Interracial Marriage in Hawaii: A Study of the Mutually Conditioned Processes of Acculturation and Amalgamation.* New York, 1937.

———. *The Japanese in Hawaii: A Statistical Study Bearing on the Future Number and Voting Strength and on the Economic and Social Character of the Hawaiian Japanese.* New York, 1924.

———. *The Peoples of Hawaii.* Honolulu, 1935.

Alcantara, Ruben R. *The Filipinos in Hawaii: An Annotated Bibliography.* Hawaii Series, no. 2, University of Hawaii, Social Science Research Institute. Honolulu, 1977.

Allen, Gwenfread E. *Hawaii's War Years, 1941–1945.* Honolulu, 1950.

Aller, Curtis. *Labor Relations in the Hawaiian Sugar Industry.* Berkeley, 1959.

Anthony, Garner J. *Hawaii Under Army Rule.* Stanford, 1955.

Barber, Joseph. *Hawaii: Restless Rampart.* New York, 1941.

Beisner, Robert L. *From the Old Diplomacy to the New, 1865–1900.* New York, 1975.

Berman, Daniel M. *A Bill Becomes Law: Congress Enacts Civil Rights Legislation.* 2d ed. New York, 1966.

Berman, William C. "Civil Rights and Civil Liberties." In *The Truman Period as a Research Field,* edited by Richard S. Kirkendall. Columbia, 1967.

Bradley, Harold W. *American Frontier in Hawaii.* Stanford, 1942.

Brookes, Jean J. *International Rivalry in the Pacific Islands, 1800–1875.* Berkeley, 1941.

Burrows, Edwin. *Hawaiian Americans.* New York, 1947.

Butler, Hugh. *Statehood for Hawaii: Communist Penetration of the Hawaiian Islands.* Washington, 1949. AH.

Campbell, Charles S. *The Transformation of American Foreign Relations, 1865–1900.* New York, 1976.

Cariaga, Roman R. *The Filipinos in Hawaii: A Survey of Their Economic and Social Conditions.* Reprint of 1936 thesis. San Francisco, 1974.

Carpenter, Edmund J. *America in Hawaii: A History of the U.S. Influence in the Hawaiian Islands.* Boston, 1899.

Carr, Robert K. *The House Committee on Un-American Activities, 1945–1950.* New York, 1952.

Clark, Thomas B. *Hawaii, the Forty-ninth State.* New York, 1947.

Congressional Quarterly Service. *Congress and the Nation, 1945–1965: A Review of Government and Politics in the Post-War Years.* Washington, 1965.

————. *Congressional Quarterly Almanac*. Vols. 1–14. Washington, 1945–1959.

Conrad, Agnes C., and Robert M. Kamins, eds. *Proceedings of the Constitutional Convention of Hawaii*. Vol. 1, *Journals and Documents*. Vol. 2, *Committee of the Whole Debates*, edited by Agnes C. Conrad only. Published under the supervision of the Attorney General's Office and the Public Archives of Hawaii. Honolulu, 1960–1961.

Conroy, Francis H. *The Japanese Frontier in Hawaii, 1868–1898*. Berkeley, 1953.

Cooke, Richard A. *The Jones-Costigan Act as It Effects the Territory of Hawaii*. Honolulu, 1934.

Creighton, Thomas H. *The Lands of Hawaii: Their Use and Misuse*. Honolulu, 1978.

Crowningburg-Amalu, Samuel. *Jack Burns: A Portrait in Transition*. Honolulu, 1974.

Daws, Gavan. *Shoal of Time: A History of the Hawaiian Islands*. New York, 1968.

Department of Planning and Research, State of Hawaii. *Historical Statistics of Hawaii, 1778–1962: A Supplement to the Statistical Abstracts of Hawaii*. Honolulu, 1962.

Dill, William C. *Statehood for Hawaii*. Philadelphia, 1949.

Dinell, Tom, et al. *The Hawaiian Homes Program, 1920–1963: A Concluding Report*. Legislative Reference Bureau Report No. 1. Honolulu, 1964.

Du Puy, William A. *Hawaii and Its Race Problem*. Washington, 1932.

Dworkin, Anthony Gary, and Rosalind J. Dworkin, eds. *The Minority Report: An Introduction to Racial, Ethnic and Gender Relations*. New York, 1976.

Eblen, Jack E. *The First and Second United States Empires: Governors and Territorial Government, 1784–1912*. Pittsburgh, 1968.

Emerson, Rupert. "America's Pacific Dependencies," and "America's Policy Towards Pacific Dependencies." Both in *America's Pacific Dependencies*, edited by Rupert Emerson et al. New York, 1949.

Estep, Gerald A. *Social Placement of the Portuguese in Hawaii as Indicated by Factors in Assimilation*. Reprint of 1941 thesis. San Francisco, 1974.

Fuchs, Lawrence H. *Hawaii Pono: A Social History*. New York, 1961.

Gardner, Arthur L. *The Koreans in Hawaii: An Annotated Bibliography*. Hawaii Series, no. 3, University of Hawaii, Social Science Research Institute. Honolulu, 1970.

Glick, Clarence E. *Sojourners and Settlers: Chinese Migrants in Hawaii*. Honolulu, 1980.

Gordon, Milton M. *Assimilation in American Life: The Role of Race, Religion and National Origins*. New York, 1964.

Graebner, Norman. *Empire in the Pacific: A Study in American Continental Expansion*. New York, 1955.

Grantham, Dewey W. "The South and the Politics of Sectionalism." In *The South and the Sectional Image*, edited by Dewey W. Grantham. New York, 1967.

Gray, Francine du Plessix. *Hawaii: The Sugar Coated Fortress*. New York, 1972.

Griffith, Robert L. *The Politics of Fear: Joseph R. McCarthy and the Senate.* Lexington, 1970.

Gruening, Ernest. *The Battle for Alaska Statehood.* Anchorage, 1967.

Haas, Michael, and Peter P. Resurrection, eds. *Politics and Prejudice in Contemporary Hawaii.* Honolulu, 1976.

Hawaii Civil Rights Congress. *Free Speech and the Smith Act?* Honolulu, 1951.

Hawaii (Territory) Equal Rights Commission. *Hawaii: Integral Part of the United States of America.* Honolulu, 1937.

Hawaii Residents' Association. *Communism in Hawaii: A Summary of the 1955 Report of the Territorial Commission on Subversive Activities.* Honolulu, 1955. AH.

_____. *Communism in Hawaii: As Revealed in the Report of the Commission on Subversive Activities to the Legislature.* Honolulu, 1957. AH.

_____. *IMUA "Spotlight" Answers the Communist Hawaii Civil Rights Congress on Free Speech—The Smith Act.* Honolulu, 1951. AH.

Hawaii Statehood Commission. *Hawaii and Statehood: History, Premises and Essential Facts of the Statehood Movement.* Honolulu, 1948.

_____. *Hawaii. . . . and Statehood: History, Premises and Essential Facts of the Statehood Movement.* Honolulu, 1951.

_____. *Hawaii U.S.A.: Showcase for Americanism.* Honolulu, 1954.

_____. *The State of Hawaii.* Honolulu, 1956.

_____. *Statehood for Hawaii: The Case of a Half Million Americans at the Threshold.* Honolulu, 1959.

Hawaii (Territory) Statehood Commission. *Hawaiian Statehood and Contiguity.* Honolulu, 1960.

Hawaiian Sugar Planters' Association. *Facts About Sugar, Hawaii's Largest Industry.* Honolulu, 1960.

Healy, David. *U.S. Expansionism: The Imperialist Urge in the 1890's.* Madison, 1970.

Higham, John. *Strangers in the Land.* New York, 1971.

Hormann, Bernard L. "The Caucasian Minority." In *Community Forces in Hawaii: A Book of Readings,* edited by Bernard L. Hormann. 2d ed. Honolulu, 1968.

_____, ed. *Community Forces in Hawaii: A Book of Readings.* 2d ed. Honolulu, 1968.

Horwitz, Robert H., and Norman Meller. *Land and Politics in Hawaii.* East Lansing, Mich., 1963.

Howells, William. *The Pacific Islanders.* New York, 1973.

Ima, Kenji. "Japanese Americans: The Making of 'Good' People." In *The Minority Report: An Introduction to Racial, Ethnic and Gender Relations,* edited by Anthony G. Dworkin and Rosalind J. Dworkin. New York, 1976.

International Longshoremen's and Warehousemen's Union. *The I.L.W.U. Story: Three Decades of Militant Unionism.* San Francisco, 1962.

International Longshoremen's and Warehousemen's Union Defense Committee. *The Plan to Get Jack Hall and Split the Union.* Honolulu, 1953.

Izuka, Ichiro. *The Truth About Communism in Hawaii.* Honolulu, 1947. AH.

Johannessen, Edward. *The Hawaiian Labor Movement: A Brief History*. Boston, 1956.

Kamins, Robert M. "The Month the Clock Stopped." In *Papers on Hawaiian Politics, 1952–1966*, edited by Daniel W. Tuttle, Jr. Honolulu, 1966.

————. "What Statehood Means." In *The New States: Hawaii and Alaska*, edited by William P. Lineberry. New York, 1963.

Key, V. O., Jr. *Southern Politics in State and Nation*. New York, 1949.

Kingston, Maxine Hong. *China Men*. New York, 1980.

Kinney, William A. *Hawaii's Capacity for Self-Government All But Destroyed: The Assassination of Hawaii as an American Commonwealth Nearing Absolute and Complete Accomplishment at the Hands of Promoters and Exploiters of Asian Immigration*. Salt Lake City, 1927.

Kosaki, Richard H. *Home Rule in Hawaii*. Legislative Reference Bureau Report No. 2. University of Hawaii. Honolulu, 1954.

Kuykendall, Ralph S. *The Hawaiian Kingdom*. 3 vols. Honolulu, 1938–1967.

Kuykendall, Ralph S., and A. Grove Day. *Hawaii: A History*. Englewood Cliffs, N.J., 1961.

La Feber, Walter. *The New Empire: An Interpretation of American Expansion, 1860–1898*. Ithaca, N.Y., 1963.

Latham, Edward, ed. *Statehood for Hawaii and Alaska*. New York, 1953.

Li, Wen Lang. "Chinese Americans: Exclusion from the Melting Pot." In *The Minority Report: An Introduction to Racial, Ethnic and Gender Relations*, edited by Anthony G. Dworkin and Rosalind J. Dworkin. New York, 1976.

Lind, Andrew W. "Hawaiian Backgrounds: The Plantation Frontier." In *Modern Hawaii: Perspectives on the Hawaiian Community*, edited by Andrew W. Lind. Honolulu, 1967.

————. *Hawaii's Japanese*. Princeton, N.J., 1946.

————. *Hawaii's People*. 3d ed. Honolulu, 1967.

————. *Trends in Post-War Race Relations in Hawaii*. Romanzo Adams Social Science Research Laboratory, Report No. 25. Honolulu, 1959.

————, ed. *Modern Hawaii: Perspectives on the Hawaiian Community*. Honolulu, 1967.

Lineberry, William P., ed. *The New States: Hawaii and Alaska*. New York, 1963.

Lipset, Seymour Martin. "The Sources of the Radical Right." In *The Radical Right*, edited by Daniel Bell. New York, 1964.

Lubell, Samuel. *The Future of American Politics*. 3d ed. New York, 1965.

McCormick, Thomas J. *China Market: America's Quest for Informal Empire*. Chicago, 1967.

McLane, George H. "The Territory of Hawaii." In *America's Pacific Dependencies*, edited by Rupert Emerson et al. New York, 1949.

Mark, Shelley M. "Emerging Patterns in Hawaiian Business and Industry." In *Modern Hawaii: Perspectives on the Hawaiian Community*, edited by Andrew W. Lind. Honolulu, 1967.

Matsuda, Mitsuga. *The Japanese in Hawaii: An Annotated Bibliography of Japanese Americans*. Hawaii Series, no. 1, University of Hawaii, Social Science Research Institute. Honolulu, 1975.

Meller, Norman. "Centralization in Hawaii: Retrospect and Prospect," (first published in *American Political Science Review* 52 [Mar. 1958]); and "The Legislative Party Profile." Both in *Papers on Hawaiian Politics, 1952–1966*, edited by Daniel W. Tuttle, Jr. Honolulu, 1966.

Mullins, Joseph G. *Hawaiian Journey*. Honolulu [1980].

Norbeck, Edward. *Pineapple Town*. Berkeley, 1959.

Nordyke, Eleanor C. *The Peopling of Hawaii*. Honolulu, 1977.

O'Brien, Thomas L. *The Plot to Sovietize Hawaii*. Hilo, Hawaii, 1948.

Ogawa, Dennis M. *Jan Ken Po: The World of Hawaii's Japanese Americans*. Honolulu, 1978.

———, ed. *Kodomo no tame ni—For the Sake of The Children: The Japanese American Experience in Hawaii*. Honolulu, 1978.

Osborne, Thomas J. *Empire Can Wait: American Opposition to Hawaiian Annexation, 1893–1898*. Kent, Ohio, 1981.

Palmer, Albert W. *The Human Side of Hawaii: Race Problems in the Pacific*. Boston, 1924.

Pendleton, Edwin C. *Labor in Hawaii: A Bibliography*. Honolulu, 1960.

Phillips, Lyle G. *The Communist Grip in Hawaii*. Paper presented at All-American Conference of National Organizations to Combat Communism, Pittsburgh, Nov. 16, 1957. Honolulu, 1957. AH.

———. An Evaluation of the Menace of Communism in Hawaii. Hawaii Residents' Association. Honolulu, 1955. AH.

Plesur, Milton. *America's Outward Thrust: Approaches to Foreign Affairs, 1865–1890*. De Kalb, Ill., 1971.

Pratt, Julius. *Expansionists of 1898: The Acquisition of Hawaii and the Spanish Islands*. Baltimore, 1936.

Purdy, Millard. "A Note on the 1946 Elections in the Territory of Hawaii." In *Community Forces in Hawaii: A Book of Readings*, edited by Bernard L. Hormann. 2d ed. Honolulu, 1968.

Rademaker, John A. "The Exercise of Union Power in 1946 and 1947." In *Community Forces in Hawaii: A Book of Readings*, edited by Bernard L. Hormann. 2d ed. Honolulu, 1968.

Rapson, Richard. *Fairly Lucky You Live in Hawaii: Cultural Pluralism in the Fiftieth State*. Lantham, 1980.

Roberts, Harold S. *Is Commonwealth the Answer for Hawaii?* Hawaii (Territory) Statehood Commission. Honolulu, 1954. AH.

Rubano, Judith. *Culture and Behavior in Hawaii: An Annotated Bibliography*. Honolulu, 1971.

Russ, William A., Jr. *The Hawaiian Republic (1894–98) and Its Struggle to Win Annexation*. Selinsgrove, Pa., 1961.

Samuels, Frederick. *The Japanese and the Haoles of Honolulu*. New Haven, Conn., 1970.

Schmitt, Robert C. *Demographic Statistics of Hawaii: 1778–1965*. Honolulu, 1968.

———. "Shifting Occupational and Class Structures, 1930–1966." In *Modern Hawaii: Perspectives on the Hawaiian Community*, edited by Andrew W. Lind. Honolulu, 1967.

Schwartz, Frederick C. *International Communism*. Hawaii Residents' Association. Honolulu, 1957. AH.

Simpich, Frederick, Jr. *Anatomy of Hawaii*. New York, 1971.

Shoemaker, John H. "Economic Transformation Since the War." In *Modern Hawaii: Perspectives on the Hawaiian Community*, edited by Andrew W. Lind. Honolulu, 1967.

Smith, Bradford. *Americans from Japan*. Philadelphia, 1948.

Smith, Drew L. *The Menace of Hawaiian Statehood*. New Orleans, 1957. AH.

Stainback, Ingram M. *A Commonwealth for Hawaii*. Honolulu, 1954. AH.

———. *Desirability of Commonwealth Status for Hawaii*. Honolulu, 1957. AH.

———. *Statehood for Hawaii*. Honolulu, 1946. AH.

Steamer, Robert J. "Southern Disaffection with the National Democratic Party." In *Change in the Contemporary South*, edited by Allen P. Sindler. Durham, N.C., 1963.

Stevens, S. K. *American Expansion in Hawaii, 1842–1898*. Harrisburg, Pa., 1948.

Stoddard, Lothrop. *The Rising Tide of Color*. New York, 1922.

Swisher, Carl B. *American Constitutional Development*. Cambridge, Mass., 1954.

Tate, Merze. *The United States and the Hawaiian Kingdom*. New Haven, Conn., 1965.

Thurston, Lorrin A. *Communism Does Not, and Never Will, Control Hawaii*. Hawaii (Territory) Statehood Commission. Honolulu, 1957. AH.

———. *Handbook on the Annexing of Hawaii*. St. Joseph, Mich., 1897.

Tuttle, Daniel W., Jr. "Contending Forces in the Island (Hawaii) Power Structure: An Analytic Essay." In *Modern Hawaii: Perspectives on the Hawaiian Community*, edited by Andrew W. Lind. Honolulu, 1967.

———. "Hawaii's Two Party System: 1959," and "Politics in Paradise." Both in *Papers on Hawaiian Politics: 1952–1966*. Honolulu, 1966.

———, ed. *Papers on Hawaiian Politics: 1952–1966*. Honolulu, 1966.

Van Slingerland, Peter. *Something Terrible Has Happened*. New York, 1966.

Volwiler, Albert T., ed. *The Correspondence Between Benjamin Harrison and James G. Blaine, 1882–1893*. Philadelphia, 1940.

Wentworth, Edna C. *Filipino Plantation Workers in Hawaii: A Study of Incomes, Expenditure and Living Standards of Filipino Families on an Hawaiian Sugar Plantation*. New York, 1941.

Wilhoit, Francis M. *The Politics of Massive Resistance*. New York, 1973.

Wright, Theon. *The Disenchanted Isles: The Story of the Second Revolution in Hawaii*. New York, 1972.

Wu, Yuan-li. *Fluctuations in Defense Spending and Their Economic Impact on Hawaii*. Honolulu, 1965.

Young, Marilyn B. "American Expansion, 1870–1900: The Far East." In *Towards A New Past: Dissenting Essays in American History*, edited by Barton J. Bernstein. New York, 1968.

Young, Nancy Foon. *The Chinese in Hawaii: An Annotated Bibliography*. Hawaii Series, no. 4, University of Hawaii, Social Science Research Institute. Honolulu, 1973.

Zalburg, Sanford. *A Spark is Struck: Jack Hall and the ILWU in Hawaii*. Honolulu, 1979.

Journal and Magazine Articles

Adams, Romanzo C. "Statehood for Hawaii." *Social Process in Hawaii* 2 (May 1936).

Anderson, Elmer. "The Americanization of a Polyglot Population." *Educational Forum* 12 (1968).

Arnold, G. E. "Self Government in United States Territories." *Foreign Affairs* 25 (July 1947).

Bailey, Thomas A. "Japan's Protest Against the Annexation of Hawaii." *Journal of Modern History* 3 (1931).

Baker, Ray S. "Human Nature in Hawaii: How the Few Want the Many to Work for Them Perpetually and on Low Wages." *American Magazine* 73 (Jan. 1912).

Ball, Harry V., and Douglas S. Yamamura. "Ethnic Discrimination in the Market Place: A Study of Landlords' Preference in a Polyethnic Society." *American Sociological Review* 25 (1960).

Bartholomew, Paul C., and Robert M. Kamins. "The Hawaiian Constitution: A Structure for Good Government." *American Bar Association Journal* 45 (Nov. 1959).

Beardslee, L. A. "Pilekias." *North American Review* 163 (Oct. 1898).

"The Big Change." *Time* 74 (Aug. 10, 1959).

Boyd, Monica. "The Chinese in New York, California and Hawaii." *Phylon Review of Race and Culture* 32, no. 2 (1971).

Brenner, Philip. "Committee Conflict in the Congressional Arena." *Annals*, Jan. 1974.

Burns, John A. "Asia and the Future: Hawaiian Statehood." *Commonwealth* 66 (Aug. 1957).

Chan, C. K., and Douglas S. Yamamura. "Interracial Marriage and Divorce in Hawaii." *Social Forces* 36 (Oct. 1957).

Chang, William B. C. "The Myth of Chinese Success in Hawaii." *Hawaii Pono Journal* 1, pt. 4 (1971).

Cheng, Ch'en-K'un. "Assimilation in Hawaii and the Bid for Statehood." *Social Forces* 30 (Oct. 1951).

"Constitutional Convention." *Parade of the Pacific* May 1950.

Cooley, Thomas M. "Grave Obstacles to Hawaiian Annexation." *Forum* 15 (June 1893).

Dedmon, Donald M. "The Functions of Discourse in the Hawaiian Statehood Debate." *Speech Monographs* 33, no. 1 (1966).

Devine, Michael J. "John W. Foster and the Struggle for the Annexation of Hawaii." *Pacific Historical Review* 46 (Feb. 1977).

Emerson, Rupert. "Puerto Rico and American Policy Toward Dependent Areas." *Annals of the American Academy of Political and Social Sciences* 285 (Jan. 1953).

Farrington, Wallace R. "Some Thoughts on Statehood." *Friend* 99 (May 1929).

Gordon, Milton M. "Assimilation in America: Theory and Reality." *Daedalus* 90 (Spring 1961).

Greer, Richard A. "University of Hawaii Theses of Interest to Students of Hawaiian History, 1923–1962." *Hawaii Historical Review* 1 (Oct. 1962).

Gruening, Ernest. "Forty-ninth and Fiftieth States: G.O.P. Betrays a Pledge."
    Nation 177 (July 11, 1953).
"Hawaii—Its Government and Scope." *Congressional Digest* 38 (Jan. 1959).
"Hawaii Moves Toward Statehood." *Congressional Digest* 38 (Jan. 1959).
Hawaii Social Science Laboratory. *Social Process.* Various vols., especially:
    "Post-War Hawaii" 11 (1945); "Primary Group Life among Immigrant
    Groups" 12 (1948); "Neglected Minority Groups in Hawaii" 14 (1950);
    "Social Problems in Hawaii" 17 (1953); "Race Relations in Hawaii" 18
    (1954); and "Race Relations and Acculturation" 21 (1957).
Hill, Howard C. "The Americanization Movement." *American Journal of Soci-
    ology* 24 (May 1919).
Hormann, Bernard L. "A Note on Hawaii's Minorities Within Minorities."
    Social Process 18 (1954).
———. "The Significance of the Wilder or Majors-Palikiko Case." *Social Pro-
    cess* 17 (1953).
———. "Some Sociological Observations on Statehood." *What People in
    Hawaii Are Saying and Doing* 14 (Jan. 25, 1948).
Hunter, Charles H. "Congress and Statehood for Hawaii." *World Affairs Quar-
    terly* 29 (Jan. 1959).
———. "Forty-ninth State? For Fifty Years Hawaii Has Sought Admission to
    the Union." *American Heritage* 2 (Spring 1951).
Jones, S. B., and Mehnert Klaus. "Hawaii and the Pacific: A Survey of Political
    Geography." *Geographical Review* 30 (July 1940).
Kamins, Robert M. "What Statehood Means to Hawaii." In *The New States:
    Hawaii and Alaska*, edited by William P. Lineberry. New York, 1963.
    (First published in *State Government* 32 [Summer 1959].)
Kinevan, Marcos E. "Alaska and Hawaii: From Territoriality to Statehood."
    California Law Review 38 (June 1950).
Kinloch, Graham, and Geoffrey Borders. "Racial Stereotypes and Social Dis-
    tance Among Elementary School Children in Hawaii," *Sociology and
    Social Research* 56, pt. 3 (Apr. 1972).
Kosaki, Richard H. "Constitutions and Constitutional Conventions of Hawaii."
    Hawaiian Journal of History 12 (1978).
Kuykendall, Ralph S. "Destined to be American: Yankee Imperialism Absorbs
    the Legendary Isles." *American Heritage* 2 (Spring 1951).
Lind, Andrew W. "Assimilation in Rural Hawaii." *American Journal of Sociol-
    ogy* 45 (1939).
———. "Recent Trends in Hawaii's Race Relations." *Race Relations* 5, nos. 3, 4
    (Dec. 1947–Jan. 1948).
Lowrie, S. Gale. "A Constitution for Hawaii." *American Political Science
    Review* 45 (Sept. 1951).
Mahan, Alfred T. "Hawaii and Our Future Sea Power." *Forum* 15 (Mar. 1893).
Matsuoka, Jirsuichi. "Race Preference in Hawaii." *American Journal of Sociol-
    ogy* 41 (1935–1936).
Meller, Norman. "Hawaii: The Fiftieth State." *Parliamentary Affairs* 13, no. 4
    (1960).
Neal, Robert. "Hawaii's Land and Labor Problems." *Current History* 12 (Dec.
    1920).

Otten, Allen L. "Here's How Twelve Men Control Congress." *Nation's Business* 44 (Feb. 1956).

Parenti, Michael. "Ethnic Politics and the Persistence of Ethnic Identification." *American Political Science Review* 61 (Sept. 1967).

Patterson, John. "The United States and Hawaiian Reciprocity, 1867–1870." *Pacific Historical Review* 7 (1938).

Paul, Justus F. "The Power of Seniority: Senator Hugh Butler and Statehood for Hawaii." *Hawaiian Journal of History* 9 (1975).

Pendleton, Edwin C. "Reversal of Roles—The Case of Paternalism in Hawaiian Labor-Management Relations." *Social Process* 25 (1961–1962).

"The Question of Granting Statehood to Hawaii." *Congressional Digest* 38 (Jan. 1959).

"The Question of New States for Our Federal Union." *Congressional Digest* 29 (Nov. 1950).

"The Question of Statehood for Hawaii and Alaska." *Congressional Digest* 33 (June-July 1954).

Roberts, Harold S. "Sound Prelude to Statehood." *National Municipal Review* 39 (Sept. 1950).

Ross, S., and E. Kiester. "Hawaii Wants Statehood Now." *Parade*, Jan. 11, 1956.

Rostow, Eugene V. "Our Worst Wartime Mistake." *Harpers* 191 (Sept. 1945).

Schmitt, Robert C. "How Many Hawaiians?" *Journal of the Polynesian Society* 76 (1969).

————. "Interracial Marriage and Occupational Status in Hawaii." *American Sociological Review* 28, pt. 5 (1963).

Shaplen, Robert. "A Reporter at Large: Islands of Disenchantment." *New Yorker*, pts. 1 and 2 (Aug. 30 and Sept. 6, 1982).

Shoemaker, John S. "Hawaii Emerges from the War." *Pacific Affairs* 19 (June 1946).

"Should Statehood be Granted to Hawaii and Alaska?" *Congressional Digest* 26 (Nov. 1947).

Shuman, Howard E. "Senate Rules and the Civil Rights Bill: A Case Study." *American Political Science Review* 51, no. 4 (1957).

"Statehood at Last?" *Newsweek* 41 (Mar. 2, 1953).

Symes, Lillian. "What About Hawaii?" *Harpers* 165 (Oct. 1932).

Varney, Harold L. "The Risk in Hawaiian Statehood." *Freeman* 4 (May 3, 1954).

Waldron, Webb. "A New Star in the Union?" *American Magazine* 122 (Apr. 1937).

"We All Haoles." *Newsweek* 54 (Mar. 23, 1959).

Wiran, A. L., and S. Rosenwein. "The Smith Act Prosecutions." *Nation* 177 (Dec. 12, 1953).

Woodyatt, Philip. "When Coconuts Dropped on the G.O.P." *Reporter* 13 (Dec. 1, 1955).

Yamamoto, George. "Political Participation Among Orientals in Hawaii." *Sociology and Social Research* 43 (1959).

Yamamura, Dennis S., and Raymond Sakumoto. "Residential Segregation in Honolulu." *Social Process* 18 (1954).

Young, Nancy. "Changes in Values and Strategies among Chinese in Hawaii." *Sociology and Social Research* 56, pt. 2 (Jan. 1972).

Newspapers and Articles in Newspapers

The following newspaper references were supplemented by editorial opinions from more than two hundred continental U.S. newspapers. These editorials, which include opinion both supporting and opposing statehood, are located in various folders titled "Clippings, Editorial Comment Etc.," HSCP; and in various folders titled "Newspapers—Editorial Comment (Statehood)," "Statehood—Editorials," and "Statehood—Clippings," FP. In addition, the *Congressional Record* includes numerous excerpts from mainland editorial opinions which were inserted by proponents and opponents during 1945–1959.

Newspapers

Evening Bulletin (Honolulu), 1898–1903.
Honolulu Advertiser, 1920–1959.
Honolulu Star-Bulletin, 1903–1959.
New York Times, 1935–1959.
Pacific Commercial Advertiser, 1898–1920.

Scrapbooks and Clippings of Newspaper Material

Hawaiian Sugar Planters' Association. *Statehood for Hawaii.* Scrapbooks, 14 vols., unnumbered. Comprises pamphlets and clippings from various newspapers and periodicals, especially the *Honolulu Advertiser* and the *Honolulu Star-Bulletin.* All newspaper clippings are placed chronologically in each volume. The pages of the various volumes are not numbered. However, situations relating to these scrapbooks in the Notes can easily be located by reference to the date of the particular newspaper item in the note.
Romanzo Adams Social Research Laboratory. Newspaper File, 1927–1941, 1948–1954. University of Hawaii Archives. Clippings on aspects of ethnicity and crime, education, politics, social life, religion, economics, etc.

Articles

Chapin, Leverett A. "Statehood for Hawaii." A series of twelve articles, originally published in *Denver Post*, Jan. 1958.
Houston, Victor S. K. "Implied Statehood Promise Given." *HA*, Aug. 15, 1957.
Hunter, Charles H. "Statehood Issues Almost Blocked Annexation." *HA*, June 23, 1959.
Hyams, Ben. "Tough Job to Get that 'Yes' Vote." *HA*, June 23, 1959.
Roberts, Harold S. "The Commonwealth Proposal." *HA*, Aug. 31, and Sept. 2, 1958.
————. "Hawaii Molds State Constitution." *Christian Science Monitor*, Aug. 7, 1950.

Index

Personal and Place Name Index

Subject Index

Production Notes

This book was designed by Roger Eggers.
Composition and paging were done on the
Quadex Composing System and typesetting
on the Compugraphic 8400 by the design and
production staff of University of Hawaii
Press.

The text typeface is Compugraphic Caledonia
and the display typeface is Compugraphic
Americana.

Offset presswork and binding were done by
Vail-Ballou Press, Inc. Text paper is Writers
RR Offset, basis 50.